TAKING SOFTWARE DESIGN SERIOUSLY

Practical Techniques for Human–Computer Interaction Design

TAKING SOFTWARE DESIGN SERIOUSLY

Practical Techniques for Human–Computer Interaction Design

Edited by

John Karat

IBM Thomas J. Watson Research Center
Yorktown Heights, New York

ACADEMIC PRESS
Harcourt Brace Jovanovich

Boston   San Diego   New York
London   Sydney   Tokyo   Toronto

Permissions for Chapter 6

Figure 1. Reprinted with permission of Academic
Press Limited from a forthcoming paper in the
International Journal of Man–Machine Studies.

Figures 2 and 3. Reprinted with permission of the
ACM. Chew, Jane Carrasco, and Whiteside, John
(eds.), Proceedings of CHI 1990 (Seattle, Washington,
April 1–5, 1990), p. 315. Copyright © 1990,
Association for Computing Machinery Inc.

Cover illustration by *Chris Eveland*.

Cover design by *Pascha Gerlinger*.

ACADEMIC PRESS, INC.
1250 Sixth Avenue, San Diego, CA 92101

United Kingdom Edition published by
ACADEMIC PRESS LIMITED
24–28 Oval Road, London NW1 7DX

Library of Congress Cataloging-in-Publication Data

Taking software design seriously: practical techniques for human
  —computer interaction design / edited by John Karat.
      p. cm.
    Includes bibliographical reference and index.
    ISBN 0-12-397710-X (alk. paper)
      1. Computer software—Development.   2. Human—computer interaction.
    I. Karat. John.
  QA76.76.D47T35   1991
  005.1—dc20   91–2550
                                                                CIP

Printed in the United States of America
91 92 93 94   9 8 7 6 5 4 3 2 1

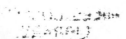

Contents

Contributors

JOHN L. BENNETT, IBM Almaden Research, 650 Harry Road, K52/803, San Jose, California 95120 (63)

ROBERT E. BRAUDES, 11504 Arrowhead Court, Fredericksburg, Virginia 22401 (195)

JAMES A. CARTER, JR., Department of Computational Sciences, University of Saskatchewan, Saskatoon, Saskatchewan, Canada, S7N 0W0 (209)

GEORGE CASADAY, Digital Equipment Corporation, 129 Parker Street, MSPK03-2/H26, Maynard, Massachusetts 01754 (45)

BERNARD J. CATTERALL, The HUSAT Research Institute, The Elms, Elms Grove, Loughborough, Leicestershire, United Kingdom LE11 1RG (315)

ANDREW M. COHILL, Systems Development 0525, 1700 Pratt Drive, Blacksburg, Virginia 24060-6361 (95)

PATRICIA A. CRAIG, Microsoft Corporation, 1 Microsoft Way, Redmond, Washington 98052 (137)

TOM DAYTON, Bellcore, RRC-1H226, 444 Hoes Lane, Piscataway, New Jersey 08854 (21)

MARGARET D. GALER, The HUSAT Research Institute, The Elms, Elms Grove, Loughborough, Leicestershire, United Kingdom LE11 1RG (315)

SUSAN HARKER, Department of Human Services, Loughborough University of Technology, Loughborough, Leicestershire, United Kingdom LE11 3TU (339)

H. REX HARTSON, Department of Computer Science, Virginia Tech., Blacksburg, Virginia, 24061 (157)

DEBORAH HIX, Department of Computer Science, Virginia Tech., Blacksburg, Virginia 24061 (157)

ELLIS HOROWITZ, Computer Science Department, University of Southern California, Los Angeles, California 90089 (257)

M. GREGORY JAMES, 211 Pinegate Circle #7, Chapel Hill, North Carolina 27514 (235)

JOHN KARAT, IBM T.J. Watson Research Center, Hawthorne, P.O. Box 704, Yorktown Heights, New York 10598 (63)

THOMAS R. LANNING, GTE Laboratories Incorporated, 40 Sylvan Road, Waltham, Massachusetts 02254 (127)

JOHN F. McGREW, Room 2E-750JJ, Pacific Bell, 2600 Camino Ramon, San Ramon, California 94583 (287)

HAROLD H. MILLER-JACOBS, TASC, 55 Walkers Brook Drive, Reading, Massachusetts 01867 (273)

CHRIS ROUFF, Computer Science Department, University of Southern California, Los Angeles, California 90089 (257)

ANTONIO C. SIOCHI, Department of Physics and Computer Science, Christopher Newport College, Newport News, Virginia 23606 (157)

JOHN C. TANG, Sun Microsystems, 2550 Garcia Avenue, Mountain View, California 94043 (115)

BRONWEN C. TAYLOR, The HUSAT Research Institute, The Elms, Elms Grove, Loughborough, Leicestershire, United Kingdom LE11 1RG (315)

DAVID A. WROBLEWSKI, MCC Human Interface Laboratory, 3500 West Balconies Center Drive, Austin, Texas 78727 (1)

Preface

What tools or techniques are useful in developing an effective computer system that people will find useful and usable in some domain? If one attempts to formulate a comprehensive software design methodology that has usability as a central focus, it is easy to be overwhelmed by the range of advice offered. High-level suggestions such as "know the users and their tasks" are of course important, but how does one go about doing this? Should we model users or tasks or both, and if so how? Are different techniques more appropriate to different domains? Since we never get the design right the first time, are there techniques that can support design that is truly iterative? How can we evaluate designs in progress and provide timely information to individuals who could use such information?

This book does not answer all of these questions, but it does offer a broad perspective on user-centered software design assembled from a number of experienced designers and researchers. The view expressed here is that the design of complex software systems involves many people exercising multiple skills and carrying out a variety of activities. If we studied a large sample of the software that is available for computer systems and asked, "How was it designed?" we would find that many methodologies have been used productively in the software design process. What is missing is some sense of how the various pieces and approaches fit in an overall picture of software design. Here we try to address design techniques, tools, and tricks, not by looking to describe a single design activity, but rather by describing a number of skills and methods that might be useful in providing a framework for deciding when to use what.

This book showcases a number of views on how to design user-centered software, with an emphasis on practical application. The chapters summarize results of a workshop held in April of 1990 in Seattle as part of the Association for Computing Machinery Conference on human factors in computing systems. As organizer, my intention was to bring together researchers and practitioners who represented a variety of views on the kinds of techniques that are useful in designing software systems that meet users' needs. In response to a general call for participation, speakers representing 22 position papers were invited to attend the workshop. While the actual workshop lasted only one day, discussions between participants have both preceded and continued after the event, and many of the chapters show the strong influence of these discussions.

I have organized the chapters in the book as follows. The book begins with several integrating views of software design. Wroblewski characterizes the design activity as craft and points out important implications of this view. Dayton describes an approach in which multiple design tools and techniques can be coordinated. Chapters by Casaday and by Karat and Bennett discuss frameworks for coordinating multiple perspectives on the system under design.

The second group of chapters discusses important individual talents or perspectives for successful design. The role of an information architect is described in the chapter by Cohill. Lanning addresses the role of eventual system users in the design of systems which will impact their work. In a case study, Tang covers some of the roles for social scientists as experienced observers of behavior, and Craig points out the importance of graphics design. These chapters do not speak to all of the skills required, but they do highlight several roles that the human–computer interaction field has not treated as central to the software design process.

The third group of chapters deals in some fashion with software design activities and the tools to support them. Siochi, Hix, and Hartson describe a technique for specifying user behavior in interacting with direct manipulation systems. Braudes describes a tool for examining conceptual models of systems that allows designers to carry out analyses early in the design. A very important topic in designing for effective human–computer interaction is the integration of user-centered approaches with more traditional software engineering approaches. While many of the chapters touch on such issues, three chapters in this book (those by Carter, by James, and by Rouff and Horowitz) provide detailed discussions of the topic and offer techniques for such integrated design. Miller-Jacobs focuses on the iterative nature of design and the importance of prototyping within the process. A technique that draws on analysis of graphs is described by McGrew. Chapters by Harker and by Catterall, Taylor, and Galer provide two perspectives resulting from the European Human Factors in Information Technology (HUFIT) project.

I wish to express my thanks to all of the people who have assisted in the completion of this book. Through their willingness to put their ideas forward carefully and then to listen to those of a number of others, each of the workshop participants helped make this a rewarding exercise. Particular thanks go to Tom Dayton who acted as workshop recorder, and who made significant contributions to the assembly and the review of the contents of the book. Additionally, I would like to thank members of the workshop who were not able to take part in this book: Meredith Bricken, Gary Klein, Allan MacLean, Larry Miller, Mark Notess, and Peter Polson. We all benefited from their discussions. Finally, I would like to thank SIGCHI for providing an environment for the workshop that led to this book.

John Karat

1   The Construction of Human-Computer Interfaces Considered as a Craft

DAVID A. WROBLEWSKI

MCC Human Interface Laboratory
Austin, Texas

I. Thesis

In this chapter I begin articulating a *craft perspective* on the construction of human-computer interfaces. The process of craft is ancient; the notion of software-as-craft has existed in the hallways of software houses since building software has been a profession. It has seldom, however, been the topic of discussion in the academic literature of computer science, psychology, or human-computer interaction. It is the premise of this chapter that the study of human-computer interfaces is rightfully and centrally concerned with the modern-day practice of craft.

I will focus on two categorical distinctions that disappear during craft processes. The first distinction is between design and manufacture, the second between tools and materials. After exploring these issues in the realm of design generally, in software development, and in the specialized subdomain of human-computer interface construction, I will examine some ideas for research, practice, and education that arise from taking seriously the notions of craft and craftsmanship.[1]

A. Design and Manufacture Unified

Let us begin by defining the word *craft*. The meaning of *craft* has changed since it was first used in the 16th century, when it referred to a forceful act, or an act of fraud, or cunning, or magic. The Oxford English Dictionary includes eight senses of *craft* describing such related but distinct notions as skillfulness in planning or acting; a device created out of such skill; an art, trade, or profession calling for special skill and knowledge; or the collective knowledge of such skill as embodied in its practitioners.

Among scientists and engineers, *craft* carries both positive and negative connotations. Negative connotations arise from the implication that its practitioners are either unaware of or incapable of articulating the principles motivating their designs, or unable to consistently reproduce the results of applying those principles. Positive connotations of *craft* come from the desirability of one-of-a-kind articles built with attention to detail, the ideal to which much engineering aspires.

For this chapter, I offer the following definition, derived from (Lucie-Smith, 1981): *A craft is any process that attempts to create a functional artifact without separating design from manufacture.* This definition provides two significant constraints. The first is that the result be a functional artifact. The construction of purely aesthetic artifacts does not qualify. This is a matter of degree, since all artifacts have some function, however small, even if it is only to evoke an aesthetic response. Painting comes close to the purely aesthetic end of the spectrum, for instance. Jewelry-making is slightly more a craft, since jewelry balances a small amount of functionality (it must be wearable in one of several ways and enhance the wearer's appearance) with a high degree of aesthetics (it must look nice.) A water pitcher thrown on the potter's wheel has significantly more functionality than jewelry (it must contain a liquid without leaking, it must afford lifting and pouring, and it must insulate its contents) and hence, we tend to consider pottery a craft.

---

[1]Throughout this discussion I will use the terms "craftsman" and "craftsmanship" to denote practitioners of either sex. I have retained these terms due to extensive usage in quoted material.

Figure 1. The 13 species of finches that Darwin observed in the Galapagos Islands, from Lack (1947). The most noticeable differences occur in the beaks, which vary due to their respective ecological niches. Reprinted with permission from Cambridge University Press.

The second constraint imposed by this definition of craft requires that the method of construction may not separate design from manufacture. Thus, routinized problem solutions, assembly-line production methods, and pure performance skills do not qualify either because they strongly enforce such distinctions or because they have no design component. Again, this is a matter of degree. Design and manufacture can be unified in craft processes either by small-grained concurrency of design and manufacture (every few seconds or minutes the maker reflects on the present form of the artifact and then returns to making) or by over-practicing the construction of the artifact, in which case the design element recedes from conscious consideration into a continuous and simultaneous influence on the making of the artifact.

B. Tools and Materials Unified

Our intuitive notions of craft are bound up with images of skill with tools or the working of materials. Indeed, most craftsmen are named by the tools they wield, the materials they use, or the products they produce: woodworkers, goldsmiths, hammersmiths, wheelwrights, and so on. We tend to forget that craftsmen produce not only handsome works but also the tools with which those works are made.

New tools arise in an evolutionary manner. A visit to the hammer shelf of the local hardware store will quickly convince you that hand tools, at least, evolve and specialize like the birds of the Galapagos Islands: different weights, different claws, different handles – each in response to a different need. Of course, not every instance of craft work produces new tools. Relatively young crafts foster rapid development of new tools and materials, while in well-established crafts new tools and materials emerge at evolutionary time scales. The agent for selection in tool evolution is the craft process itself.

New tools also arise on-the-spot, playing roles we hardly take time to name. It can be hard to recognize these tools as tools at all. In ordinary cases, e.g., when we cut a piece of lumber with a handsaw, the tool is the component that changes the least as a result of the interaction. But consider a shim. Shims are handy for carpenters like myself, who always find they have missed their cuts by an eighth of an inch (or more). Suppose I build shims on-the-spot to help steady some parts in preparation for assembly. Are the shims tools or materials? Their status is ambiguious precisely because it changes so quickly.

As you might expect, this categorical breakdown is complete in situations where the craftsman's trade involves working the very materials from which his tools are made. Dougherty and Keller (1982) discuss precisely this phenomenon in their observations of blacksmiths at work:

> Similarly, the smith is not constrained by a given inventory of tools, but is largely free to create new tools as the need arises. For example, tongs are manufactured to hold

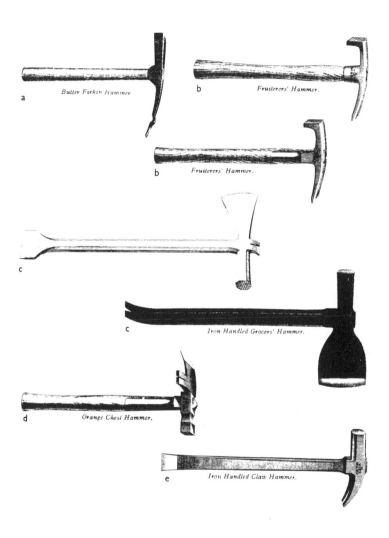

Figure 2. A selection of grocer's and warehouse hammers, taken from Salaman (1989). The most noticeable differences occur in the claws, which vary due to their respective ecological niches. Reprinted with permission from Harper Collins Publishing.

standard stock endwise and sideways. If a special shape stock is used, or a standard size significantly modified, the blacksmith can reforge the jaws to create a new set of tongs. The discontinuities evident in a tool inventory at any given point in time are not perceived as fixed boundaries within which one must work, but as the arbitrary result of tools assembled for past tasks.

In other cases, tools need not be manufactured for novel situations, but objects intended (and named) for some other purpose may serve a blacksmith's needs. In making a gun spring, for example, one smith used a small sardine can for a tempering container, and the can well served the needs of the task. Another illustration of this kind of improvisation appears in Pirsig's (1975:50-51) *Zen and the Art of Motorcycle Maintenance*. The author offers to tighten his friend's motorcycle handle bars using a piece of an aluminum beer can as shim stock. Although the friend indignantly refuses the offer, the aluminum can is perfect as stock for shims. (Dougherty and Keller, 1982, p. 769)

All partially finished work acts both as tool and material. For example, in knitting, the first row of knits are put on a needle in a process known as *casting on*. This first row guides the knitting of subsequent rows, and thus is simultaneuously both a tool and a material. Here is another example: Agre and Batali (1990) collected protocols of pairs of subjects assembling a piece of furniture, in this case a redwood deck glider. Among the resources the subjects used to make sense of the assembly instructions are the features of the parts and the state of the job so far; Agre and Batali observe that a sort of "logic of the object" guides the work:

...the instructions and materials both participate in 'codes' within a particular 'system', so that reciprocal interpretation becomes a matter of the situated commensuration of these codes.... In the materials, the 'code' includes things like the symmetries of the materials, the discrete types into which the pieces fall, the definite functions associated with these types, the clear definition of each feature.... (Agre and Batali, 1990, p. 53)

Like the distinction between design and manufacture, the distinction between tools and materials is a simplification of what really happens during craft work, and tends to disappear when examined closely. The dissolution of these categorical boundaries can be used as an indicator, a symptom, that craft work is taking place.

II. Evidence for a Craft Viewpoint

I have offered two categorical distinctions – design versus manufacture and tool versus material – whose boundaries dissolve during craft work. In this section I will argue in steps of increasing specificity that design in general, in the construction of computer software, and in the specialized subdomain of HCI construction, are crafts.

A. *Design Viewed as a Craft*

An extensive literature exists on the design process and its role in past and present society. It is generally agreed that the designers we see today can trace their professional roots to the craftsmen of antiquity. Lucie-Smith (1981) identified three stages in the history of craft, each of which has gradually led to the next. In the first stage, all objects were made through craft, whether for utilitarian, ritual, or decorative purposes. At this stage, all design was accomplished by craft evolution, in which repeated practice produced better and better artifacts. After the European Renaissance, a distinction arose between craft and fine art; artists were presumably concerned with aesthetic artifacts while craftsmen focused on the utilitarian. Finally, the Industrial Revolution removed from the realm of craft those products for which one constant design could be specified, and construction could be relegated to a machine. Where once there had been only the craftsman, there were now the artist, the craftsman, and the designer.

Mass production forced the separation of design from manufacture, but some objects were industrialized more readily that others. Coins, for example, have nearly always been mass-produced since they are useless unless there are many, virtually identical, copies. For more functional objects, the separation of design from manufacture has taken much longer, when it has happened at all. Jones (1981) discusses the account of George Sturt, who apprenticed to a wagon-maker in the late nineteenth century, and who, in 1923, published a book entitled "The Wheelwright's Shop" describing the craft of wagon-making as he learned it. The wagons he described were well-integrated into their work environment but had been designed only through craft evolution. The form of each wagon was influenced by many things: the type of material it was to haul, its dimensions, the type of soil through which the wagon would travel, and the kinds of horses that would pull it. The resulting features were nontrivial. They included dished wheels and a waist to reduce the turning radius of the cart. The dished wheels in particular have taken on an iconic quality in the literature of design methods, representing the dual qualities of exceptional design success accompanied by ignorance of the principles governing the design:

> There is probably no one "true" reason for the dishing of the cartwheels but rather a great number of interrelated advantages. This is very characteristic of the craft-based design process. After many generations of evolution the end product becomes a totally integrated response to the problem. Thus if any part is altered the complete system may fail in several ways. Such a process served extremely well when the problem remained stable over many years.... Should the problem suddenly change however the vernacular or craft process is unlikely to yield suitable results. If Sturt could not understand the principles involved in cartwheel dishing how would he have responded to the challenge of designing a wheel for a steam-engine or even a modern petrol-driven vehicle with pneumatic tires? (Lawson, 1980, p. 14)

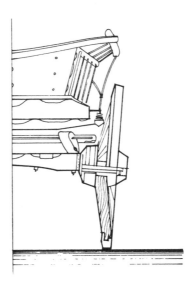

Figure 3. Sturt's dished wagon-wheel. Reprinted with permission from Eastview Editions, Inc.

How was the wagon-maker able to confidently begin a new wagon with no blueprint? There were two reasons for confidence. First, he had made similar wagons; an architectural precedent had been established and proven by experience. Second, the wagon-maker trusted the craft process as a way of thinking – situated and responsive instead of removed and analytical. Although the successful completion of the wagon could not be guaranteed, the craftsman could respond to emerging problems continuously throughout the construction process and take steps to repair them. The result could be quite effective: "Farm-waggons had been adapted, through ages, so very closely to their own environment that, to understanding eyes, they really looked almost like living organisms." (Jones, 1988, p. 220)

As Lawson points out, craft evolution begins to fail when the environment changes faster than the forces of craft evolution can cope. Tools, materials, situations of use, and performance requirements all change in the modern world much faster than in the wheelwright's shop of the 1860's. Without a deeper, explicit knowledge of the principles behind successful designs, the craftsman has no way to prioritize alternative responses to change. We are left with a model of the craftsman toiling to produce artifacts whose design he neither understands nor controls.

Some thinking on design has come full circle, however. Schön (1983) examines the complementary crisis existing today: the technical knowledge or scientific basis for most professional design does not guide the actual practice of design as an investigation into the unique properties of each individual problem. Nor does the act of designing itself appear to be adequately described as the rigorous application of this technical knowledge, however complete, to some predetermined goals. Instead, significant other activities take place before technical knowledge can be effectively applied. Before problem *solving* can begin, claims Schön, problem *setting* must occur. In problem setting, we as designers "interactively *name* the things to which we will attend and *frame* the context in which we will attend to them." And even after the problem has been set, the designer engages in a sort of dialogue with the problem situation to uncover the most appropriate means and goals, rather than through the rigorous application of technical knowledge toward predefined ends. The model of design that Schön suggests is called "reflection-in-action":

> A designer makes things.... Typically, his making process is complex. There are more variables... than can be represented in a finite model. Because of this complexity, the designer's moves tend, happily or unhappily, to produce consequences other than those intended. When this happens, the designer may take account of the unintended changes he has made in the situation by forming new appreciations and understandings and by making new moves. He shapes the situation, in accordance with his initial appreciation of it, the situation "talks back," and he responds to the situation's back-talk.... In answer to the situation's back-talk, the designer reflects-in-action on the construction of the problem, the strategies of action, or the model of the phenomena, which have been implicit in his moves. (Schön, 1983, p. 78)

Similarly, Rittel and Webber (1973) introduced the notion of *wicked problems*, that is, problems whose formulation is neccesarily vague and whose optimal solution cannot practically be found or measured. Design is clearly one of these wicked problems. Rittel and Webber claim that each wicked problem is "essentially unique": similar problems and their solutions can guide the solution of a wicked problem but cannot guarantee it, for a critical difference may always be discovered that invalidates the analogy between the old problem and the new.

We are left with a model of the modern designer as one who struggles to change systems whose behavioral properties are often too complex to fully understand, who must resort to *in situ* experimentation merely to uncover those properties, and whose store of technical knowledge is useful only when the playing pieces have been named, the problem has been framed, and the major design decisions have been made. This model is, after all, not so different from the craftsman of old.

B. Software Construction Viewed as a Craft

In this section, I will make the case that software construction is sometimes practiced as a craft. I will discuss evidence that the design and manufacture of software is, at least sometimes, unified. Also, I will make the case that the categorical boundaries between tools and materials completely disappear during the practice of software construction.

Until recently, it has been a tacitly accepted goal of software engineering research to drive the craft out of software development to make it as predictable, schedulable, and manageable as possible. The resulting models were based on an analogy to the manufacture of physical goods and were intended primarily to benefit software management, not as an accurate model of how such efforts usually proceed (Curtis, Krasner, Shen, and Iscoe, 1987). In fact, the meaning of the word "manufacture" requires a nontrivial mapping into the construction of software, since the work of producing the program is done in programming, and the duplication of the media for distribution is trivial in comparison.

Not surprisingly, recent work has brought this goal into question. Guindon and Curtis (1988) summarize the results of several studies of software designers by describing such activities as being an opportunistic discovery process. They stress that the parameters of the problem emerge during attempts to build solutions; some attempts fail but reveal previously unrecognized constraints in the solution space.

There is an abundance of anecdotal evidence that some software construction efforts are craft-like. A telling comment comes from Jones (1988):

> The more I see of software designing the more I notice resemblance not to design in other fields but to craftsmanship. In each the designing, if such it can be called, is done by the maker, and there is much fitting, adjusting, adapting of existing designs, and much collaboration, with little chance of a bird's eye view, such as the drawing board affords, of how the whole thing is organized, though, in craft evolution, if not in software, the results have the appearance of natural organisms or of exceptionally well integrated designs. But there is an important difference: software is increasingly made by modifying the actual material of previous pieces of software, as a building may be altered for a new use, whereas a waggon-maker, for instance, modifies the form, but does not reuse the material, in making each small step in the gradual evolution of his product. (Jones, 1988, p. 219)

The reality is that building software has been successfully practiced both as a craft and as an engineering endeavor. When a reliable specification of the problem is available, the problem can be tackled by conventional programming languages and methodologies. When the specification is difficult to state or unreliable, however, only more craft-like efforts have succeeded (Sheil, 1984). When problems do crop up in larger, apparently well-specified projects, it is the individual "superconceptualizer" who steps in to repair the design (Curtis, Krasner, Shen, and Iscoe, 1987).

The categorical breakdown between tools and materials is complete in the crafting of software. As Jones points out, programs have the unique property of serving as the raw materials for new programs. In our lab, for instance, we routinely make new programs by copying and editing old ones. Subroutine libraries (either tools or materials, depending on your perspective) often arise from the systematic extraction of code developed for a particular application, whose generality and value to other programmers is recognized. Additionally, new software tools arise when building or testing an application. For instance, imagine building a simple program to monitor network traffic to help debug latency and collision problems for a distributed computing application. The intended result is the distributed computing application, but the network traffic analyzer might be noticed by someone else who then uses it for entirely different purposes. The software craftsman works in a virtual toolsmith's shop, where all materials can become tools, and all tools are raw materials.

C. Human-Computer Interface Construction Viewed as a Craft

In the construction of human-computer interfaces, a craft perspective is not only in evidence but inevitable. Several recent attempts to make psychological theory more relevant to HCI practice suggest the same model of the HCI design problem: to change, by the introduction of a new artifact or the modification of an existing one, an ecology of tasks and artifacts whose behavioral properties are so complex as to be difficult or impossible to predict with accuracy or detail (Carroll, 1990; Landauer, 1990; Suchman, 1987; Winograd and Flores, 1986; Wixon, Holtzblatt, and Knox, 1990).

This problem is often experienced by the designer as a problem of "details." As Carroll (1989) notes, every interface is a theory of how a task ought to be supported. A major feature in the interface is a claim that such functionality is central to completing the task. The absence of a feature is also a claim that the corresponding subtask is incidental enough to be considered a detail. Sometimes a strange switch in figure and ground happens when the tool is fielded for evaluation. The details begin to appear more central to the task than originally thought while the major features are ignored, misused, or cursed by the user. For instance, Erikson (1989) is devoted almost entirely to the discussion of such unexpected problems in several CSCW systems, including difficulties with seating arrangements, the unexpected desirability of ambiguity in office communication, and the inadvertent usurping of a corporate status hierarchy. Most or all the systems considered had strong theoretical underpinnings and were built by accomplished interface designers. Nevertheless, when placed in realistic settings, the designers witnessed the Necker-cube flip of details and features. This is reminiscent of Rittel and Webber's "wicked problems": similar problems do not necessarily lead to similar solutions. Details can have disproportionate effects.

Experiences such as those described in Erikson's paper, although still largely undocumented in the HCI literature, are pervasive and lead to statements like this, from Wixon, Holtzblatt, and Knox (1990):

Principles alone are not enough in the design of artifacts. Design involves not only a broad architecture but a myriad of details which are not obvious until observed in practice. (Wixon, Holtzblatt, and Knox, 1990, p. 333)

Carroll (1990) agrees:

An important body of work in current HCI stresses that designed artifacts cannot be understood apart from the situations in which they are used....These investigators emphasize that even small details can have substantial effects on the usefulness of an artifact, that such details emerge from the situation of use, and hence can be neither predicted outside of that context nor meaningfully abstracted from it. (Carroll, 1990, p. 322)

Schön (1983) argues that the problem is one of expectations. He has seen the same phenomenon in other design disciplines, such as architecture and urban planning. His characterization of the design process as a "reflective conversation with the materials of the situation" exactly fits the *in situ* experimentation that has been suggested in HCI to help better predict results.

However, don't misunderstand this argument: It is *not* about the presence or absence of a basis for informed design decisions in practice. On the contrary, I assume all conscientious practitioners are well-versed in the state of theory in HCI, psychology, and computer science. Instead, it is an observation that building human-computer interfaces involves applying the relevant knowledge in a complex problem-solving context to systems of tasks and artifacts too complex to be completely understood. In practice, the distinctions between design and implementation are necessarily so blurred that the construction of human-computer interfaces can surely be considered a craft.

III. Implications for HCI Research and Practice

If the construction of human-computer interfaces is a craft, then we might rethink some current strategies for researching, managing, and teaching it. Most obviously, any project management decision that separates HCI design from implementation risks the disuse or ineffective use of the resulting interface. However, we might also explore more constructive alternatives that, though they break with tradition in this field and within the software professions generally, are worth considering.

First, we can acknowledge that craftsmen value facile tools and responsive materials above all else and make the development of such tools a priority in HCI research. Facile tools free craftsmen from worrying about the mechanics of building and focus attention on the properties of the task/artifact ecology to be changed. In most current interface design systems, building human-computer interfaces is a complex, tedious task characterized by clumsy tools, catastrophic consequences resulting from minor errors, and attention to microscopic implementation tactics rather than macroscopic design strategies. Techniques for evolving interface-building tools as a result of individual design episodes are primitive or nonexistent.

I am suggesting here that more facile tools and responsive materials *alone* can bring about the next revolution in human-computer interfaces. One advantage of this approach is that it can proceed without a comprehensive model of the design process. Facile tools are facile no matter what your theory of design is, even if it is nonexistent, just as good musical instruments don't inherently commit to a particular school of music. Its main drawback is the same, however. It is possible that we would never build a theory of interface design by concentrating exclusively on building tools and materials to support the practice.

A. *Researcher as Articulate Craftsman*

My second suggestion is to recast the researcher's role to be consistent with his membership in a community of craftsmen. What is it like to do research in HCI construction? How about glass-blowing? Pottery? Authorship? The traditional answer has been to investigate and describe the physical and logical processes at work within the work materials, or the psychological processes that guide human performance in the appreciation or use of the craft product. Unfortunately, much information generated this way is not used in practice because it is not posed in a form useful to making decisions in the context of crafting actual products.

There are alternatives. Another role we could play is that of the *articulate craftsman*. In this role, the researcher reports the forces that shape crafted artifacts as a result of undertaking the craft activities, in a form meaningful to the practice context, though not necessarily useful in traditional analytic or quantitative techniques. In particular, sets of design trade-offs, which I will call *design economies*[2], seem to arise from and strongly guide work in the practice context. Sometimes these design economies are instantiations of more general principles or conservation laws (for example, the well-known space vs. speed trade-off in computer programs), and other times they are quite particular to the design situation, and their generality is unclear (for example Wroblewski, 1987, describes a problem-specific design economy found in a graph unification algorithm.)

Such design economies do exist in human-computer interface construction. Norman (1983) poses several, and attempts a quantitative analysis of one, called "information versus time," which manifests itself in a messaging system as a

---

[2]Also called "exchanges" in (Minsky, 1987).

problem of choosing how much screen space to devote to permanently visible menus, and how much to leave for user workspace. Another trade-off, made famous in (Norman, 1988) is "knowledge in the head versus knowledge in the world." Even more recently, Grudin (1989) and Grudin and Norman (1990) have examined the trade-offs between ease of learning (consistency in the interface) and ease of use (inconsistent, but optimized interfaces.) Other research has taken the approach of studying finished artifacts in order to glean the extant design economies from them, in a process called "claims extraction" (Carroll, 1990).

B. Researcher as Craft-Methodologist

We can also undertake the role of *craft-methodologist*, by studying craft activities in a variety of domains, ranging from almost purely aesthetic crafts, such as authorship and glassblowing, to the production of more functional artifacts in such bastions of mature design as mechanical engineering, electrical engineering, and architecture. The benefits of such a course of inquiry are straightforward but profound, clarifying and refining our models of the craft process, our understanding of the nature of facility in tools, and extending our models of how design knowledge is formed and used in the practice context.

Perhaps you have a hard time imagining that, for instance, authors of fiction struggle with the same problems of craftsmanship as designers of human-computer interfaces. Consider then the following passage from John Gardner, a highly regarded writing teacher and author, discussing what he calls "the fictional process," with eerie similarily to the craft processes we have discussed so far:

> It was once a fairly common assumption among writers and literary critics that what fiction ought to do is tell the truth about things, or, as Poe says somewhere, express our intuitions about reality. Viewed in this way, fiction is a kind of instrument for coming to understanding. But we can see that there are problems to be solved if that view is to be defended. The realist says to us: "Show me, by a process of exact imitation, what it's like for a thirteen-year-old girl when she falls painfully, faintingly in love." And he folds his arms, smug in the conviction that *he* can do just that. But questions dismay us. Shall we tell the truth in short, clipped sentences, or long smooth gracefully ones? Shall we tell it using short vowels and hard consonants or long vowels and soft consonants?...A common answer at the present time is that that is the question the serious writer spends his whole life trying to work out by means of the only kind of thinking he trusts; that is, the fictional process. (Gardner, 1983, pp. 37-38)

Or another from John Steinbeck:

> Although it must be a thousand years ago that I sat in a class on story-writing at Stanford. I remember the experience very clearly. I was bright-eyed and bushy-brained and prepared to absorb the secret formula for writing good short stories, even great short stories. This illusion was canceled very quickly. The only way to write a good short

story, we were told, is to write a good short story. Only after it is written can it be taken apart to see how it was done. (Steinbeck, 1989, p. 216)

In this case, for instance, the craft-methodologist can begin to see a theme of trust in the investigative properties of craftsmanship that cuts across domains of expertise. Other parallels surely hold.

C. Teaching HCI Construction: Apprenticeship Learning

In Terry Winograd's closing address at the 1990 ACM CHI conference, he asked the question "what can we teach about human-computer interaction?" It is an especially troublesome question if HCI construction is a craft, for teaching craft has been problematic. The traditional method of teaching a craft is through apprenticeship, and contemporary apprenticeship is alive and well in many fields, including medicine, architecture, and even software engineering. What varies is the degree to which the apprenticeship is a formal part of the education process and who pays for it.

There are two sets of processes involved in most apprenticeship systems. The first, and one we will not consider here, concerns the socialization and social control of the apprentice (Graves, 1989). The second is the notion that learning craft skills requires individual coaching, since significant elements of the craft cannot be well-communicated via classroom lectures, texts, or other nonparticipatory techniques. After studying Sturt's account of the wheelwright's shop, for instance, Jones concludes

> It may be necessary to read the whole of Sturt's book, and perhaps to serve as an apprentice oneself, if one is to understand more fully how the craftsman's blend of know-how and ignorance can produce works that a scientist would find hard to explain and in which the artistic eye can perceive a high level of formal organization. (Jones, 1981, p. 19)

Schön considers this issue at length. After examining examples of "professional artistry" in urban planning, architecture, and psychiatric therapy, he concludes

> Perhaps, then, learning *all* forms of professional artistry depends, at least in part, on conditions similar to those created in studios and conservatories: freedom to learn by doing in a setting relatively low in risk, with access to coaches who initiate students into the "traditions of the calling" and help them, by "the right kind of telling," to see on their own behalf and in their own way what they need most to see. We ought, then, to study the experience of learning by doing and the artistry of good coaching. We should base our study on the working assumption that both processes are intelligent and – within limits to be discovered – intelligible. And we ought to search for examples whenever we can find them – in the dual curricula of the schools, the apprenticeship and practicums that aspiring practitioners find or create for themselves, and the deviant traditions of studio and conservatory. (Schön, 1987, p. 17)

It is also instructive to consider that many human-interface designers have been making apprenticeship a part of the normal interface design process for quite some time. This idea is that to effectively design a human-computer interface, one must become an expert in the task domain. How is this to be done? Of course, by apprenticeship to those domain experts available. Several researchers have begun to formulate design methodologies that capitalize on this apprenticeship model, such as the participatory design methodology articulated by Ehn (1988), or the contextual design techniques of Wixon, Holtzblatt, and Knox (1990).

D. Teaching HCI Construction: Use of Paradigmatic Examples

Another method of teaching craftsmanship can be called "teaching by paradigmatic examples."[3] This technique rests on the assumption that access to a repertoire of interfaces could provide the learner with useful landmarks in the design space. These landmarks become the initial passes of the design process, and subsequent design iterations may take the designer arbitrarily far away from the starting point. Choosing the proper starting point is dealt with by analysis of the task domain and matching to the repertoire. If several examples apply along different dimensions, then the learner chooses the relevant properties of each example and uses it in guiding the new design where appropriate. When no example from the repertoire applies, the designer must find other means to guide the process.

In order for this technique to work, several problems must be addressed. First, one must be able to choose those members of the repertoire most applicable to the new problem. A comparison of the design economies at work within the new problem and within the examples in the repertoire could fill this gap, for an important measure of similarity must be the primary design economies at work within that problem space. Another problem with this approach is that the final form of an artifact does not capture design decisions that were tried but failed (Jones, 1981). Clearly, the absence of a design feature can sometimes be cause for concluding it doesn't work, but not always. One response is to include negative examples in the student's repertoire to provide landmarks to steer away from. Again, these landmarks require a level of analysis to emphasize the design economies at work and why they failed. Recent techniques to capture the design rationale of the artifact during the design process, such as Issue-Based Information Systems (McCall, 1986) and computer-based critics (Fischer and Morch, 1988), begin to address these issues.

------

[3]Thanks to Michael Williams of IntelliCorp™ for these ideas and access to his own paradigmatic example of using these ideas to teach design skills in the slides for his presentation "The Craft of Building Intelligent User Interfaces."

IV. Summary

In this chapter, I have considered the notion that building human-computer interfaces is a craft, with all the advantages and disadvantages that that entails. My main points follow:

1. A craft is any process that attempts to create a functional artifact without separating design from manufacture.

2. Significant by-products of the craft process are new tools and materials as well as the intended artifact. The distinction between tools and materials begins to dissolve when viewed this way.

3. Creating software is sometimes, but not always, a craft. The degree of variability in practice is due to the availability of a reliable specification.

4. Creating a human-computer interface is usually, and perhaps always, a craft, because of the investigative nature of each designing.

5. Productive HCI research can take the form of facile tools and responsive materials, articulate craftsmanship, or craft-methodology.

6. We can begin to codify operational design knowledge by searching for and articulating design economies at work within individual interfaces.

7. Two approaches to teaching HCI as a craft are apprenticeship and exposure to paradigmatic examples.

The future of software practice and HCI construction belongs to those who take their craft most seriously and least respect the bounds of tradition, be they craft or science. I have argued that it is instructive to study other craft and design professions, but we must also be mindful of the limits to such analogies. Fundamentally, the materials shape the craft. Computer programs are unlike any other material, and the form of craftsmanship in software will surely be unique.

V. Acknowledgments

Many members of the MCC research community reviewed, supported, and improved this paper through hours of discussion, especially Will Hill, Tim McCandless, Loren Terveen, Elaine Rich, and Jim Hollan. Jean McKendree was particularly helpful in providing insight on the issues of apprenticeship and exemplar learning. During the workshop, Alan MacLean was especially enthusiastic, and afterward, Tom Dayton and John Karat were gracious and accommodating in letting me submit drafts late, and contributed several useful suggestions and lots of encouragement. Don Norman, Gerhard Fischer, Jonathan Grudin, Terry Winograd, Mike Williams, and Tom Erickson provided useful feedback, suggestions, and encouragement. Finally, Patricia Stuhr of the Ohio State University Art Education Department helped guide me into the literature of craft and craft education.

VI. References

Agre, P. and Batali, J. (1990). "Collaborative Instruction Use in Furniture Assembly." In Nigel Gilbert (Ed.) *AAAI Workshop on Complex Systems, Ethnomethodology, and Interaction Analysis,* (pp. 41-56).

Carroll, J. M. (1989). "Artifact as Theory-Nexus: Hermeneutics meets theory-based design." *Proceedings of the CHI'89 ACM Conference on Human Factors in Computing Systems.* (pp. 7-14). New York: ACM.

Carroll, J. M. (1990). "Infinite Detail and Emulation in an Ontologically Minimized HCI." *Proceedings of the CHI'90 ACM Conference on Human Factors in Computing Systems.* (pp. 321-327). New York: ACM.

Curtis, B., Krasner, H., Shen, V., and Iscoe, N. (1987). "On Building Software Process Models Under the Lamppost." *Proceedings of the IEEE 9th International Conference on Software Engineering,* (pp. 96-103).

Dougherty, J. and Keller, C. (1982). "Taskonomy: A Practical Approach to Knowledge Structures." *American Ethnologist,* Volume 9, Number 4, 763-774.

Ehn, P. (1988). *Work-Oriented Design of Computer Artifacts.*   Stockholm: Arbetslivscentrum.

Erickson, T. (1989). "Interfaces for Cooperative Work: An Eclectic Look at CSCW '88." *SIGCHI Bulletin,* Volume 21, Number 1, 56-64.

Fischer, G. and Morch, A. (1988). "Crack: A Critiquing Approach to Cooperative Kitchen Design." *Proceedings of the International Conference on Intelligent Tutoring Systems.* (pp. 176-185). New York: ACM.

Gardner, J. (1983). *The Art of Fiction: Notes on Craft for Young Writers.* New York: Vintage Books.

Graves, B. (1989). "Informal Aspects of Apprenticeship in Selected American Occupations." In Michael W. Coy (Ed.), *Apprenticeship: From Theory to Method and Back Again,* (pp. 51-64). Albany, NY: State University of New York Press.

Grudin, J. (1989). "The Case Against User Interface Consistency." *Communications of the ACM,* Volume 32, 1164-1173.

Grudin, J. and Norman, D. A. (1990). "Lessons for System Design from the Study of Natural Language Evolution." Manuscript submitted for publication to CHI'91.

Guindon, R. and Curtis, B. (1988). "Control of Cognitive Processes During Design: What Tools Would Support Software Designers?" *Proceedings of the CHI'88 ACM Conference on Human Factors in Computing Systems.* (pp. 263-268). New York: ACM.

Jones, J. C. (1981). *Design Methods: Seeds of Human Futures.* New York: John Wiley and Sons.

Jones, J. C. (1988). "Softecnica." In John Thackara (Ed.), *Design After Modernism:*

Beyond the Object, (pp. 216-226). New York: Thames and Hudson Publishing.

Lack, D. (1947). *Darwin's Finches: An Essay on the General Biological Theory of Evolution*. Cambridge, England: Cambridge University Press.

Landauer, T. (1990). "Let's Get Real: A Position Paper on the Role of Cognitive Theory in the Design of Humanly Useful and Usable Systems." Bellcore Technical Memorandum TM-ARH-016841. Also to appear in J. Carroll (Ed.), *Designing Interaction: Psychology at the Human-Computer Interface*. Cambridge, England: Cambridge University Press.

Lawson, B. (1980). *How Designers Think*. New Jersey: Eastview Editions, Inc.

Lucie-Smith, E. (1981). *The Story of Craft*. New York: Van Nostrand Reinhold Company.

McCall, R. (1986). "Issue-Serve Systems: A Descriptive Theory of Design." *Design Methods and Theories*, Volume 20, Number 3, 443-458.

Minsky, M. (1987). "Form and Content in Computer Science." In *ACM Turing Award Lectures: The First Twenty Years, 1966-1985*. (pp. 219-242). New York: ACM. [Originally published as Minsky, M. (1969). "Form and Content in Computer Science", *Journal of the ACM*, Volume 17, Number 2, (pp. 197-215.)]

Norman, D. (1983). "Design Principles for Human-Computer Interfaces." *Proceedings of the CHI'83 ACM Conference on Human Factors in Computing Systems*. (pp. 1-10). New York: ACM.

Norman, D. (1988). *The Psychology of Everyday Things*. New York: Basic Books.

Pirsig, R. (1975). *Zen and the Art of Motorcycle Maintenance*. New York: Bantam.

Rittel, H. and Webber, M. (1973). "Dilemmas in a General Theory of Planning." *Policy Sciences*, Volume 4, Number 2, 155-169.

Salaman, R. A. (1989). *Dictionary of Woodworking Tools*. Newport, Connecticut: The Taunton Press, Inc.

Schön, D. (1983). *The Reflective Practitioner*. New York: Basic Books.

Schön, D. (1987). *Educating the Reflective Practitioner*. San Francisco: Josey-Bass.

Sheil, B.A. (1984). "Power Tools for Programmers." In D. Barstow, H. Shrobe, and E. Sandewall (Eds.), *Interactive Programming Environments*. (pp. 19-30). New York: McGraw-Hill.

Steinbeck, J. (1989). "John Steinbeck." In B. Strickland (Ed.), *On Being a Writer*. (pp. 216-218) Ohio: Writer's Digest Books. (Originally published 1963.)

Suchman, L. (1987). *Plans and Situated Actions*. Cambridge: Cambridge University Press.

Winograd, T. (1990). "What Can We Teach About Human-Computer Interaction?" *Proceedings of the CHI'90 ACM Conference on Human Factors in Computing Systems*. (pp. 443-449). New York: ACM.

Winograd, T. and Flores, F. (1986). *Understanding Computers and Cognition*. New York: Addison-Wesley Publishing.

Wixon, D., Holtzblatt, K., and Knox, S. (1990). "Contextual Design: An Emergent View of System Design." *Proceedings of the CHI'90 ACM Conference on Human Factors in Computing Systems*. (pp. 329-336). New York: ACM.

Wroblewski, D. (1987). "Nondestructive Graph Unification." *Proceedings of the 6th National Conference on Artificial Intelligence*. (pp. 582-587). Seattle: AAAI Press.

2 Cultivated Eclecticism as the Normative Approach to Design

TOM DAYTON

Bell Communications Research
Piscataway, New Jersey

In this overview and interpretation of the Taking Design Seriously workshop from CHI '90 (this book, plus Braudes, 1990; Carter, 1990; Catterall, Harker, Klein, Notess, & Tang, 1990; Hix & Casaday, 1990; Karat & Dayton, 1990), I make a case for taking diverse techniques seriously as the major part of an eclectic approach to design. The workshop format's allowance of simultaneous discussion of all the methods, the participants' constant interrelating of the methods, and the conceptual frameworks proposed by some of the participants, suggested to me that a set of methods might be sufficient and coherent as a grand approach to design. Against such a purely methodological approach to HCI stands a workshop on a theme quite different from ours—the role of theory in HCI (Carroll, 1991-a); those papers convinced me that local theories and descriptive global theory can also be useful. Both workshops mentioned both theories and methods, and the theme emerged that a *variety* of methods, theories, and people is *necessary* for design.

But individual ad hoc methods are not enough to improve the design process, and it is toward this further goal that our workshop made the most, though

I did much of this work while a postdoc at IBM's Watson Research Center in Yorktown Heights, New York, and the rest while in my current position at Bellcore. The views expressed herein are mine, and not necessarily Bellcore's or IBM's. I thank John Karat for conversations about these ideas, and I thank Robert Campbell, Andy Cohill, and Dave Wroblewski for comments on the manuscript. My current address: For e-mail, tdayton@ctt.bellcore.com. For snail-mail, Bellcore RRC-1H226, 444 Hoes Lane, Piscataway, NJ 08854.

perhaps implicit, progress. Most convincing was the spontaneity of the discussion's interrelation of methods, since the workshop call was not for the construction of a unified approach to HCI based on methods but only for individually useful methods. Though I will point to many of the methods from the other chapters as being useful individually for improving the design process, passive eclecticism is incapable of rapidly *driving* improvement in the design process. So I point to some of the chapters as providing global methods that allow us to be more active in designing the design process. But I think we also need a grand conceptual framework for HCI design, which accommodates all methods and theories and which *suggests* new ones; I close the chapter by suggesting we take much more seriously the notion of evolution of artifacts as species.

I. Techniques Are Valuable

The call for this workshop was very pragmatic. The result—methods collected without regard to their theoretical underpinnings or post hoc rationales—could be regarded as useful but unexciting, for how could the future of HCI be *driven* by a collection of methods? Surely an order of magnitude improvement in the design process cannot be gotten from selecting, by hearsay and intuition, some of the product of unprincipled proliferation of techniques! But McDonald and Schvaneveldt (1988) did settle on methods as the best approach to HCI:

We have thus far dismissed guidelines as unsupported by data and of little value for specific applications, and creative insights as unreliable. What are the alternatives? We contend that the strengths of scientific disciplines, such as cognitive psychology, lie in their use of theories and methodologies. Empirical methodologies have the dual characteristics of *generality*, meaning they can be applied in a wide range of situations, and *validity*, meaning the answers produced by their application are legitimate for the situations to which they are applied. Thus, we propose a methodological approach to interface design. (p. 292)

Broadbent (1990) agreed with the strength of the methodological approach, at least in comparing their chapter to others in that book: "This chapter stems from psychological method rather than theory, but it straddles psychology and computing more than the others do. It therefore offers more hope of an advance that is both rational and applicable. Many readers will regard it as the best in the book" (p. 235).

Note that these statements did not exclude theory, or laud methods as always superior, but acknowledged that methods can play at least as strong a role as theory. Our workshop was created to bring together whatever methods, tools, and people are useful for designing human-computer interfaces. The call did not exclude theory, but theory was mentioned at the workshop only as another component of the design process instead of the sole solution. Evidence for the eclecticism of design was the lack of dominance of any of the methods people brought in response to this open-ended call. It is tempting to conclude simply that optimal design requires many people doing many different things, but I think more is needed if we want to rapidly improve the design process. What we need is a framework for thinking about these valuable methods that helps us recognize good methods when they arise and that suggests invention of even better ones. Perhaps the very eclecticism that is disconcerting about our workshop's product can be turned into an identifiable, normative, and improvable approach to design.

II. HCI Design Is Currently and Ideally Eclectic

A. Evidence from Our Workshop on Methods for HCI Design

Why must design involve many different people doing many different things? Wroblewski's chapter opens our book because it answers that question by claiming design is inherently a craft activity. Other people at the workshop also pushed this point, and my impression is that everyone soon came to agree that design as a whole is a craft. As such it comprises many activities, including science, guidelines, principles, art, trial and error, intuition, shared wisdom, apprenticeship, and accident. Different workshop participants had different notions of the relative contributions of all these activities—both the current contributions and the ideal contributions—but no one claimed that HCI design could be made entirely science or engineering.

The eclectic theme is expanded in the book's first section, Coordinating Design Activities, which does more than describe methods for helping members of groups communicate explicitly. Casaday's chapter describes a general framework that can help all the people involved in design, whatever their specialized activities, to think about the other activities. Even if these people never meet or communicate overtly, their work influences each other's by virtue of being part of the same design process. Therefore, the process can be improved if each person tries to take advantage of information available from the other activities and tries to do her activity so it provides leverage for the other activities. During much of the workshop discussion we got perspective on the assorted methods being discussed, by placing them in Casaday's framework. Casaday's chapter demonstrates his framework by noting where all the other chapters fit into it. By providing a single view on the diverse activities of design, it allows specialists in the different activities to consider their work as complementary to instead of competitive with others' work. Yet it acknowledges the differences among the activities, not constraining them even so much as by placing them in a temporal order. In this way Casaday's chapter points to eclecticism as the way to do grand design.

Karat and Bennett's chapter also reviews the other chapters, but it is focused more narrowly than Casaday's on techniques to help design groups communicate through meetings and shared representations. It is important to note that Karat and Bennett were not just concerned with communication among *people* who differ, but also with communication among design *activities* that differ. For instance, their four-walls representation of the design space guarantees that pragmatic constraints such as financial limits and marketing deadlines are just as visible as pure usability issues are. Some readers might object to this, claiming that the job of HCI designers is to make interfaces usable and that management should set constraints only after it has seen what levels of product quality the various levels of financial and temporal support can buy. I agree there is a place in HCI for some people who are concerned with usability regardless of such constraints, but I am now convinced that the design process as a whole must include *all* the activities, people, and objects that influence the final form of the artifact and the context of its use.

The second section of the book, Who to Involve In Design, deals less with frameworks and methods for coordinating different people and more with the identities of the people to involve. However, Cohill's chapter might easily have gone instead into the first section, because it suggests that the coordination of design activities and people can better be done by a person with that as his only role, than by a bunch of different people with specialized interests trying to give appropriate credence to others. Just as architects of buildings have ties to engineering, art, finance, construction, geology, and geography, Cohill's *information architect* would be the means of communication for, and the instrument of, the eclectic design approach.

The remaining three chapters in this section also can be used as support for the eclectic approach to design. Lanning's, Tang's, and Craig's chapters advocate design approaches that cannot be condensed into tools, techniques, or even frameworks. Lanning separated design into several subtasks, each requiring a different kind of information about users and their tasks. He insisted that the only way to get this information is to bring in experts—the users themselves. Tang's approach is an anthropological analysis of interface use. I believe Tang's approach is not an algorithm, nor even an explicable heuristic, but a set of attitudes, knowledge, skills, and experiences that can be adequately instilled and combined only through anthropology graduate education, reading the books Tang's chapter recommends, and apprenticing. Similarly, Craig called not for handing out graphic design guidelines to interface designers, but for using a professional graphic designer as a source of esthetic sense and years of practical experience and artistic schooling. None of these three authors claimed their approach is sufficient for design, and they denied that their approaches can be packaged for quick reference by people without relevant backgrounds. Therefore, no overarching theory of interface design, nor any single person, can include all the necessary approaches to design; an eclectic approach is required.

Though most of the techniques described in the book's Methods section are narrower than those in the first two sections, many of the Methods chapters explicitly mention the eclectic nature of design and how their techniques enhance it. Everyone at the workshop—even those proposing specialized methods—talked about eclecticism. For example, some workshop participants were mostly concerned with finding methods for the relatively narrow problem of representing interfaces. This discussion kept returning to the necessity of notations being comprehensible to people with varied backgrounds; for instance, potential users of the interface often are brought into the design team briefly, on short notice, with no training in human factors or computers. This prompted the suggestion of prototypes, pictures of screens, scenarios, and natural language as concrete, readily understood representations. But those representations lack the conciseness needed by other members of the design team—members who are schooled in computers and human factors. Even professionals on the team have favorite notations and languages peculiar to their disciplines—anthropology, psychology, sociology, computer science, art. Multinational teams have the extra problem of finding *which* natural language to use as the representation. Thus, all the way through to the proponents of the most focused methods, in the workshop discussion and chapters I see the fundamental assumption that design is and must be composed of many different people doing many different things.

B. Agreement from a Workshop on the Role of Theory in HCI

The HCI literature tends toward acknowledgment of eclecticism as the proper description of design as currently practiced, but it is just starting to recognize eclecticism as the normative approach as well. Especially telling is the collection of papers from a recent workshop on a quite different topic from our workshop on techniques—the Kittle House workshop on the role of theory in HCI (Carroll, 1991-a). One dimension along which all the chapters in their resulting book could be organized is optimism about the utility of scientific theory for application to design. But the resulting ranks are confusing: It is possible to see the Lewis (1991) and Barnard (1991) chapters allied in optimism, contrary to the pessimism of the rest of the chapters. But it is also possible to see Barnard (with Carroll, 1991-b; Carroll, Kellogg, & Rosson, 1991; and Payne, 1991) as more optimistic for a universal role for theory than Lewis and everyone else. Another sign that the workshop participants' attitudes cannot easily be classified on this dimension is that Greif (1991) and Bannon and Bødker (1991) did not consider themselves pessimistic about theory, because their versions of theory included a wealth of detailed contextual information. Yet some of the other participants thought those very details made the theories so unparsimonious as to reduce their values both as theories and as practical orientations.

I think eclecticism makes a better organizing dimension for the theory work-shop's chapters, and lets it easily relate to our technique workshop. The three chapters of Barnard (1991), Payne (1991), and Carroll *et al.* (1991) seemed to pursue the dream of a single, theory-based approach that would use science to bring faster improvements to design than can be gotten from a consciously eclectic approach. Lewis's (1991) and diSessa's (1991) chapters were more eclectic, and therefore supported the utility of basic theory *when it is used in concert with other approaches.* DiSessa gave a physical science example of how theory can be important even when contextual details make it insufficient: The design of a piece of material may depend on a parameter of the material's strength, but theory may not predict the parameter's value. Though the strength must be found by measurement, theory makes an enormous difference by inter-preting *strength* in a more meaningful way and by allowing practical implica-tions to be drawn from the parameter's value in one direction or the other. Karat and Bennett (1991-b), Henderson (1991), Landauer (1991), and Tetzlaff and Mack (1991) were also especially supportive of the need for multiple approaches. For a workshop on the role of theory, there was a lot of discussion of techniques (Tetzlaff & Mack (1991) summarized them). I take the theory workshop's attitude as evidence converging with our technique workshop's atti-tude, in support of eclecticism as the normative approach to HCI. There were some dissenters at the theory workshop, but I think my next section shows their objections are weak.

C. *Three Poor Alternatives to Eclecticism*

Though consensus on the desirability of eclecticism is rising from both the theoretical camp (the theory workshop—Carroll, 1991-a) and the meth-odological camp (our workshop), there are some principled objections. I believe the complaints derive from the observations that eclecticism has been the standard approach to interface design for decades and that the resulting interfaces have not been good. We know current interfaces are poor, despite the lack of ideals from theory or practice as standards for comparison, because potential improvements often seem so obvious to users, to other designers, and even to the same designers, after the interfaces are put in use.

A natural response to the poverty of current design is to radically change the approach from eclecticism to something else. The first such shift was toward the simplicity and generality of scientific theory, especially psychology (e.g., Card, Moran, & Newell, 1983), but it proved woefully inadequate due to its oversimplification of the phenomena (as contended, for example, by the major-ity of the theory workshop participants in Carroll, 1991-a). The second shift was in the opposite direction—abandonment of attempts to simplify, generalize, or systematically observe (e.g. Winograd & Flores, 1986). This radical contextualist approach, too, is being rejected, because it does not help designers cope with the enormous complexity of their task.

Most recently Carroll and colleagues have proposed a noneclectic hybrid of the two previous noneclectic methods. To show that it is no better than the first two approaches I must spend some time on it, as it has not yet gotten the literature's critical attention. I think their "usability-innervated invention" (Carroll, 1989) is a craft approach in scientific garb, rather than a novel and useful cross of the contextualist and theoretical frameworks. Some of their methods may be valuable, but their anti-eclectic insistence on interpreting them as a unified scientific approach detracts from the methods' comprehensibility and usability.

Carroll and colleagues rejected the radical contextualist approach because it offered little understanding—little generalization and abstraction about HCI—but they despaired of the traditional scientific approach because of its inadequate handling of the complexity of real use (Carroll, 1989, p. 72). They claimed an approach could be built around the assumption that HCI artifacts in their natural situations of use "embody implicit theories of human interaction with software. Indeed, they embody theory of a sort that melds the need for some abstraction with the need for task details and design examples" (Carroll, in press).

I object to this use of interpretations-of-artifacts as substitutes for theory, because they do not serve all the functions of good theory. Even Carroll and Campbell (1989) did not assert they serve more than the falsifiability and formal explanatory functions. Good theory must also serve parsimony, comprehensibility, fruitfulness, and prediction, though I do not go as far as the contextualists do in deemphasizing falsification (Jaeger & Rosnow, 1988, p. 71). I believe artifacts (aside from their interpretations, to which I turn next) score miserably on those other dimensions. As for explanatory function, though formal cause and effect relations can be seen in artifacts' relations with users and tasks, it is only in that formal sense that artifacts *explain* anything. Artifacts do not convey the gut sense of comprehension—the connection of the target phenomenon to our general knowledge—that a good theory does.

The very notion of *interpreting* artifacts—of extracting claims from them—sits poorly. On one hand, it should not be possible to construct useful claims simpler than the artifact, because "it seems likely that artifacts are in principle irreducible to a more conventional theory medium. . . . [because] the design of software may be of an order of complexity beyond that which conventional theories can explain or predict" (Carroll, 1989, p. 65). On the other hand, the artifacts *must* be interpreted: "The artifact, as the common ground, is the appropriate *source from which to construct* [italics added] sharable understandings of the relationship of user experience and design" (Kellogg, 1990). All of the concrete examples of their approach used verbal claims as explications of the theories implicit in the artifacts; they did not use just the artifacts, because the artifacts are not general and abstract enough (e.g., Bellamy & Carroll, 1990; Kellogg, 1990).

In some of their writings, there seems to be no distinction between their task-artifact centered approach and the theoretical approach they decried. I say this because I do not see a distinction between constructing claims by observing artifacts, and constructing theories by observing natural phenomena. One possible distinction is that artifacts might be said to be built by people using theories, so the artifacts are a more concentrated source of theory than natural phenomena are. But Carroll and company denied this: "It is *not* a claim about the *intentions* of the designers of Smalltalk, it is a claim about psychological consequences for users of Smalltalk. Our approach to design rationale does not attempt to externalize the designer's reasoning process . . . but rather attempts to externalize the psychology inherent in the designed artifact and its use" (Carroll & Rosson, in press). Okay, then maybe they are just using the artifacts as explications of *un*intentional claims of the designers—of their *im*plicit theories. In that case, any knowledge elicitation methods would be appropriate, such as multiattribute decision theory (Edwards, 1977) and psychological scaling (Davison, 1983). But they never used such methods of collecting designers' opinions; instead they got other people to extract the claims from the artifacts and tasks. Indeed, Carroll and Rosson (in press) stated that the claims about the utility of demonstrations in their Smalltalk utility were claims made *by Smalltalk* as a theoretical entity.

If "claims" are not intentionally placed in artifacts by designers, then teleology cannot be the distinction between Carroll and colleagues' target phenomena and biologists' target phenomena. How, then, can biologists successfully use scientific theory? Surely their phenomena are no less complex than ours! Surely their organisms are as intertwined with their environments as our artifacts are! Why do biologists not eschew the traditional language and concepts of science in favor of treating organisms and species as embodiments of claims about their survivability? If, instead, claims extraction is no different from theory construction, why should we expect claims extraction to succeed as a grand strategy, when we (well, many of us, including Carroll and company) have rejected all grand theoretical approaches as unworkable because of the complexity of our targets? We shouldn't; I think the extent to which claims extraction succeeds in designing particular artifacts (and this remains to be seen, since no artifacts have been designed this way) will be owed to the craft of the designer. Carroll and company have some possibly good but ill defined methods that are abstract and general (science- and engineering-like) enough to be transmitted to other people, but artful enough for their transmission to require more than verbal description—they require apprenticeship. This is a good example of what many of our workshop's participants called craft—a practice in between art and science/engineering (Wroblewski, 1991).

I think Carroll and colleagues needlessly tried to justify their methods as science; their contention that interpretations of artifacts are similar to theory buys nothing. The methods can stand alone as craft, as revealed in two paragraphs of Carroll and Rosson (in press, Section 2.1, the paragraphs starting with "To a great extent" and "The approach"). Those two paragraphs contain the most straightforward and lucid of all their published descriptions of their methods, because there they did not try to justify their methods as science but merely described how the methods could improve the craft of design.

This burial of potentially useful methods in rationalizations of those methods as science is a severe disadvantage of Carroll and colleagues' conceptual framework for HCI. Their approach's handicap is as large as those of the previous two approaches, which either deny the spotlight to techniques that aid the design process without specifying the actual design (the science/engineering framework) or which refuse to allow strong intrusion into the design process for fear of disrupting the task-user-artifact ecology (the contextualist framework). What we need is a framework that acknowledges the power of all techniques, including scientific theories, art and craft, and techniques not directly concerned with the designer or the conscious act of design. Even without a grand theoretical framework, such an eclectic approach need not be chaotic and can be improved by research.

III. The Eclectic Approach Is Improvable

When I asked why many researchers put most of their energy into trying to expand the role of science in design while virtually ignoring techniques such as speeding the design-test cycle, Jack Carroll responded that he wanted to *do* something. He was afraid that an eclectic approach would be the same as no approach, and that without principled criticism of design and of research on design, the HCI discipline would become unproductive chaos. When I asked Steve Payne the same question about the emphasis on theory, he said "presumably that's where the leverage is."

But eclecticism does not mean absence of theory, just absence of global, dominating theory. It is a mistake to interpret the coincidence of our dramatic technological progress with our astounding scientific success, as evidence of an all-encompassing scientific framework that assists the translation of basic theory into technology. But it is also a mistake to think that basic theory rarely contributes to technology, as Carroll sometimes has written. Lewis (1991) and diSessa (1991) were optimistic for theory in HCI because they recognized that basic scientific theory in domains such as medicine has been powerful in pockets of time and topic, and has even connected these pockets, without being the only source of advance in either science or technology. Carroll and company were more pessimistic about direct contribution by basic science than Lewis and diSessa were and ironically were more optimistic about the utility of an overall scientific orientation. Carroll and colleagues have been trying to create something like science out of the entire enterprise of design, whereas Lewis and diSessa have allowed a plethora of other activities to dominate the design process, with theory playing only one role. Meteorology is a good example of how to deal with complex phenomena eclectically: Forecasts are produced by combining empirical data and empirically derived models (as Landauer (1991) supported), large doses of human experience, expertise, and intuition, and some deep qualitative and quantitative scientific theories.

Local *methods* also work well, and I think they have the potential to improve HCI design far more than do local theories, at least for several decades. This conclusion was reached even by some participants of the theory workshop (Tetzlaff & Mack, 1991). The Methods section of our book describes several innovative local techniques and tools. Siochi, Hix, and Hartson opened the section with a report on User Action Notation of interfaces. It is a good example of what I consider one of the narrower methods, not because it is of limited utility but because it is focused on a narrowly defined problem; obviously—and this came up during our workshop discussion—the interface representation can play a pivotal role in the design process. The chapters by Braudes, Carter, and James are broader in that they propose techniques explicitly encompassing most of the design process. There is a continuum of chapters on prototyping: Craig's focuses on very quick prototyping of appearance and simple function of interfaces (in the book's Who to Involve in Design section), Miller-Jacobs's includes more interface function but still prefers limited function for the sake of rapidity, and Rouff and Horowitz's goes into a particular and ambitious scheme for prototyping much deeper function. Catterall, Taylor, and Galer's describes an entire set of tools intended to make it easy for designers with no training or proclivity for human factors to include usability in their product's development. McGrew's chapter is a description and demonstration of a method specialized for menu design; the technique is unusual in its use of the context of graph theory to inspire task analysis. The Methods section and the book are closed by Harker's report of experiences with real designers using various methods, some of which were described in the previous chapters.

The key to consciously improving the eclectic approach, and in fact the reason it can be considered an identifiable approach, is the global methods that tie all these local theories and methods into a unified design process. The largest in scope are the methods grouped in our book's section on Coordinating Design Activities, though several of the chapters in the Methods section are coordinators within narrower domains. To an extent, the book's section on Who to Involve in Design is part of global methodology, because the people recommended there are experts who serve as summaries of vast quantities of information. Such an expert not only ties together his own subdiscipline (such as the task domain in which the artifact will be used), he dynamically links that subdomain appropriately with the other aspects of design. Cohill's information architects are the most global of the experts, because they connect *all* the components of the design process.

Well, almost all the components. Some methods for improving the design process are too far-reaching to fit into Cohill's notion of information architecture or even into a simple framework of eclecticism, and other methods are accommodated by simple eclecticism but aren't given proper due. Worse yet is the failure of a passive, simple, eclectic framework to *suggest* new theories and methods to *drive* progress in the design discipline. To get these benefits I suggest we adopt the perspective of interfaces as members of evolving species.

IV. Evolution-of-Artifacts as a Framework for Improving Eclectic Design

Many researchers and developers are sure that improving the speed of the design-prototype-test cycle would dramatically increase the influence of usability on design (e.g., Brooks, 1987, p. 17; Nielsen, 1989). But none of the frameworks I've described so far (science/engineering, claims extraction, contextualism, passive eclecticism) gives proper due to the power of this technique or to any of the others described in our book. Much of the problem is that frameworks for thinking about design have usually focused on the intentional act of design—how designers think or act and what materials or guidance can be given to them to assist their thinking and acting. In effect, designers are users of tools, and we have usually tried to design good tools for them by getting inside their heads. But acknowledging the utility of, for instance, design-prototype-test cycle rapidity as a useful tool requires stepping out of the designer's perspective, because the designer is inside the first part of that cycle.

The contextualists (e.g., Bødker, 1989; Whiteside, Bennett, & Holtzblatt, 1988; Winograd & Flores, 1986) extended the scope of design to include as influences (and sometimes as co-designers) the users of the artifact, the people who affect the situation in which the artifact is used, and the social context of the artifact. This definition of design is satisfyingly broad, but it has the bad effect of dealing with the overwhelming web of influences on HCI by tangling designers in the web. Another approach, the unelaborated concept of design as craft, is similar to contextualism in its leaving us somewhat helpless for sources of ideas on how to improve the design process, because craft is improved by its practitioners slowly refining their experience and knowledge and passing them on to other craftspeople. That craft conception leaves as our major recourse just waiting for better design practice to evolve, and that is slow if we can train new craftspeople only by apprenticeship; Wroblewski (1991) pointed to this as a good focus for research. Another trouble of the craft conception is that it undervalues techniques, such as speeding of the design-prototype-test cycle, that are distant from hands-on, direct, intentional design activity. This is a consequence of craft's emphases on one-of-a-kind artifacts, the mingling of design with manufacture, and the mingling of tools with materials (Wroblewski, 1991).

Both these problems of contextualist and craft orientations—failure to suggest how to improve the design process and failure to acknowledge good methods that are outside the orientations' scopes—can be solved by stepping back from the designer's perspective even farther than the contextualists have. We need to adopt a perspective that contains the entire design process, with *all* the influences on the final form of the artifact. But passive, simple eclecticism will not do. The new framework must be *actively* eclectic; it must be a scheme that helps us discover ways to improve the multitude of things in the very broadly defined design process.

Henderson (1991) came close to this perspective by thinking of artifacts as continually developing organisms. He acknowledged virtually all the influences on artifact development, including the usually ignored but powerful effect of marketing. But he did not step back quite far enough to get all the relevant influences into a coherent picture: He wisely emphasized that design is never really finished because artifacts never stop changing, and he recognized that its change is intrinsically cyclic (there are successive versions of interfaces). But he failed to recognize that biologic organisms don't develop cyclically and so differ from interfaces. A closely related problem is that the speed of development has no meaning in the context of an individual organism's development, whereas the speed of iterative design-test cycles is very important in the development of interfaces.

Taking Henderson's biological analogy one step farther back eliminates these problems. If we think of HCI artifacts as members of species, and each design-to-test cycle as the birth-to-birthing lifetime of one organism, then the iterations leading to a marketable product are the evolution of a species. The speed of iteration matters because the species' final form must meet the requirements of its changing environment's current state, including production deadlines. The environment includes influences (such as marketing demands, fads, limits of current hardware and software, and the bias we and users have from doing tasks in the current ways) that go well beyond the designer's intentional activity or awareness, so the designer's craft is but one influence on the species' form, and *all* influences are given proper due. The evolution-of-artifacts perspective lets us retain craft as our conception of the designers' activity, but makes the artifact the focus of a wider picture in which the designers' intentional activity is but one influence on the artifact species.

The notion of evolution of technology stretches back for nearly a century (Dunlavy, 1989). Norman (1988, p. 21) quoted a designer making that connection: "The 'R' button [on British telephones] is a kind of vestigial feature. It is very hard to remove features of a newly designed product that had existed in an earlier version. It's kind of like physical evolution. If a feature is in the genome, and if that feature is not associated with any negativity (i.e., no customers gripe about it), then the feature hangs on for generations."

There are selection pressures in the evolutionary environment of HCI artifacts. Another of the designers with whom Norman spoke (p. 29) described one: If an artifact fails in the marketplace two or three times, no one dares introduce it again, even if it is improved over the original. Since five or six redesigns are necessary to get the design right, and the redesigns must be informed by feedback from the marketplace, then good designs are unlikely to evolve, because the species fails to live through all the necessary marketplace tries. This is analogous to biological evolution's requirement that the species be hardy enough for a reproductively viable population to exist continuously, so deviant individuals can reproduce, so any subtle survival advantages of their genotypes can be strengthened to overcome other genotypic disadvantages.

Unlike a radical contextual framework, the evolutionary framework allows researchers to take strong action to quickly improve the design process. An example is doing extensive usability testing outside of the marketplace, so the species has time to adapt without being decimated. Since only limited time will ever be available for testing and redesign before the artifact goes to market, we need a second technique: speeding of the design-prototype-test cycle to allow greater adaptation within the given time. These methods allow us to powerfully improve artifacts' structures without forcing us to grapple with the impossible task of direct specification of artifacts' structures (as still favored by Long & Dowell, 1989).

A. The Evolutionary Framework Suggests Improvements of Design and Design Process

1. Design by Management Instead of by Specification

The biological analogy serves the additional purpose of forcing us to acknowledge that interfaces are too complex to be designed entirely analytically, just as biological organisms and species are. Brooks said as much in 1987 though he was not exclusively concerned with usability, but with software engineering in general: "The conceptual structures we construct today are too complicated to be specified accurately in advance, and too complex to be built faultlessly, . . . [so] we must take a radically different approach. . . . The secret [of the brain] is that it is grown, not built. So it must be with our software systems" (p. 18).

Even outside the computer domain, many artifacts have always been too complex to be designed purely by decomposition into manageable units (contrary to Long & Dowell's 1989 claim that decomposition is central to engineering's success). Many are too complex for their design to be contained in any one person's head, so external representations act as cognitive and sensory extensions; these tools run the gamut from mnemonics, to drawings on paper, to prototypes, to mathematical models. Someone using such tools is no longer doing purely analytic design but is creating and managing a design process. Some objects are too complicated to be understood by any one person even with external representations, so the design process must be subdivided among people. In a design team, if anyone can be labeled *the* designer, that person is doing design by creating and managing the social design process. In our book, this person is Cohill's *information architect*, and some methods that person can use were described by Karat and Bennett.

Some artifacts are so complicated, or the goals they will serve so ill defined, that their goals cannot even be entirely explicated for assignment to team members. Instead the designer specifies the processes by which the artifacts are created or the environment from which they arise. This type of design is actually covered by standard definitions of design, such as, "design is the successive application of constraints until only a unique product is left" (Richard W. Pew quoted in Norman, 1988, page 158). Pew probably intended "constraints" to mean explicit specification of the object's structure, but it can also mean specification only of the *process* by which the object's structure is evaluated against the goals and the results fed back to change the structure.

Design by process has as long a history as does design by analysis. Providing an environment for an artifact's growth, self-assembly, or construction by other agents (e.g., making pearls by seeding oysters) is traditional agriculture. Agricultural versions of analytic design are much newer—tree grafting and genetic engineering, in contrast to selective breeding. These examples illustrate the difference between specifying a process to build the artifact we have analytically designed and using process *to* design. In selective breeding agriculture, the desired characteristics sometimes are known in advance, and agents or environments are designed to build objects having those features. But often agriculturists don't know the exact identities of the desired characteristics. They only know that they want plants that produce much grain; they don't know what particular characters are responsible for high grain production. Science may reveal that the needed character is resistance to salt, in which case the design becomes more analytical. But often the features producing high grain production are so numerous and interdependent that the design process is merely the act of selecting plants that produce much grain. Empirical design is necessary in these cases because the complexity of the artifact precludes analysis. Are we not forced to do the same with interfaces?

2. An Example of Design by Managing the Design Process

An excellent example is the design of connectionist AI systems (McClelland, Rumelhart, & the PDP Research Group, 1986; Rumelhart, McClelland, & the PDP Research Group, 1986). The connectionist system's complete design is not just its initial set of links and nodes but the final weights of its links. Most of those weights are not specified by the designers but are built by the system from its own activity during exposure to an environment chosen by the designers. Part of the designer's job is to figure out which environment produces networks that behave in the desired way. Connectionist systems do not work perfectly the first time, so the design process is iterative. Often the designers have little idea, even after the fact, why the successful artifacts are successful. The advantage of such design by managing the design process is that the artifact's specific structure need not be known in advance. The disadvantage is that the designers often learn little about the artifact's structure that they can turn into a prescription for creating other artifacts, just as early agronomists didn't learn that resistance to salt was the key to their success with plant breeding.

Part of a connectionist system's final form is of course due to its genetic structure—the portion of its structure that was intentionally designed. One of the purer examples of intentional design in this domain is Rumelhart and McClelland's (1986) use of phonemic units as the base of the genotype of their past-tense word producer. Even so, much of their design was empirical, because a connectionist system reaches its phenotype via interaction of its genotype with its environment. So Rumelhart and McClelland had to design not just the genotype but also the growth environment. Such iterative, empirical design does not fit the model of artifacts as individual organisms. Brooks (1987) and Henderson (1991) envisioned artifacts as growing entities, but they treated them as individuals; to contain iterative, empirical design, our framework must extend to species.

B. The Evolutionary Framework Suggests a Type of Grand Science for HCI

The evolutionary perspective allows us to do science without rationalizing our craft activity as science (as in Carroll and colleagues' claims extraction). It does this by suppressing the details enough to bring the topic into the scope of good science. A lesson from evolutionary biology is that stepping away from phenomena can make their study tractable without losing either the productivity of study or the scientific nature of study. In biology, meteorology, and other disciplines, a recent and extreme example of stepping back is scientists resorting to the mathematics of chaos in order to cope with complexity that overwhelms their traditional approaches. When it became apparent that the situations they were investigating were too sensitive to initial conditions, they receded far enough to see regularities—for instance, chaotic attractors—that allow them to continue theorizing despite their inability to specify the details of the processes (Pool, 1989).

At the same time that the evolutionary framework simplifies the phenomena enough for us to do science, it meets the contextualists' demand that we consider simultaneously the entire ecology of HCI—artifacts, tasks, users, and more—including the important fact that artifacts influence the evolution of their environments as much as vice versa. Biology has an important, descriptive branch that is the first line of attack on such daunting complexity:

> Systematics, the study of biological diversity, is sometimes portrayed as the mere classification of organisms, but in fact its range and challenge are among the greatest in biology. . . . Because of the largely unknown nature of diversity, systematics remains a fountainhead of discoveries and new ideas in biology. If a biologist is well trained in the classification of the organisms encountered, the known facts of natural history are an open book, and new phenomena come more quickly into focus. (Wilson, 1985, p. 1227)
>
> Systematics is not simply the identification of specimens, it is the reconstruction of evolutionary history; and it should be supported not just because it has practical applications (which it does) but because it is a fundamental scientific discipline. (O'Hara, Maddison, & Stevens, 1988, p. 276)
>
> Systematics matters to biology because it embodies the process theories of organisms' existence. . . . The most remarkable collective property of organisms is not their diversity, but their many shared traits through which that diversity is expressed. . . . Systematics tries to identify these traits and reconstruct the hierarchy of relationships. So systematics is not only taxonomy—the description of organisms in an ordered system of words—or only the collection and identification of organisms. It is, most generally, the study of how to best compare the results of evolution. (O'Grady & Mooi, 1990, p. 1594)

The evolutionary framework justifies the advocacy of description by Brooks (1991) and Pylyshyn (1991) as the proper role for theory in HCI. As the preceding quotes about the role of description in biology attest, the result is far more than static categorization for convenience. Systematics represents the history of species, including the many influences that contextualists insist are relevant. Unlike, say, the Goms approach, this kind of simplifying theory for complex phenomena is within our ability and includes sufficient detail to be relevant. Unlike the radical contextualist approach, it suppresses enough complexity to reveal actions we can take to manipulate artifacts powerfully but indirectly, by manipulating many facets of their evolutionary environment. Evolution of artifacts thus accommodates and encourages all the various methods described in our book.

C. The Evolutionary Framework Explains Eclecticism's Optimality

Jaeger and Rosnow (1988) emphasized that many theoretical and methodological perspectives are needed to deal with human action. Even traditional scientists do not work the way they represent themselves in journal articles; instead they think Yiddish while writing British (p. 67). Formal experimentation definitely "can play a role in describing certain relational patterns or identifying causal properties," but it is needed in addition to other approaches, such as hermeneutics (p. 69). "While contextualism and mechanism constitute different world views, there is nonetheless a certain affinity between them; mechanism can lend a certain substance and basis to contextualism while contextualism, in turn, can give a life and reality to mechanistic accounts" (p. 72). We need a framework for the HCI discipline that permits all these conceptions to be used when and where they are appropriate, without having one conception—be it science, engineering, craft, or art—squeeze out the others.

1. Proper Credit to All Techniques That Help Design

The framework I found for my overview of the Taking Design Seriously workshop is that artifacts and the evolutionary niches they fill should be taken more seriously than the intentional act of design. This perspective of evolving artifacts changes the question for methods creators from "how do we help designers," through "how do we improve the design process," to "how do we modify the evolutionary process so artifacts more quickly attain desirable forms?"

Brooks, a software engineer rather than a human factors specialist, wrote:

It is really impossible for a client, even working with a software engineer, to specify completely, precisely, and correctly the exact requirements of a modern software product before trying some versions of the product. Therefore, one of the most promising of the current technological efforts, and one that attacks the essence, not the accidents, of the software problem, is the development of approaches and tools for rapid prototyping of systems as prototyping is part of the iterative specification of requirements. (1987, p. 17)

What strikes me about Brooks's prescription is that it has nothing to do with scientific theory, and nothing to do with engineering principles that specify artifact structure. Rather, he thought the most leverage is in methods. My favorite example of such a method is improvement of the speed of the cycle of design-prototype-test; it is superficial in the applied science, engineering, and claims extraction conceptions of HCI, yet it promises to be more powerful than those approaches. With Brooks's general prescription and the accepted utility of this particular technique, why does an auspicious technique like this get so little research resources?

I suspect our current frameworks for thinking about HCI are what prevent us from taking seriously methods such as those in this book. In contrast, the evolutionary framework forces us to see the importance of all tools and techniques. Most relevant to this workshop is the evolution framework's broadening of focus beyond the designer, to all influences on the artifact. By relegating intentional design to being just one influence of many, the evolutionary viewpoint frees us to examine and manipulate factors outside the designer. That is fortunate, for if the designer's activity is craft there is little we can do to help, because most of that activity is nonconscious, informal, and implicit (Wroblewski, 1991). Many of the methods in this book help design by influencing things, such as communication among team members, that are outside the individual designer's intentional work on the artifact. The evolutionary framework helps us explain why those methods help design, by revealing the things the methods influence.

2. Proper Credit to Analytic Design (Genetic Engineering)

Evolution has long battled revolution as an historical view of technological change: Do new artifacts arise gradually through modifications of extant ones, or are radical designs proposed suddenly? Recently Basalla (1988) tried to close the argument in favor of continuity, by taking the analogy with biological evolution to a new depth. He thought of artifacts' designs as being continuous through their generations but he also recognized that evolution requires sources of novelty and selection pressures. But Dunlavy (1989) wrote that Basalla's deeper analogy with biological evolution may have eliminated the argument about evolution versus revolution, by changing the meaning of technological *evolution* from *continuous* to the more technical biological meaning. In this deep sense evolution requires not only selection pressures, which I have discussed for HCI, but also genetic diversity on which the selection pressures can operate. Such a conception can be extended to evolution in HCI technology.

To get genetic diversity, even connectionists directly modify the genotypes of their neonates. In HCI, designers can intentionally use themes (e.g., object orientation) in creating the original interfaces they inject into the evolutionary process, so they need not rely on random genotype sources. This is where science and engineering can play important roles—even if they find only a few good principles or themes, designers can use those as seeds for evolutionary fine tuning.

Molecular biology provides the lesson that absolute control over genetics—something we have in HCI—is insufficient; we need knowledge of which genetic structures to create. Molecular engineers now have the ability to create precisely whatever simple genetic sequences they desire. But often theory is insufficient to dictate which sequences to create for particular purposes. So some molecular engineers are using random sequences as inputs to artificial evolution, with the selection pressures designed to favor traits suitable for the applications (Beardsley, 1990). Even when a solution is known from theory or accident, there is always the possibility that it is only locally optimal—that there is some drastically different solution that cannot be found from the current gene pool or from intentional tinkering with the current genetic sequence. Similarly, in HCI we will never be certain that the interface themes we have found through science and engineering, or even through the contextualist approach of asking users and examining their work environments, are globally optimal. We need to foster diversity by adopting brainstorming techniques, by scouring hardware and software labs, and maybe by using randomization as the molecular engineers do. Perhaps we can even draw by analogy from the methods used to prevent local settling in mathematical procedures. The need for such methods is revealed far more by the evolutionary framework than by the science and engineering frameworks.

V. Conclusions

An eclectic approach to HCI produces a large number of widely differing interface ideas, some from local theory, some from global descriptive theory, some from users, some from tasks and work situations, some from accident, some from tradition, and some from the clear blue sky. The evolutionary analogy makes us realize that this diversity is necessary, so the analogy reveals the value of methods that increase the number and diversity of interface ideas. In contrast, diversity is restricted by frameworks that attempt to be all-encompassing guides to design. Such restriction is good only in narrow domains, because there is no universally best design; there *are* some very narrow domains (of task, user, and interface feature) in which there are optimum designs, and some of these designs can be created from theory. Eclecticism recognizes their existence and therefore values the local theories and craft wisdom that point to them, along with the situation-specific empirical approaches necessary for the many other cases. Many of the methods in this book cultivate eclecticism by encouraging diversity of the initial pool of design ideas. Some do this by fostering communication among design team members, thereby giving all species of artifacts the chance to be evaluated by the really important selection forces instead of by mere obscurity. Some methods, such as rapid prototyping, encourage diversity by giving design ideas the chance to be evaluated in fully developed form and in test environments very similar to the real environments. Thus, the fostering of diversity can be expressed as several concrete, narrow, achievable goals such as fostering communication and easing prototyping. HCI researchers can deliberately and quickly improve the general design process by building methods to support those concrete goals, and HCI designers can improve designs of particular interfaces by using those methods. So eclecticism need not be passive or unguided.

Just as a source of diverse genotypes is useful only if combined with effective selection, diversity of HCI designs is useful only if powerful methods are available for finding the good designs. As many of our workshop participants emphasized, we need good usability testing methods to serve as selectors.

These methods must fairly represent the selection pressures in the real world, for example by representatively sampling users or by testing in real work situations.   Communication among the design team members is important for guaranteeing that the test results serve the selection function, by guaranteeing that the people who make the final decisions seriously consider the results. Some methods for this communication are letting the users design, having an information architect explicitly in charge of integrating all the activities and people, representing the test results on the walls of the same room that displays other information relevant to the design, and illustrating test results with video clips.   In the selection component of evolution as in the diversity component, eclecticism need not be passive. Though there are many test methods that conflict because they serve different goals, such as external versus internal validity, the data from the different methods need not conflict.   As this book demonstrates, we can build methods that give all testing results their proper places in the design process.

After empirical forces have selected a good genotype from the diverse population, the third component of evolution comes into play: extensive reproduction of that individual's most beneficial traits, thereby forming a species. Craft wisdom and local theory can perform this distilling and propagating function, and this is often the way that theory and wisdom arise: After an excellent design emerges, theory is used or created to explain it, so the best features can be deliberately used again in other artifacts. Once again, there is no single best way; some artifacts' best features and the circumstances of their use are describable by scientific theory, but most are describable only as craft tradition. Communication is as important in this evolutionary phase as it was in the previous two phases, but here the need is more for transmission of the information through time. Many of the methods described in this book recognize the multiple generations of artifact species and have mechanisms to enhance the survival of good traits by easing their entry into the craft database, be it a formal database or informal shared wisdom. In this reproduction phase, too, eclecticism is needed but need not be passive: Designers can search hard for, and use previously discovered, good interface features. Researchers can create methods that ease this reuse, such as modular prototyping to permit good features to be easily retained as an interface evolves.

Many different people doing many different things are needed for good interface design. But the lack of dominance of any one design approach does not doom us to the pace of natural evolution of artifacts, as long as our deliberate improvement of the design process includes improving *all* the influences on artifacts. Evolution of artifacts as species is a framework that encompasses all these influences and which suggests new methods. This framework has places for all the methods in this book and makes apparent the need to use any methods that help design, even if they are not theoretically motivated or concerned with individual designers' intentional work directly on the artifact. The evolutionary framework lets us take methods seriously as tools for actively and studiously cultivating eclectic design.

References

Bannon, L. J., & Bødker, S. (1991). Beyond the interface: Encountering artifacts in use. In J. M. Carroll (Ed.), *Designing interaction: Psychology at the human-computer interface*. New York: Cambridge University Press.

Barnard, P. (1991). Bridging between basic theories and the artifacts of human-computer interaction. In J. M. Carroll (Ed.), *Designing interaction: Psychology at the human-computer interface*. New York: Cambridge University Press.

Basalla, G. (1988). *The evolution of technology*. Cambridge, England: Cambridge University Press.

Beardsley, T. (1990). New order: Artificial evolution creates proteins nature missed. *Scientific American*, October, pp. 18, 24.

Bellamy, R. K. E., & Carroll, J. M. (1990). Redesign by design. In D. Diaper, D. Gilmore, G. Cockton, & B. Shackel (Eds.), *Human-computer interaction—Interact '90* (pp. 199–205). Amsterdam: North-Holland.

Bødker, S. (1989). A human activity approach to user interfaces. *Human-Computer Interaction, 4*, 171–195.

Braudes, B. (1990). Report of the design methodologies subgroup. *SIGCHI Bulletin, 22*, 42–45.

Braudes, R. E. (1991). Conceptual modelling: A look at system-level user interface issues. In J. Karat (Ed.), *Taking software design seriously: Practical techniques for human-computer interaction design*. Boston, MA: Academic Press.

Broadbent, D. (1990). A problem looking for solutions [Review of *The psychology of human-computer interaction* and *Cognitive science and its applications for human-computer interaction*]. *Psychological Science, 1*, 235–239.

Brooks, F. P., Jr. (1987). No silver bullet: Essence and accidents of software engineering. *Computer, 20*(4), 10–19.

Brooks, R. (1991). Comparative task analysis: An alternative direction for human computer interaction science. In J. M. Carroll (Ed.), *Designing interaction: Psychology at the human-computer interface*. New York: Cambridge University Press.

Card, S. K., Moran, T. P., & Newell, A. (1983). *The psychology of human computer interaction*. Hillsdale, New Jersey: Lawrence Erlbaum.

Carroll, J. M. (1989). Evaluation, description and invention: Paradigms for human-computer interaction. In M. C. Yovits (Ed.), *Advances in computers* (Vol. 29, pp. 47–77). San Diego: Academic Press.

Carroll, J. M. (Ed.). (1991-a). *Designing interaction: Psychology at the human-computer interface*. New York: Cambridge University Press.

Carroll, J. M. (1991-b). Designing interaction: Psychology at the human-computer interface. In J. M. Carroll (Ed.), *Designing interaction: Psychology at the human-computer interface*. New York: Cambridge University Press.

Carroll, J. M. (in press). Making errors, making sense, making use: Science and design in an ecology of tasks and artifacts. In Budde, Floyd, Keil-Slawik, & Zullighoven (Eds.), *Software development and reality construction*. Berlin: Springer-Verlag.

Carroll, J. M., & Campbell, R. L. (1989). Artifacts as psychological theories: The case of human-computer interaction. *Behaviour and Information Technology, 8,* 247–256.

Carroll, J. M., Kellogg, W. A., & Rosson, M. B. (1991). The task-artifact cycle. In J. M. Carroll (Ed.), *Designing interaction: Psychology at the human-computer interface.* New York: Cambridge University Press.

Carroll, J. M., & Rosson, M. B. (in press). Deliberated evolution: Stalking the View Matcher in design space. *Human-Computer Interaction.*

Carter, J. A. (1990). The universe of design is unfolding (as it should!). *SIGCHI Bulletin, 22,* 46–48.

Carter, J. A. Jr. (1991). Combining task analysis with software engineering in a methodology for designing interactive systems. In J. Karat (Ed.), *Taking software design seriously: Practical techniques for human-computer interaction design.* Boston, MA: Academic Press.

Casaday, G. (1991). Balance. In J. Karat (Ed.), *Taking software design seriously: Practical techniques for human-computer interaction design.* Boston, MA: Academic Press.

Catterall, B. J., Harker, S., Klein, G., Notess, M., & Tang, J. C. (1990). Group HCI design: Problems and prospects. *SIGCHI Bulletin, 22,* 37–41.

Catterall, B. J., Taylor, B. C., & Galer, M. D. (1991). The HUFIT planning, analysis and specification toolset—easing I.T. designers effectively into a consideration of human factors as a normal part of the I.T. product design process. In J. Karat (Ed.), *Taking software design seriously: Practical techniques for human-computer interaction design.* Boston, MA: Academic Press.

Cohill, A. M. (1991). Information architecture and the design process. In J. Karat (Ed.), *Taking software design seriously: Practical techniques for human-computer interaction design.* Boston, MA: Academic Press.

Craig, P. A. (1991). The role of graphic designers in interface design. In J. Karat (Ed.), *Taking software design seriously: Practical techniques for human-computer interaction design.* Boston, MA: Academic Press.

Davison, M. L. (1983). *Multidimensional scaling.* New York: John Wiley & Sons.

diSessa, A. A. (1991). Local sciences: Viewing the design of human-computer systems as cognitive science. In J. M. Carroll (Ed.), *Designing interaction: Psychology at the human-computer interface.* New York: Cambridge University Press.

Dunlavy, C. A. (1989). Technological change [Review of *The evolution of technology*]. *Science, 245,* 991.

Edwards, W. (1977). How to use multiattribute utility measurement for social decision making. *IEEE Transactions on Systems, Man, and Cybernetics, SMC-7,* 326–340.

Greif, S. (1991). The role of German work psychology in the design of artifacts. In J. M. Carroll (Ed.), *Designing interaction: Psychology at the human-computer interface.* New York: Cambridge University Press.

Harker, S. (1991). Human factors inputs to the design of computer systems: A review of requirements specification and the role of prototyping in current practice. In J. Karat (Ed.), *Taking software design seriously: Practical techniques for human-computer interaction design.* Boston, MA: Academic Press.

Henderson, A. (1991). A developmental perspective on interface, design, and theory. In J. M. Carroll (Ed.), *Designing interaction: Psychology at the human-computer interface.* New York: Cambridge University Press.

Hix, D., & Casaday, G. (1990). Report of the working group on interface design decisions and representation. *SIGCHI Bulletin, 22,* 34–36.

Jaeger, M. E., & Rosnow, R. L. (1988). Contextualism and its implications for psychological inquiry. *British Journal of Psychology, 79,* 63–75.

James, M. G. (1991). PRODUSER: PROcess for Developing USER-interfaces. In J. Karat (Ed.), *Taking software design seriously: Practical techniques for human-computer interaction design*. Boston, MA: Academic Press.

Karat, J., & Bennett, J. L. (1991-a). Using scenarios in design meetings—A case study example. In J. Karat (Ed.), *Taking software design seriously: Practical techniques for human-computer interaction design*. Boston, MA: Academic Press.

Karat, J., & Bennett, J. (1991-b). Working within the design process—supporting effective and efficient design. In J. M. Carroll (Ed.), *Designing interaction: Psychology at the human-computer interface*. New York: Cambridge University Press.

Karat, J., & Dayton, T. (1990). Taking design seriously: Exploring techniques useful in HCI design. *SIGCHI Bulletin, 22*, 26–33.

Kellogg, W. A. (1990). Qualitative artifact analysis. In D. Diaper, D. Gilmore, G. Cockton, & B. Shackel (Eds.), *Human-computer interaction—Interact '90* (pp. 193–198). Amsterdam: North-Holland.

Landauer, T. K. (1991). Let's get real: A position paper on the role of cognitive theory in the design of humanly useful and useable systems. In J. M. Carroll (Ed.), *Designing interaction: Psychology at the human-computer interface*. New York: Cambridge University Press.

Lanning, T. R. (1991). Let the users design! In J. Karat (Ed.), *Taking software design seriously: Practical techniques for human-computer interaction design*. Boston, MA: Academic Press.

Lewis, C. (1991). Inner theory in HCI. In J. M. Carroll (Ed.), *Designing interaction: Psychology at the human-computer interface*. New York: Cambridge University Press.

Long, J., & Dowell, J. (1989). Conceptions of the discipline of HCI: Craft, applied science, and engineering. In A. Sutcliffe & L. Macaulay (Eds.), *People and computers V: Proceedings of the fifth conference of the British Computer Society Human-Computer Interaction Specialist Group* (pp. 9–32). Cambridge, England: Cambridge University Press.

McClelland, J. L., Rumelhart, D. E., & the PDP Research Group. (1986). *Parallel distributed processing: Explorations in the microstructure of cognition: Vol. 2. Psychological and biological models*. Cambridge, MA: MIT Press, Bradford Books.

McDonald, J. E., & Schvaneveldt, R. W. (1988). The application of user knowledge to interface design. In R. Guindon (Ed.), *Cognitive science and its applications for human-computer interaction* (pp. 289–338). Hillsdale, New Jersey: Lawrence Erlbaum.

McGrew, J. F. (1991). Tools for task analysis: Graphs and matrices. In J. Karat (Ed.), *Taking software design seriously: Practical techniques for human-computer interaction design*. Boston, MA: Academic Press.

Miller-Jacobs, H. H. (1991). Rapid prototyping: An effective technique for system development. In J. Karat (Ed.), *Taking software design seriously: Practical techniques for human-computer interaction design*. Boston, MA: Academic Press.

Nielsen, J. (1989). Usability engineering at a discount. *Proceedings of the Third International Conference on Human-Computer Interaction, 3*, 1–8.

Norman, D. A. (1988). *The psychology of everyday things*. New York: Basic Books.

O'Grady, R. T., & Mooi, R. (1990). Support for systematics [Letter]. *Science, 248*, 1594–1595.

O'Hara, R. J., Maddison, D. R., & Stevens, P. F. (1988). Crisis in systematics [Letter]. *Science, 241*, 275–276.

Payne, S. J. (1991). Interface problems and interface resources. In J. M. Carroll (Ed.), *Designing interaction: Psychology at the human-computer interface*. New York: Cambridge University Press.

Pool, R. (1989). Chaos theory: How big an advance? *Science, 245*, 26–27.

Pylyshyn, Z. (1991). Some remarks on the theory-practice gap. In J. M. Carroll (Ed.), *Designing interaction: Psychology at the human-computer interface.* New York: Cambridge University Press.

Rouff, C., & Horowitz, E. (1991). A system for specifying and rapidly prototyping user interfaces. In J. Karat (Ed.), *Taking software design seriously: Practical techniques for human-computer interaction design.* Boston, MA: Academic Press.

Rumelhart, D. E., & McClelland, J. L. (1986). On learning the past tenses of English verbs. In J. L. McClelland, D. E. Rumelhart, & the PDP Research Group, *Parallel distributed processing: Explorations in the microstructures of cognition: Vol. 2. Psychological and biological models* (pp. 216–271). Cambridge, MA: MIT Press, Bradford Books.

Rumelhart, D. E., McClelland, J. L., & the PDP Research Group. (1986). *Parallel distributed processing: Explorations in the microstructure of cognition: Vol. 1. Foundations.* Cambridge, MA: MIT Press, Bradford Books.

Siochi, A. C., Hix, D., & Hartson, H. R. (1991). The UAN: A notation to support user-centered design of direct manipulation interfaces. In J. Karat (Ed.), *Taking software design seriously: Practical techniques for human-computer interaction design.* Boston, MA: Academic Press.

Tang, J. C. (1991). Involving social scientists in the design of new technology. In J. Karat (Ed.), *Taking software design seriously: Practical techniques for human-computer interaction design.* Boston, MA: Academic Press.

Tetzlaff, L., & Mack, R. (1991). Perspectives on methodology in HCI research and practice. In J. M. Carroll (Ed.), *Designing interaction: Psychology at the human-computer interface.* Cambridge, England: Cambridge Univ. Press.

Whiteside, J., Bennett, J., & Holtzblatt, K. (1988). Usability engineering: Our experience and evolution. In M. Helander (Ed.), *Handbook of human-computer interaction* (pp. 791–817). Amsterdam: Elsevier Science Publishers B.V., North-Holland.

Wilson, E. O. (1985). Time to revive systematics. *Science, 230,* 1227.

Winograd, T., & Flores, F. (1986). *Understanding computers and cognition: A new foundation for design.* Norwood, New Jersey: Ablex.

Wroblewski, D. A. (1991). The construction of human-computer interfaces considered as a craft. In J. Karat (Ed.), *Taking software design seriously: Practical techniques for human-computer interaction design.* Boston, MA: Academic Press.

3 Balance

GEORGE CASADAY

Digital Equipment Corporation
Maynard, Massachusetts

I. Introduction

When I laid aside programming to concentrate on human factors issues in software, I was told this: You are beginning an exploration of a region that is mostly uncharted terrain. In your travels, you may discover something that works especially well. If you do, you have a responsibility to share it by writing it down. And so this contribution is a report of some of my practice and experience with a framework for interface design that I use and that I have been able to teach to others. It is not a research result, although in my experience this framework is a powerful conceptual tool. I share it in hopes that you may find that you can adapt it for your own use.

I have used and evolved this conceptual framework during about three years of software development, human interface design, teaching, and consulting in an industrial context. Participation in the workshop that is the source of this book (Karat and Dayton, 1990) was an important positive influence on my thoughts.

The framework helps teams of designers and engineers to be more effective in designing human interfaces. It facilitates shared understanding by creating a structure for identifying the important human interface design issues and by providing a context for understanding statements about design. It promotes powerful decision making by supporting designers in the eclectic, often chaotic, processes of creative design and by supporting them in their need to discuss, make, record, and communicate clear and clearly justifiable design decisions. It can be the basis for a flexible discipline for the human interface designer.

Taking Software
Design Seriously

45

Since some of you work, as I do, as teachers or consultants for design teams, I will try to present my ideas in a form that you can use in that context. The model of human interface design is simplified – it is one of the approximate theories Norman (1986) advocates for pragmatic use. Abstractions are supported by concrete examples, real and imaginary. Explanations that I have found to communicate well are pointed out, especially ones that are humorous or attention-getting.

The chapter brings together three lines of thought. One concerns empirical studies of how design teams work, especially observations that show designers navigating freely, creatively, through their design spaces rather than moving in a linear sequence. Another is current practice in software engineering, particularly object oriented analysis, that provides ways of making very clear and robust models of subjects as complex as the human interface design space. The last, from the artificial intelligence literature, is information on giving advice that shows that the most powerful advice clarifies issues rather than gives solutions. The synthesis is an object oriented model of the human interface design space that supports creative design by providing a clear representation of the human interface design issues.

II. All the Real Issues

Let us begin with a question: What is the appropriate center for human interface design? Many very different human interface design centers have been fashionable during the past decade. Karat (Karat and Dayton, 1990) points out that "For awhile, there was almost a search for a single Holy Grail of design techniques." Examples are tool kits incorporating good design principles, user centered design, task centered or work centered design, graphic design, and design centered in the social implications of the designed artifact. Indeed, there are many candidate centers.

I have used many of these design centers with human interface design teams. I have had some success but also two negative outcomes. First, when a single design center dominates, the result is not a complete design but rather a fragment of a design expanded out of proportion – for example, a beautiful graphic design that cannot be implemented within schedule or a highly usable system that does not support the user's real tasks. Second, when one center takes control of the design process, it is usually sponsored by a member of a design team with expertise in that area. Other team members, with other specialties, are alienated: they fight back, damaging the design process and the design product. As consultants we may call that client resistance, but it results from a flaw in the design process.

With that introduction, here is my central premise: What is most needed for effective design is not a center but rather balance. Rubinstein and Hersh (1984) put the point elegantly. "The essence of engineering is creating constructive compromises among many conflicting goals. Integrated design can occur only when all the real issues are allowed to exert an influence." Engineering is concerned with trade-offs, and good management of trade-offs creates balance.

If balance is essential in human interface design, what specific support will help in achieving it? If the true center for design comes from the creative tension among all the real design issues, what is a conceptual structure where all the real issues can get fair representation? It is impossible to specify rules for making trade-offs in the details of individual designs, for those compromises depend on the designer's intimate knowledge of the particular application domain. Therefore, this chapter offers not design guidelines but rather a framework for organizing thoughts about design. By analogy with government, the framework is less like a collection of laws and more like a constitution, a document that does not legislate directly but that does provide a framework in which laws can be made in an orderly and balanced way.

Several chapters in this volume take a similarly broad view of human interface design (James, Karat and Bennett, Lanning, Wroblewski).

III. Modeling Human Interface Design

A practical model of the human interface design space is the most useful support I can offer to designers. Research on effective advice (Woods and Roth, 1988) shows that assistance in understanding a problem space is much more useful than prescriptions of solutions or of courses of action; an appropriate model is exactly that kind of assistance. Models are precisely chosen collections of labeled categories and the relationships between them – simplified and abstracted representations of pieces of the world. Models are useful for organizing thoughts and communication. They may be useful parts of a conceptual architecture without posing as scientific theories. By supplying labels, they help us focus on individual topics. By supplying a context for our words, they help us communicate clearly. Models are different from scientific theories in that they are judged by their usefulness rather than by their correctness.

I intend the model presented in this chapter to represent, at a useful level of detail, all the real issues relevant to human interface design. But it is easily modifiable to handle the issues I have missed in spite of my good intentions. Most of all, I intend the model to be practical, and I have found it to be so.

A. Object Orientation

A model of human interface design could begin with either the design as a work product, an object, or design as a process, a distinction pointed out by Rouff (Karat and Dayton, 1990). Of course both must be represented, but the question is where to begin?

I choose to model design in an object oriented way for several reasons. Software engineering practice shows that an object oriented decomposition is generally more stable and more robust than a procedural decomposition (Shlaer and Mellor, 1988; Coad and Yourdon, 1990). Besides stability, there are other advantages for the object oriented approach to understanding human interface design. The entities in the model of design are design deliverables – decisions represented in documents, graphics, prototypes – so there is a seamless transition from the designer's model of the design work to the human interface design itself. Also the relationships between entities are usually constraints rather than data flows or control flows, so it is possible to make design decisions in any natural order and still maintain a discipline. In addition, object oriented techniques are becoming well known in the software engineering community. So an object oriented model tends to be acceptable, understandable, and attractive to engineers. That is, it tends to build upon their existing skills. This is important because engineers are usually major contributors to human interface design.

B. Fundamental Object Is the Decision

In this model, the fundamental object is the individual human interface design decision, for example, a decision to use a color rather than a monochrome display, or to use a menu rather than a command line, or to use a specific word for a command. So a decision is a selection from a set of alternatives for a feature of the artifact being designed. Activities, such as testing or prototyping, are purposely excluded from the model; the model includes decisions but not procedures for making decisions.

C. Decision Foci

To be practical — explainable, comprehensible, usable — the model must collect the many types of design decisions into a small number of categories. Therefore, the model distinguishes six types of human interface design decisions, referred to as decision foci. The word *focus* is chosen to suggest that the purpose is to direct attention to the issues but not to define categories with definite boundaries. The foci are *Context for Design, User Mental Activities, User Physical Activities, Functional Human Interface Design, Physical Human Interface Design,* and *Implementation Policies.*

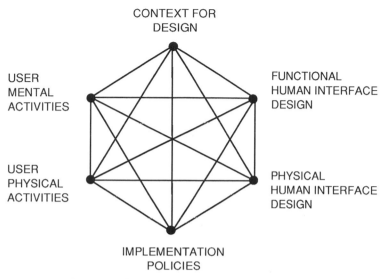

Figure 1. The human interface decision foci.

Figure 1 is a graphical representation of the foci that I use in explaining the concepts to consulting clients. By its form, the graphic suggests balance. It suggests that design issues of each type are related to issues of all other types in a network of constraints. It suggests that the design center is not in any focus but is like the center for a centripetal force that prevents the components from flying apart.

D. Advantages of this Model

There are many ways to model any domain, including human interface design, and they are all somewhat arbitrary. I have tried many, but I have been most successful with the one I am describing here for several reasons.

- These foci can be easily identified, explained, and illustrated. That is, they can be directly tied to concrete experience.

- The six foci give good coverage of the human interface design space for most problems. Nearly all decisions can be discussed under one of them. When that is not the case, it is simple to add another focus. For example, one designer found it useful to replace *Context for Design* with two foci, *Physical Context* and *Social Context,* to encourage sufficient attention to each of these issues. The object orientation of the model makes this type of adaptation very easy.

- The relationships among the six foci tend to be fairly simple compared with the relationships within each focus; in classic software engineering terms, they have good coherence and loose coupling. Therefore, we can handle each focus somewhat independently.

- This model is at a useful level of granularity because each of the foci can be covered by a single individual. Therefore, it can be a basis for dividing design work and for pointing out areas where a design team has a need for more expertise.

- This decomposition fits fairly well into the standard documents of a waterfall development processes.

I need to stress that, although I have found this to be a useful model, it is only a model. It is not a theory of design: No testable hypotheses can be derived from it, it cannot be true or false, and it will not yield any deep insights into the nature of design. Like any model, it is simply a summary description intended to aid comprehension and communication in a complex subject area.

E. Using the Model

The model of the human interface design activity is most useful for aiding communication among collaborating designers.

I have found it useful for communicating the true scope of the human interface design activity to design teams. For example, engineers are often helped by seeing how the task analysis and user psychology issues relate to the implementation issues and how essential they are for a balanced design. And human factors specialists are helped in coming to grips with the implementation issues.

The foci help make statements meaningful by putting them into a context. For example, the word "menu" in the context of *Implementation Policies* probably refers to software components in a particular user interface tool kit. In the context of *Functional Human Interface Design,* "menu" probably refers to many ways of making a selection from a short list without regard to appearance or implementation. By being clear about the context for a statement, designers with very different backgrounds can communicate effectively.

This model offers no advice on what technique to use in making a design decision. That is an intentional omission, which makes the model stable, robust, and tolerant of changing technique and technology. But the model can help designers appreciate just what kind of decision a chosen technique can help with. So, this model is not a formula for doing design; rather, it is a framework for investigating what design is.

IV. Details of the Decision Foci

This section details the six decision foci. Figure 2 is a summary.

A. *Context for Design*

Context for Design concerns objects and events external to the system being designed. Examples are information on how potential users structure their work, what procedures they use or could use, which user tasks are supported and which are ignored, types of users supported, learning time requirements, and time to market requirements. This focus includes, but is not limited to, the task level of Moran (1981) and the user's goals of Norman (1986).

Typical information gathering techniques for this focus are contextual interviews, focus groups, market surveys, and traditional task analysis. Typical tests for checking decisions in the focus are mockups, games, and storyboards.

Focus	Context For Design	User Mental Activities	Functional HI Design	User Physical Activities	Physical HI Design	Implementation Policies
Location	World	User's mind	Designer's mind	User's body	Device surfaces	Program code
Typical entry	Work Tasks Frequency Impact Goals Subgoals Users	Task model System model Strategy Memory limits Processing capacity	HI Entity Attributes Relations HI States Transitions Triggers Effects	Position of hands Direction of gaze	Graphics Language Menu Command Syntax Mouse Keyboard	Platforms Hardware Software Tool kits Resources
Typical document	Requirements Functional spec.	Functional spec.	Functional spec.	HI design spec.	HI design spec. Prototype	Implementation design Code Development plan

Figure 2. Summary of the decision foci.

The focus exists to help system designers make the very difficult distinction between benefits to the user, which exist in the context for the system, and the features of the system itself. Therefore, it is best to avoid reference to the system being designed while discussing decisions in the *Context for Design* focus.

The decisions derived from study of the *Context for Design* are best recorded in a requirements document to separate them from the list of system features that typically constitute the functional specification.

Several chapters in this volume address issues in this focus, primarily by describing techniques used in analysis of requirements and tasks (Braudes; Carter; Catterall ,Taylor, and Galer; Cohill; Harker; McGrew; Miller-Jacobs; Tang).

B. User Mental Activities

The *User Mental Activities* focus concerns how the system being designed will influence the user's thoughts. Examples are a user's view of the task, a user's view of the functionality and operation of the system, and a user's view of a means for achieving the task goals by using the system, a work strategy. The focus includes concerns about human cognitive performance such as limitations on short term memory or processing capacity. It also includes the user's model of the system (Norman, 1986) and the aspect of the semantic level of Moran (1981) that concerns the user's concepts.

There is an intuition about effective ways of thinking about work that can come from immersion in the task domain through research, experience, and contact with potential users. This may be the most useful source of information leading to decisions in the *User Mental Activities* focus. It is possible to test much of a design at this level with paper and pencil tests and with techniques such as the cognitive walkthrough described by Polson (Karat and Dayton, 1990; Lewis *et al.*, 1990).

The focus exists to encourage designers to take responsibility for the influence they exert on the user's thoughts. Beginning designers naturally tend to design a system and then ask how the design might influence the user's experience. The *User Mental Activity* focus suggests first designing the user's experience and then asking what system might cause that result. This change of design perspective can be very powerful.

I have been able to fit these decisions into the functional specification, although I have rarely seen them discussed in traditional project documentation. Two chapters in this volume directly address user mental activities (Braudes, McGrew).

C. User Physical Activities

The *User Physical Activities* focus concerns the physical movements the user makes to interact with the system, but it does not concern the meanings of the movements. Examples are the user's posture, shift of gaze to and from the screen, movement of the hands between the keyboard and mouse, and speed and coordination required for the user's hand movements. This is the traditional realm of ergonomics.

This focus exists to help designers make the sometimes useful distinction between the user's physical activities and physical aspects of the human interface. For example, movement of a cursor with mouse or keyboard are physical aspects of the human interface – the mouse, keyboard, and cursor are all parts of the computer system. Movement of the mouse with the left hand, right hand, or foot are aspects of the user's physical activities.

Most current computer systems have such limited input capabilities that there are very few design decisions to make in this focus. (In fact, no chapter in this book addresses user physical activities.) On the other hand, this area is very important for users with unusual physical characteristics or limitations, and it may become more generally important as input devices become more capable in the future.

The decisions for this focus can appear in a human interface design specification. Alternatively, they may be placed in a traditional functional specification.

D. Functional Human Interface Design

Functional Human Interface Design concerns decisions about the human interface expressed in a way that is as nearly device-independent as possible – the semantics, flow, and logic of the human interface, as distinguished from the physical interaction mechanisms. Typical entities for this focus are 1) the human interface objects and their relationships augmented with preliminary sketches of screen graphics and 2) the human interface states with their transitions, triggering conditions for transitions, and side effects. This focus includes the computer system aspects of the semantic level of Moran (1981) and the design image of Norman (1986).

There are analogous abstract levels in many subdisciplines of software engineering. Logical versus physical design of databases and algorithm versus program are examples. The main problem I have encountered with this level of design is that it has not been done traditionally for human interfaces, even though it is widely practiced in other areas of software engineering. Therefore, it is sometimes difficult to convince the reviewer of a design document that a human interface specification can be meaningful without final, committed pictures of physical screens.

This focus exists because the gap between a description of the supported tasks and the physical human interface design is often too great to be spanned in a single step; an intermediate abstract description is needed as a bridge. When this bridge is omitted, the result can be a premature commitment to physical design that hides flaws in the underlying logic. When the bridge is included, it can be part of an effective design pattern that begins with a user's model of the task and system and proceeds through increasingly more detailed sketch designs to a final physical interface design.

The decisions for this focus preferably appear in a human interface design specification. Alternatively, they may be placed in a traditional functional specification.

Several chapters in this volume concern issues of *Functional Human Interface Design* (Siochi, Hix, and Hartson; Miller-Jacobs; Rouff and Horowitz; Tang).

E. Physical Human Interface Design

Physical Human Interface Design concerns the surfaces of physical I/O devices such as screens and keyboards, and thus it includes look and feel. Examples are precise graphic renderings at the pixel level, fonts, mouse-button syntax, keyboard bindings, exact words for menus and dialog boxes, and command line syntax. In other words, this is the subject matter of most style guides. The focus includes the syntactic and interaction levels of Moran (1981) and the system image of Norman (1986).

This focus exists primarily to emphasize its relationships with the other foci. Some designers, especially the less experienced, consider human interface design to be *only* physical design. An important purpose of this chapter is to show how physical design is connected in and takes its significance from a network of other concerns.

The decisions in this focus can be recorded as annotated drawings in a typical system design document, in system prototypes, and in the human interface facade.

Several chapters in this volume concern *Physical Human Interface Design* (Craig; Siochi, Hix, and Hartson; Miller-Jacobs; Rouff and Horowitz).

F. Implementation Policies

Implementation Policies concern implementation decisions that constrain the rest of the human interface design. Actual software design is not within the scope of this focus. Included decisions are hardware and software platforms, tool kits, level of resources committed, and schedule.

Given an appropriate physical design, implementation can be fairly straight-forward. However, platforms and tools usually come into the design process very early as constraints, which are often not negotiable. Therefore, a success-ful human interface design effort must usually include implementation exper-tise.

Implementation decisions fit naturally into the system implementation design document but may also naturally appear in the requirements document or even the project management documents.

One chapter in this volume addresses *Implementation Policy* issues, describ-ing a system that can be used in implementation (Rouff and Horowitz).

V. The Design Meeting

A. *Opportunistic Design*

I believe the design meeting is a crucial component of the process of design-ing human interfaces for software. Establishing a shared understanding among people of very different experiences, competencies, vocabularies, and interests is critical for success in the design meeting. To conclude this chapter I will ex-plain how I use the model to organize human interface design meetings.

There is now convincing evidence that creative design is not at all linear, one-step-at-a-time; it is neither top-down nor bottom-up. Design is better described as a search than as a computation (Simon, 1969; Rowe, 1987). Designers actu-ally jump around, following semantic links, constraint relations in the design space, and needs of different designers to assure that individual viewpoints are represented (Rasmussen, 1988; Guindon, 1989). The process has been referred to as *opportunistic*.

On the other hand, software projects are traditionally managed using a se-quential process that emphasizes successive transformations of information from requirements definition, to functional specification, to design, to imple-mentation — the waterfall model. The advantages of this approach for plan-ning, monitoring, and control are obvious.

Parnass suggests doing software design in the opportunistic style as much as necessary and documenting it in the sequential style by "faking rational de-sign," as he puts it (Parnass, 1986). My approach to human interface design meetings follows that suggestion by looking at the human interface design space in a way that enables designers to discover information in any order and then to assemble the information into a coherent linear story.

I find the label *schema driven design* communicates the idea well to design teams. There are a limited number of schema items, the foci; they must all be addressed, but they can be visited in any convenient order. To summarize the feel of the style, I sometimes call it designing by jumping around; that phrase resonates with some. Sometimes I use a quote from a popular British television science fiction series, Dr. Who: "One thing at a time. First things first. But not necessarily in that order." In any case, I find that it is important to give inexperienced designers *permission* to use their creative ablities this way. Then they are more able to be creative while maintaining a discipline based on the decision space model.

B. Linear Report and Review

For understandably communicating the reasoning behind a collection of related design decisions, I find the following sequence for visiting the foci most useful (Figure 3):

- Context for Design
- User Mental Activities
- Functional Human Interface Design
- User Physical Activities
- Physical Human Interface Design
- Implementation Policies

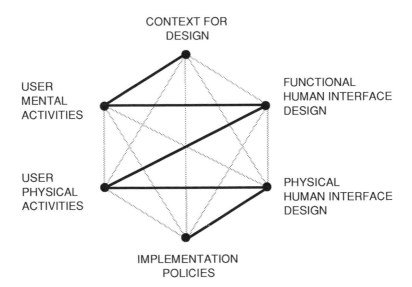

Figure 3. A linear form of the model.

This sequence corresponds to top-down or outside-in approaches and maps well onto the traditional waterfall paradigm. It is the sequence I have used for Figure 2 and Figure 4.

C. Example

The following paragraphs and Figure 4 use a fictitious and very simple design problem to present an informal worksheet notation that I have evolved for using the model in human interface design meetings. It is almost always useful to improvise variations on the notation for individual design problems.

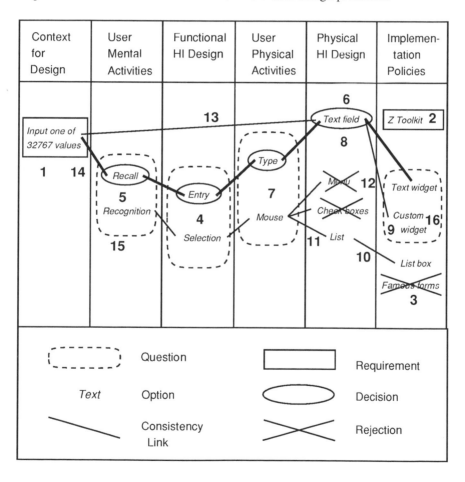

Figure 4. Design Worksheet

Figure 4 represents an imaginary design conversation and the resulting design decisions as they might be recorded on a whiteboard or on paper. A plausible imaginary history of the design conversation follows: the numbered statements in the script correspond to the numbers in Figure 4. This example illustrates use of the decision foci: in my experience real design meetings are rarely so orderly or complete. It is more typical of one of my classroom exercises. The following terminology is adapted from MacLean (Karat and Dayton, 1990; MacLean *et al.*, 1989):

- *Options* are grouped by means of *Questions*
- A *Decision* is selection of an *Option*
- *Consistency Links* connect *Options*

D. Script of a Fictitious Design Meeting

1. The design is required to support the task *Enter one of 32,767 possible values*. This is a small subtask in an application; from this viewpoint the rest of the system is external context. The designers place this phrase in the *Context for Design* column and box it to indicate that it is a requirement.

2. They also record and box the requirement to use the *Z-toolkit* under *Implementation.*

3. *Famous Forms* is considered as an additional implementation platform and recorded as an option. However, it is finally crossed out to indicate explicit rejection. This leaves enough evidence so that we can be sure that it was not missed by oversight. An annotation explaining why it was rejected might be useful.

4. The designers then consider two familiar input options, *Entry* and *Selection,* at the *Functional Human Interface Design* level. They phrase the issue as the question of which option to use but defer the decision.

5. They realize that *Entry* will constrain the *User's Mental Activity* to *Recall* while *Selection* will require only *Recognition*. They enter *Recall* and *Recognition* in the *User Mental Activities* focus and indicate the *Entry-Recall* and the *Selection-Recognition* constraints with consistency links.

6. The designers then search through their repertoire of *Physical Human Interface Design* elements corresponding to *Entry* and *Selection*. As options they list one entry method, *Text field,* and three *Selection* methods, *Menu, List,* and *Check boxes*. No clear question is formulated to organize these options, perhaps because they are very familiar.

7. *Type* and *Mouse* are entered as options under *User Physical Activities* and grouped as a question.

8. The designers record with consistency links, that *Text field* is related to *Type* and *Entry* on the left and to *Text widget,* which is entered on the right.

9. One person notes that a *Custom widget* for a special kind of *Text field* might be constructed. To avoid an unproductive argument, *Custom widget* is allowed to stand as an option. It is grouped with *Text widget* in a question and the issue is deferred to the software design team for feasibility assessment.

10. Someone mentions that the *List* written down refers to the particular kind of mechanism supplied by the Z-toolkit *List box.* This fact is recorded. Although it is noted and logged, it is not referred to again.

11. As the conversation has moved to this area, *Menu, List,* and *Check Boxes,* are belatedly connected with consistency links to *Mouse,* which is then connected to *Selection.*

12. *Menu* is rejected and crossed out as inappropriate for this class of interaction, based on past experience. *Check boxes* are rejected because they allow more than a single value at one time. The designers are not quite able to give up on *List* because of an unclear intuition that it might somehow be used to support selection in this situation. But they begin to favor the *Text field* as their only known way of supporting input of such a large number of possible values.

13. The designers prefer *Selection* but are not able to think of a *Physical Human Interface Design* mechanism that could support selection from as many as 32,767 alternatives. They record that issue as a consistency link.

14. Finally, the designers make the decision to choose *Recall-Entry-Type-Text field,* which they indicate by circling the decisions and darkening the consistency links connecting them. Thus, they accept a tentative design that displays a clear path from the requirement to at least one implementation.

15. The *Recognition-Selection* pair are not finally rejected (they are not crossed out), because of the single designer who still has a vague intuition that something creative can be done with the *List* mechanism. This single optimist commits to work offline and to report back success or failure.

16. The programming member of the design team commits to look into the cost of the *Custom widget.*

The meeting adjourns.

VI. Conclusion

In using this model, and sometimes the worksheet, I have made several observations that I want to note.

The design worksheet spans a wide range of issues in a concise graphic form. Therefore, it is possible to see large parts of a design as a whole and in a way almost impossible with text descriptions. Creative compromises are encouraged. Opportunistic design is supported, but an organized design story emerges as a useful base for writing formal documents in the traditional waterfall style.

Because decisions and links are explicitly noted, hidden issues are sometimes revealed, and logical inconsistencies are exposed. Rationales are revealed by consistency links and the annotations that designers often attach to them. Impoverished questions, that is, those with only a single option, are brought up for scrutiny. Options remain until explicitly rejected, reducing errors of oversight.

The worksheets can become unruly because they encourage creativity. The format serves best as a brainstorming notation, but it is not a presentation format. As in the example above, much is not explicitly said or recorded.

In many cases no worksheet is constructed. Rather, designers use the model as an aid to clear communication in natural language and diagrams. They draw parts of the worksheet to address particularly difficult points, or they draw separate worksheets for separate subcomponents of a design. In that case, the major benefit is the ability to separate the concerns represented by each of the foci.

Blank columns in the worksheet indicate an unbalanced design – some issues are not getting the consideration they require. Difficulty filling in a column indicates an unbalanced design team. If all the columns are filled in, then all the issues are being addressed at some level of detail even though there is no guarantee that the decisions are correct; that is left to the skills of the designers.

The views and opinions expressed in this chapter are solely those
of the author and not of Digital Equipment Corporation.

References

1. Coad, P. and Yourdon, E. (1990). *Object Oriented Design*. Prentice Hall, Englewood Cliffs, NJ.
2. Guindon, R. (1989). "The Process of Knowledge Discovery in System Design," *Designing and Using Human-Computer Interfaces and Knowledge Based Systems*. Elsevier. Amsterdam, p. 727.
3. Karat, J. and Dayton, T. (1990). "Taking Design Seriously: Exploring Techniques Useful in HCI Design," *SIGCHI Bulletin,* **22,** 2.

4. Lewis, C., Polson, P., Wharton, C., and Rieman, J. (1990). "Testing a Walkthrough Methodology for Theory-Based Design of Walk-Up-And-Use Interfaces," *Proceedings of CHI'90: Human Factors in Computer Systems*. ACM, New York.

5. MacLean, A., Young, R., and Moran, T. (1989). "Design Rationale: The Argument Behind the Artifact," *Proceedings of CHI'89: Human Factors in Computing Systems*. ACM, New York.

6. Moran, T. (1981). "The Command Language Grammar: A Representation for the User Interface of Interactive Computer Systems," *International Journal of Man-Machine Systems,* **15**, 3.

7. Norman, D. (1986). "Cognitive Engineering," in *User Centered System Design,* (D. Norman and S. Draper, eds.). Lawrence Erlbaum, Hillsdale, NJ.

8. Parnass, D. and Clements, P. (1986). "A Rational Design Process: How and Why to Fake It," *IEEE Trans. Software,* **SE-12,** 251.

9. Rasmussen, J. (1988). "Models for Design of Computer Integrated Manufacturing Systems," *First Intl. Conf. on Ergonomics of Advanced Manufacturing and Hybrid Automated Systems*. Louisville, KY.

10. Rowe, P. (1987). *Design Thinking*. MIT Press. Cambridge, MA.

11. Rubinstein, R. and Hersh, H. (1984). *The Human Factor*. Digital Press, Bedford, MA.

12. Shlaer, S. and Mellor, S. (1988). *Object Oriented Systems Analysis*. Yourdon Press, Englewood Cliffs, NJ.

13. Simon, H. (1969). *The Sciences of the Artificial*. MIT Press, Cambridge, MA.

14. Woods, D. D. and Roth, E. M. (1988). "Cognitive Systems Engineering," in *Handbook of Human-Computer Interaction,* (M. Helander, ed). North-Holland, Amsterdam.

4   Using Scenarios in Design Meetings - A Case Study Example

JOHN KARAT and
JOHN L. BENNETT

IBM T. J. Watson Research Center
Yorktown Heights, New York

I. Introduction

The design of complex systems involves many people exercising multiple skills and carrying out a variety of activities. If we surveyed a large sample of the software that is available for computer systems and asked "How was it designed?" we would find many methodologies used in the software design process. Put another way, we do not understand design sufficiently at this time to write a text prescribing one procedure that would reliably lead to successful development of such a cross-section of software systems. Nevertheless, much has been written about aspects of software system design and development. For example, contextually rich and detailed accounts of particular experiences are provided by Lammers (1986), Kidder (1982), Guindon, Krasner, and Curtis (1987), and

Rosson, Maass, and Kellogg (1988). None of these are comprehensive in scope.

Design is a complex synthesis involving trade-offs among multiple perspectives. An important aspect of the design process is a search for workable answers. Managing the evolution of a design in this situation is so challenging that issues not clearly represented as a part of the design activity simply become lost. In our work we have been particularly interested in developing and maintaining a user-centered perspective on design of software systems intended to support effective human-computer interaction. We assume that this must be done in concert with engineering realities of function to be provided, schedules to be met, and development costs to be managed. By user-centered we mean that the total system function is crafted to meet requirements for effective user learning and efficient user access to that function. That is, the eventual users must see the system as useful and usable. In addition, the design must be compatible with the already present engineering perspective of an affordable, logically complete, and technically sound system.

Over the last several years we have looked for ways to raise the probability of having usable systems emerge from design activities. This has led us to focus on early design activities, particularly design meetings in which small teams meet to work out a system design at initial stages of specification. We have described elsewhere the general framework that we have found useful for such meetings (Karat & Bennett, 1990, 1991). In these papers we have discussed the role of representations in focusing design discussions and the effects of facilitation activities on the outcome of the design process. We have noticed the importance of examples for explaining our activities to others. In this chapter we will describe in some detail how we have used scenarios as one form of representation to give us insight for design. This is presented in the form of a case study.

II. Establishing a Context for Design

We note the increased attention paid to the overall process of design of computer systems. A growing body of work portrays human-computer interaction design as an activity that engages the varied skills of participants in design meetings as they work to manage a complex design context (see the chapters by Wroblewski and by Cohill in this volume for examples). In some cases authors suggest that researchers look at design in a different way (e.g., as a "craft" in Wroblewski, 1991). Others suggest that design difficulties can be overcome through use of integrated "frameworks" (Casaday, 1991) or skilled design architects (Cohill, 1991).

A. Representing a Design

The system design process can be supported in various ways (many of the chapters in this volume discuss the benefits of different kinds of representations). For example, various formal notations might be used to describe a design, and differing techniques have been suggested to aid in human-computer interaction design (e.g., Siochi, Hix, & Hartson, 1991; Braudes, 1991). Of particular interest to us are techniques that can support finding answers to the kind of questions that come up in design.

We have already described the "design room" framework we use for displaying representations intended to bring out aspects of a design for creative discussion (Karat & Bennett, 1990, 1991). We provide here a brief overview as a background for this chapter.

To facilitate a user-oriented overview, we bring together on the walls of a design room (large enough for a team of 2 to 8 people, small enough so that the walls are nearby) an organized and high-level view of the entire context of discussion. The use of walls provides a large space with distinct regions (usually different walls) to help in the separation of complex issues within the array of problems typically encountered in design.

We have used a variety of representations in developing and maintaining an effective perspective on the user. Examples we have found important in design settings are as follows:

- *Objectives for the system* -- goals, often usefully presented in tabular formats, including those relating to usability (Whiteside, Bennett, & Holtzblatt, 1988). These can provide specific indicators for knowing when the objectives are met.
- *Guidelines for style* -- abstract statements of guiding visions for design including the qualities to be experienced by users as they carry out tasks (e.g., design guidelines such as in IBM, 1989). These provide partial guidance.
- *Abstract, generic objects and actions* -- types of objects such as "containers" and actions such as "copy." Concrete objects important to users and the actions that users can take on those objects (Wegner, 1987) can be related to these types.
- *Screen pictures* -- representative images extracted from current documentation, storyboard sequences, or design prototypes to provide realistic illustrations and a sense of sequence dynamics and to serve as a basis for design iteration (Gould, Boies, Levy, Richards, & Schoonard, 1987).

- *Resources and tools available for system construction* -- aids for soft-ware engineering, rapid prototyping, or user interface screen design that are in common use within the organization (e.g., data base support, data interchange architectures, libraries of existing programs). While such tools support system design and development, invariably they also place constraints on what can be designed.
- *Sample scenarios* -- sequences illustrating the flow of specific user actions needed for a result, concentrating on what the user will see, what the user must know to interpret the display, and what the user can (or in some cases must) do to achieve the needed task results (Karat & Bennett, 1991).

Some combination of such representations can be valuable in different situations. Walls are useful because they provide a surface for easy manipulation of a variety of representations within a context (all the walls) readily visible to the group. The separation onto different walls can highlight distinctions such as general system requirements (from which specific system objectives and goals are extracted) on the one hand and specific design decisions (means and mechanisms) intended to meet requirements on the other hand. In the same way, the tools used to implement the design are viewed as separate from the design itself. The material on some of the walls (e.g., constraints and resources) might seem remote from user-centered concerns. But we find that bringing these concerns within the broader context of objectives and design-in-progress facilitates discussions that balance such concerns.

We do not hold any particular arrangement of wall content in a design room as fixed (i.e., many different distinctions appropriate for a particular study can be used in laying out content). When to use a particular representation is far from clear. For example, work comparing the use of various analytical techniques in design has not provided any indication of which techniques are best for a given context, but instead it has suggested a variety of features useful in design settings (Bellotti, 1990). This is in many respects similar to the experience reported in quality assurance processes, where a variety of techniques can be described (King, 1987), but where their effective use is sensitive to context and requires skilled facilitation.

B. Facilitating the Design Process

The social context in which a design activity takes place is an important factor in the quality of the resulting design (Bennett, 1986, 1987; Bennett & Karat, 1990; Casaday, 1991). As a result of our experiences we have become particularly interested in the role of those who facilitate meetings, the formal or informal leaders of the meeting. While some design tasks may be carried out by individuals or small teams in close contact, most commercial system development involves a fairly large group of people. Even those design breakthroughs created by individuals are explained and worked out in groups. In these cases, and in the case of work in large teams, it is particularly important to achieve a shared understanding of the objectives and of the suggested design as it evolves.

Within our design room environment the process of laying out the representations on walls has invariably led to questions and discussions that explore the reasons for the content of that wall. Any explicit representation will include a background of assumptions that may not initially be shared by all in the design group. Each wall serves as a focus for particular design questions, and the whole room provides an arena for holding questions open while the team searches for solutions. Some of the discussion may simply lead to clarification, but often we find that it points to areas in which something overlooked is recognized or disagreement surfaces. Through group discussion the participants can develop a common vision of system requirements and how to meet them.

C. The Role of an Example in Understanding Design

Because we do not know at this stage how to prescribe generically for success in design processes, we seek increased understanding through examples - descriptions of particular events. The case study we describe here is one in a dozen or so series of events in which we have participated over the last several years. Other meeting sequences have addressed stages in the design cycle ranging from initial sketches of ideas to system assurance walk-throughs. They include activities such as helping to formulate a plan for managing development resources, facilitating a comparison of the user interfaces for two systems, and conducting usability analysis of competitive user interfaces.

In presenting our case study we concentrate on the use of scenarios (descriptions of situations suggesting the need for computer support for tasks) by a design team working within the design for a larger system. If we refer back to the kinds of representations listed above, the system objectives had been established as background, given as part of the larger system design. Similarly, guidelines for style were in the background and were referred to only in passing during the work. Consideration of abstract objects and actions was important, but the focus was relatively narrow. The design work done by this particular team did not progress to the level of screen pictures. And finally, the resources and tools available for system construction did not enter discussion at this stage.

With respect to the need for facilitation techniques, the four people participating at the stage we describe had all worked together for some time. Though the backgrounds were varied, all participants were already focused on the results that were possible from the series of meetings. Therefore, facilitation support was not a key factor.

III. A Sample Experience - A Design for Connecting Objects

In this example we highlight the use of scenarios as one representation technique useful in focusing design discussions. For the project described here our small design team was provided with a short (3 page) description of typical activities to be accomplished by users through connecting objects in a system. This scenario involved paragraphs describing 15 variations of what was described as a generic linking function. The resulting design was to provide support for typical known uses of object connection (e.g., linking two text locations in a hypertext system) and a range of possible functional extensions, (e.g., allowing data flow between objects such as tables of data and graphs of that data). For the purpose of this case study report, we present only five parts of the larger scenario.

Our team of four people met about three times a week for two-hour sessions over a period of about six weeks (about 30 hours total) to develop a high level specification for connecting objects. Our work was carried out as an additional project on top of an already full schedule of other precommitted activities. We were given little in the way of objectives for the design other than that it meet the functional requirements (i.e., that some method be provided to enable users to carry out the tasks). Additionally, the design that we produced was to fit within a general user interface style defined by guideline document (IBM, 1989).

For this project our team had access to a design room in which we were able to post paper notes on three of the walls. The fourth wall contained a white-board we used for additional illustrations and note taking. Figure 1 presents a rough outline of the room layout, along with a sketch of the information that was placed on the various walls. We tended to use the white board for drawing pictures of the designs we were discussing. For the most part these were not saved as final designs, but rather they were used for brief discussions and then erased. We placed notes written on 3 by 5 cards and various printed pages on the other walls of the room. Information on these walls was fairly dynamic, rearranged numerous times during the discussions. The content of the walls was preserved over the course of the project.

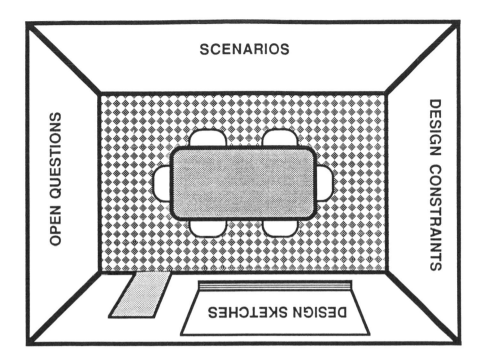

Figure 1.   Room layout for four-walls design environment.

An initial set of constraints and assumptions influenced our work. The design was to cover a system-wide connecting function to be used along with already defined capabilities for presenting and manipulating windows and with icons representing objects such as files of data. Within this system guidelines had been established for using a mouse to select and drag objects and for the appearance and use of a menu bar in windows. Also present were guidelines for the appearance and use of "context menus." These menus, available for any object in the system, offered actions that could be taken on the object. Context menus were presented on request by the user. Additionally, all objects in the system had properties that could be listed and changed through use of a property sheet associated with each object.

We also were given some information from earlier work done on the design. This called for the link itself to be considered as an object in the system and to have a distinct visual appearance. Thus, it was possible that a link object would itself have a context menu and its visual ap-

pearance would have context-sensitive properties. We considered this
work as preliminary, and we were free to make changes. We did not attempt to do much with the graphic appearance of the link object, and
we were comfortable working with the assumption that the connection
itself would be an object.

We initiated our user-centered focus by concentrating on what the users
would see when interacting with the system, what they would need to
know to understand the system-displayed information, and what they
would need to do to complete the tasks. As we developed our work, we
used the walls of the room as the initial record of our design and as a
reminder of the objectives and constraints on the design. The walls also
held notes that we made and questions that we raised during our discussions.

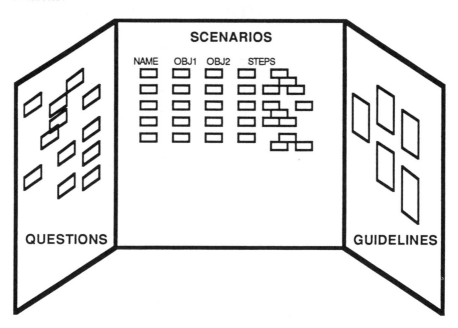

Figure 2.   Schematic of room for
             link design meetings.

Figure 2 outlines the content of the walls of the room at the end of the
work described here. The main focus of our discussion was on the wall
containing the scenario descriptions. At the end of the work, this was
laid out almost entirely on 3 by 5 cards with columns describing the scenario task, the objects involved in the connection, and various sketches

of the steps involved in accomplishing the task. At various stages the wall contained information on other topics (e.g., it was used in breaking down the larger scenario into parts, deciding how to describe the tasks, and initially for holding some open questions). We recorded questions that arose during our discussion on cards and later placed them on a separate wall, grouped by topic. We also kept the guidelines that influenced our work on another wall in the room, though we referred to these infrequently.

A. Decomposing a Scenario

Soon after we began our design process we developed a way of analyzing the scenario paragraphs that had been supplied to us from outside our team. To keep things manageable, we worked on one of the 15 scenario paragraphs at a time. In our meetings we stepped through the paragraphs a number of times, adding detail to our discussion on each iteration. As we worked we developed a specific structure for describing the scenario pieces, which we found very useful in the design activity. We decomposed each scenario part into a *Name*, a textual *Situation Description*, a description of the *Logical Essentials*, the *Generic Steps* that would be needed, and finally the *Specific Steps* needed to carry out the task for a particular design solution. A brief description of each of these components is given in Table 1.

The scenario *Name* is a brief descriptive phrase provided for easy reference to the scenario.

The *Situation Description* for a scenario contains text describing the function to be supported and the task to be carried out. This is intended to provide a high-level easy-to-read summary of the task rather than a complete definition of details. In the course of describing the situation in story form and making the description interesting, we have found that the author often includes extraneous details (see examples). In addition, some important facts may be missing.

The *Logical Essentials* for a scenario represent our analysis of the scenario into components that are seen as necessary (i.e., required information for the situation) to carry out the task. This includes details important for the specific type of objects being identified (e.g., it contains an explanation of what it might mean to connect various objects). For example in the link scenarios we decided that for all connections it is necessary to

1. identify two objects (or sets of objects) and
2. indicate that the objects are to be connected.

Scenario Component	Level of Detail
Name	A short label used when referring to a scenario.
Situation Description	Running prose giving a concrete illustration of a situation.
Logical Essentials	With respect to the system, information that must be supplied in order to achieve the desired result within the system. With respect to the user, the representations and actions that must be made available by the system to the user. Information at this level is intended to be implementation-independent, what would be needed regardless of methods used to achieve the result.
Generic Steps	The sequence of user steps (sometimes ordered) that must be performed regardless of implementation method.
Specific Steps	A particular design will presume a series of user steps with particular devices and with system feedback to the user as each step is taken. Error analysis (what happens if a user makes a misstep or if information needed by the system is missing) can also be considered at this level.

Table 1. Summary of Scenario Decomposition

The *Generic Steps* for a scenario describe actions needed to complete the scenario at an implementation-independent level. They represent an expansion of the logically essential elements interpreted as a set of steps.

For the link scenarios we identified three generic steps that might occur in any sequence:

- Identify Object 1
- Identify Object 2
- Identify Connection

Another essential element for linking is specification of the kind of connection between the two objects. It is possible (though not logically essential) that the user might have to identify explicitly the different types of connections. For example, connections might allow the user to move a focus of attention directly from one object to another, or connections might support transfer of data from one object to another. We assumed that many types of connections might be useful in a system with general linking capabilities, though we did not try to enumerate all of them.

We did not require that the user must carry out all three steps through some explicit action (e.g., one object might be assumed as source or target, or a link might automatically happen if the system somehow "knows" that the user intends to link identified objects). Further, it may not be necessary that the steps be done in a particular sequence, though we may decide that it is a good idea to impose an order in the design that follows from consideration of the structure. Because we believed these steps were the same for all of the scenarios we considered (i.e., they are generic to link tasks), we did not describe them in the summary table (see Table 2).

The scenario *Specific Steps* provides a description of the user actions to carry out the scenario in a proposed design at some level of detail. Many levels of detail are possible (from conceptual steps to fine motor actions), and we suggest that deciding on an appropriate level of detail for a particular analysis be a group decision. This decision can be weighted by many factors such as desired outcome of the analysis. If we were developing an architecture as contrasted with a particular design, we might stop at a higher, less detailed level of analysis.

With this basis for analysis we now turn to our study of selected parts of the overall scenario. A structure representing five parts of this scenario is outlined in Table 2. Because "scenario analysis" (in a way similar to the related subject of "task analysis") is a process with many possible interpretations, we found it necessary to develop a common understanding of how we were going to proceed.

In Table 2 the Object 1 and Object 2 columns represent information from our *Generic Steps* analysis above. We have labelled Object 1 as source and Object 2 as target, though we do not necessarily mean to imply directionality (it was simply easier for our discussions to refer to them as source and target). Included in the summary columns under Object 1 and Object 2 are the types of objects that need to be identified for the particular scenario part. It is essential for scenario completion that some mechanism be provided for identifying these sources and targets (e.g., text, data, point, symbolic pattern, and whole object). Rather than inventing a new way to indicate a source or a target, we used the selection mechanisms that we assumed would be used in the rest of the system as we developed the link scenarios.

While each scenario has one set of *Generic Steps*, different designs can imply different *Specific Steps*. For the link scenarios we outlined two possible specific designs - direct manipulation as a method and menu dialog (or menu-sequence) as a method. The steps described in this chapter are incomplete in that we did not consider all details of what the presented menus would contain, but we just carried the description to what seemed to be an appropriate level given the time available to us.

Scenario Name	Object 1 (source)	Object 2 (target)	Specific Design: Direct manipulation as a method	Specific Design: Menu dialog as a method
Scenario 1. Between documents link	Text: visible	Text: visible	Select source Context menu Select target Drag	Select link item Select source Select target Close dialog
Scenario 2. Within document link	Point: visible	Point: not visible	Select source Context menu Make target visible Select target Drag	Select link item Select source Make target visible Select target Close dialog
Scenario 3. Future document link	Text: visible	Object: named, not yet existing	Select source Context menu Select handle Property sheet Enter target name Close dialog	Select link item Select source Enter target name Close dialog
Scenario 4. Term indexes another document	Symbol: visible or not	Text: visible	Select source Context menu Select handle Property sheet Select "all occurrences" Select target Drag	Select link item Select source Cascade to new menu Select "all occurrences" Select target Close Dialog
Scenario 5. Static target data linked direct to document	Data	Point	Select source Context menu Select point Drag Context menu Create inset Make graph from target template	(Not designed)

Table 2. Summary of Selected Parts from the Overall Scenario for Connecting Objects

B. Selected Parts from the Overall Scenario

Each *Situation Description* below is followed by a description of our work in the design room. As much as is possible the discussion reflects the sequence of the design group deliberations. Occasionally our focus shifted as we made discoveries during the course of our discussion, and it is difficult to present this coherently in linear text. Our approach for this project was to iterate through the scenarios, going to finer levels of detail on each pass through the set. Our stopping rule for each cycle through the scenarios was one of reaching a group consensus that we should change the level of detail in our discussion and begin again.

SCENARIO 1 - Between Documents Link

Situation Description

> Pat, an over-ambitious author, decides to produce a large composite document. After having written a substantial chunk of it, he goes back to the start and establishes a link between a word in one of his initial paragraphs and text in another document shown in another window. He expects that, when the reader decides to activate the link, the reader's view of the document will transfer to the other document.

Much is assumed in the situation description (e.g., in this design environment the user is expected to understand that text seen in a window is a view on an underlying object). Because of verbosity that would obscure the main point of the situation described, it might not be useful to explain in detail all that is assumed. We should be aware, however, of some important assumptions in any description (we will note many in the following sections).

Logical Essentials

We decided that the design must be able to address the following:

1. Users must be able to identify arbitrary strings of existing text to serve as object 1 and as object 2 for the link.
2. Users must be able to indicate that they want to create the link.
3. Users must be able to indicate that they want to use the connection (e.g., to navigate the link).

In our early work on the design we focused on creation of connections rather than on the use one might make of such connections. Thus, for this design work, we took as given that the functionality of the mechanism we designed would be useful. For many design activities this is a risky assumption (we noted it as a question for consideration on our design room wall). Our concentration was on the usability of designs we proposed.

Generic Steps

- Identify Object 1
- Identify Object 2
- Identify Connection - something to be done with the two objects.

This provides a basis for expanding the design discussion by considering specific designs (a few of the many possible). On the wall we were careful not to confuse generic steps with (possibly arbitrary) specific design decisions.

Specific Steps - Direct Manipulation as a Method

1. Purpose: Identify source object to the system
   Method: SWIPE SOURCE TEXT
   (WITH FIRST MOUSE BUTTON)
   At this point we began to move our discussion from a high level, design-independent analysis to specific design issues. A number of questions were posed about what the user would actually do to create a link. Does the user have to begin with the source? What if an object is already selected as part of another action? Can it be used as one end of a link? Does one set up the link and then specify directionality? Are links bidirectional?

   It may not be wise (or feasible) to decide the answer to such questions on the basis of one situation. For example in Scenario 3 we considered linking to a document that does not yet exist (i.e., considered connecting to a "place holder"). If the user sets up 50 links to this currently phantom document from a variety of sources, and if each link points to the beginning of the place-holder for the second document, then the user is going to need some way to get back to each source in order to determine the target within the created document where it should be attached. This could be done as the second document is created. Or would the user prefer to make the attachments after the second document is completed? Here we begin to see the importance of an effective "style of use" implied by a particular design.

   We also begin to consider some aspects of the physical device involved in the selection. Some guidance is provided by guidelines for use of mouse buttons in the system, and we assume that "swiping" will be done by moving the mouse over an area to be selected with the first button held down. This still allows for some discussion of how swiping should work in various domains (e.g., text, graphics, and spreadsheet), but we delayed those for the time being.

2. Purpose: Indicate to the system that a link is to be made
   Method: BRING UP CONTEXT MENU (POINT TO SOURCE
            AND CLICK SECOND BUTTON), then
            SELECT "CREATE LINK"

Note that we have made several design decisions here. First we assume that a context menu is something that is available for arbitrary text objects, and second we assume that "CREATE LINK" is an option appearing on it.

In the system design within which the connection mechanism is to exist, menus may be associated with objects. These context menus are obtained through a mouse button click while pointing to an object. Again, we did not attempt to create a method for bringing context menus up, but used the method prescribed by the interface guidelines (click second mouse button). At this point we began to see that the user may have an option to do many things to a source from this context menu, not just set up a link as in the situation description. We have to consider all possibilities including establish a link. Second, an order is implied in the way steps are specified (select object, select action on object, select target). This is the style recommended in the system (object selection first, then action designation), and the sequence seemed to be a "natural" way of creating a link.

We had many open questions at this point in our discussion about the appearance and behavior of a connection that we expected to address in continuing the scenario analysis. The following were some specific questions that we recorded on the wall for later discussion:

- The connection needs to be made visible to the user. We assume that a link icon will appear (the visible representation of the link object), and that it will have a "HANDLE" that can be dragged to the target (this was part of the initial design presented to us). How is it represented on the display (the initial design was not specific on appearance)?
- What else is on the context menu?
- What will the display look like after the user selects the "CREATE LINK" option (e.g., what objects are currently selected)?
- How will modifications to the text at the source or target be handled? What will the effect on the link be if the text is later modified, moved, or copied?

3. Purpose: Identify target object to the system
   Method: SWIPE TARGET TEXT

   We found that much the same discussion applied here as that for source. We did not find any special considerations in specifying the target. We took this as a good architecture and usability sign, since we did not feel that selection distinctions based on the use of an object would be desirable.

4. Purpose: Complete the link
   Method: DRAG LINK ICON HANDLE TO TARGET

   We assumed for this scenario that the source and target are both visible at the same time so that this operation is possible. Scenario 2 specifically called out the situation where they are not both simultaneously visible, and we asked whether we knew how to do direct manipulation in this case. The answer was that we do not (it might require some extension of the direct manipulation design to accommodate the case). We considered a second design, partially in the belief that direct manipulation techniques will not always be appropriate.

   Several other questions were raised at this point. Our general strategy was to defer detailed discussion of most questions that we believed could be postponed in favor of a breadth-first discussion of several scenarios. We then returned later to address the questions stored on the wall.

   Presumably several types of links are possible, so the link once established must be identified as to type. (Note that this was not explicit in the situation description as we received it.) Is there any logical reason why the type has to be identified by the user before the link is established? Can it be identified after the user has established it? What is the possibility of a system defaulted type?

   Some kind of (visible) cue must be given to the user for the existence of a link once it is established. We decided that it would be desirable if the display of this cue could be an option that users could turn on or off (i.e., show links, or do not show links, as an option under user control).

Specific Steps - Menu Dialog as a Method

At this point we decided to consider an alternative technique for creating a link - one involving the use of menus rather than the dragging operations of the first design. Part of the reason was an uneasiness with the general applicability of the direct manipulation method, and we saw development of a menu method as a way to compare relative usability of the two methods.

1. Purpose: Indicate to the system that a link is to be made
   Method: SELECT "LINK ITEM" FROM MENU BAR
   We did not know where this item would be in the menu structure that was part of the system (because this is a system-wide function and many functions relate to specific windows, we were not sure where to place it). Selecting the item from some menu would initiate a dialog in which the user could indicate source, target, and perhaps other parameters (such as link type). Our assumption was that source and target objects could be identified through a variety of techniques (e.g., by direct manipulation pointing or swiping or by supplying an object name). We noted the question about location of the menu item and continued on.

2. Purpose: Identify source object to the system
   Method: SWIPE SOURCE TEXT
   Success of this method seemed related to intelligent use of defaults. If an object was already selected prior to step 1, we assume that it is indicated as the default source object in the dialog (this would permit some variation in order of steps for users - this is a known usability plus). We discussed, but were not committed to, a "moded" design in which the user would be sequentially prompted to select source, target, and possibly link type (the guidelines for our system discourage use of such modes).

   On the next iteration through the analysis we noted that we would need to consider how the user would indicate that a swiped object was to be treated as the source (i.e., completing this design requires more than we have here - swiping the text does not necessarily mean that the system would recognize this as identifying the source rather than identifying the target or some object unrelated to the linking operation).

3. Purpose: Identify target object to the system
   Method: SWIPE TARGET TEXT
   As with the direct manipulation method, we find that much the same discussion applies here. We did not find any special consider- ations in specifying the target (again a good architecture and usability sign).

4. Purpose: Complete the link
   Method: CLOSE THE DIALOG BOX

This may happen automatically on completion of the needed information or it may require explicit user action. Again, guidelines for dialogs were given in the existing system environment, and we did not spend time inventing a way to indicate the end of such a dialog.

Summary Observations

Roughly one-third of our total meeting time (about 10 hours spread over the six weeks) was spent on discussion of the first scenario. As we moved on to discussion of other parts of the overall scenario, we typically returned to this first scenario as an anchor point. Because we could reconstruct the context easily in our review of the walls, we did not go completely through the whole scenario on each of the four iterations. For each pass we stopped when it seemed appropriate to the group.

SCENARIO 2 - Within Document Link

When the discussion of the first part of the overall scenario seemed complete enough for the moment, we moved on to explore additional parts. We used a group consensus that it was time to move as our stopping criteria. We knew we had 15 situations to analyze in the overall scenario (five parts discussed here), and we worked (within time constraints) in a delicate balance between depth and breadth.

Situation Description

Pat now establishes a link between a point in the document where he would like to put the word "glossary" (this might be a button with a label), and a subsequent section many pages away from the link anchor. This, of course, involves some form of scrolling to get to the later page.

Logical Essentials

We observe that this scenario description contains many hidden design assumptions (as do most scenario descriptions). Notice that the scrolling mentioned in the text is not logically essential for completion of the task, nor is it necessary that "a button with a label" be created. We suggest that authors of future scenarios be careful not to include implementation-dependent solutions as part of the description.

Scenario 2 is very similar to the previous scenario (we selected parts in order to build toward gradually more complex situations). The new additions here are

1. source and target cannot be easily viewed simultaneously (we could open multiple views on the same object and proceed as in Scenario 1, but we were looking for easier methods here), and

2. source and targets are logical points rather than existing text.

The scenario requires methods for the user to handle these.

Generic Steps

This is similar to Scenario 1. Identifying the objects will require a different method than above, and some discussion of symbolic object reference (e.g., to relative points rather than specific objects) began.

Specific Steps - Direct Manipulation as a Method

1. Purpose: Identify source object to the system
   Method: SELECT "POINT" WITH FIRST MOUSE BUTTON
   We were not sure how this should be done. It seemed likely to us that linking to a logical point (such as the beginning of a chapter or the end of the document) would be something that we would like to be able to do (expressing some of the "user" in each of us). In order to understand this, we needed to explore questions such as how someone would select a point or how the point moves when a text document changes (and whether this might be different for text than for a graphic).

   We also discussed providing the word "glossary" as a labeled button by modifying attributes of the link object (which assumes that links are viewed as objects with a number of attributes). We did not expand on that discussion at this time, since it seemed to be the next level of detail in this analysis. Labeling the points remains an open question at this level of analysis.

2. Purpose: Indicate to system that a link is to be made
   Method: BRING UP CONTEXT MENU ON "POINT", then
   SELECT "CREATE LINK"
   With the exception of some discomfort about how a user could point to a point, this was viewed as much the same as Scenario 1.

3. Purpose: Make target visible
   Method: SCROLL TO TARGET AREA
   This is called out because the act of making the target visible might cause the source to be scrolled off the screen (or overlaid by another window). We assumed that the link icon handle would stay with the source as the user scrolled, and thus would not be visible when the target was found. This would create the undesirable situation of

having the subgoal of making the target visible undoing the subgoal of making the source visible. Our discussions did not lead to a satisfactory solution to this problem, and it remained an open question on the wall of the design room.

4. Purpose: Identify target object to the system
    Method: SELECT "POINT" WITH FIRST MOUSE BUTTON
    We assumed the same method would be used for selecting the target as was used for selecting the source.

5. Purpose: Make source and target visible
    Method: ?
    We believed that linking through direct manipulation would lead to a general problem when both the link icon handle and the target had to be visible at the same time in order to complete a link. We developed and discussed some "new" ideas for addressing this, but we found no clear solution. These difficulties indicated the need for an additional method (such as the menu dialog).

6. Purpose: Complete the link
    Method: DRAG LINK ICON HANDLE TO TARGET
    No new discussion took place at this point.

Specific Steps - Menu Dialog as a Method

1. Purpose: Indicate to system that a link is to be made
    Method: SELECT "LINK ITEM" FROM MENU BAR
    We assumed that this step would be the same step as in Scenario 1. For our early discussions we decided that there would be a single item on the menu bar that would provide access to all activities related to links.

2. Purpose: Identify source object to the system
    Method: CLICK ON SOURCE POINT
    This has the same meaning as in Scenario 1, menu dialog. We noted on the wall that we still needed to work out the details of the dialog in further iterations. Questions that remained included the following:

    *   Do we enter a mode, saying that "I will now identify the source," and then allow a click on a point to identify it? Selecting a point here may have much in common with the issues raised in the previous direct manipulation discussion.
    *   How do we identify "symbolic points" such as end-of-chapter or after-this-table so that the "right things" happen when the docu-

ment changes? We felt we may need to consider a number of issues related to symbols, but we decided not to do so at this point.

3. Purpose: Make target visible
    Method: SCROLL TO TARGET AREA
    Scrolling to the target did not seem to lead to a problem in the menu dialog. We do not need to keep the source visible, and we assume that the menu does not disappear or scroll off the screen. This seemed easier to do than finding a way to keep the link icon visible during scrolling.

4. Purpose: Identify target object to the system
    Method: CLICK ON TARGET POINT
    We view this as the same as in selecting the source object in this scenario.

5. Purpose: Complete the link
    Method: CLOSE THE DIALOG BOX

Summary Observations

In general, the time spent in the discussion of the two design methods for Scenario 2 was much less than that for Scenario 1 (2 hours compared to 10 hours). Many outstanding questions discussed in the earlier scenario were noted again, but held open, during Scenario 2. The group had a general feeling of increased understanding of the important issues.

SCENARIO 3 - *Future Document Link*

On each iteration we reached a point in the discussion where it seemed most useful for us to broaden our understanding by moving to the next part of the overall scenario. In general, we spent less time on each successive part.

Situation Description

Still on the first page, Pat decides to establish a link from a word on the first page to another document that does not yet exist. He does this in the knowledge that, by the time anybody attempts to traverse the link, he will have written the other document. Thus, he expects this link to just go to the start of the second document and not to any specific point within it.

Logical Essentials

The scenario required that the user know how to identify the link once the new document is created, but it does not require creating a dummy document to serve as a temporary target. Such a special action could be a coping behavior that users would employ if the system allowed only existing objects to be the source or target of links). We were not convinced that the situation posed in the scenario is important or common (though without working with a system that has this capability it is hard to be certain). However, because completing a future connection between things that the user knows how to identify in some fashion (whether they exist or not) seemed important to us, we did discuss the scenario.

Generic Steps

These were similar to previous scenarios. Identifying the target will be slightly different since the user can not point to a document not yet created.

Specific Steps - Direct Manipulation as a method

1. Purpose: Identify source object to the system
   Method: SWIPE SOURCE TEXT

2. Purpose: Indicate to system that a link is to be made
   Method: BRING UP CONTEXT MENU ON POINT, then
   SELECT "CREATE LINK"
   The first two steps are the same as in previous scenarios. Nothing new needed to be added to the selection of the source because of the change in target. At this time we believed that the general pattern of link construction was robust and would accommodate various new tasks.

3. Purpose: Indicate to system that the target is a named file
   Method: SELECT HANDLE, then
   PRESS MOUSE BUTTON TO VIEW PROPERTY
   SHEET
   Here we see that a link might be an object with properties. Previous work by another designer (not part of our group) had resulted in proposals for properties that objects in the system might have (e.g., appearance of the link icon, name of source, name of target). It seemed reasonable to us that a link should have such properties and that the target name should be entered on the property sheet. We did have some questions for the next round of discussion:

   • What mouse button would be pressed to get a property sheet rather than a context menu or selection action? The giudelines that called for property sheets were unclear on this. We were concerned that too many distinctions on mouse button presses were being called for.

- What else is contained on the property sheet, and how deep in the dialog would one go to find "target name"? Other discussions of object properties seemed to be placing many items on the property sheet (e.g., the direction for changing the appearance of the link icon), and we were not sure how complex this would become.

  We had a similar concern in our discussion of the menu dialog method for this scenario, and we felt that the next level of detail should include a description of what is contained in the various menus.

- What is the structure and appearance of the general property sheet, and is this what users would expect? Again, more discussion seemed necessary (along with finding out about guidelines for property sheets as an aspect of the system). We noted the need to be aware of design developments in areas outside of our primary concern in order to complete our work.

4. Purpose: Identify target object to the system
   Method: TYPE IN THE TARGET NAME
   We assumed that this will be done in the same way as in other dialogs (i.e., the same as in other places in the system where names are entered). We were not sure how (or whether) nonexistent file names could be entered. For example, what will happen if a user tries to use a navigation link before the target is created? We also did not consider how link objects would be named (what will be in the property sheet for a source or target that is a segment of text, not a complete file?). These issues also apply to the menu dialog method.

5. Purpose: Complete the link
   Method: CLOSE PROPERTY SHEET DIALOG
   This has now become a partial direct manipulation method because of our use of the property sheet and symbolic name. The link must be completed eventually by the user through use of a dialog to fill in the target name.

Specific Steps - Menu Dialog as a Method

1. Purpose: Indicate to system that a link is to be made
   Method: SELECT "LINK ITEM" FROM MENU BAR

2. Purpose: Identify source object to the system
   Method: SWIPE SOURCE TEXT

We determined that the first steps could be the same as in previous scenarios for the menu dialog.

3. Purpose: Identify target object to the system
   Method: TYPE IN THE TARGET NAME
   We assumed that this directly follows the pattern established in the previous scenarios and that property information such as target name could be found under a single link item entry on the menu bar. However, as mentioned above, we were becoming uneasy with the complexity of the menu structure we were calling for. Though we still had not determined exactly where or how the user would create link properties, we knew that source and target identifiers would be required. We assumed that identifying a named object would proceed in the same fashion as with other dialogs.

4. Purpose: Complete the link
   Method: CLOSE THE DIALOG BOX

Summary Observations

The introduction of a new kind of object (a to-be-created target) led to difficulty in Scenario 3. Nearly all of the 2 hours of discussion on this scenario was devoted to design possibilities for specifying such a target. The exact content of the link property sheet, the context menu, and the link item on the menu bar remained as open questions. Resolving this content was viewed as a driving question for the next iteration in our design discussion.

SCENARIO 4 - A Term is Used to Index to Another Document

Situation Description

Pat then decides that it would be useful for the reader to be able to link directly to a target from anywhere in the source document that the words "Share Prices" occur. Naturally, he does not want to go through the source document to find every single use of these words - he expects the machine to do this for him. In fact, since he hasn't finished writing the document, there will be many more uses of these words as the long day wears on.

Logical Essentials

The request here is to be able to connect "automatically" from many occurrences of a pattern in the source document to a single point in a target document. The function seemed potentially useful to us. We decided that we must be able to distinguish between a string as an object itself and a string as a matching pattern to be used in a search. This led us to a discussion of how to accommodate symbols as objects within the design.

Generic Steps

Identifying the source would now involve indicating that a pattern will lead to the creation of a link to a target wherever that pattern occurs in the source document. We can see this as a useful glossary reference function (also for uses such as table or figure references).

Specific Steps - Direct Manipulation as a Method

1. Purpose: Identify source object to the system
   Method: SWIPE SOURCE TEXT

2. Purpose: Indicate to the system that a link is to be made
   Method: BRING UP CONTEXT MENU ON POINT, then
   SELECT "CREATE LINK"
   The beginning steps seemed very similar to Scenario 3. The insight from earlier design discussions suggested that indicating the source was a pattern (rather than a literal) should be done through the property sheet of the link. An alternative might be a system-wide symbol definition process, but we decided to work out the method we had started.

3. Purpose: Indicate to the system that the link is to a target identified
   by a pattern
   Method: SELECT HANDLE then
   PRESS BUTTON TO VIEW PROPERTY SHEET
   The property sheet would have to contain this new kind of item (i.e., it is not just the identity of the objects that are being connected but some properties of the targets). The composite scenario led us to consider symbols as important (the need was seen in a number of places). It was not clear whether we should consider symbols as part of the linking design specifically or part of a more general system design (we believed the latter).

4. Purpose: Indicate to the system that the source is a symbol
   Method: SELECT "ALL OCCURRENCES" FROM PROPERTY
   SHEET
   We assumed that some sort of "cascade" in the menus presented would lead the user from the source to properties of the source. We did not try to work out the details on this iteration through the scenario.

5. Purpose: Identify target to system
   Method: SELECT WHOLE DOCUMENT
   This was included because we were not sure of the direct manipulation technique for identifying a target in all cases (e.g., is the method different if the document is represented as an icon than if it is open in a window?).

6. Purpose: Complete the link
   Method: DRAG LINK ICON HANDLE TO TARGET
   Assuming we understand how the previous step works, we did not seem to need new discussion at this point.

Specific Steps - Menu Dialog as a Method

We sketched out a design (summarized in Table 2). We will not provide the details here, since little in the way of new questions or insight emerged beyond that already discussed in the direct manipulation design.

Summary Observations

Discussions of Scenarios 3 and 4 introduced new features that we did not completely work out. However, we felt we had reached a sufficient understanding of linking for navigation to proceed to the other uses of linking that were envisioned for the system. On each iteration through the 15 parts of the scenario, we went at least as far as considering these parts as a test of whether our discussions were appropriately broad in scope.

SCENARIO 5 - Static Target Data Linked Directly to Document

Objects may be connected so that data can be passed between them (e.g., between a spreadsheet and a graph). Several parts of the overall scenario required this type of linking.

Situation Description

Since the document concerns stock share prices, and realizing that a picture is worth a thousand words, Pat decides to incorporate a line plot of the share prices over the last five years into the document. So, he leaves the document for a moment and produces a graph. This involves establishing a link from the small file he has (small because it only contains 5 records - one for each of the last five years) to a standard chart definition. This produces a plot, which he grabs and embeds into the document.

Logical Essentials

Our discussion deviated somewhat from the scenario as written. Notions such as "leaves the document" or considerations of what would be in a "standard chart definition" seemed tied to particular implementations rather than requirements of a given task. As our discussion developed, the scenario was interpreted to require that a user be able to include a graph of some data in a document. A data source needs to be identified in this simplified scenario, and a way to view the data (the particular type of graph that is to be developed) needs to be specified along with the point in the document where it is to be displayed.

Generic Steps

We discussed the way this task is normally carried out in current systems. Where it is possible to get this result, it seems to be done through creating a graph and copying (or cutting and pasting) it into another document. It did not immediately occur to us that this was a link scenario (i.e., it might not be obvious to a user that this requires a connection between separate objects). After some thought we decided to proceed with the link analysis; we thought that the function might be useful (e.g., enabling one to find the data source of a graph).

We were unclear in which of two directions to proceed. The summary in Table 2 presents one solution for this scenario. The full discussion was quite complex. We spent a considerable time designing a two step link process (following the words used to describe the task). After a first iteration, we changed to viewing the task as connecting a data source to a place in the document in a single connection. The appearance of the graph on the display was to be determined through use of a graph template.

Specific Steps - Direct Manipulation as a Method

1. Purpose: Identify source data to the system
    Method: SWIPE SOURCE DATA
       We found that several new issues emerged when we analyzed a slightly different scenario. Though we think we reached a reasonable understanding of the text navigation (hypertext) scenarios, we were less clear on the data link scenarios. Selecting data items to be included in a graph might be quite different from selecting strings of text. To simplify our discussion, we assumed that users would select data to be used from underlying data displayed for selection in a spreadsheet format. In this tabular view we could see that the methods for selecting text would extend to data cells (i.e., swiping

could easily apply). However, in order to understand this better, we felt that we would need to spend considerable time looking at data base issues (again, this required understanding how other parts of the system would support such functions).

To simplify our analysis, we assumed that selecting data was outside our current scope. We proceeded assuming that it had been selected through use of a standard method established across the system (e.g., spreadsheet swipe or data-base query).

2. Purpose: Indicate to system that a link is to be made
    Method: BRING UP CONTEXT MENU, then
                SELECT "CREATE LINK"

3. Purpose: Identify document location for graph
    Method: SELECT POINT IN DOCUMENT
    We treated this as another case of identifying a point as an object. Though we did not resolve how this would be done (see Scenario 2), we felt that once the procedure for identifying a point had been designed, this would just be a case of its use.

4. Purpose: Complete the link
    Method: DRAG LINK ICON HANDLE TO TARGET
    This step could be carried out in other locations in the method. It does not complete the scenario here.

5. Purpose: Identify point as graph inset
    Method: SELECT CONTEXT MENU ON POINT, then
                SELECT "CREATE INSET" FROM CONTEXT MENU
    This analysis is much more preliminary in its details and conclusions than the earlier scenarios. We need to specify a transformation of the data to a particular representation. After some discussion, we decided that this would be dependent on the area in the document in which the graph would appear. We considered having it be a property of the link, but we decided that this was putting too much "weight" on the link. In our meetings we called this a decision to design "light" rather than "heavy" links (i.e., to place less responsibility for knowing about things like data transformations on links than on the data objects themselves). As another alternative we talked about placing "graph templates" in the document. We did not dismiss this as undesirable, but we did decide that it touched on issues that were outside of our scope.

6. Purpose: Complete the graph description
    Method: DIALOG WITH GRAPH TEMPLATE

We assumed that designing this dialog is done in some other part of the system development process.

Specific Steps - Menu Dialog as a Method

We did not discuss the details of the menu dialog for this or the next part of the scenario. A combination of time constraints and a belief that it would result in much the same analysis as the direct manipulation method led us to conclude that we did not need to do the analysis further at this level.

IV. General Discussion

In this chapter we have illustrated some of the complexity in a design activity rather than provided a particular set of answers. We still had many unanswered questions, as can be seen from the previous discussion. We had, however, uncovered important issues. This clear identification of issues relating to the use of the system was a necessary step in developing a user-centered design. As we discussed our results with others in the larger design process, we were able to present the issues convincingly by recreating scenarios of use and associated questions. In the iterations that followed, typical additional questions were

What cues offered to user on the next action in sequence to take?
What happens if the user makes a mistake?
What is the recovery path?
What kind of answer to the user's "Where was I?" question is available if the user is interrupted to take a phone call?
What path is the beginner likely to take while learning?
What is the most frequent user path through the set of scenarios?
What kind of interactive performance (response time) does the user need and expect?

We found that the iterations through the parts of the overall scenario were valuable. We considered most of the design to be a workable first cut compatible with our design constraints.

Should we have expected more results from the resource we put into the analysis? This is difficult to answer. Work at the larger system level to resolve the questions and to complete the design is still in progress. In subsequent design discussions we have built on these results without "throwing away" our previous work.

V. Conclusions

From this work, what have we learned about the development of useful guidance for design meetings? We have given an example of the complex synthesis/analysis iterations typically found in a human-computer interaction design situation. We have described steps we took to keep a user-centered perspective while simultaneously considering the engineering constraints of practical system design. Scenarios representing successive decomposition from broad user intentions into specific user sequences of actions help build an understanding of an evolving design. We see this as a constructive technique, one among many, to help raise the likelihood of achieving a needed design result.

We consider it important to continue inventing and refining techniques that aid in the search for workable solutions. Techniques that can be used at early design stages and that continue to be applicable as the design develops are especially interesting to us. This chapter describes our experience in practical work with one design team. We have also applied the techniques in other design situations. For example, while it is generally accepted that scenarios centered on user tasks lead to valuable discussion in such meetings, we often find little agreement on how to formulate them, and we have heard of groups achieving only partial success in using them. Our previous experience included meetings in which participants confused logically essential task steps (e.g., identify an object to be copied) with task steps that are dependent on a particular design implementation (e.g., use of a mouse to identify an object). Our method for scenario decomposition (see Table 1) has proven useful in avoiding such errors in our scenario-based design discussions.

Other ways of representing user interactions with systems are also useful in such meetings. GOMS (Goals, Operators, Methods, Selection Rules) analysis (Kieras, 1988) and User-Action Notation (Siochi, Hartson, & Hix, 1991), are two that provide additional structure to the less-formal scenario analysis we describe in this chapter. Both of these techniques quantify the complexity of the user dialog under analysis in order to provide a basis for design decisions. Our experience suggests that such analyses might be particularly valuable in later design discussions (once the design is constrained to relatively few choices). For earlier design work, where it is important to consider many alternatives, we feel that design needs support of a very flexible nature. Though we continue to discuss ways for technology to provide formalized support, we have been most successful using simple scenarios and "low technology" techniques (walls, paper, tape, scissors) to create and maintain a user-centered perspective.

REFERENCES

Bellotti, V. (1990). A framework for assessing the applicability of HCI techniques. In D. Diaper, D. Gilmore, G. Cockton, & B. Shackel (Eds.), *Human-Computer Interaction - Interact'90*. Amsterdam: North-Holland, 213-218.

Bennett, J. (1986). Observations on Meeting Usability Goals for Software Products. *Behaviour and Information Technology*, 5, 183-193.

Bennett, J. (1987). Collaboration of UIMS Designers and Human Factors Specialists, *Computer Graphics*, 21, 102-105.

Bennett, J., & Karat, J. (1990). Facilitating a user-centered perspective in design meetings, *IBM Research Report RC 16282*, Yorktown Heights, NY.

Braudes, R. (1991). Conceptual modelling: A look at system-level user interface issues. In J. Karat (Ed.), *Taking Software Design Seriously: Practical Techniques for Human-Computer Interaction Design*. Boston: Academic Press.

Casaday, G. (1991). Balance. In J. Karat (Ed.), *Taking Software Design Seriously: Practical Techniques for Human-Computer Interaction Design*. Boston: Academic Press.

Cohill, A. (1991). Information architecture and the design process. In J. Karat (Ed.), *Taking Software Design Seriously: Practical Techniques for Human-Computer Interaction Design*. Boston: Academic Press.

Gould, J., Boies, S., Levy, S., Richards, J., & Schoonard, J. (1987). The Olympic Message System: A case study in system design. *Communications of the Association for Computing Machinery, 30,* 758-769.

Guindon, R., Krasner, H., & Curtis, B. (1987). Breakdown and processes during early activities of software design by professionals. In G. Olson, E. Soloway, & S. Sheppard (Eds.), *Empirical Studies of Programmers - Second Workshop*. Norwood, NJ: Ablex.

IBM Corporation (1989). Common User Access, Advanced Interface Design Guide, Systems Application Architecture, SC26-4582.

Karat, J., & Bennett, J. (1990). Supporting effective and efficient design meetings. In D. Diaper, D. Gilmore, G. Cockton, & B. Shackel (Eds.), *Human-Computer Interaction - Interact'90*. Amsterdam: North-Holland, 365-370.

Karat, J., & Bennett, J. (1991). Working within the design process -- supporting effective and efficient design. In J. Carroll (Ed.), *Designing Interaction: Psychology at the Human Computer Interface*. Boston: Cambridge University Press.

Kidder, T. (1982). Soul of a new machine. New York: Avon.

Kieras, D.E. (1985). Towards a practical GOMS model methodology for user interface design. In M. Helander (Ed.), *Handbook of Human-Computer Interaction*. Amsterdam: North-Holland.

King, B. (1987). Better Designs in Half the Time; Implementing QFD quality function deployment in America. Bob King, GOAL/QPC, Methuen, MA.

Lammers, S. (1986). Programmers at Work. Redmond, WA: Microsoft Press.

Rosson, M., Maass, S., & Kellogg, W. (1988). The designer as user: building requirements for design tools from design practice. *Communications of the Association for Computing Machinery, 31,* 1288-1299.

Siochi, A., Hix, D., & Hartson, R. (1991). The UAN: A notation to support user-centered design of direct manipulation interfaces. In J. Karat (Ed.), *Taking Software

Design Seriously: Practical Techniques for Human-Computer Interaction Design. Boston: Academic Press.

Wegner, P. (1987). Dimensions of object-based language in design. In N. Meyrowitz (Ed.), *Object-Oriented Programming Systems, Languages, and Applications (OOPSLA) Conference Proceedings.* New York: ACM, 168-182.

Whiteside, J., Bennett, J., & Holtzblatt, K. (1988). Usability Engineering: Our experience and evolution. In M. Helander (Ed.), *Handbook of Human-Computer Interaction.* Amsterdam: North-Holland.

Wroblewski, D. (1991). The construction of human-computer interfaces considered as craft In J. Karat (Ed.), *Taking Software Design Seriously: Practical Techniques for Human-Computer Interaction Design.* Boston: Academic Press.

5 Information Architecture and the Design Process

ANDREW M. COHILL

Virginia Polytechnic Institute and State University
Blacksburg, Virginia

I. Introduction

The software industry, almost from it's inception, has tried to overcome the ubiquitous problems of development cost overruns, late delivery, poor product performance, and dissatisfied users. Much of the effort to resolve the situation has focused on the use of development methods of one kind or another that attempt to provide a structure for development that prevents some or all of these problems from occuring.

However, success has been limited. One need only pick up any industry trade magazine to find articles on both the problems and "solutions" offered for sale. The reason that these solutions have never been entirely successful for software development problems is due to an underlying confusion about the nature of software development.

Lyytinen (1987) described problems he found in a study of information systems development. Project goals were ambiguous and narrowly defined, and new technology was not applied properly for fear of unknown changes. Poor communication among developers and poor or nonexistent quality control

Taking Software
Design Seriously

hampered development. Neglect of behavioral issues in the end user organization created implementation difficulties. Finally, a highly rationalistic model of the development process rarely matched reality: a strongly idiosyncratic effort driven by a few high achievers and plagued with mistakes and setbacks before completion of the product.

While most view software development as an engineering problem, it is in fact a design problem, which requires a different approach. The software methodologies that are offered for sale are made to solve software engineering problems and are erroneously applied to software design problems. As an illustration, writing a command line parser is an engineering task (well defined inputs and outputs), but determining the task functions supported by an application and building an interface to support them is a design task (poorly defined inputs and outputs).

However, the command line parser is invisible to the end user of the system, while the interface and task capabilities are highly visible. It is the task of an engineer to build a parser that correctly translates command lines into an internal syntax; it is the task of a designer to build an application and interface that performs in a way that users expect and fits well into the work environment of the user.

This chapter discusses some differences between engineering and design and proposes that a new kind of information system developer is needed--the information architect (Cohill, 1989), who has overall design responsibility for a system and who may supervise a variety of engineering tasks. These engineering tasks are linked coherently by a design, and the information architect works

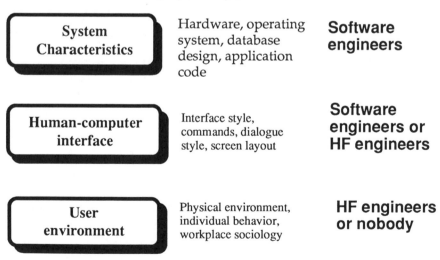

Figure 1. Components of an information system

toward a system solution using a design process rather than an engineering methodology.   Engineering and design models in the architecture of physical structures illustrate these differences.

Terry Winograd, in his closing address to CHI '90, called for a examination of the way computer science is taught and suggested that it should be based on the learning process used to educate architects (Winograd, 1990).   He also cited Mitch Kapor, CEO of On Technology, as a supporter of his views.   Regrettably, he ends this speech with a suggestion that as an experiment, this should be tried in a single class before attempting to reorganize an entire college level computer science curriculum.   I believe there is simply no way to compress the experience of design to a single course and make any meaningful statements about the value of such a class.   It trivializes the notion of design and in the long run will impede efforts to solve the underlying problem of inadequate information systems.

II.   Information Systems and Information Architecture

If we are to overcome intractable development problems and poor communication among software engineers, human factors engineers, and end users, a new approach to system design is needed.   Developers must become more aware of the effects of computer systems on users and their environment. This is more than the localized effects on task performance; it includes effects on the workplace environment and effects on the social and organizational behavior of users.   Increasingly, we are seeing computer systems used to increase organizational performance at the expense of individual well being.   Lyotard (1984) calls this the "terrorism of performativity."

Information systems are composed of three separate and distinct parts, as described below and illustrated in Figure 1.

- *System characteristics* -- the characteristics of an information system are the hardware and software needed to implement it.   This includes a central processor, disk storage, visual displays, an operating system, low-level application code, optional tools like a database package or a communications package, and the application-specific code.

- *Human-computer interface* -- the software that implements the user interface.   This software determines user interaction style, the kinds of commands available, and screen layout, and can greatly affect both user and system performance.

- *User environment* -- the exogenous variables that can affect how well the system is accepted by users and individual performance. These include physical environment characteristics like temperature control, ambient lighting, and workspace arrangement. Also critical are organizational factors like information flow, managerial power structures, and informal social structures in the workplace.

The work of thinking about and accounting for these three components of information systems development--system characteristics, application and interface, and the user environment--is often assigned haphazardly or not at all. System characteristics receive the most attention because most developers have the appropriate background in computer science and programming.

The interface often receives inadequate attention because this item is still frequently assigned to programmers and analysts, who often lack the prerequisite knowledge of task analysis, evaluation of human performance, theories of human-computer interaction, and cognitive modeling. Human factors engineers are trained in these areas, and if one is assigned to a software project, these areas receive more attention. However, if the project manager has a background only in systems analysis and programming, system characteristics may still receive a disproportionate share of development resources.

The last component, the user environment, often receives the least attention. Human factors engineers are qualified to make recommendations about workspace design, temperature control, and lighting, but these things often are not perceived as part of the information system and are given little attention by the project manager or by managers of the user population. Behavioral issues in the workplace are usually ignored completely. The introductions of information systems often change and disrupt both formal and informal behavioral patterns, yet rarely is anyone on an information systems development project qualified to either study or make recommendations about them.

The practice of using software professionals such as programmers and analysts as project managers is problematic; it is as if, when we decide to build a house or an office building, we hire the plumber to design the building and to supervise the construction. That practice almost certainly guarantees that the toilets will flush properly, but it does not bode well for the design of other components of the building.

When we build a house, we hire an architect, whose basic grounding is design and who also possesses much knowledge about the components of a house: the plumbing, the electrical circuits, the foundation and walls, and the roofing. The

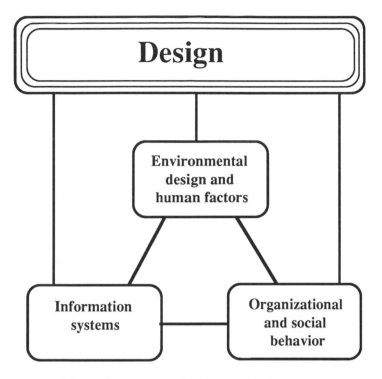

Figure 2. Linkage of design with other areas

architect possesses enough knowledge of water supplies, plumbing fixtures, and waste systems to write high level specifications for a plumber but leaves it up to the plumber to actually install the system and make any minor changes needed to deliver a working system.

In the future, we may see the high level design work now performed by a systems analyst performed by a member of a new discipline called information architecture; the practitioners of this discipline would be information architects. The foundation of such a discipline would be training in design, and the primary role of the information architect would be to discover the deep structure of information environments, rather than on the shallow structure of data, the focus of current systems. Structure as defined by Piaget (1977)—a whole, self-regulating, system of transformations—would serve as a model.

Rather than having a narrowly focused education in software production or human factors engineering, this information architect would have a broad education covering both disciplines. He or she would also have training in environmental and organizational behavior. This concept is illustrated in Figure 2.

Information architects would possess the skills of Hartson and Hix's (1989) synthetic mode: creativity, free-thinking, and behaviorally oriented. System design would be approached as inquiry through action (Archea, 1988). An analogy already exists for this kind of endeavor; the building architect is a specialist in design who works with contractors and structural engineers to build three dimensional spaces that enhance human life. The information architect would work with and coordinate the activities of the human factors and software engineers to build information structures that enhance human intellectual capabilities.

 The notion of information architectures is not new; Brancheau and Wetherbe (1986) proposed using a high-level map of the information requirements of an organization as an important aid to systems development. But their model of information architecture excludes consideration of personnel and organizational structures and problems. Although the two authors recognize the effects that end users may have on a system, they believe that information requirements can be imposed from above by considering strictly how information is used for business purposes. There is some value in this approach, but Zuboff (1988) provides striking examples of the difficult problems that can arise when systems are developed with little consideration of their effect on those that are required to use them.

 There are six principles in information architecture that form the philosophical foundation.

1) Design is a process; it is circular, repetitive, and unpredictable.

2) Design is intimate and idiosyncratic; it is a process that can be learned only through personal exploration and experience; it cannot be taught.

3) Design is an act of exploration; it is feedback–oriented, it requires a willingness to change, and it requires a sensitivity to the aesthetics of the final product.

4) Information architecture is concerned with information environments; these environments can be represented as self–contained, self–regulating structures composed of elements defined by interconnecting relationships.

5) The elements of an information structure are computers (hardware and software), people, and the physical and social environment in which people and computers communicate.

6) Information architects are designers. A fundamental grounding in design, combined with expertise in computer systems, organizational behavior, and ergonomics provide them with the knowledge to design information structures.

III. Method and Process in Design Models

The Human Factors Society Committee on HCI Standards (1990) has made a useful distinction between method and process. A *method* tells you what you need to start and what you have when you finish. A *process* is an instance of a method or set of methods. That is, a method (or algorithm) is static, producing the same results each time it is used, while a process is dynamic and may be different every time.

Individual development methods are not inherently bad; problems arise when systems developers try to apply the same method to a variety of problems. Adopting a process approach to development gives the designer the freedom to choose development methods and tools heuristically, applying and using them as the need arises and as they fit the particular situation.

Rouse's design model (1986) is typical of the method approach to design; it has four phases: formulation of goals, synthesis, analysis, and optimization.   The synthesis portion of the model involves what Rouse calls divergence, and the analysis portion he terms convergence. The synthetic phase is where the creative part of the work occurs. Although Rouse agrees that design is an iterative process, he sees problem formulation as the critical problem in design. However, he believes that this must happen first, so iteration is intended to refine solutions to match the goals.

Malhotra and his colleagues (1986) espoused a similar model. Design is a problem-solving activity that begins with goal elaboration, whereby major goals

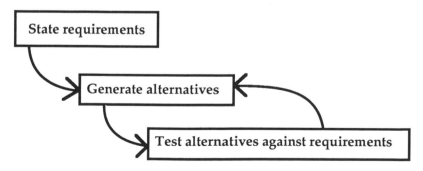

Figure 3. Classic software process model

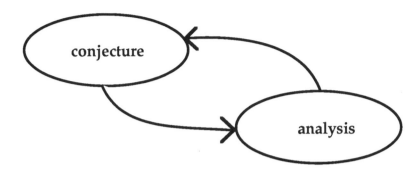

Figure 4. Hillier's design process

are decomposed in subgoals. Design generation follows; design elements are developed, and an organization is imposed upon them. Finally, an evaluation follows, measuring the proposed design against the stated goals. Herbert Simon (1969) states most clearly the rationalistic design model.

1) State the requirements.
2) Generate alternatives.
3) Test alternatives against the requirements.
4) Cycle through 2 and 3 as needed.

These approaches presuppose a great deal of information about the user environment, and the effects of the yet nonexistent system on the user. This is the top down approach to design, yet as every system developer knows, the goals of a project change constantly as development proceeds. What these models fail to account for is that the introduction of a new system changes the operating environment on which the original goals were based; the operating environment for which the system was designed *does not exist* when it is delivered.

The act of designing changes the world, and only a design model that incorporates feedback as a basic tenet will be robust. Furthermore, it is the goals that must be allowed to change, not just the solution. Many of the problems of software design and development arise because iteration does not allow the system requirements to change as the project matures. If iteration is used in the development model, it is is only to try to match the finished product more closely to the original specifications. Iteration is seldom used as a tool to change the requirements of the problem itself. Thus, the typical mechanistic design model is as appears in Figure 3.

The consequence is a delivered system that meets the original specifications perfectly but which is used indifferently. Introducing a new system, a new *structure*, into a work environment changes that environment and voids the original specifications.

In Figure 4, Hillier's design process is a continuous cycle of conjecture and analysis (Hillier, 1976). In the conjecture phase, the designer plays with possible solutions, and in the analysis phase he or she evaluates them for fit against what is known about the design problem. A design solution is permitted to exist early in the process, although there may be many iterations through the loop. Conjecture and problem specification proceed side-by-side, not sequentially. The notion of feedback is critical to this model, and Amkreutz (1975) has also specified a design model using feedback.

Hartson and Hix (1989), in their studies of interface development, have postulated two development modes; one is synthetic, corresponding to Hillier's conjecture phase, in which designers exercise creativity and work in an ad hoc fashion to develop new ideas. Like Hillier, they call the other mode analytic; in this phase the designers organize and structure data known about the developing system.

The act of drawing is an integral part of architectural design, and in large part the CAD programs currently available are only sophisticated drawing tools—they offer little aid to *design*. Laseau (1980) postulates six types of design drawing, or graphic thinking as he calls it:

- Representation
- Abstraction
- Manipulation
- Discovery
- Verification
- Stimulation

These six types of drawing can be used to classify the kind of cognitive activity that engages the designer as he or she works. Graves (1977) presents a simpler but no less useful set of categories for design drawings.

- The referential sketch, serving as a record of discovery, a diary; a metaphorical base for later use.

- The prepatory study, which documents the process of inquiry; experimentally produced in series, but not wholly linear.

- The definitive study, final and quantifiable in proportion, dimension, and detail; an instrument to answer questions, not to pose them.

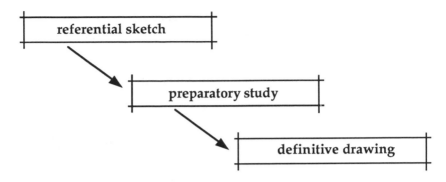

Figure 5. Graves' design model

These two classification systems (Laseau and Graves) offer a way to compare and analyze the the artifacts of the design process. Pye's model (1964) focuses on the act of finding. Pye believes that this process must precede the development of a successful design. He further partitions the process into a set of three interconnected requirements:

- requirements of *use*

    1) must correctly embody the essential principle of arrangement
    2) components must be geometrically related in whatever ways suit these objects and the intended result
    3) components must transmit and resist forces as needed for the intended result
    4) access must be provided (a special case of 2)

- requirement for *ease* and *economy*

    5) cost must be acceptable

- requirement of *appearance*

    6) appearance must be acceptable

These models of design have several words or related words in common: finding, discovery, and conjecture.

Michael Heim has investigated the effects of the computer on writers, examining the way electronic word processing systems affected the writing process. He has

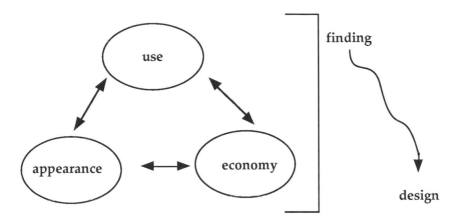

Figure 6. Pye's design process model

proposed a three-stage model of document design that seems remarkably similar to the kind of mental work conducted by architects (Heim, 1987).

- The writer engages in a process of *manipulation*, arranging symbolic domains. For the writer, this encompasses writing and accessing texts. For the information architect, this involves describing the components of an information system: data, functions, and users.

- *Formulation* is a mental activity; the writer responds to the text and attains a certain presence of mind that leads to the generation of forms. For the information architect, it would be the stimulation provided by images that lead to more focused elements of an information systems design.

- Finally, a process of *linkage* occurs: a network of symbols is combined to form a homogeneous system. An information system is exactly that.

Lyytinen (1987) stresses that every information systems problem may require its own type of theory building and research. Note that this view of design as a process does not proscribe the use of development methodologies; it does, however, suggest that methodologies should not be blindly applied to every development project. Rather, they should be chosen on a case-by-case basis, considering the unique environment of every system development effort.

IV. The Components of Information Architecture

The foundation of information architecture is design expertise, and upon that base three areas of technical skill are added:

- Information systems development, including database management and design, information storage and retrieval, and software engineering.

- Organizational behavior, including organizational psychology, motivation and leadership theory, and workplace sociology.

- Ergonomics, including environmental design and behavior, anthropometry, cognitive psychology, and human performance.

A. Design as a Process of Discovery

The foundation of information architecture is the recognition of the central role of design in development. In the first half of this century, philosophers like John Dewey and A. N. Whitehead began to develop a theory of learning that emphasized considerable freedom for the student to explore the world of knowledge, rather than the prevailing view which emphasized rote learning over freedom of expression. Whitehead was opposed to the division of education into discrete areas of study, preferring instead to let the student decide what to study. He did not, however, deemphasize the role of the teacher; he viewed the teacher as a guide, providing direction and encouragement to students and adapting general goals to each student's individual needs.

In the sixties, Jerome Bruner (1966) followed up on this work, describing in detail the components of learning, based on empirical studies of school children. Bruner stressed that all intellectual activities, at any age, involve learning and that the structure of the learning experience is critical to the outcome. He tried to shift the emphasis in education away from the acquisition of skills (training) to the development of basic tools and processes that enable the learner to grow intellectually without constant supervision.

There are many models of the design process but not much agreement on the nature of the process or on its steps. As a very general model, I favor Hillier's two part model: conjecture and analysis, linked in a loop. A solution may exist very early in the process, or there may be many design iterations but without the notion of convergence that exists in the engineering model. That is, successive designs do not reduce the number of potential solutions. Rather, each trial design is used to learn more about the problem. One outcome may be that the designer redefines the problem itself.

Brancheau and Wetherbe (1986) noted that the development of information requirements is a poorly structured task using poorly understood, soft tools. This is indeed the case; an academic background in computer science (logic, systems analysis, and numerical analysis) prepares one poorly for coping with and understanding the vagaries of human behavior. Lyotard (1984) argues that the technology's emphasis on efficiency has been detrimental to the development of systems of high quality, because it is difficult to measure quality. Instead, quantitative performance, inherently measurable, has become the goal of system developers.

User satisfaction is elusive, so systems are specified according to the number of transactions processed, or in microsecond response time, ignoring all the while the stress imposed on users by the forced pace of computer-based transaction processing.

Design is an uncomfortable topic with programmers; Rosson (1988) found that few programmers liked to discuss or talk about it. Typically, when asked about design, they responded with jokes and nervous laughter, suggesting that they do not see themselves as designers first. An information architect, with a strong grounding in design skills, will adapt more readily to changing project needs and will be more sensitive to organizational and environmental problems.

B. Information Systems Development

An information architect must be able to understand the technical complexities of systems development to maintain control over the project design. Training in programming, algorithm construction, database design and management, project management, and information storage and retrieval technology will give the architect the ability to design feasible solutions.

Sethi and Teng (1988) have outlined the components of information requirements analysis (IRA), a methodology that attempts to consider the factors that affect the content of data required in a system. They note that both organizational and individual characteristics should be considered when trying to define the kind of data to be manipulated in a system. Brancheau and Wetherbe (1986) also include IRA as part of their model of systems development, along with assessing the cost of storing and distributing information and the development of models of information allocation among users.

Prototyping must be considered a critical tool in the development of information systems. Mason and Carey (1983) have studied the use of prototyping tools in the commercial development environment and found that their use increases the likelihood that useful systems will be developed, and that the development cycle will be shortened. Iterative design works because it tacitly recognizes that each design problem is different and that the solution to a particular problem is unlike previous problems. Iterative design gives developers the freedom and flexibility to adapt the development process to the particular needs of the problem. The emphasis has changed from method to process.

Boland and Hirschheim (1987) warn against relying too heavily on data as the force of information systems design. They note that language and dialogue are the real organizational process, not structured data, and that the goal of a "perfect" information system is unattainable.

C. Organizational Behavior

The effects of information systems on organizations are rarely considered, but those effects are real. Zuboff's (1988) extensive analysis of them (in a variety of blue and white collar settings) documents the political, sociological, and cognitive changes that may take place as workers adjust to using advanced information systems.

Abdel-Hamid and Madnick's empirically developed model of software development (1989) includes human resource management because they found that the kind of people assigned to a project affected the time of the project's completion and the quality of the work. In a study of the impact of technology through the end of the century, Straub and Wetherbe (1989) found that organizational change was considered a major problem, with new technology changing the way workers interact with each other and with management. Cohill, Harper–O'Donnell, and Curran (1985) found that the management of office political entities was more critical to system success than the design was.

Campbell and Campbell (1988), in a study of informal communication in work organizations, had several conclusions with implications for information systems development. They found that informal communication strengthens the individual's sense of identification with and commitment to the organization, and that face-to-face communication increases job satisfaction. Not surprisingly, Zuboff found increased dissatisfaction with organizations in which the introduction of new information systems, relying heavily on electronic communication, discouraged and minimized face-to-face encounters and informal lines of information flow. Sankar (1988) also found that new technology tends to increase the social distance between workers.

Rowe (1987), in a case study of a new sales order processing system, found that management tends to focus on technical factors when problems arise with a new system, because that is what they understand best. Some of the problems were a failure to identify information communication channels in the organization, failure of management to use the system while requiring line workers to use it, and changes in job status by those who were required to use the system.

These problems are all organizational, not technical, and it is unrealistic to expect a project manager trained only in systems analysis and computer programming to anticipate or to consider them. The effects of systems development are not always negative, but as a new system is developed, it is important to predict how the flow of paperwork may be altered, whether or not formal and informal lines of communication in an office may change, whether or not the new system will change job descriptions or force a redistribution of tasks, and how the system may concentrate or dilute sources of organizational power.

To cope adequately with behavioral problems in systems development, an information architect would be grounded in the theories of organizational behavior and organizational psychology, as well as theories of individual behavior and motivation. Maslow's hierarchy of needs (1943) provides a framework for understanding worker motivation in organizations; Herzberg's motivation-hygiene theory (1959) based on growth needs and avoidance of discomfort, also offers insights into worker behavior.

Markus (1983) has postulated several theories of resistance to information systems that can be used to help understand and anticipate organizational problems when designing and implementing information systems. Olson and Lucas (1982) have also considered the impact of technology on organizations and have listed seventeen propositions that they feel must be considered, including changes in the physical boundaries of departments, possible effects on management span of control, possible changes in level and quality of communication among departments in an organization, and increased efficiency in communication among workers and departments.

There are many other behavioral theories and techniques that can increase the chances of a successful introduction of new information systems. However, this knowledge can also be applied not only to the end user organization but also in the management of the development team, which is an end user community too, though of a different sort.

D. Ergonomics

In the past decade there has been an increasing awareness of the importance of human factors input to software projects. Human factors engineers are now often included as part of development teams, but their work is not always well integrated into the final product. The human-computer interface is now recognized as a critical part of the system, but blending interface design with the computational portion of the system is difficult to do using linear or hierarchical models of development.

Another, less visible problem is the effect of systems on the user environment. New systems often force unwanted changes in working conditions. The user's personal workspace (desk height, chair characteristics, desktop space, storage space, etc.), room temperature, opportunities for communication with others, and work pacing are just some of the variables that should be routinely considered.

Proshansky, Ittelson, and Rivlin (1976) discuss territorial and privacy issues in how people use and adapt to their environment. For example, electronic information systems provide management with a whole set of unobtrusive, automated tools that can be used to invade worker privacy. Privacy also extends to the physical environment, and the introduction of new technology may crowd an employee's workspace if the proper furniture or additional floor space is not allocated.

DeGreene (1970) recommends using task analysis to determine what the system should do, noting that this procedure can aid in defining the problem (constraints, resources, operational environment, etc.), and in understanding what the system should do (boundaries, interfaces, functions, environment, subsystems, and interactions).

Wixon, Holtzblatt, and Knox (1990) have had much success with a technique called contextual design, in which human factors engineers work closely with the users of a system in the user environment, rather than transporting users to a usability laboratory. They found the data collected in the user work context is richer and more meaningful and frequently includes insights that could not have been anticipated in the design of a controlled study. This approach to the collection of human factors data is much closer to the spirit of design (as a process) than controlled experiments, because it allows for change and feedback.

Experimentally controlled studies of human behavior are useful and important for certain classes of problems, but the methodology is inadequate for coping with the complexity of work-life information structures that encompass hardware, software, the physical environment, and the intellectual and emotional environment. Hermeneutic phenomenology, on which Wixon and Whiteside base their work, offers designers a better set of tools for exploring existing environments. Winograd and Flores (1986) have advocated this approach to data collection, and Hycner (1985), Seung (1982), Wertz (1984), and others offer guidelines and advice on the process.

Straub and Wetherbe's study suggests that there is still enormous room for improvement in the human factors of systems; that is, the usability of a system, and that major advances in system use in the 1990s will come not from increased computational power but from greater ease of use. This will only come to pass if human factors engineering is tightly coupled with the rest of the development activity.

V. Summary

Information systems development is no longer dependent on advances in technology to provide increased functionality. Operating systems, compilers, databases, and communications packages are sufficiently mature that poor systems performance cannot be blamed entirely on limitations in hardware or software. Performance is increasingly becoming an issue of design, not just of the tangible hardware and software but also a design issue of the organization and its behavior and a design issue of the physical environment.

It was, perhaps, easier to ignore environmental and organizational issues when computers were contained in a glass walled, environmentally controlled, centrally managed operation. But computers are now part of the background of most business operations, decentralizing the flow of information, changing the control points of the business, and often dominating the work environment of individual employees.

Good design is no longer an aspiration, it is a necessity. To achieve it requires a shift away from a reliance on rigid development methodologies, and recognition that no two information problems are alike. Design is a process of exploration and a uniquely human activity that cannot be easily explained, categorized, or packaged as a set of rules.

The principles of information architecture attempt to describe a basic framework in which to create better systems. Systems design is a multidimensional process that requires a new kind of project manager--the information architect--who has the knowledge and experience to develop information structures that account for the multiple levels and layers of interaction among humans, machines, and the physical environment.

References

1. Abdel-Hamid, Tarek K., and Stuart E. Madnick (1989) Lessons learned from modeling the dynamics of software development. *Communications of the ACM*, Vol. 32, No. 12, pp. 1426 - 1438

2. Amkreutz, J. H. A. E. (1975) Cybernetic model of the design process. *Computer-Aided Design,* 8, pp. 187-191

3. Archea, John (1988) The myth of application: Rethinking the relationship between inquiry and action. *Design Research News,* Vol. 19, No. 1

4. Boland, Richard, and Rudy Hirschheim (1987) *Critical Issues in Information Systems Research.* New York: John Wiley and Sons

5. Brancheau, James C., and James C. Wetherbe (1986) Information architectures: methods and practice. *Information Processing and Management*, Vol. 22, No. 6, pp. 453 - 463

6. Bruner, Jerome (1966) *Toward a theory of instruction.* Cambridge, Mass. : Belknap Press of Harvard University

7.   Campbell, David E., and Toni A. Campbell (1988)   A new look at informal
      communication: The role of the physical environment. *Environment and Behavior*, Vol.
      20, No. 2, pp. 211 - 226
8.   Cohill, Andrew M. (1989) The human factors design process in software development. In:
      Proceedings of the 3rd International Conference on HCI. Boston, MA, September 18-22,
      1989
9.   Cohill, A.M., L. Harper-O'Donnell, and F. P. Curran (1985) Sociological factors in
      software development. In: *Proceedings of the 27th Annual Conference of the Human
      Factors Society*. Santa Monica, CA: HFS
10.   DeGreene, Kenyon B. (1970) *Systems Psychology*. New York: McGraw-Hill
11.   Dreyfus, Hubert L. (1986) *Mind over machine: the power of human intuition and
      expertise in the era of the computer.* New York: Free Press
12.   Graves, Michael   (1977) The Necessity for Drawing: Tangible Speculation.
      Architectural Design, June, 1977, pp. 384 - 394
13.   Hartson, H. R., and D. Hix, (1989) Toward empirically derivedmethodologies and tools
      for human-computer interface development. In: *International Journal of Man-Machine
      Studies*,
14.   Heim, Michael (1987) *Electric Language: A philosophical study of word processing.*
      New Haven: Yale University Press
15.   Herzberg, F., B. Mausner, and B. Snyderman (1959) *The motivation to work.* New
      York: John Wiley and Sons.
16.   Hillier, William J., John Musgrove, and Pat O'Sullivan (1976) Knowledge and design.
      In: *Environmental Psychology*, edited by Proshansky, H. M., W. H. Ittelson, and L. G.
      Rivlin pp. 69 - 82
17.   Human Factors Society Committee on Human-Computer Interaction (1990) Draft
      standard on system design. Santa Monica, CA: HFS
18.   Hycner, Richard M. (1985) Some guidelines for the phenomenological analysis of
      interview data. *Human Studies*, 8,   pp. 279 - 303
19.   Laseau, Paul (1980) *Graphic Thinking for Architects and Designers.* New York: Van
      Nostrand Reinhold
20.   Lyotard, Jean-Francois (1984) *The postmodern condition: a report on knowledge.*
      Minneapolis: Univ. of Minnesota Press
21.   Lyytinen, Kalle (1987) Different perspectives on information systems: problems and
      solutions. *ACM Computing Surveys*, Vol. 19, No. 1, pp. 5 - 46
22.   Malhotra, Ashok, John C. Thomas, John M. Carroll, and Lance A. Miller (1980)
      Cognitive processes in design. *International Journal of Man-Machine Studies*, 12, pp.
      119 - 140
23.   Markus, Lynne M. (1983) Power, politics, and MIS   i m p l e m e n t a t i o n .   I n :
      Communications of the ACM, Vol. 26, No. 6, pp. 430 - 444
24.   Maslow, A. H. (1943) A theory of human motivation. *Psychological Bulletin*, 50,
      pp. 370 - 396.
25.   Mason, R.E.A., and T.T. Carey (1983) Prototyping interactive information systems.
      Communications of the ACM, Vol. 26, No. 5, pp. 347 - 354
26.   Olson, Margrethe H., and Henry C. Lucas, Jr. (1982) The impact of office automation
      on the organization: Some implications for research and practice. *Communications of the
      ACM*, Vol. 25, No.11, pp. 838 - 847
27.   Packer, Martin J. (1985) Hermeneutic inquiry in the study of human conduct. *American
      Psychologist,* Vol. 40, No. 10, pp. 1081 - 1093

28. Piaget, Jean (1977) *The Essential Piaget.* H. E. Gruber and J. J. Voneche (Ed.).   New York: Basic Books

29. Proshansky, Harold M., W. H. Ittelson, and L. G.Rivlin (1976) Freedom of choice and behavior in a physical setting. In: *Environmental Psychology*, edited by Proshansky, H. M., W. H. Ittelson, and L. G. Rivlin pp. 170- 180

30. Pye, David W. (1964) *The nature of design.* New York: Reinhold Publishers

31. Rosson, Mary Beth, Susanne Maass, and Wendy A. Kellogg (1988) The designer as user: building requirements for design tools from design practice. *Communications of the ACM*, Vol. 31, No. 11, pp. 1288-1298

32. Rouse, William B. (1986) On the value of information in system design: a framework for understanding and aiding designers. *Information Processing and Management,* Vol. 22, No. 2, pp. 217 - 228

33. Rowe, Christopher J. (1987) Introducing a sales order processing system: the importance of human, organizational, and ergonomic factors. *Behaviour and Information Technology,* Vol. 6, No. 4, pp. 455 - 465

34. Sankar, Y. (1988) Organizational culture and new technologies. *Journal of Systems Management*, 4, pp. 10 - 17

35. Sethi, Vijay, and James T. C. Teng (1988) Choice of an information   requirements anaylsis method: an integrated approach. *INFOR* Vol. 26, No. 1, pp. 1 - 16

36. Seung, T. K. (1982) *Structuralism and Hermeneutics.* New York: Columbia University Press

37. Simon, Herbert A. (1969) *The Sciences of the Artificial.* Cambridge, MA: MIT Press

38. Straub, Detmar W., and James C. Wetherbe (1989) Information technologies for the 1990s: An organizational impact perspective. *Communications of the ACM*, Vol. 32, No. 11, pp. 1328 - 1339

39. Wertz, Frederick J. (1984) Procedures in phenomenological research and the question of validity. *Studies in the Social Sciences*, Vol. 23, pp. 29 - 48

40. Winograd, Terry (1990) What can we teach about human-computer interaction. In: *proceedings of CHI, 1990.* New York: ACM, pp. 443 - 449

41. Winograd, Terry, and F. Flores (1986) *Understanding Computers and Cognition.* Norwood, NJ: Ablex

42. Wixon, Dennis, Karen Holtzblatt, and Stephen Knox (1990) Contextual Design: An emergent view of system design. In: *Proceedings of CHI*, 1990, Seattle, WA, April 1-5 pp. 329-336 New York: ACM

43. Zuboff, Shoshana (1988) *In the age of the smart machine.* New York: Basic Books

6 Involving Social Scientists in the Design of New Technology

JOHN C. TANG[+]

Xerox Palo Alto Research Center
Palo Alto, California

I. Introduction

Recent trends in design methodologies have led to design processes that include understanding the needs of the users (Gould & Lewis, 1985), understanding the context in which users work (Wixon *et al.*, 1990), or even involving users in the design process (Namioka & Schuler, 1990). However, translating these trends into practical methods that designers can employ is problematic. Part of the problem is that the interaction between users and technology is a complex human activity. Understanding this interaction requires applying skills and observational methodologies not usually found in the curriculum for computer interface designers. However, methodologies for studying and understanding human activity can be found in the social sciences. Working together with social scientists can help designers understand the needs of users and help them design technology that supports the users' work activity.

[+]Current affiliation: Sun Microsystems, Inc., Mountain View, California.

Taking Software
Design Seriously

115

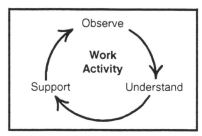

Figure 1. Iterative research approach[*]

An interdisciplinary group of anthropologists, designers, and computer scientists at the Xerox Palo Alto Research Center (PARC) has been studying how people accomplish their work activity as part of the process of designing technology to support that activity (Suchman, 1987; Tang, 1989; Henderson, in press). This research is premised on the need to understand what users actually do in their work activity in order to guide the design and development of tools to support their work. This iterative process of observing, understanding, and supporting a work activity is represented in Figure 1.

Our research draws upon video-based interaction analysis techniques (Goodwin, 1981; Heath, 1986) to study and understand human activity. In particular, we apply interaction analysis techniques to identify implications for the design of technology to support a work activity. One focus of our interdisciplinary work group has been studying collaborative drawing activity (Tatar, 1989), the writing, drawing, and gesturing activity that occurs when a small group of people collaborate over a shared drawing surface (e.g., chalkboard, pads of paper). These studies have been guiding the design and development of prototype tools to support collaborative drawing (Tang & Minneman, 1990; Minneman & Bly, 1990). This process not only leads to a better understanding of collaborative drawing activity but also leads to the design of better tools to support that activity. Furthermore, reflecting on this process of using interaction analysis methods in the development of new technology leads to an understanding of how studying users can be an integral part of the design process.

This chapter distinguishes two ways in which designers have worked together with social scientists to study users in our research:

[*]I would like to acknowledge Scott Minneman for initially composing this representation for the relationship of observing, understanding, and intervening in an activity (Minneman, 1988).

- *User* Studies: Given a target end user population and a work activity of interest, intensively analyze how the users accomplish their work in order to identify design implications for new technology to support their activity.
- *Usability* Studies: Given a functional prototype and some tasks that can be accomplished on that prototype, observe how users interact with the prototype to accomplish those tasks in order to identify improvements for the next design iteration.

After describing these two approaches, an example is presented that illustrates integrating both user studies and usability studies as part of the design of technology to support users' work.

II. User Studies

User studies involve an intensive analysis of the users' work activity that can lead to the development of a new technology to support that activity. Studying and understanding how users accomplish their work helps identify their needs and formulate implications for the design of technology to satisfy those needs. Conducting user studies before beginning to design a new technology is a *proactive* way of involving users in the design process; the observations from studying the users can produce insights that lead to innovative design concepts for new technology to meet their needs.

Our user studies at Xerox PARC draw upon a methodology from the social sciences known as video-based interaction analysis. This methodology has been used to study the accompanying non verbal behavior in conversation (Goodwin, 1981; Heath, 1986), the interaction between humans and technology (Suchman, 1987), and the collaborative drawing activity of small groups (Tang, 1991). Applying this methodology to conduct user studies in a design context can accomplish the initial crucial step in design of identifying the users' needs.

Video-based interaction analysis involves a careful study of videotape records of realistic work activity to understand how that activity is accomplished through the participants' interactions with their environment. This focus on externally visible interaction contrasts with a cognitive approach that interprets human activity in terms of the internal mental processes of the participants. In interaction analysis, there is a methodological commitment to recording work activity as it would naturally happen in a real (or as realistic as practical) work environment, since that context has a major influence on the work activity. This contextual setting contrasts with the experimental psychology approach, which studies isolated tasks in a laboratory environment.

Videotape is used to capture as complete a record as possible of the activity for repeated review and analysis later. In order to minimize the potential distraction of observing the participants, the cameras are unobtrusively mounted on tripods and not moved or re-aimed for the duration of the session. This "passive" observational methodology is less disrupting than controlled experiments or "thinking aloud" protocol analysis. In the sessions observed using this methodology, the groups were focused on their collaborative task and there was no visible evidence that the video observation significantly affected the group's activity.

The videotapes of work activity are studied as an interdisciplinary group, including the designers of the tool, computer science implementers, anthropologists who study the interaction between people and technology, and sometimes even the users. This approach brings together insights from a variety of perspectives on the video data. Since the group members come from different academic disciplines and viewpoints, they each bring different sensitivities with which to examine the video data. Furthermore, they are each forced to demonstrate their claims about the activity by observable evidence from the video data, rather than relying solely on characterizations of human activity that are specific to their own discipline. Interdisciplinary group analysis helps assure that the resulting observations are based on observable evidence from the data.

The tapes are carefully studied to understand how the participants accomplish their activity through their interactions with their environment. This goal is rather open-ended but, when set in a design context, the analysis is often directed toward identifying new technology for supporting the participants' work activity. A central technique for studying the video data is to collect repeated patterns of activity—either common mechanisms for accomplishing work or recurring problems. Comparing and contrasting among this collection of patterns leads to identifying what resources the participants use to accomplish their work and what hindrances they encounter in the course of their work. Based on this understanding, technology can be designed to support their work activity by augmenting resources while removing obstacles.

III. Usability Studies

Conducting usability studies is a common practice in interface design that involves observing how representative users work with functional prototypes to evaluate the prototype and suggest improvements to the design of the tool (see, for example, Schneier & Mehal, 1984). A variety of methods for quickly prototyping user interfaces through computer tools (e.g., Hypercard), video (Vertelney, 1989), or simulations (Gould *et al.*, 1983) have been discussed in the literature.

At Xerox PARC, we videotape sessions of users working on realistic tasks using functional prototype tools. These tapes are analyzed by a group of anthropologists, designers, and computer scientists (and sometimes the users) to identify specific examples of trouble (or accomplishment) in the users' work activity. Reviewing the video data together as an interdisciplinary group helps raise specific issues and suggests improvements to the design of the tool from a variety of perspectives.   Problems experienced by the user are often not perceived by the designer but can be noted by the anthropologist or the user. Likewise, the tool designers can often readily suggest design improvements to the tool once they are confronted with problems observed in the videotape. In our experience, it is far more effective for designers to actually see for themselves the problems that the users encounter rather than relying on second hand reports on the results of usability studies. Involving the designers in the usability studies or collecting videotape samples for the desingers to view is an effective vehicle for engaging the designers with the users' needs.

Usability studies lead to evolutionary design improvements for the next iteration prototype of the tool, which can in turn be observed in use. This cycle of refining and observing can be repeated until all the design and user requirements are satisfied, or time and money constraints force the design into production. Usability studies depend on a design method that iterates quickly between rapid prototyping and observing these prototypes with real users. However, usability studies are *reactive* in that the users' responses can be collected only after a functional prototype has been built and the users have an opportunity to interact with it. This after-the-fact nature of usability studies tends to limit the impact that they can have on the design, since many features of the design will have been largely fixed by the time a functioning prototype is constructed. Thus, the effectiveness of usability studies in design is greatly enhanced when coupled with user studies that help guide the design in advance.

IV. Applying User and Usability Studies to Develop a Shared Drawing Tool

An example of a design process that incorporated user studies and usability studies is the development of VideoDraw (Tang & Minneman, 1990). VideoDraw is a prototype, video-based tool that provides a shared "virtual sketchbook" among collaborators who may be in remote locations. A schematic of a 2-person VideoDraw is

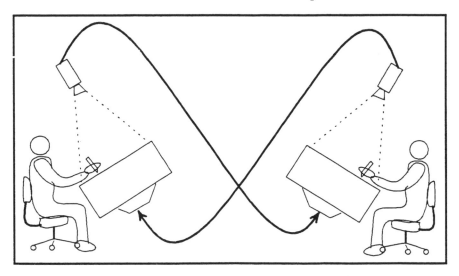

Figure 2. Schematic diagram of 2-person VideoDraw

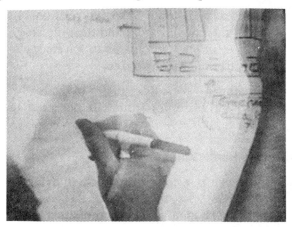

Figure 3. Participant's view of a VideoDraw screen

shown in Figure 2. It consists of an interconnection of video cameras aimed at the display screens of video monitors. The collaborators use dry erase whiteboard markers to draw directly on the display screens. As each collaborator draws on the screen, the video camera transmits those marks *and* the accompanying hand gestures to the other collaborator, enabling them to effectively share a drawing space. Figure 3 shows a view of a VideoDraw screen as seen by a participant.

Previous to the development of VideoDraw, an interdisciplinary work group at PARC was studying how small groups of people collaborate around shared drawing surfaces, such as whiteboards, large sheets of paper, or notebooks. By analyzing these tapes over the course of several months, we identified several resources that the collaborators use to accomplish their work, as well as obstacles they encountered. Collaborators used hand gestures as a resource to act out ideas, to refer to objects in the drawing space, and to help mediate their interaction (e.g., waving a hand to indicate wanting the next turn of talk). They used the *process* of creating and referring to their drawings to convey information that was not contained in the resulting drawings themselves. Often more than one collaborator was active in the drawing space at the same time, and this concurrent access was used as a resource to help them negotiate sharing the drawing space.

On the other hand, not being able to clearly see each other's gestures and what those gestures refer to was sometimes a problem when the group worked face-to-face. Also, when two collaborators sat facing each other, they saw the drawings that their partner was making at an improper orientation (i.e., upside-down), making it difficult to perceive or add onto each other's drawings. The resources and obstacles identified from studying shared drawing activity are illustrated in a videotape summarizing this research (Tang, 1990).

These observations on the resources and obstacles in collaboration may seem unremarkable, since they are such a natural part of everyday, face-to-face interaction. Yet, in considering the design of tools to support shared drawing activity, especially between remote collaborators, these observations have significant design implications. Most existing computer tools do not convey gestural activity, do not convey much about the process of creating and using marks, and often introduce time delays that can make it difficult to negotiate having multiple users active in the same drawing space at the same time.

The design of VideoDraw addresses these issues. Video is able to very effectively convey hand gestures and the process of creating marks and referring to them. Furthermore, the overlaid video images allow the collaborators' hands to interact more closely than would be physically possible if they were sharing the same drawing surface, giving them even more concurrent access to the drawing space than if they were working face-to-face. VideoDraw also allows the collaborators to see each other's gestures with respect to their referents in the drawing space. Each collaborator can also see the jointly constructed drawing in the proper, upright orientation, enabling them to easily interact over each other's drawings.

The development of VideoDraw demonstrates how user studies lead both to a better understanding of human collaborative activity and to the design of new technology. Identifying specific resources and hindrances in collaborative work not only provided a better understanding of collaborative drawing but also guided the design of VideoDraw to augment resources (e.g., gestures) while eliminating obstacles (e.g., upside-down orientation) in that activity. Attempting to both understand an activity and design tools to support it can be complementary pursuits. In our research, the design interest to support collaborative drawing activity often led to new insights into understanding the activity, and a more specific understanding of the activity often led to concrete design implications for tools to support that activity.

Once the new technology is embodied into a working prototype, it can be subjected to usability studies, leading to iterative improvement of the design. Our initial usability studies of VideoDraw have confirmed that users utilize the way that VideoDraw conveys gestures, conveys process, allows concurrent access to the drawing space, and preserves a proper orientation to the drawing space. VideoDraw enables people to do new things (*remotely* share a drawing space) in familiar ways. This familiar nature of VideoDraw comes from the understanding gained through user studies of how collaborators share a drawing space in face-to-face collaboration.

The usability studies also identified some limitations in the use of VideoDraw. The size of the display and the limited resolution of standard video constrains the amount of information that can be legibly conveyed through VideoDraw. Because each participant's marks are made on the surface of the video display while their collaborator's marks appear on the phosphor of the display, each participant can erase only their own marks, and not those made by their collaborator. Furthermore, because of the thickness of the glass of the display screen, a noticeable amount of parallax can make it difficult to correctly align marks between the participants.

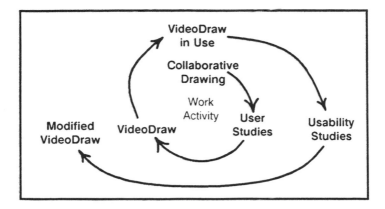

Figure 4. Iterative development through use and usability studies

Conducting usability studies to develop concepts initially identified through user studies is represented in Figure 4. VideoDraw has already gone through two more design iterations in response to the initial usability studies of the first prototype.

V. Conclusions

Involving anthropologists who are skilled at analyzing human activity with designers who are skilled at translating those analyses into design prototypes leads to designing new technology that meets users' needs. An important characteristic of our research is that it has involved anthropologists with an expertise in interaction analysis methods. It is often their training and sensitivities in analyzing human activity that have enabled the group as a whole to come to a better understanding of the work activity being studied and how to better support it. Since interaction analysis focuses on how people accomplish their activity through interactions with their environment, it is especially well suited to study user interface (i.e., people interacting with technology) and collaboration (i.e., people interacting with other people) issues.

The video-based observation methods described in this chapter tend to be rich yet time consuming analyses of how users interact with technology. User studies are very open-ended and can take months or years of research but have a potential in fundamentally shaping the design of innovative technology. Usability studies can be more timely and narrowly focused but are typically limited to more evolutionary modifications to the design of technology. Due to the time investment required, only a few samples of activity can be subjected to in-depth user or usability studies. In an actual product development program, this methodology would be complemented by other methodologies (e.g., user interviews, market surveys, focus groups) for a broader indication of how users would interact with the technology.

A fundamental tension does arise between anthropologists, who are trained not to disturb the activity that is being observed, and designers, who are committed to changing the world to meet the needs of users. The anthropologists sometimes expressed reluctance to intervene in an activity before coming to a better understanding of it. The designers, on the other hand, were often quick to propose solutions to problems observed in the activity and anxious to try prototype designs to see how the users would respond to them. Although this tension sometimes became problematic in our experience, it was mediated in practice by conducting a balanced amount of analysis *before* moving into an implementation cycle. The anthropologists and designers need to have equal commitment, investment, and responsibility at the outset of the project in order to negotiate that balance.

Our experience of having anthropologists and designers working together has been a very productive one. Intensive user studies led to innovative insights into the design of new technology, and usability studies led to evolutionary improvements in iterative design. Together, user studies and usability studies have been leading to a better understanding of collaborative activity and to improved prototype tools to support that activity. Although it would be premature to call this approach a design method, we are beginning to reflect on this approach in ways that could generalize to other design projects.

Acknowledgments

I would like to acknowledge the other colleagues who have been involved in this research integrating studies of use with design: Sara Bly, Francoise Brun-Cottan, Austin Henderson, Brigitte Jordan, Scott Minneman, Lucy Suchman, and Deborah Tatar. I especially acknowledge Scott Minneman, who has been working together with me on the design and development of VideoDraw.

References

Goodwin, C. (1981). *Conversational Organization: Interaction Between Speakers and Hearers*, New York: Academic Press.

Gould, J. D. and Lewis, C. (1985). "Designing for Usability: Key Principles and What Designers Think," *Communications of the ACM*, **28** (3), pp. 300-311.

Gould, J. D., Conti, J. and Hovanyecz, T. (1983). "Composing Letters with a Simulated Listening Typewriter," *Communications of the ACM*, **26** (4), pp. 295-308.

Heath, C. (1986). *Body Movement and Speech in Medical Interaction*, Cambridge: Cambridge University Press.

Henderson, A. (in press). "A Development Perspective on Interface, Design, and Theory," *Designing Interaction: Psychology at the Human-Computer Interface*, John M. Carroll, Ed., Cambridge: Cambridge University Press.

Minneman, S. (1988). Ph.D. qualifying exam presentation, Stanford University.

Minneman, S. L. and Bly, S. A. (1990). "Experiences in the Development of a Multi-user Drawing Tool," *Proceedings of the Third Guelph Symposium on Computer Mediated Communication*, Guelph, Ontario, pp. 154-167.

Namioka, A. and Schuler, D. Eds., (1990). *PDC '90: Participatory Design Conference Proceedings*, Seattle, WA, Computer Professionals for Social Responsibility (CPSR).

Schneier, C. A. and Mehal, M. E. (1984). "Evaluating Usability for Application Interfaces," *Human-Computer Interaction*, G. Salvendy, Ed., Amsterdam: Elsevier Science Publishers B.V., pp. 129-132.

Suchman, L. A. (1987). *Plans and Situated Actions: The Problem of Human-Machine Communication*, Cambridge: Cambridge University Press.

Tang, J. C. (1989). *Listing, Drawing, and Gesturing in Design: A Study of the Use of Shared Workspaces by Design Teams*, Xerox PARC Technical Report SSL-89-3 (Ph.D. Dissertation, Stanford University).

Tang, J. C. (1990). "Observations on the Use of Shared Drawing Spaces," videotape, Xerox Corporation, Palo Alto Research Center.

Tang, J. C. (1991). "Findings from Observational Studies of Collaborative Work," *International Journal of Man-Machine Studies*.

Tang, J. C. and Minneman, S. L. (1990). "VideoDraw: A Video Interface for Collaborative Drawing," *Proceedings of the Conference on Computer Human Interaction (CHI) '90*, Seattle, WA, pp. 313-320.

Tatar, D. (1989). "Using Video-Based Observation to Shape the Design of a New Technology," *SIGCHI Bulletin*, 21 (2), pp. 108-111.

Vertelney, L. (1989). "Using Video to Prototype User Interfaces," *SIGCHI Bulletin*, 21 (2), pp. 57-61.

Wixon, D., Holtzblatt, K., and Knox, S. (1990). "Contextual Design: An Emergent View of System Design," *Proceedings of the Conference on Computer Human Interaction (CHI) '90*, Seattle, WA, pp. 329-336.

7   Let the Users Design!

THOMAS R. LANNING

GTE Laboratories Incorporated
Waltham, Massachusetts

I. Introduction

Almost by definition, user-centered design requires user involvement in the design process. Since the design process requires many types of information from users, it requires involving users throughout the process in a variety of ways. In this chapter we define several roles users and professional designers can play in the design of human-computer interfaces and discuss the impact these roles have on product and service quality.

Before we explore the benefits and problems of including users in the design process, we will quickly review a simplified model of the design process and discuss the players in that process.

II. A Simple Model of the Design Process

The design process can be viewed as several overlapping tasks:

1. define the problem,
2. list the requirements any solution must satisfy,
3. select an abstract solution concept,
4. specify the general parameters of the solution, and
5. create a detailed implementation plan for the solution.

These activities are illustrated in the following story. An island-bound farmer's customers were on the nearby shore of the mainland. The farmer soon discovered a problem, "My produce must be transported to the customer on the other shore." A refined statement of this discovery would become the problem definition (task 1). The farmer may decide on the amount of money available, along with how much produce any solution should be able to transport. These are examples of items included in a requirements list (task 2). The farmer may decide that he should build a bridge. "Build a bridge," "build a boat," "build an airplane," or "dig a tunnel" could be example solution concepts. The farmer would select a concept, perhaps "build a bridge" (task 3). The farmer would then continue to elaborate on the selected concept, perhaps specifying a "wooden pontoon bridge with a planked surface," (task 4). The detailed implementation plan would include enough detail to build the bridge, maybe including details such as plank sizes and pontoon diameters (task 5).

Each of these tasks can be viewed as an iterative cycle composed of four overlapping subactivities:

1. gather background information,
2. collect and/or generate alternatives,
3. select an alternative, and
4. evaluate the validity of the decision.

For example, someone defining requirements might study the work patterns of several users (gather background information). That person might hypothesize that the new product needs concurrent user access (generate a new requirement). If the design team decides to include this requirement (select alternative), someone should verify that concurrent user access is really needed (evaluate the validity of the decision).

The model presented here does not completely describe any real design process. However, it does provide enough common language to describe how users should be involved in the design process.

III. The Players

There are many players involved in the design process:

- the users,
- the customers, who might be different than the users,
- the designers,
- the engineers that implement the product or service,
- the company producing the product or service,
- the retailer, which might be different than the producer,
- competing companies, which might be setting industry standards,
- governments, which might be regulating design options, and
- communities different than users and customers affected by the design.

Although there are many important players in the design process, in this chapter we will focus on the professional designers and users.

A. Professional Designers

One critical group of players in the design process is the professional designers. These professional designers develop and practice the art and science of design. Their primary function is to create new products and services. Usually, professional designers are only involved with a product or service until it is implemented, and then they move on to other assignments. Therefore, we can assume most professional designers will not routinely use the products or services they design. As part of that job, however, we can usually assume professional designers strive to understand why and how users interact with the things they design. We will also assume professional designers must deal with issues and constraints that may be in direct conflict with identified user interests, such as technical limitations, legal restrictions, and corporate strategies. Finally, we will assume professional designers have limited resources available for the design process.

B. Users

Users are the group of people that use a product or service. Unlike the professional designers, users do not focus on the product or service; they focus on what they can *achieve* with the product or service.

Users can play three different roles in the design process: the subject, the evaluator, and the designer. These three roles are introduced next.

1. Subject

The user, as a subject, is a creature to be studied and whose needs should be satisfied. This passive role portrays users as something to design for, not something to design with. The subjects may not even know they are involved in a design process. They can provide general information about themselves, their environment, and the tasks they attempt. Task analysis, market research opinion surveys, and cognitive modeling are some techniques that can collect subject information.

2. Evaluator

The user, as an evaluator, is a living tool used by professional designers to measure the user-perceived value of design alternatives or design decisions. The evaluator, unlike the subject, will actually interact with the design before the product or service is "finished." The evaluator may be used to predict acceptance levels of the final design and can provide performance, preference, and intent-to-purchase information. Experimental usability and utility studies are typically used to collect evaluator information.

3. Designer

The user, as a designer, is a member of the design team. In this role the user actively makes strategic design recommendations, suggests alternatives, and helps define acceptance criteria. The designer can generate alternatives and make design decisions. Envisionment (Buxton 1989), collaborative storytelling (Evenson, Rheinfrank, and Wulff 1988), brainstorming, lead-user analysis, and some applications of think-aloud protocol can help include the user as a designer.

IV. Involving Users in the Design Process

A. The User as Subject

A design is more likely to be user-centered if designers consider accurate information about users and their environment during each design activity. Professional designers certainly have a better chance of generating high-quality design alternatives and making better user-related design decisions if they use background information obtained from the user as subject. However, designers can only collect a subset of all possible user-related information because of cost and time constraints. How do designers know what subset to collect? How do designers know when enough information has been collected? It is unlikely that designers, by themselves, will ever know the absolute answers to these questions.

Many professional designers cope with this problem by using their intuition to select the subset of background information to collect. Sometimes their intuition is correct; however, many times it is not. A design process that does not involve the user beyond the user as a subject, is highly sensitive to the skill (and luck?) of the professional designers. Excellent designers can create wonderful user-centered designs. However, as Gould and Lewis (1985) point out, the high probability of user-perceived errors appearing in the work of most designers is unacceptable.

B. The User as Evaluator

The number of user-perceived errors in a design can be reduced by validating the professional designers' decisions. The user, as an evaluator, can be utilized to ensure the professional designers make reasonable user-perspective choices. If the evaluator determines that a design decision is inappropriate, the designers can go through another full iteration of gathering more or different background information, generating and collecting new alternatives, selecting a different alternative, and then finally evaluating the new decision.

Validating decisions not only places safeguards on the quality of the background information gathered but also ensures that professional designers make acceptable decisions. It also helps improve the process of gathering background information, the process of generating alternatives, and the process of decision making by discovering design errors soon after they are made. Boehm (1981) found errors could be as much as 50 times more costly if not corrected early. Validating decisions made during each activity helps prevent the costly propagation of design errors. If feasible, decisions should be validated before any other downstream decisions based on them are made. Imagine discovering after six months of design work that the original problem definition was incorrect!

However, evaluating every decision made during each definition task can be costly. If professional designers are confident of the decisions they made and the cost of making a bad decision is small, they can postpone the evaluation. However, postponing the evaluation can squander precious resources. For example, suppose a survey indicates users want a touch screen instead of a mouse. Also, let us assume the cost of creating and evaluating a new detailed implementation plan incorporating the touch screen is minimal. It might seem foolish to evaluate the new requirements, concept, specification, and implementation plan. If the survey is interpreted correctly and the intermediate definitions are correct, then indeed much is saved if the intermediate validations are skipped. However, if the survey is not interpreted correctly, valuable resources will be wasted on all the downstream activities based on that faulty interpretation. Thus, this shortcut can be dangerous if used incorrectly. I have observed that it is very easy to underestimate the cost of bad decisions and to place too much confidence in the designers' decisions. The cost of a bad decision must include all the resources allocated downstream to activities based on that bad decision. In general, the cost of errors increase as each validation point is postponed. Design teams should carefully examine the full cost of this shortcut before using it.

Promising work by Nielsen (1989) and Virzi (1989, 1990) on discount usability engineering demonstrates that reliable validation does not have to be expensive or time consuming. They have found, repeatedly, that five users can identify approximately 80% of the existing interface related problems. Their techniques are currently being used to validate decisions made during the concept, specification, and implementation plan tasks. Similar techniques that also reduce the number of required users and that simplify the interpretation of data may be possible for the problem and requirements definition tasks.

Given enough time and money, professional designers utilizing only the user as an evaluator, can create an acceptable design. However, creating a design using only user validation would be similar to reconstructing what I did today by asking me questions I can answer with only a "yes" or "no." Such reconstruction, and design, is possible but far from optimal. Professional designers that only allow users to pass judgment on what they have produced are utilizing the same sub-optimal technique. Professional designers that incorporate information obtained from the user, as a subject, have a better chance of presenting good alternatives or making good decisions. Utilizing both user roles is a definite improvement but still not optimal.

C. The User as Designer

Up to this point, we have assumed that only professionals design new products. We have assumed that these professionals need to understand the user, the user's environment, and how the user operates in that environment. We have also assumed that the user does not need to understand much about the design process. This position is at one end of a range of possibilities. At the other end, *users* design new products and services.

If users wanted to utilize professional designers, the users would need to understand the professional designers, their environment, and how they operate in their environment. We could also assume that much of the burden of gathering user-related background information and representing users' needs would be transferred from the professional designers to the users. The professional designers would ensure other appropriate perspectives are represented and would provide expert guidance on employing design techniques. The professional designers would help the user, as designer, to organize background information, to collect and/or generate design alternatives, and to make good design decisions. This extreme position should certainly ensure more user-centered designs. However, Ehn, Grudin, and Thoresen (1990) and others point out that this level of user involvement does have problems. Many professions and companies would need to change political structures and organizational boundaries. User environments may be large and diverse, making it difficult to even find people that can serve as "representative" users. Even if a workable number of representative users can be found to serve on a design team, it may be difficult to find users who want to invest the time and energy necessary to design a new product or service. Anyway, if users wanted to design new products, they would have become professional designers, instead of what they currently are! It is also not clear that everyone has the skills and temperament to help lead a design project.

Luckily, professional designers can tap the users' domain knowledge and design insights without requiring restructuring, without finding small representative samples of users, and most importantly, without requiring the users to become professional designers. There are various creative techniques available, such as those mentioned in Buxton (1989) and Gould and Lewis (1985), that can help users reason about design issues and then help them communicate their thoughts. Some techniques, such as creative groups and interactive storytelling, allow professional designers to interact in real-time with the user as designer. This can greatly speed the design process by allowing the professional designers to ask questions, interpret responses, and quickly follow up on new or interesting information.

With the help of experienced guides, users can provide strategic design information and participate with the professional designers on a design project. If users help direct the collection of background information, it is less likely that the professional designers will overlook important information; possibly avoiding costly redesign efforts. Professional designers can produce better designs if users are allowed to propose alternatives that they may have overlooked. Designs will be more user-centered if the users are allowed to voice their opinions when design decisions are made. Finally, acceptance criteria will be more complete and realistic if users help.

Probably the most important reason users, as designers, should be included in the design process is their ability to add perspectives, insights, and information that professional designers just do not realize they are missing. It is easy for professional designers to make an error of omission. For example they could proceed without stating an essential requirement, or without realizing a desirable alternative was not discovered, or that a beneficial metaphor was missed. LeMaster and Merz (1990) discuss how users proposed valuable alternative truck packing representations that the professional designers missed. Adding the user to the design team should not be mistaken as simply adding more pseudo-random information that will statistically increase the chance of finding something important. Users are natives of the environment where the new product or service will be introduced and hence have an understanding of that environment that most professional designers will never fully acquire. Users usually do not reason about their environment in the same way the professional designers do, or as Norman

(1988) puts it, designers are not typical users. This difference can be an asset or liability for the design process. If the user and professional designers work together, the different perspectives can add to the effectiveness of the design process.

Including the user, as a subject, as an evaluator, and as a designer, is still not enough to ensure user-centered design. It is possible to utilize each user role and still fail. Information provided by each user role must make it to the core of the decision making process. A great resource is wasted if the designer's recommendations collected in the sales department, the evaluator's data collected in the product test group, and subject's information collected in the human factors department are not used by the professional designers. Grudin and Poltrock (1989) describe a survey of how software organizations operate today. Unfortunately, the survey indicates there is not enough sharing of user-related information. If organizations do not allow this information to move easily to the designers, optimal user-centered design is still doomed.

V. Summary

A simple, but incomplete, model of the design process was introduced. The model included several overlapping tasks:

1. define the problem,
2. list the requirements any solution must satisfy,
3. select a solution concept,
4. specify the general parameters of the solution, and
5. create a detailed implementation plan for the solution.

Each task was comprised of four activities: gather background information, collect and/or generate alternatives, select an alternative, and then evaluate the validity of the decision. Three roles users can play in a design process were defined: subject, evaluator, and designer.

Professional designers can not gather every desirable piece of background information about the user, as subject, due to resource limitations or perspective blindness. Users, as designers, can help select what information should be gathered, what alternatives should be considered, and how alternatives should be selected. Users, as evaluators, help ensure the design process is producing user-centered designs by validating the selected alternatives.

Since most users utilize products in environments different than the environments designers inhabit, including users will potentially result in a larger set of alternative ideas to be considered. If more ideas are considered, the chance of deciding on an optimal design is increased.

When users are incorporated throughout the design process, design errors are detected and corrected before they propagate and become expensive or impossible to correct. This not only improves designs but also the design process.

References

Boehm, B. W. (1981). *Software Engineering Economics*. Prentice-Hall, Englewood Cliffs.

Buxton, B. (1989). "Drama and Personality in User Interface Design," *Proceedings ACM CHI'89 Conference*. Austin, TX.

Ehn, P., Grudin J., and Thoresen K. (1990). "Participatory Design of Computer Systems," *Proceedings ACM CHI'90 Conference*. Seattle, WA.

Evenson, S., Rheinfrank, J., and Wulff, W. (1988). "Storytelling as a Collaborative Approach To Multi-Disciplinary User Interface Design," *Proceedings ACM CIII'88 Conference*. Washington, DC.

Gould, J. D. and Lewis, C. (1985). "Designing for Usability: Key Principles and What Designers Think," *Communications of the ACM*. Volume 28, Number 3, March 1985.

Grudin, J. and Poltrock, S. E. (1989). "User Interface Design in Large Corporations: Coordination and Communication Across Disciplines," *Proceedings ACM CHI'89 Conference*. Austin, TX.

LeMaster, R. and Merz, U. (1990). "Design of a Loading Plan Format for an Expert Cargo Loading System," *Proceedings ACM CHI'90 Conference*. Seattle, WA.

Nielsen, J. (1989). "Usability Engineering at a Discount," *Proceedings Third International Conference on Human-Computer Interaction*. Boston, MA.

Norman, D.A. (1988). *The Psychology of Everyday Things*. Basic Books, New York.

Virzi, R.A. (1989). "What Can You Learn From A Low-Fidelity Prototype?" *Proceedings Human Factors Society 33rd Annual Meeting*. Denver, CO.

Virzi, R.A. (1990). "Streamlining Design: Running Fewer Subjects," *Proceedings Human Factors Society 34th Annual Meeting*. Orlando, FL.

8 A Graphic Designer's Perspective

PATRICIA A. CRAIG

Microsoft Corporation
Redmond, Washington

I. Introduction

Although the interface team is composed of many different professionals - such as graphic designers, software engineers, cognitive psychologists, and writers - this chapter will focus on the relationship between a graphic designer and a software engineer. My experience of working with software engineers has convinced me that it's possible for a collaborative relationship to work between graphic designers and software engineers.

In order to understand how this collaborative relationship can work, it's necessary to understand the evolution of design in the industrial world as well as to arrive at a common definition of design and to agree upon the roles of the graphic designer and the software engineer. Design in the preindustrial world was united with craft in a single act of design and creation. In the industrial world, as production became more complex, the act of design and creation were separated. Design gradually developed closer ties to research and development.

Many professionals refer to their activities as *design*: software engineers design algorithms and graphic designers design the appearance of the user interface. Because the outcome of design activity is widely different from profession to profession, arriving at a common definition of design is difficult. The definition must be general enough to encompass the wide variety of design activities, but it must be specific enough to enhance understanding. One way to define design is to say that the purpose of design is to create objects that appropriately communicate their intent, to satisfy the needs of the audience, and to work as fully as possible within the medium. Although this definition of design allows for a broad definition of *object*, the audience and the medium are more narrowly defined for interface designers: the audience is the user and the medium is the computer. The definition of the object may be a different meaning for the software engineer that it is for the graphic designer.

II. Who Is the Designer?

The word *designer* is used broadly in the computer industry and it does not mean the same thing to professionals in the field of interface design. A software engineer is considered a designer when he or she designs and writes the system software for interactive computer systems (Rosson, 1987). A graphic designer is considered a designer when he or she designs and creates the appearance of interactive computer systems (Carpenter, 1989). The role of designer has aspects of both the craftsperson and the artist, as well as unique characteristics that are peculiar to the act of design in a technological world.

A. Software Engineer

The craft of software engineering brings order to a disorderly collection of variables, records, code segments, and algorithms. Code and algorithms are beautiful in their simplicity. The skillfulness in executing the logical flow of the code, in creating complex algorithms, and in planning a usable and extendable data structure are the components of the craft of software engineering.

B. Graphic Designer

The craft of graphic design facilitates communication between users and the computer. The communication needs to be transparent so the user can forget about using the computer and concentrate on his or her task. The visual presentation and the user interaction are beautiful when they are appropriate to the tasks. The skillfulness in executing an appropriate user interface, in creating the visual interface elements, and in planning the user-computer interaction are components of the craft of graphic design.

C. Synthesis of the Two Professions

Both of these crafts are essential to the production of the user interface. But the skills of the software engineer and the graphic designer do not make these individuals designers. The task of the designer is to conceptualize the essential elements of the user's perspective, tasks, and preferences. Frank Lloyd Wright clearly states the designer's task for an architect:

> In the arts every problem carries within its own solution, and the only way yet discovered to reach it is a very painstaking way — to sympathetically look within the thing itself, to proceed to analyze and sift it, to extract its own consistent and essential beauty, which means common sense truthfully idealized. That is the heart of the poetry that lives in architecture. (Meehan, 1987).

The poetry of interface design is a high goal that makes possible the transparency of user-computer interaction and a highly desirable interface. The consistent and essential beauty is not a responsive or pretty interface but an interface that is appropriate. Beauty is only one of the aspects of appropriateness, and since beauty lies in the eye of the beholder, it is a by-product rather than a goal. In nature, beauty is the expression of some function - such as the color of flowers that attract bees for pollination. This is why words like *elegant*, *appropriate*, and *beautiful* can be considered synonymous.

The sympathetic investigation is an analytical and perceptual investigation into the meaning of the user-computer interaction. The conceptual elements such as the meaning of the visual symbols, the intention of the verbal message, and the mode of interaction create the *feel* of the interface. The mental picture that is created from the conceptual elements must be appropriate to users. The task of the designer is to make the interface transparent to users from a visual and technical perspective. The visual aspects facilitate communication, and the technical aspects make possible the interaction.

D. Graphic Designer and Software Engineer as Designer

Because interface design is complex, it is difficult to find a single person with the abilities and skills that are necessary for a designer. Together, the graphic designer and the software engineer function as designer. Their two perspectives balance the design of the user interface. The work of these professionals blends into a finished product that will satisfy the user's needs. The graphic designer does not create the interface in its entirety and neither does the software engineer, but both work together as craftsperson, artist, and designer.

III. What Is Design?

Design can be described fairly clearly up to a point, but its essence remains elusive (Nelson, 1983). Although the purpose of design can be defined, how to accomplish the purpose is not clear and requires careful investigation. The purpose of interface design is to create a human-computer dialog; to satisfy the needs of the user; and to use the constraints of the target system and operating software.

To create the human-computer dialog, it is necessary to understand how clearly communication occurs between user and computer. The primary intent of a software engineer is to design a system that is highly responsive and that uses the system software effectively. When software responds quickly and provides the necessary tools to the user, the human-computer dialog is enhanced. The primary intent of the graphic designer is to design an interface that clearly communicates to the user. When the product is both easy to learn and use as well as enjoyable, the human-computer dialog becomes transparent.

To satisfy the needs of the user, it is necessary to understand clearly the users - who the users will be and how they will use the computer. An initial user description is not sufficient. A comprehensive list of user characteristics should be detailed and updated throughout the design and development process. Graphic designers and software engineers must observe real users in action. Characteristics of both novices and expert users must be tracked. When both the graphic designer and software engineer take the user characteristics seriously and do not assume that they themselves represent typical users, it is possible to design a user interface that satisfies the needs of the user.

To work as fully as possible with the target system and operating software, it is necessary to understand clearly the technology used for the target computer, including features and limitations of the system software. The software engineer needs to mold algorithms and data structures into a finished product that utilizes the features and de-emphasizes the limitations of the system software. The graphic designer needs to utilize knowledge of composition, color, and type specifications as represented in the new environment of computers to use the features and hide the limitations of the medium.

A. Comparison of Design and Craft

The design philosophies of design and craft are similar, although the process of craft does not parallel the design process. Design and craft are concerned with the creation of practical and appropriate objects. Appropriateness is judged by the user's ability to use the product. The emphasis is on the object's ability to do something: scissors have to cut, keys must unlock doors, and chairs must provide a place to sit.

Craft is the skillfulness in planning the production of the product. The emphasis is on the act of creation rather than on specifying the creation. Craft concerns itself with unique objects that are created primarily by one individual for one individual, whereas design concerns itself with mass-produced objects that are created by a group of individuals for mass consumption. Design is a process that anticipates others will take control of the production of the product. Essential to design is understanding the ripple effect of every single choice that is made that the designer will no longer control after his or her role in the process is complete.

B. Comparison of Design and Art

The philosophies of design and art are vastly different, although the design process has characteristics similar to the creative process of art. Art is a personal expression of the artist's world view, whereas design is a personal expression of the society's world view. Design expresses the taste and the style of the society in which it is created. Design is largely centered on the application of practical aesthetics - a focus that differs from that of purely aesthetic endeavors such as painting (Diffrient, 1983). Practical aesthetics is concerned with an object that is in complete harmony with its function.

Both art and design are predominantly nonlinear. The design process and the creative process of art are similar because they are seemingly chaotic. They both need elements of disorder and serendipity to allow creativity to grow. One of the requirements of the creative act is that something has to be destroyed before something else can be created. At the core of the design process, one is likely to find someone with an ability to identify and to deal with the creation-destruction polarity (Nelson, 1983).

IV. Evolution of the Design Philosophy and Process

As with many creative problems, interface design problems are often obvious but the solutions are not. Finding interface solutions requires a painstaking investigation. To find the essential character of the user interface requires more than pragmatic tools and methods; creative thinking is necessary. A discussion of the evolution of design philosophy and process reveals how the craftsperson, artist, and designer discover the essential characteristics of the finished product. The discussion starts with the preindustrial designer and moves to the industrial designer and, finally, ends with a new model that consists of a collaborative relationship between artist and technician.

A. The Preindustrial Designer

The preindustrial designer was primarily a craftsperson who both planned and executed the production of finished products. The craftsperson's design emphasizes the uniqueness of the object, and the production process emphasizes the individual technical ability of the craftsperson.

1. Design Philosophy

The craftsperson's practice of design is often an unconscious act that guides and influences the production of the finished product. Many of the standard principles of industrial design were known by preindustrial societies, though those principles were not consciously formulated by them. The design of finished products developed in a harmonious relationship with the technical know-how and aesthetic expression of the craftsperson. Often design was subservient to the act of creation. Preindustrial societies were not marked by the great number of innovations or inventions. Design modifications were gradual and occurred over a long period of time. The slow rate of innovation was the result of combining design and production in the creation of craft objects.

Creating appropriate objects is the aim of the craft design, which includes both meeting the user's needs and using appropriate materials and tools to create the finished product. Products created by a craftsperson have a high appropriateness to the user because they are often created for a single user. Personal dialogue occurs between the craftsperson and user. The negotiation can deal specifically with the details of the materials or tools that are used. Both the craftsperson and the user can make appropriate design trade-offs. Cabinetmaking is a good example of when to use appropriate materials for the finished product. When a cabinetmaker works with rosewood, the cabinet will have a higher value than the same cabinet made with pine, since rosewood is a more valuable and precious wood. Because users will place a higher value on the rosewood cabinet, this cabinet will be used in a formal living room, for example, rather than in a utility room. If the cabinet was meant to be used as a utility cabinet, then using rosewood is an inappropriate use of the material.

2. Design Process

The technical ability of the craftsperson as well as the materials and methods that are at his or her disposal determine the outcome of the finished product. The craft of cabinetmaking shows how the cabinetmaker's aesthetic judgement and dexterity combine to produce cabinets of lasting beauty. When the cabinetmaker works with wood to reveal the grain, he or she uses technical know-how to improve the aesthetic qualities of the product.

The actual design of the finished product wholly encompasses the act of planning and creating in the unity of time and place. For the craftsperson, design and creation occur simultaneously. Design is not a thought process but rather a hand process. The craft designer *thinks* through his or her hands; physical contact with the material is essential to the development of design. The craftsperson works in a society where the integration of function and meaning grew spontaneously out of unity of design, creativity, and production.

B. Emergence of Industrial Design

Industrial design is the occupation of determining the form of objects that are made by mass-production methods for mass distribution. The model of one individual working specifically for one customer is foreign to industrial design. To design products for mass production, the industrial designer must first plan the product's structure, operation, and appearance, then plan these specifications to fit into an efficient production method.

1. Design Philosophy

Design of the outward appearance of the finished product is one of the tasks of an industrial designer. Industrial designers are asked to provide the protective case for the product; the inner workings of the product are left to engineers. Complicated mechanical or electronic assemblies need protective coverings for safety and orderly appearance. Often industrial designers are accused of superficial embellishment or styling of the product. In other words, making the product pretty.

It is not enough for industrial designers to design only the outward appearance. The idea that design is not an afterthought during the research and development process took a long time to establish. The industrial designer gradually came to be seen as an essential part of the whole process of production. Designers started to be involved in the initial stages of the research and development phase of product development. Successful design activity can fluctuate between art and technology without favoring one extreme at the expense of the other. By balancing both the design and technical aspects of product development, it is possible to make the product's interface more usable.

Even in the beginning of the industrial revolution, industrial designers were well acquainted with the notion that use must be allowed to dictate form, since design is more than simply packaging. This is reminiscent of Donald Norman's belief that "design has reflected the capitalist importance of the marketplace, with an emphasis on exterior features deemed to be attractive to the purchaser. Usability is not the primary criterion in the marketing of home and office appliances" (Norman, 1988).

2. Design Process

Among the far-reaching effects of the industrial revolution is the separation in time and space of the act of design and the act of production. Because the design and production processes are separated, a new design role broadens the scope of possibilities. The designer is in a key position between technical, aesthetic, and usability concerns in the development of the product.

Because the design process is both a self-contained and a complex process, it can develop close ties to the activities of scientific and technical research. There is necessarily a fundamental relationship between scientific and technical research and the role of the designer. One example of how design became tied more closely with scientific and technical research is the development of the Studebaker Manufacturing Company. Studebaker was the world's largest producer of horse-drawn vehicles in the preindustrial era. In 1899, Studebaker entered the auto industry as body maker and three years later the company produced their first electric car (Karolevitz, 1968). The research and development that started in 1899 led to Studebaker's technical advancement and the company's ability to compete in modern industry. Studebaker used what it learned from the design of the operation and structure of horse-drawn vehicles and applied that knowledge to a mechanized vehicle. Studebaker continued to be successful as it produced automobiles that merged technical, aesthetic, and usability concerns. A continued openness toward innovative and alternative directions in research is necessary because new research will lead to better products.

Since it is difficult for a single person to have a complete grasp of all aspects of the product development, the role of the designer becomes increasingly concerned with the integration of the technical and aesthetic components. In addition to creative capabilities, the designer must have the specific capacity to coordinate and integrate diverse development activities. Although appearance, operation, and structure are ingredients for the product's design, the designer must fit the product's specifications into an efficient production method. Clear and detailed specifications that can be reproduced during production are necessary. Production methods must be understood by the designer. Each aspect of production may either enhance the design or have an adverse effect on the design. When the designer can anticipate the effects of production, the product's design will be able to work as fully as possible within the medium.

C.   Collaboration of Designers and Engineers

A new development is the collaborative relationship between designers and engineers. The relationship between the industrial designer and the engineer is often ambiguous because specific functions of design tend to influence other functions. For instance, the inner workings of the finished product sometimes limit the outward appearance, and the outward appearance may not utilize the technical features of the underlying system.

1.   Design Philosophy

To believe in a design philosophy that necessitates a collaborative relationship between designer and engineer means that each profession is viewed as providing valuable input to product development. The outward appearance and the inner working of the finished product are equally important; neither aspect has a higher priority. The designer's work is more than simply making the product pretty. Likewise, the engineer does more than making the product an engineering accomplishment. The goal of both of these professionals must be to make the product usable.

2.   Design Process

A unique situation developed in the mid-20th century: scientists and artists started to collaborate on various projects. Many research labs - such as Jet Propulsion Lab in Pasadena, CA - invited artists to work alongside scientists. In many instances, scientists needed assistance in visualizing scientific data. The Voyager Project is a good example of the value that can be added by an artist's perception of color and movement. The Voyager simulations used the artist's ability to define color to provide a clearer presentation of the scientific data and to describe the movement of astronomical objects and Voyager spacecraft.

Although the activities of scientific research are separate from the activities of a designer such as a colorist or an animator, these activities can influence each other. The final product will be dramatically different because the two sensitivities of these professionals are involved. If an artist alone were involved, the actual data might be inaccurate or misrepresented because a particular color palette was used. If a scientist alone were involved, the actual data might be difficult to analyze because there was not enough variety in the color palette. The Voyager is an interdisciplinary project. An interdependence between practicing artists and scientists evolved to produce works of art and scientific investigation. The Voyager simulations are elegant, appropriate, and beautiful.

V. Application of Design Philosophy to UI Design

Although there are elements of craft, design, and art in the philosophy of interface design, the craftsperson model and industrial designer model have the most similarities to interface design.

A. User Interface Design as a Craft Activity

Skillfulness in the creation of interface elements such as the visual appearance of the interface and the system code of the underlying data structure for the interface are valuable skills for the production of software products. When interface design is considered a craft, rules are formulated from the skills of the graphic designer and the software engineer. Rules can be developed for the design of software code as well as for the visual appearance of the interface, though these rules are most effective when applied by professionals in these areas because such professionals have a theoretical understanding of the discipline. These rules are often viewed as guidelines or principals to follow rather than as hard-and-fast rules. When people try to apply the rules from another profession, the result is often inappropriate and the rules are often misapplied.

After working on a computer animation film for my master's project, I recognize that writing code is more than simply applying a series of rules and that writing the most elegant and simple code is a worthy design goal. It took a year of writing code before I came to that conclusion. I also realized that, after writing code and designing the data structure for handling the objects in my film, I was only beginning the training necessary in order to become a software engineer. My goal was not to become a software engineer but to use tools such as Pascal programming to produce my personal vision. After working on my master's project, I have a high respect for software engineers.

To make a statement that anyone can design the visual components of an interface after learning a few rules of graphic design is like saying that anyone is competent enough to write a complex application program after learning the rules of C programming. Learning the craft of programming requires more effort than simply learning the rules of C programming. Likewise, graphic design is a craft that requires a long training period as well as practice. More specifically, it takes a while to become acquainted with a particular medium before being able to take advantage of the unique abilities and limitations of that medium. This medium could be either C programming or computer graphic design.

B. Interface Design as a Design Activity

Often the graphic designer is accused of being concerned only with the outward appearance of the user interface, and the software engineer is accused of being concerned only with the underlying system software. In order to create interfaces that are usable, the outward appearance and inner workings of the interface must be developed side by side.

The industrial designer is a good model for the graphic designer who is working on user interfaces. Like the industrial designer, the graphic designer must create objects that not only work as intended but that clearly indicate what their function is - things that speak a visual language. Anyone who is likely to use the objects or see the visual display must be able to understand their meaning. Both the industrial designer and graphic designer must deal with the way in which things are perceived as well as with the way in which they objectively exist.

The industrial engineer is a good model for the software engineer. Both engineers work on the inner workings of the product. Both engineers work towards merging discoveries from the research and development process into the production process. An important role is the technological advancement of mass-produced products.

C. The Interface Team Philosophy

Interface design is a complex activity that needs the expertise of both graphic designers and software engineers. Graphic designers need the support and expertise of software engineers for a better understanding of the capabilities and limitations of the system software. Software engineers need the support and expertise of graphic designers for a better understanding of how visual design influences the usability of the interface. The graphic designer and software engineer are successful when the outward appearance and inner workings are joined to become a transparent interface. It is possible to join these two elements only when there a strong collaborative relationship between software engineer and graphic designer. These two professionals must work together from the initial stage of product development because decisions made by either professional may have an unforeseen impact on the design of the finished product.

At the beginning of the computer revolution, the users of application and system software were scientists and researchers, so the user interface was developed by software engineers. Now, mass-produced graphic interfaces for many applications are being used by a wide variety of people. Graphic designers are accustomed to working with visual elements and communicating with a wide variety of people, so it makes sense for the outward appearance of the user interface to be developed by graphic designers. A balanced and pleasing design invites use of an interface, while confusing design discourages use. Interfaces must be enjoyable as well as facilitate efficiency of users' tasks. Presenting information that communicates is essential to the design of user interfaces. Likewise, the display of graphics and animation remains a complex computing problem, so it makes sense to *free* the engineer from the problems of the visual appearance of the product to work on the problem of displaying the graphical elements with greater speed and efficiency.

Engineers sometimes become frustrated with designers when the outward appearance does not use all the technological features that are possible. Designers sometimes become frustrated with engineers when the underlying system software limit the outward appearance. The interface team must design and create products that are appropriate for the user and the medium. The team works best when there is mutual respect and cooperation between team members. The interdisciplinary approach assumes mutual dependence and respect for each professional's work and perspective.

VI. Application of Design Process to UI Design

Which aspect of the creative process is emphasized depends on the specific type of product. If the product is just like a thousand other products that the development team has developed, then design and production is more like a craft. The process of both design and craft emphasize the known features and limitations; these processes work best when there are fewer unknown variables. The skillfulness of design and craft are valued, and it is easy to reward and manage this team. If the product is a new type of product such as an information product or a virtual reality research project, then design and production is more like an art form. The process of both art and design emphasize the unknown, and artists and designers want to leave things open-ended (a characteristic of all creative endeavors). The creative process is the most staggeringly complex of all mental processes, and therefore it is one of the more difficult processes to manage. It is difficult to know when or how the seemingly disorganized creative process will create a product.

A. Graphic Designer and Software Engineer as Craftspersons

Both the graphic designer and software engineer take great pride in the skillfulness and manual dexterity that they display in creating the user interface. The skills of the graphic designer make the visual elements easy to view and understand. When the graphic designer is successful, the finished product is easy to use as well as enjoyable. The skills of the software engineer make the code easy for other software engineers to read and understand. When the software engineer is successful, the finished product is easy to maintain.

1. The Graphic Designer as Craftsperson

Like a craftsperson, the graphic designer works directly with tools and materials to schematically layout all visual components of the interface. This facilitates communication between the user and computer through visual symbols, typeface, color, spatial arrangement of interface elements, and the usage of two-dimensional, three-dimensional, and animation.

Visual symbols and icons must be culturally significant and easy to recognize. These symbols must be drawn with great technical ability. The graphic designer must be able to depict the symbols on electronic paper. The skills of a draftsperson are valuable for a graphic designer who will be drawing small symbols and icons for the user interface.

The style of typeface can both change the meaning of the interface and make the information in the interface more readable. The graphic designer must specify the typeface based on how it will be used in the interface. The skills of a typographer are useful when laying out the type specifications for the user interface.

Color both gives meaning to the interface and makes the interface easy to view. Sometimes, color can have specific meaning in the interface, so special considerations are necessary concerning the use of meaningful color and how meaning changes when the color preferences are defined by the user. The skills of a colorist and an understanding of the physiological effects of color are helpful when defining color in the interface.

The spatial arrangement of interface elements can improve the user's working environment by allowing the user to maneuver the mouse with greater adeptness than is possible with poorly arranged interface elements. The graphic designer needs to determine the appropriate amount of information to be displayed so the user does not scroll excessively through list boxes. By composing the screen in an appealing manner, the interface will not be crowded with unnecessary information. After creating separate elements of the user interface, the graphic designer needs to consider how each element fits into the appearance of the entire product.

Every technical advance gives rise to difficult aesthetic issues regarding the nature of style and content. New advances in the area of multimedia require advice from a graphic designer regarding the use of graphics and animation. Determining the effectiveness of two-dimensional or three-dimensional graphics is one of the tasks of the graphic designer. Sometimes interface elements are better described when using three-dimensional graphics because it makes the interface more real to users who are accustomed to a three-dimensional world. If animation is used in the interface, then graphic designers need to design the motion of the various elements in the interface. Animation makes an interface fun to use.

2. The Software Engineer as Craftsperson

Likewise, the software engineer works directly with the programming language to create windows and file management systems for the user interface. Since other software engineers will be working on the software product, a particularly useful skill is the ability to write easy-to-read code.

The crafting of tools for application building is another important aspect of software engineering. The Apple Macintosh is a good example of an interface tool kit. Many of the toolbox procedures and functions for creating the basic interface elements are built into the computer. The development of the interface tools also provides consistent implementation of the interface features. Software engineers will use the existing procedures and functions instead of recreating them - thus, the basic interface features are consistent from application to application. Both users and software engineers win: users have consistent interfaces and software engineers can devote more time and energy to more complex sections of the user interface.

A primary difference between design and craft is the process. Design and production are joined in the craftsperson's work, whereas design is joined with research and development. Thus, design can be more innovative. The outcome of the finished product is wholly dependent on the craftsperson's ability, whereas with design the outcome is dependent on the product team.

B.   Graphic Designer and Software Engineer as Industrial Designers

In industrial design, it is clear that there is a delicate balance between the visual appearance of the interface and the system software. A good example of how the graphic designer and the software engineer are designers is the interface development of the 8010 "Star" Information System. This was one of the first times that graphic designers were hired to determine the arrangement and appearance of objects on the computer screen. Software engineers determined the window and file manager level of the interface as well as the usage of the desktop metaphor with icons and iconic file management; graphic designers applied visual design principles to the design of window headers and borders, the desktop background, the command buttons, the pop-up menus, the property sheets, and the desktop icons.

Software engineers applied principles of software development in order to make the Star interface more transparent and appropriate, and graphic designers applied principles of visual design. The most important principles applied by graphic designers were the illusion of manipulable objects, visual order and user focus, revealed structure, consistent and appropriate graphic vocabulary, and matching the medium. A clear figure/ground relationship makes the illusion of manipulable objects possible because the icons appeared to stand by themselves and on top of the desktop background. By using visual principles of intensity and contrast, the user's attention is drawn to the most important features of the interface. The principle of visual order and user focus is so important that the Star designers made sure that the display hardware could address the unaddressable border of the screen so the grey desktop would appear to bleed to the edge of the monitor. White is used for the color of the window content to simulate paper, and black is used very infrequently such as to show and emphasize the current selection. Revealing the structure of an object is equally as important. For instance, understanding the difference between a rectangle and four straight lines that form a rectangle is important when editing objects with a graphic editor. An interface is more usable if a consistent graphic vocabulary is used. The sensitivities of a graphic designer are most apparent when creating a consistent graphic quality in graphics that are appropriate to the product and that make the most of the given medium (Johnson, 1989).

Through the diverse integration of the various design components, a renewed creativity is possible that can respond to social needs in a coherent, expressive context. In the early 1980s businesses needed computers that were easy to use and that could be used by occasional users such as office workers. An important design goal for the Star computer was to make the computer *invisible* to users - this design goal would have been impossible without the integration of the ideas and work of graphic designers and software engineers. The Star computer succeeded in making a transparent interface by applying a commonplace metaphor such as a desktop metaphor. The development of a metaphor that is primarily the conceptual aspect of the user interface is just as important as the development of the graphic presentation and system code. Each development activity can play a role by nurturing, serving, and caring for the user, rather than fighting the user. Most appealing systems have an enjoyable user interface.

C. Collaboration between Graphic Designers and Software Engineers

Designing a user interface is a complex and highly creative process that blends intuition, experience, and careful consideration of numerous technical issues. Graphical interface products must be the result of interdisciplinary effort. An interdependence between graphic designers and software engineers must evolve so user interfaces can be usable and enjoyable.

The collaborative relationship works because each professional has significant and distinct contributions to make. An important factor is the difference in the training of graphic designers and software engineers. While learning about a particular medium such as computer graphics, the graphic designer learns to think visually and to speak a visual language. Communication is an important part of the training of graphic designers. Although psychology is not taught in the graphic design curriculum, understanding the psychology of the audience is an important aspect of communication. Likewise, while learning specific knowledge about programming and data structures, the software engineer is learning to think analytically as well as to create simple and elegant data structures.

As a result of different training and different perspectives, the views of graphic designer and software engineer are different. The graphic designer looks at the interface from the outside in, much as real users would view the interface, whereas the software engineer looks at the interface from the inside out (Akscyn, 1988). The outside in method aims to create an interface that is transparent to users, whereas the inside out method aims to create an interface that utilizes the system software to maximum effect. Which aspect of the interface comes first - the user interface or the data model - is reminiscent of the chicken-and-egg discussion. There is no correct answer; rather the two different aspects must be developed jointly. The development of an underlying data model with the development of the user interface is a give-and-take process that is only possible when a collaborative relationship is developed between graphic designer and software engineer.

VII. Why Is Interface Design So Hard?

Most interface problems are often obvious, but the solution is often not as obvious. To paraphrase Frank Lloyd Wright, every problem carries its own solution, but it's often painstaking to discover it. Since the solution may involve both a visual solution as well as a technical solution, the best solutions will develop from a working collaborative relationship between graphic designer and software engineer. The designer is no longer one individual but a union between graphic designer and software engineer. Both the craft of graphic design and software engineering are essential to the production of the user interface. Through the entire design process there is steady movement in the direction of a solution that is ultimately seen not as beautiful but as appropriate.

References

1. Akscyn (1988), Robert Akscyn, Elise Yoder, Donald McCracken, "The Data Model is the Heart of Interface Design" in *SIGCHI 1988 Conference Proceedings*, p. 115-120, Washington, D.C.

2. Berton (1989), John Andrew Berton, Jr., "Film Theory for the Digital World: Connecting the Masters to the New Digital Cinema" in *Leonardo: Journal of the International Society for the Arts, Sciences, and Technology*, p. 5-13, Pergamon Press, Oxford, United Kingdom

3. Brazendale (1976), Kevin Brazendale, Enrica Aceti, *Classic Cars: Fifty Years of the World's Finest Automotive Design*, Exeter Books, New York, New York

4. Carpenter (1989), Rachel Carpenter, John Derry, Claire Barry, Peter Conn, Vibeke Sorensen, "Digital Canvas: Artists and Designers in the 2D/3D Marketplace" in *SIGGRAPH 1989 Conference Panel Proceedings*, p. 75-92, Boston, Massachusetts

5. Diffrient (1983), Niels Diffrient, "Design and Technology" in *Design Since 1945*, p. 11-16, (Kathryn B. Hiesinger and George H. Marcus, ed.), Philadelphia Museum of Art, Philadelphia, Pennsylvania

6. Erickson (1990), Thomas D. Erickson, "Creativity and Design: Intorduction" in *The Art of Human-Computer Interface Design*, p. 1-5, (Brenda Laurel, ed.), Addison-Wesley Publishing Company, Reading, Massachusetts

7. Hooper (1988), Kristina Hooper, *Interactive Multimedia Design 1988, Technical Report #13*, Apple Computer, Inc., November 1988

8. Johnson (1989), Jeff Johnson, Teresa L. Roberts, William Verplank, David C. Smith, Charles H. Irby, Marian Beard, Kevin Mackey, "The Xerox Star: A Retrospective" in *IEEE Computer*, p. 11-26, September 1989

9. Kaprow (1988), Alyce Kaprow, Joel Slayton, Paul Souza, Rob Haimes, "Computer Graphics and the Changing Methodology for Artists and Designers" in *SIGGRAPH 1988 Conference Panel Proceedings*, p. 1-23, Atlanta, Georgia

10. Karolevitz (1968), Robert F. Karolevitz, *This Was Pioneer Motoring*, Superior Publishing Company, Seattle, Washington

11. Kim (1990), Scott Kim, "Interdisciplinary Cooperation" in *The Art of Human-Computer Interface Design*, p. 31-44, (Brenda Laurel, ed.), Addison-Wesley Publishing Company, Reading, Massachusetts

12. Lucie-Smith (1983), Edward Lucie-Smith, *A History of Industrial Design*, Van Nostrand Reinhold Company, New York, New York

13. Meehan (1987), Patrick J. Meehan, *Truth Against the World: Frank Lloyd Wright Speaks for an Organic Architecture*, John Wiley & Sons, New York, New York

14. Mountford (1990), S. Joy Mountford, "Tools and Techniques for Creative Design" in *The Art of Human-Computer Interface Design*, p. 17-30, (Brenda Laurel, ed.), Addison-Wesley Publishing Company, Reading, Massachusetts

15. Nelson (1983), George Nelson, "The Design Process" in *Design Since 1945*, p. 5-10, (Kathryn B. Hiesinger and George H. Marcus, ed.), Philadelphia Museum of Art, Philadelphia, Pennsylvania

16. Norman (1988), Donald A. Norman, *The Psychology of Everyday Things*, Basic Books, Inc, New York, New York

17. Rheingold (1990), Howard Rheingold, "An Interview with Don Norman, in *The Art of Human-Computer Interface Design*, p. 11-16, (Brenda Laurel, ed.), Addison-Wesley Publishing Company, Reading, Massachusetts

18. Rosson (1987), Mary Beth Rosson, Susanne Maass, Wendy A. Kellogg, "Designing for Designers: An Analysis of Design Practice in the Real World" in *SIGCHI 1987 Conference Proceedings*, Toronto, Canada

19. Shneiderman (1987), Ben Shneiderman, *Designing the User Interface: Strategies for Effective Human-Computer Interaction*, Addison-Wesley Publishing Company, Reading, Massachusetts

20. Sparke (1986), Penny Sparke, *An Introduction to Design and Culture in the Twentieth Century*, Harper & Row Publishers, New York, New York

21. Tufte (1990), Edward Tufte, *Envisioning Information*, Graphics Press, Cheshire, Connecticut

22. Vertelney (1990), Laurie Vertelney, Michael Arent, Henry Lieberman, "Two Disciplines in Search of an Interface: Reflections on a Design Problem" in *The Art of Human-Computer Interface Design*, p. 46-46, (Brenda Laurel, ed.), Addison-Wesley Publishing Company, Reading, Massachusetts

23. Wurman (1989), Richard Saul Wurman, *Information Anxiety*, Doubleday, Inc., New York, New York

24. Zanuso (1983), Marco Zanuso, "Design and Society" in *Design Since 1945*, p. 17-22, (Kathryn B. Hiesinger and George H. Marcus, ed.), Philadelphia Museum of Art, Philadelphia, Pennsylvania

9

The UAN: A Notation to Support User-Centered Design of Direct Manipulation Interfaces*

ANTONIO C. SIOCHI

Christopher Newport College
Newport News, Virginia

DEBORAH HIX and
H. REX HARTSON

Virginia Tech
Blacksburg, Virginia

I. Introduction

X, Motif, OpenLook, Mac Toolbox—we as an interface design community are fortunate to have so many design and development aids at our disposal. Or are we? The past few years have seen an increase in the variety of software tools to

---

* This chapter is based on a paper by the same authors in ACM Transactions on Information Systems. Permission has been granted by ACM to reproduce sections and figures of that paper.

157

support the development of interactive computer systems. One common theme that has emerged is applying software engineering approaches to the production of user interfaces. However, it has been realized that software engineering methods do not necessarily produce user interfaces with high usability. Because of the difficulty of specifying and building user interfaces, the view of the user has been difficult to maintain. Developers know better how to construct (implement) a system than how to specify what it is to accomplish and how it is to interact with the user. The development community has excellent tools for the construction of software but needs behaviorally oriented tools for the design of user interfaces. We are seeking to complement constructional methods by providing a tool-supported technique capable of specifying the behavioral aspects of an interactive system—the tasks and the actions a user performs to accomplish those tasks. Integration of behavioral techniques into the constructional development process can lead to a more effective method of creating user interfaces that are both useful and usable.

A. *Interface Design*

As can be seen from the other chapters in this book, interface design is a very complex business. It occurs at several levels, is domain-sensitive, and is affected by management concerns, resource constraints, and the need to communicate with a myriad of developer roles. Interface design may also be affected by the type of interface being designed. Today this can range from command line interfaces to direct manipulation interfaces. Command line interfaces are characterized by a turn-taking paradigm, in which the user interacts along a single dimension. Direct manipulation interfaces, on the other hand, present the user with a model (Hutchins, Hollan, & Norman, 1986) where the user interacts with objects of a two dimensional world, for example, windows, icons, and trash cans. Hutchins, Hollan, and Norman refer to these two interface types as the conversational world metaphor and the model world metaphor, respectively.

Support for designing command line interfaces and simple menu and form-based interfaces exists in the form of state transition diagrams, grammar-based notations such as production systems, and scenarios or sequences of screens. These work fairly well for these types but not for the more interactive and asynchronous direct manipulation interfaces. The problem arises in the handling of closely coupled dialogues such as those with semantic feedback (e.g., highlighting a folder as an icon is dragged over it) and in the need for explicit specification of control flow (e.g., as a result of mouse clicks and cursor positions). Grammar-based notations only describe the task structure of an interface, not the feedback. More accurately, grammars assume a *glass teletype* interface, in which the feedback is always a printed error message, so grammars specify only the error message's content. State transition diagrams suffer from combinatorial explosion with the large number of states in real user interfaces.

The need for explicitly specifying control flow in both these techniques (and also in procedural programming languages) hinders the clear design of interfaces as well. Users can and do change their intentions during the performance of a task. In general, user interfaces that are rigid, and hence unsupportive of such *intention shifts*, typically have poor usability. Consequently, a substantial difficulty in designing interfaces is *accommodating a user's intention shifts* while at the same time *maintaining a focus on the primary function of the task*. This problem is familiar to anyone who has ever had to write a program in which error and condition-checking code interferes with readability of the primary function of the program. Incorporating such considerations into a task description can obscure the sequence of actions required for normal accomplishment of the task, yet it is precisely those considerations that help shape the usability of a system. This problem is especially acute for direct manipulation interfaces, whose asynchronous nature practically guarantees the occurrence of user intention shifts.

As a result, interface developers turned to object-oriented techniques and event-based UIMSs. These alleviated the control flow problem elegantly, reducing the problem to one of modeling objects in the interface. However, this approach is system-centered, rather than user-centered. By this we mean that the interface design is described in terms of what the system must do to interpret user actions, rather than in terms of the actions a user performs to accomplish a task using the system—a *constructional* view of the system as opposed to a *behavioral* view. This may seem like splitting hairs, but the proper viewpoint in design contributes to good design (Norman & Draper, 1986). Consider the problem of describing the design for a lock. If you imagined yourself inside the lock, viewing the tumblers and cylinder, you would describe the task *open the lock* as follows: "Tumblers A, B, and C are retracted 2, 3, and 6 mm, and the cylinder assembly is rotated counterclockwise 90°, releasing the locking bolt." However, if you were outside the lock, you could describe the same task as "Insert key into lock and turn counterclockwise until the lock opens." Both descriptions are of the same task, yet if you are trying to design a lock that is easy to open, it is easier to evaluate the ease of use of the lock from the second description than from the first. Note, however, that neither description alone is sufficient—each addresses different design needs. For example, to construct the lock, the second description must be translated into the first. But since usability is a goal of an interface designer, a design representation that supports a user-centered view is also necessary.

B. Mountains of Paper

In the Spring of 1987, as part of the Dialogue Management Project at Virginia

Tech, we started work on a UIMS that had a direct manipulation user interface. We followed a fairly common development methodology that involved the production of a requirements document, both for system functionality and for the user interface. This process involved a task analysis for each of the tools in the UIMS and resulted in a set of tasks for each tool. We then designed the interface to support the task set, by drawing a basic prototypic screen picture, making several copies of that picture and drawing on it the changes corresponding to manipulations the user was to make for each task. These figures were accompanied by copious amounts of prose describing in painful detail how users were to accomplish each task. This amount of writing and drawing tended to interfere with design thought processes and became quite tedious after the first revision of the first tool in our UIMS. Our designers got tired of writing a mountain of prose and our implementers got tired of reading and trying to understand it.

To overcome this problem, we developed and refined an interface representation notation as an alternative to the text-based techniques just described. This notation, the *User Action Notation (UAN)* (Siochi & Hartson, 1989), *is a task- and user-oriented notation for behavioral representation of asynchronous, direct manipulation interface designs.* The UAN is used to describe the user actions necessary to accomplish a task in a direct manipulation interface, as well as corresponding feedback and system state changes that result from those actions. Based on our experiences and that of others, we have found that the notation is concise, yet precise enough in representing the design of an interface, so that details are not left to the imagination or best guess of its implementers. We have also found that the UAN is easy to read with minimal training and facilitates communication between designers and implementers. The UAN is being used by growing numbers of interface developers and researchers.

In this chapter we present a practical, rather than theoretical, introduction to the UAN. We also briefly examine the UAN's relationship to the overall development process, especially with respect to the six foci for design decisions discussed in Casaday's chapter. In particular, we are addressing the specific needs of a user interface designer designing a direct manipulation interface. Our hope is that an interface designer, after reading this chapter, can read and write the UAN.

In teaching use of the UAN to designers, we have found that the most effective approach is by example. Therefore, we begin this chapter with a simple example.

II. A Simple Example

Imagine a hypothetical description in a user manual for the task of selecting a file icon. This task might be described in prose as

1. Move the cursor to the file icon.
2. Depress and immediately release the mouse button.

The user action portion of the UAN description for this task is

1. ~[file_icon]
2. Mv^

The ~ denotes moving the cursor, in this case into the context of the file icon. The second line represents depressing (v) and releasing (^) the mouse button (M). Even this simple example illustrates the brevity and readability of the UAN. This describes only the user action part of the UAN description; the full task description will be revealed in later sections of this chapter.

Let us describe another task, moving a file icon, which can be stated in prose as

1. Move the cursor to the file icon. Depress and hold down the mouse button.
2. With the button held down, move the cursor.
3. Release the mouse button.

The user action portion of the corresponding UAN description is

1. ~[file_icon] Mv
2. ~[x,y]* ~[x',y']
3. M^

Reading this task description, we again note moving the cursor into the context of the file icon and depressing the mouse button. In the second line, ~[x,y] indicates movement of the cursor to an arbitrary point x,y on the screen. The * (Kleene star for expressing iterative closure in regular expressions) means to perform, zero or more times, the task to which it is attached. Thus, ~[x,y]* ~[x',y'] means to move the cursor in a succession of zero or more arbitrary points about the screen, ending at the point x',y'. Finally, in the third line the mouse button is released.

III. Behavioral Design Representation

Historically, and practically, many user interfaces have been designed by software engineers and programmers as part of the software of interactive systems. The result has been interfaces of varying quality and usability. Much work in the field of human-computer interaction has been directed toward new approaches to user interface development in hopes of improving quality and usability. Among these new concepts is the notion that design of software to construct a user interface is different from design of the interface itself and that interface design has requirements not shared by software design. A major distinction is that good interface design must be user-centered, whereas software design is system-centered. Being user-centered means focusing on the behavior of the user and what the user perceives while performing tasks with the computer. To underscore this distinction we use the terms *behavioral domain* and *constructional domain*. The first refers to the context of user interface design and development, whereas the second refers to the context of the design and development of software to implement those interfaces.

In the behavioral domain one gets away from the software issues of interface design into the processes that precede, and are inputs to, software design. These processes include task analysis, functional analysis, task allocation, and user modeling. The people in various development roles must have a representation of the interface design in order to do their work. Thus, the concept of design *representation* itself is very important. High usability of an interface stems from a good design. Good designs depend on the ability of each person in a developer role—for example, designer, implementer, evaluator, customer, bidder—to understand and evaluate (and thereby improve) interface designs in the development process. Understanding and evaluating designs depends, in part, on the methods used to *represent* those designs. Design and representation are very closely related; design is a creative, mental, problem-solving process and representation is the physical process of capturing or recording that design.

It follows that each domain ought to have representation techniques tailored to its perspective and needs. As Richards, Boies, and Gould (1986) state about tools for mocking up user interface prototypes, "Few of these provide an interface specification language directly usable by behavioral specialists." Many existing interface representation techniques, especially those associated with UIMSs, are constructional. *But it is in the behavioral domain of the user that interface designers and evaluators do their work.* Thus, there is a need for behavioral representation techniques coupled with supporting interactive tools to give a user-centered focus to the interface development process.

Behavioral descriptions can be thought of as *procedures executed by the user*. Behavioral design and representation involve physical and cognitive user actions and interface feedback, that is, behavior both of the user and of the interface as they interact with each other. Each behavioral design must be translated into a constructional design that is the computer system view of how the behavior is to be supported. Because the UAN supports task description, which is important in many early interface development activities, it is suitable for use by behavioral specialists. The UAN is used to describe how a user performs a task but not how the system is implemented to interpret user behavior. Because the UAN is in the behavioral domain, it should not be confused with, for example, specification languages for program behavior. Interface designs represented in the UAN must still be translated, manually or automatically, into the constructional domain. Therefore, *the UAN is not a replacement for constructional representation techniques; it just serves in a different domain.*

One behavioral technique that has long been used both formally and intuitively is scenarios (or storyboards) of interface designs. While this technique is effective for revealing a very early picture of interface appearance, because a scenario is an example (extension) of the interface, it cannot represent the complete design (intension). Scenarios can show much about screen layout but do not adequately or efficiently show the user's behavior while interacting with the computer.

The UAN is a task-oriented notation that describes the behavior of the user and the interface during their cooperative performance of a task. The primary abstraction of the UAN is a task. A user interface is represented as a quasi-hierarchical structure of tasks that are asynchronous (i.e., sequencing within each task is independent of that in the others). User actions, corresponding interface feedback, and state information are represented at the lowest level. Levels of abstraction are used to hide these details and represent the entire interface. At all levels, user actions and tasks are combined with temporal relations such as sequencing, interleaving, and concurrency, to describe allowable temporal user behavior. The UAN is used to supplement scenarios, indicating precisely how the user interacts with screen objects shown in a scenario. The need for detailed scenarios and task descriptions was articulated by Gould and Lewis (Gould & Lewis, 1985): "Another method is to construct detailed scenarios showing exactly how key tasks would be performed with the new system. It is extremely difficult for anybody, even its own designers, to understand an interface proposal, without this level of description."

IV. Related Work

Other techniques for representing user interface designs can be divided into the general categories of behavioral or constructional techniques. The behavioral techniques describe interaction from the user's view and are generally task-oriented. These include the GOMS model (Card, Moran, & Newell, 1983), the Command Language Grammar (CLG) (Moran, 1981), the keystroke-level model (Card & Moran, 1980), the Task Action Grammar (Payne & Green, 1986), and the work by Reisner (Reisner, 1981) and Kieras and Polson (Kieras & Polson, 1985). Design of interactive systems, like most kinds of design, alternates analysis and synthesis (Hartson & Hix, 1989). Most of the techniques just mentioned were originally oriented toward analysis; that is, they were not intended to capture a design as it is being created, but to build a detailed representation of an existing design with the purpose of predicting user performance for evaluating usability. Synthesis includes the activities that support the creative mental act of problem solving (creating new interface designs) and the physical act of capturing a representation of (i.e., documenting) the design. The UAN shares the task orientation of these other behavioral models but is presently more synthesis-oriented, because it was created specifically to communicate interface designs to implementers. In practice, most of these techniques can be used to support synthesis as well, but typically they do not represent the direct association of feedback and dialogue states with user actions. Also, many of these techniques—GOMS, CLG, and keystroke in particular—model expert error-free task performance in contiguous time (without interruption, without interleaving of tasks, and without considering the interrelationships of concurrent tasks), but these are not suitable assumptions for the synthesis-oriented aspects of interface design.

The GOMS model is a foundation of task analysis for interface design. The amount of detail generated in a GOMS description of an interface supports thorough analysis but can be an enormous undertaking. GOMS and UAN have similarities, especially at higher levels of abstraction where tasks are described as sequences of subtasks. The keystroke-level model includes actions other than keystrokes but at the same level of time granularity (i.e., single, simple, physical user actions). The CLG formalism offers a thorough and broad framework for describing many aspects of a user interface. Description at each level (task, semantic, syntactic, and interaction) contains procedures, written in a language much like a high level programming language. The work of Reisner with the ROBART graphics system interface uses an action language grammar and applies metrics to predict user performance, to compare alternative designs and to identify design choices that could cause users to make mistakes. TAG is a formal, production-rule based description technique for representing mental models of users in task performance. Similarly, the work by Kieras and Polson is used to model user tasks and apply metrics to measure the complexity of user knowledge required in performing specific tasks.

Among the earliest representation techniques for dialogue control flow (sequencing) are those based on formal, machine-processable production-rule grammars represented in, for example, Backus Naur Form (e.g., SYNGRAPH (Olsen & Dempsey, 1983)). Grammatical representations tend to be behavioral because they describe expressions that come from the user, but they are difficult to use and so are not used much now. Multi-party grammars (Shneiderman, 1982) are an interesting extension to the production-rule based techniques. By representing the computer system as one of the interacting parties, the multi-party grammar allows direct association of interface feedback to user inputs. The multi-party grammar, however, is not easily adapted to the variety of user actions found in a direct manipulation interface.

State transition diagrams (STDs) and their variations (Jacob, 1985; Wasserman & Shewmake, 1985; Yunten & Hartson, 1985) are similar in expressive power to BNF but show control flow explicitly in a graphical form (e.g., the system is in state X; if user input A is sensed, then the system makes a transition to state B). BNF and STDs are used to represent mainly state change information but not interface feedback or screen appearance.

Event handlers (Green, 1985; Hill, 1987) are used to represent events that result from user actions. Because event handlers represent the system view of an interface (e.g., cause computational procedures to be invoked in response to an event), they are constructional. Event handlers offer an object orientation and have more expressive power than BNF or STDs (Green, 1986). Concurrent programming concepts have also been used to specify or implement the interface (Cardelli & Pike, 1985; Flecchia & Bergeron, 1987).

Other work has involved specifying interfaces by demonstration (e.g., PERIDOT (Myers, 1987)). This is a novel and creative approach, but it produces only program code, with no other representation of the interface that conveys its design or behavior, or that can be analyzed. On the other hand, this approach is very suitable for producing rapid prototypes. An interface can also be generated from a set of application functions (Olsen, 1986). This is a quick constructional method of producing a default interface and is also useful for prototyping. Another technique combines two constructional techniques, state diagrams and object orientation (Jacob, 1986). In this case a mutually asynchronous set of state diagrams represents the interface, avoiding the complexity of a single large diagram. Another approach (UIDE (Foley, Gibbs, Kim, & Kovacevic, 1988)) involves building a knowledge base consisting of objects, attributes, actions, and pre- and post conditions on actions that form a declarative description of an interface, from which interfaces are generated.

V. More on the UAN

A. Interface Feedback

The simple example at the beginning of this chapter showed how to describe the *user actions* necessary for a task. Comparing the UAN description to the prose in that simple example, we find that the prose contains feedback and semantic information as well as user actions. Such *interface feedback* information—interface responses to user actions—allows a more complete description of user and interface behavior, as seen in Figure 1.

TASK: move a file icon	
USER ACTIONS	**INTERFACE FEEDBACK**
~[file_icon] Mv	file_icon!
~[x,y]* ~[x',y']	outline of file_icon follows cursor
M^	display file_icon at x',y'

Figure 1. Interface feedback in response to user actions

TASK: select an icon	
USER ACTIONS	**INTERFACE FEEDBACK**
~[icon] Mv^	icon!

Figure 2. UAN description of the task *select an icon*

TASK: select an icon	
USER ACTIONS	**INTERFACE FEEDBACK**
~[icon] Mv	icon!
M^	

Figure 3. Precise correspondence of feedback to user actions

This task description is read left to right, top to bottom, and indicates that when the user moves the cursor to the file icon and depresses the mouse button, the icon is highlighted (file_icon!). As the user moves the cursor around the screen, an outline of the file icon follows the cursor, and upon release of the mouse button, the file icon is displayed at the new position. *Note the line-by-line association of feedback with the corresponding user action*; this level of precision is lost in the prose description, where actions and feedback are intermingled. For example, consider this description of selecting an icon:

1. Move the cursor to the icon.
2. Click the mouse button and the icon will be highlighted.

The corresponding UAN task description is shown is Figure 2.

In the Macintosh™ interface[1], highlighting occurs when the mouse button is depressed (rather than when it is clicked—depressed and released). Figure 3

---

[1]The UAN is not limited to the Macintosh™ nor is it oriented toward any one specific graphical direct manipulation interface style. However, we have taken advantage of the popularity of the Macintosh™ desk top to illustrate use of the UAN.

TASK: select an icon	
USER ACTIONS	INTERFACE FEEDBACK
~[icon_x] Mv	icon_x!, icon_y-! where ∀icon_y: icon_y≠icon_x
M^	

Figure 4. Complete feedback

TASK: move a file icon	
USER ACTIONS	INTERFACE FEEDBACK
~[file_icon_x] Mv	file_icon_x!
~[x,y]* ~[x',y']	outline(file_icon_x) > ~
M^	@x',y' display(file_icon_x)

Figure 5. More concise and formal feedback description

shows how the UAN can be used to represent, more precisely than in Figure 2, this correspondence between feedback and separate user actions in the sequence.

The feedback in Figure 3 is still not complete, however. Since the shift key is not depressed, selection (and, therefore, highlighting) of icons is mutually exclusive. This means that this task is technically the task to *select one icon and deselect all others*. The feedback in Figure 4 has been extended to include this notion, where ∀ and : mean for all and such that, respectively.

If the designer feels that the added information about dehighlighting the icon_y's clutters the feedback description for icon_x, abstraction can be used to hide those details. For example, the definition of !, the highlighting for icon_x, can contain the unhighlighting behavior for all other icons in the same mutually exclusive set. This abstraction is assumed in the examples that follow.

While the feedback column of the example to move a file icon in Figure 1 is easy to read, it can be more concise and formal. In particular, the symbology X > ~ is used to denote object X following the cursor. The exact behavior of the outline as it follows the cursor in the second line and displaying the file icon in the third line can be encapsulated as feedback functions, defined precisely in a single place. The task description then appears as shown in Figure 5.

Making the feedback description more formal detracts little from readability but improves precision and consistency of the resulting interface by not leaving these design details to the discretion of the implementer. In addition, formal feedback specifications can be included in a consistency analysis of the interface.

TASK: move a file icon		
USER ACTIONS	INTERFACE FEEDBACK	INTERFACE STATE
~[file_icon] Mv	file_icon!	currentObject=file_icon, file_icon is selected

Figure 6. Interface state information

TASK: move a file icon			
USER ACTIONS	INTERFACE FEEDBACK	INTERFACE STATE	CONNECTION TO COMPUTATION
~[file_icon] Mv	file_icon!	currentObject= file_icon, file_icon ∈ selected	
~[x,y]* ~[x',y']	outline(file_icon) > ~		
M^	@x',y' display(file_icon)		location(file_icon) =x',y'

Figure 7. Connection to computational semantics

B. State Information

In addition to feedback, it may be necessary to include some *state information*, both for the *interface* and for its *connections to the computation*, associated with user actions. For example, if the interface design includes the concepts of selectable objects and current objects, details about how these attributes are applied to objects must be communicated to the implementer. Figure 6 shows just the first line of the task description from Figure 5 for moving a file icon. Here it is clear that depressing the mouse button when the cursor is over an icon makes it current and selected.

Suppose the location of the icon is significant to the computational (non-interface) component of the application. In this case, any task involving movement of the icon must inform the computational component, shown in the lower right hand cell of Figure 7.

C. Conditions of Viability

Consider the description of the task of selecting a file icon given in Figure 8.

To show that this task applies only to a file icon that is not already selected, we use *conditions of viability*. In Figure 9 the condition of viability is file_icon-!:, which is read as *file_icon is not highlighted*. The scope of the condition of

TASK: select a file icon		
USER ACTIONS	**INTERFACE FEEDBACK**	**INTERFACE STATE**
~[file_icon] Mv	file_icon!	currentObject=file_icon, file_icon is selected
M^		

Figure 8. UAN description of the task *select a file icon*

TASK: select a file icon		
USER ACTIONS	**INTERFACE FEEDBACK**	**INTERFACE STATE**
file_icon-!: (~[file_icon] Mv	file_icon!	currentObject=file_icon, file_icon is selected
M^)		

Figure 9. Condition of viability (i.e., file icon is not already highlighted)

TASK: select a file icon		
USER ACTIONS	**INTERFACE FEEDBACK**	**INTERFACE STATE**
~[file_icon-!] Mv	file_icon!	currentObject=file_icon, file_icon is selected
M^		

Figure 10. Alternative form (built-in binding) for condition of viability

viability is indicated with parentheses. A condition of viability acts as a precondition, or guard condition, that must be true in order for user actions within its scope to be performed as part of this task. A condition of viability with a false value does not mean that a user cannot perform the corresponding action(s); it just means that the action(s) will not be part of this particular task. The same actions, however, might be part of another task in the overall set of asynchronous tasks that an interface comprises.

The term file_icon in the condition of viability is bound to the same term in user actions within its scope, like a bound variable in first order predicate logic. In Figure 10 the condition of viability in Figure 9 is written as a built-in binding, which is more concise and easier to read. In this form, conditions quite naturally provide specific instructions for user behavior (i.e., *move the cursor to an unhighlighted file icon*).

TASK: delete file			
USER ACTIONS	INTERFACE FEEDBACK	INTERFACE STATE	CONNECTION TO COMPUTATION
~[file_icon-!] Mv	file_icon!	currentObject= file_icon, file_icon is selected	
~[x,y]*	outline(file_icon) > ~		
~[trash_icon]	trash_icon!		
M^	erase(file_icon), trash_icon!!		mark file for deletion

Figure 11. UAN description of the task *delete a file*

D. Another Example

The task description in Figure 11 ties together many of the previous concepts; it represents one version of the task of deleting a file from the Macintosh™ desk top by dragging that file's icon to the trashcan icon.

VI. Further Discussion of the UAN

A. Actions Applied to Devices

At a detailed design level, the UAN describes physical user actions that are applied to physical devices. Determination of the symbols to be used in representing an interface design requires identification of the devices and the operations that can be performed on them. For example, consider the class we call switch-like devices. These are devices that can be depressed and released, thereby causing transmission of a single character or signal. Switch-like devices include, for example, the mouse button (M), the control key (CNTL), the shift key (S), all special and function keys, and possibly devices such as knee switches, foot pedals, and *puff and sip* tubes. Pressing and releasing this kind of device is represented in the UAN with v and ^, respectively, as shown in the preceding examples. An idiomatic shorthand for clicking (depressing and immediately releasing) is v^, as in Mv^, for example. Clicking on the left button of a three-button mouse can be indicated by M_Lv^.

Another class contains devices from which user actions result in character strings. Examples are keyboards and voice recognition devices. Although keyboards are made up of keys, the individual keys are abstracted out of the description because the significant feature is the character string. An example of the UAN for such devices is K"abc," the description of the user action of typing the literal string abc, and K(user_id), the description of the user action of typing a value for a string variable named user_id. In addition, a regular expression can be used inside the parentheses to specify the lexical definition of the variable to be entered by the user, for example, K(user_id = [A-Z][A-Z 0-9]+).

B. Cursor Movement

The mouse is composed of two or more devices—a cursor position controller and one or more buttons. The buttons are switch-like devices, as described above. Unless it is important to address the details of how the user physically and cognitively interacts with the cursor controlling device, the UAN represents user actions that cause *cursor movement* in terms of where the cursor is moved. At this level of abstraction the cursor controlling devices have the same behavior in the sense that the notation ~[X] specifies, in a somewhat device-independent manner, that the user moves the cursor to the context of X. The notation does not indicate how this is done, for example, by mouse, joy stick, track ball, arrow keys, touch panel, or eye tracker.

At a lower level of abstraction, pragmatic differences between devices cannot as easily be represented. It may be possible to produce detailed UAN descriptions of the task of using each device to move the cursor, but it would require perceptual, cognitive, and decision making actions, and perhaps even kinesthetics of the physical actions, all in a very tight feedback loop. While acknowledging the importance of carefully deciding the issues of device pragmatics, we assume these issues are settled and that the implementer and the user know the device pragmatics.

C. Context of Objects

The UAN symbology ~[X] describes the user task of moving the cursor into the *context* of the interface object X. Moving out of the same context is denoted by [X]~. The context of an object is that *handle* by which the object is manipulated, such as the object itself. Other handles may include a rectangle circumscribed about the object or a small grab handle (e.g., of the kind used to manipulate lines and corners in MacDraw[TM2]). The context is modal in that it remains until explicitly changed. For example, in the expression ~[X] Mv, it is assumed that pressing the mouse button occurs within the context of X.

---

[2]MacDraw is a trademark of Claris, Corp.

D. Feedback

UAN symbology describing *feedback* includes X!, for describing the highlighting of object X, and X-! for its dehighlighting. X!! is used to indicate a different type of highlighting. X!-! means to blink the highlight; (X!-!)^3 means to blink three times. The effect of X! (or X-!) is null if it is already the case that X! (or X-!). In addition, there are functions for displaying and erasing objects in the feedback. Dragging an object is indicated by X > ~, and rubberbanding an object as it follows the cursor is shown by X >> ~. The difference between these last two is illustrated by the difference in moving a box on the screen and resizing that box by rubberbanding one of its handles.

E. Temporal Relations

In addition to the need for a behavioral view, another problem arises from new styles of interaction involving direct manipulation of graphical objects and icons. These interaction styles are more difficult to represent than the older styles of command languages and menus. User actions in these interfaces are asynchronous, having rather more complex temporal behavior than those of earlier interfaces that were largely constrained to predefined sequences. A brief introduction to these concepts is given in this section; Hartson and Gray (Hartson & Gray, 1990) gave a more detailed discussion of *temporal aspects* of the UAN.

The most basic temporal relationships we have identified are the following:

- sequenced with
- order independent
- interruptible by
- interleavable with
- concurrent with

These are listed in decreasing order of temporal constraint. *Sequencing* is the most constrained temporal relation; the first action must be performed completely before the next, until all actions are completed. In many sequential interface designs, this constraint is arbitrary and even opposed to the cognitive and task needs of the user. For example, initiation of a second task in the middle of a first task may be required in order to get information necessary to the completion of the first task. It is very desirable that the second task can be interleaved with the first, so it will not destroy the context of the first task.

With *order independence*, all actions must be performed and each completed before another is begun, but the constraint on the specific ordering of actions is removed. An example of order independence at a very low task level is seen in the task of entering a *command-X* in a Macintosh™ application, a combination of the ⌘ and X keys. Since the ⌘ key must be depressed before the X key, but the order of their release does not matter, the task is defined in UAN as

<u>Task</u>: command-X
⌘v Xv (⌘^ & X^)

While order independence relaxes the sequentiality constraint, *interleaving* removes the constraint of a task or action having to be performed to completion before beginning another action; that is, it allows an action to be interrupted.

User actions are mutually interleavable if and only if they can *interrupt* each other without damage to either; a period of activity of either action can interrupt a period of activity of the other. Consider the case of *help* as a facility available during some complex user action such as editing a document. Suppose that help information, when invoked, appears in a window separate from the document being edited. The editing and help actions are interleavable since the user may alternate the focus of attention, and therefore task performance, from one window to the other.

With interleavability, user actions can be alternated among tasks; with *concurrency*, user actions for two or more tasks can occur simultaneously. Concurrency is a temporal relation that has not been greatly exploited in user interfaces. Nevertheless, it has been shown (Buxton, 1986) that there are cases in which it is possible and, indeed, preferable, to carry out more than one task at the same time—for example, via input techniques that rely on the simultaneous use of both hands.

Time intervals are also important in task descriptions. For example, the prose description of a double click with the mouse button might tell the user to click the mouse button and immediately click it again. This task can be represented precisely in the UAN. Note that waiting a certain amount of time (i.e., not doing any action for that interval) is itself a user action. The UAN task description for double clicking is

Mv^ (t<n) Mv^,

where the value of n can be controlled by the user via a control panel setting, and an appropriate default value can be empirically determined by developers.

Analysis of the various temporal relations gives the interface designer the ability to distinguish task types that are significantly different but which, without these relations, would be difficult to identify. Furthermore, adding operators to the UAN to express these relations gives the designer a powerful means of specifying such interfaces.

TASK: move a file icon	
USER ACTIONS	INTERFACE FEEDBACK
~[file_icon]; Mv;	file_icon!
~[x,y]* ~[x',y']	outline of file_icon follows cursor
M^	display file_icon at x',y'

Figure 12. Task interruptibility indicated by semicolons

F. Task Interruption

So far we have assumed that once a user starts a task it is continued to completion, but this is not always the case. From a human-computer interface development view, a user task consists of a sequence of user actions or subtasks, the last one marking the end of the task (i.e., task *closure*). Thus, in the task of moving a file icon (Figure 12), the action of releasing the mouse button (M^) signals task closure. Each task is associated with a user intention. A user performing all and only the user actions of that task achieves task closure without an intention shift. Should the user change intention in the middle of a task and perform some action other than the next in the sequence, we say that task is *interrupted*. In the task in Figure 12, if the user positions the cursor over the file icon, but then moves the cursor away without depressing the mouse button, the task of moving the file icon is interrupted; there is a user intention shift. This point of interruptibility is indicated in a task description by a semicolon, as shown in the first line of the user action column in Figure 12.

The semicolon in a UAN task description allows a designer to accommodate intention shifts by indicating where a task can be interrupted without having to specify details of how the user interrupts the current task. This has the benefit of preserving the clarity of a UAN task description—the designer can concentrate on the actions for the task at hand, while acknowledging (yet delaying) resolution of the ways in which that task can be interrupted. In addition, the semicolon is helpful to implementers because it shows the points at which they must handle special user events.

Users can interrupt tasks by *interleaving* or *abandoning*, reflecting different intention shifts. Both classes of interruption are specified in the UAN with semicolons. Interleaving was discussed in the previous section on temporal aspects; here we will discuss abandoning. Abandoning requires identification of explicit user actions that bring about closure, with intention to abort the task. For example, the user can abandon the task of using a dialogue box by clicking on a cancel button, abandon the task of choosing an item in a pulldown menu by moving the cursor off the menu and then releasing the mouse button, and abandon the task of deleting a file by moving the file icon back into its original

TASK: select item from pulldown menu		
USER ACTIONS	**INTERFACE FEEDBACK**	**INTERFACE STATE**
~[menutitle] ; Mv;	menutitle! show (pulldownmenu)	
(~[menuitem] [menuitem]~)* ;	menuitem! menuitem-!	
~[menuitem'] M^	menuitem'! menuitem'!! hide (pulldownmenu)	menuchoice = menuitem

Figure 13. Selecting an item from a pulldown menu

window instead of releasing it into the trash can.

As further illustration, consider the task of selecting an item from a pulldown menu. The UAN task description in Figure 13 shows the sequence of actions a user takes to select an item from a pulldown menu, together with exact points in the sequence where this task can be interrupted (i.e., the semicolons). The first semicolon indicates a point where users can change their mind about pulling down this menu at all. The second and third semicolons indicate points where the user may decide not to pick any of the items in this menu. Note that the actions that cause this interruption are not explicitly specified in the task description (this is covered in the section on task transition diagrams). This makes reading and writing the actions for this task straightforward while allowing for a user's intention shifts.

G. Analytic Potential of the UAN

The abstraction provided by UAN descriptions helps designers detect problems. Consider the move and select tasks in MacDraw™ (which are similar to the tasks of Figures 1 and 2). Users commonly move an object accidentally when they had intended only to select it. These tasks actually have a common prefix in their UAN descriptions: ~[object]Mv. The select task is closed by immediately releasing the mouse button, whereas the move task requires first moving the cursor to some other screen location. The degree of hand-eye coordination a user has will affect the amount of inadvertent movement that occurs during a select task. Since any movement results in a move task, the designer should incorporate some timing considerations or slack movement (free play) in order to reduce the chances of moving an object when the intent was only to select it.

H. Design Aspects of UAN Symbols

We chose the UAN symbols with specific requirements in mind:

- usage separate from definition
- typeable from a standard keyboard
- mnemonically meaningful

The first requirement provides a locality of definition similar to that in programming. It allows the designer, for example, highlighting before the method of highlighting is defined. It also preserves consistency by requiring a single modification of the definition of highlighting for a class of objects.

Although computer-based tools can provide specialized, even graphical, symbols for the UAN, it is desirable that the symbols be producible with regular word processing (possibly with an extended font for some mathematical symbols), and that specific parts of designs be usable within other text documents. This allows use of standard keyboards for writing UAN task descriptions.

For mnemonic purposes the symbols were chosen to be visually onomatopoetic. For example, ~ carries the impression of movement and [X] conveys the idea of a box around X. Similarly, ! attracts attention as highlighting and > reflects the notion of following, while >> is following but stretching out (rubberbanding).

I. Summary of UAN Symbols

We have deliberately kept open the definition of the UAN, in the sense that interface developers can add and modify symbols or columns for their particular design situations. Many of the symbols and idioms we have found useful are summarized in Table 1. See (Hartson & Gray, 1990) for a more formal definition of the UAN, especially its temporal aspects.

VII. Using the UAN at Higher Levels of Abstraction

So far we have discussed the UAN as it is used to represent low level physical user actions directly associated with devices. It is possible to build, on these physical actions, levels of abstraction to represent the complete task structure for an entire application. We shall use the terms *task* and *action* interchangeably here to underscore the fact that the higher level tasks and the lower level physical

Table 1.
Summary of Some Useful UAN Symbols

Action	Meaning
~	move the cursor
[X]	the context of object X, the *handle* by which X is manipulated
~[X]	move cursor into context of object X
~[x,y]	move the cursor to (arbitrary) point (x,y) outside any object
~[x,y in A]	move the cursor to (arbitrary) point within object A
~[X in Y]	move to object X within object Y (e.g., to OK_icon in dialogue_box)
[X]~	move cursor out of context of object X
v	depress
^	release
Xv	depress button, key, or switch called X
X^	release button, key, or switch X
Xv^	idiom for clicking button, key, or switch X
X"abc"	enter literal string, abc, via device X
X(xyz)	enter value for variable xyz via device X
( )	grouping mechanism
*	iterative closure, task is performed zero or more times
{ }	enclosed task is optional (performed zero or one time)
A B	sequence; perform A, then B (same if A and B are on separate, but adjacent, lines)
OR	disjunction; choice of tasks (used to show alternate ways to perform a task)
&	order independence; connected tasks must all be performed, but relative order is immaterial
⇔	interleavability; performance of connected tasks can be interleaved in time
‖	concurrency; connected tasks can be performed simultaneously
;	task interrupt symbol; used to indicate that user may interrupt the current task at this point (the effect of this interrupt is specified as well; otherwise it is undefined, as though the user never performed the previous actions)

Feedback	Meaning
!	highlight object
-!	unhighlight object
!!	same as !, but use an alternative highlight
!-!	blink highlight
$(!\text{-}!)^n$	blink highlight n times
@x,y	at point x,y
@X	at object X
display(X)	display object X
erase(X)	erase object X
X > ~	object X follows (is dragged by) cursor
X >> ~	object X is rubberbanded as its follows cursor
outline(X)	outline of object X

actions have many of the same properties when combined into a task structure. Following are some definitions that show how tasks can be combined in the UAN:

- The physical actions on devices described so far are tasks. Examples include all actions such as ~[X] and Mv^.
- If A is a task, so are (A), A*, and {A}.
- If A and B are tasks, so are A B, A OR B, A&B, A⇔B, and A ‖ B.

Thus, a task description written in the UAN is a set of actions interspersed with logical and temporal operators. Tasks built up as combinations using these rules can be named, and the name can be used as a reference to the task. A task is invoked by using its name as an action within another task, in the manner of a procedure call in a computer program. This leads to higher levels of abstraction, necessary for understanding by readers and writers of the notation, and a quasi-hierarchical calling structure of tasks. Use of a task name as a user action corresponds at runtime to the invocation of a user-performed procedure.

Task descriptions are eventually written at the low abstraction level of user actions. This level is the *articulation point* between two major activities within the development life cycle: task analysis and design. Because these task descriptions are at once the terminal nodes of the task analysis hierarchy and the beginnings of a user interface design, *it is a case where task analysis quite naturally drives the design process*.

As one example of the way symbols are used together in higher level task descriptions, consider the symbol OR, used to indicate a disjunction of choices. For example, A OR B OR C denotes a *mutually exclusive* three-way choice among user actions or tasks. A common high level construct in the UAN is seen in this example of a repeating disjunction:

(A OR B OR C)*

This notation means that tasks A, B, and C are initially concurrently available. Once a task is begun, it is performed to completion, at which time the three tasks are concurrently available again. The cycle continues arbitrarily, each time any one of the three tasks is initiated and performed to completion. Note that this notation is a compact high level description of the use of a menu.

The use of task names as abstractions—for modularity, consistency, and reusability—is illustrated in the following example, using the task of deleting multiple files from the Macintosh™ desk top. To begin, Figure 14 shows the task description without use of abstraction.

Note that S denotes the shift key. Also note the condition of viability applied to the file_icon in the second line. The icon must not be selected as the user enters this task. If an icon is selected and the user depresses the shift key, moves the cursor to that icon, and depresses the mouse button, this task description simply does not indicate what would happen. Since the condition of viability is not met

TASK: delete multiple files			
USER ACTIONS	**INTERFACE FEEDBACK**	**INTERFACE STATE**	**CONNECTION TO COMPUTATION**

(Sv
  (~[file_icon-!]
       Mv
 	
      M^)*
S^)*
	file_icon!	currentObject=
		file_icon,
		file_icon ∈ selected	

~[file_icon!] Mv ~[x,y]*	outline(icons!) > ~		
~[trash_icon]	trash_icon!		
M^	erase(icons!), trash_icon!!		mark selected files for deletion

Figure 14. UAN description of the task *delete multiple files*

TASK: delete multiple files			
USER ACTIONS	**INTERFACE FEEDBACK**	**INTERFACE STATE**	**CONNECTION TO COMPUTATION**
select_multiple_ files			
delete_selected_ files			

Figure 15. Using higher levels of abstraction

for this task, then the user is *not performing this task*. There may, however, be another task within the set of asynchronous tasks that comprise the interface (perhaps a deselect task) whose condition of viability is met and whose description matches these user actions. That task description would say what results in this case.

This task of deleting multiple files can be decomposed into two tasks:

1. Select files (the top block in Figure 14)
2. Delete selected files (the other three blocks in Figure 14)

Both these tasks are performed often and will appear as part of other tasks as well. Figure 15 shows how the overall task description of Figure 14 is stated in terms of names for these lower level tasks, which are then defined elsewhere.

TASK: select multiple files			
USER ACTIONS	INTERFACE FEEDBACK	INTERFACE STATE	CONNECTION TO COMPUTATION
shift_multiple_ select			
OR			
drag_box_ multiple_select			

Figure 16. OR: showing alternative methods

TASK: shift multiple select			
USER ACTIONS	INTERFACE FEEDBACK	INTERFACE STATE	CONNECTION TO COMPUTATION
(Sv (~[file_icon-!]			
Mv	file_icon!	currentObject= file_icon, file_icon∈ selected	
M^)* S^)*			

Figure 17. One method of performing *select multiple files*

TASK: drag box multiple select			
USER ACTIONS	INTERFACE FEEDBACK	INTERFACE STATE	CONNECTION TO COMPUTATION
~[x,y] Mv		x,y is fixed corner of rectangle	
~[x',y']*	draw dotted rectangle with corner diagonally opposite fixed corner following the cursor		
~[x",y"] M^	items intersected by rectangle are !	all intersected items ∈ selected	

Figure 18. Another method of performing *select multiple files*

Also, as indicated in Figures 16, 17, and 18, the task of selecting multiple files can be done in at least two ways: by using the shift key, as described in the first block of Figure 14, or by dragging out a selection rectangle with the mouse. Figure 16 is the higher level task description, stated as a disjunction of the names

TASK: drag box multiple select			
USER ACTIONS	**INTERFACE FEEDBACK**	**INTERFACE STATE**	**CONNECTION TO COMPUTATION**
~[x,y] Mv		x,y is fixed corner of rectangle	
~[x',y']*	dotted rectangle >> ~ **see figure** *selection rectangle*		
~[x",y"] M^	items intersected by rectangle are !	all intersected items ∈ selected	

Figure 19. Referring to a scenario figure

of the tasks in Figures 17 and 18, which give the lower level details of each method for selecting multiple files.

The task, *shift multiple select,* of Figure 17 is the same as the first block in Figure 14.

Figure 18 defines the task *drag box multiple select..*

VIII. Complementary Representation Techniques

The UAN is intended for describing user actions in the context of interface objects, along with feedback and state information. It does not, however, describe screen layouts, nor state transition information (that is often distributed among task descriptions). Therefore, designers have found it useful to augment UAN with other representations.

A. *Scenarios*

Because feedback describing drawing out the rectangle in Figure 18 may not be enough to convey the task completely, a screen picture can be used to augment the task description. Figure 19 is the task description of Figure 18 with a reference to a *scenario* figure (shown in Figure 20) added to the feedback column of the second row.

Note that the screen picture of Figure 20, which shows the layout of the screen objects, is also annotated with UAN descriptions.

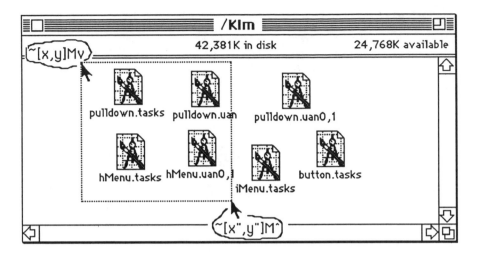

Figure 20. The scenario figure *selection rectangle*

B. Task Transition Diagrams

As already discussed, the UAN contains a mechanism—the semicolon—for specifying points in a task where user interntion shifts may occur. There is often a need to know not just where a task can be interrupted, but what the user can do to interrupt a task. For example, at the second or third semicolon in Figure 13, the user could move the mouse to another menu title (indicating a change of which menu to pull down) or move the mouse off the menu completely (indicating the user's intent of not selecting any of the items). Such detail is more efficiently and effectively presented at a level higher than the actions in this task description—a level that shows the relationships among these tasks.

State transition diagrams are a well-known method for showing a constructional view of the system. The system can be in one of a set of states (represented by nodes), and the transition (represented by arcs) from one state to another is governed by events, for example, sensing user input. Similarly, a *task transition diagram* (TTD) shows a set of related tasks a user can perform with a system. A task is represented as a node. The relationship among tasks reflects the various possible intentions of a user. For example, an arc from task A to task B indicates that a user performing task A may intend to perform task B. There is no labelling of arcs, or rather there is an implicit labelling of an arc with the intent to perform the task to which the arc leads. Hence, for each semicolon in the task description, we can include in the TTD nodes that indicate what the user can do to abandon the original task.

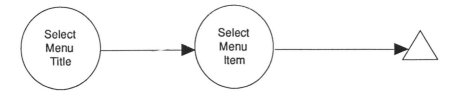

Figure 21. Initial TTD showing sequence of subtasks

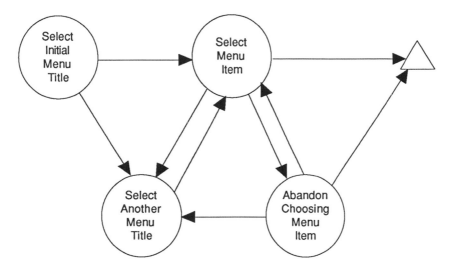

Figure 22. TTD showing how a user can interrupt the pulldown menu task

In the pulldown menu example from Figure 13, Figure 21 shows the relationships among the subtasks of selecting a menu item from a pulldown menu. Note that a path from the first subtask through the last shows completion of the task, task closure being indicated with the triangle. Thus, the user selects a menu title, selects a menu item, then closes the task. This simple figure corresponds to the UAN task description of Figure 13 without the semicolons: the subtask of selecting a menu title corresponds to the user actions in the first line of Figure 13, while the subtask of selecting a menu item corresponds to the user actions in the second and third lines of the same figure. A designer looking at the TTD in Figure 21 might ask, "What if the user wants to abort this task, or discovers that the wrong menu is pulled down?" Figure 22 answers these questions by showing *interruptor tasks* (e.g., select another menu title, abandon choosing menu item) that are available to the user at points indicated in the UAN task description by semicolons. These interruptor tasks are themselves defined by other UAN task descriptions.

It is not sufficient to maintain a separate notational scheme identifying these interruptor tasks. It is equally important to know the exact points *within* a task at which a user may shift to the interruptor tasks. A complete view of the principal task and its interruptor tasks thus requires both a UAN description of the principal task, as well as a TTD identifying the interruptor tasks and showing the relationships among all these tasks.

C. Discussion Sheets

Because an interface design document is a working document as well as a means for communicating among developer roles, designers are encouraged to include as part of the design representation, their comments about trade-offs faced and reasons behind design decisions. These comments appear on *discussion sheets* that augment UAN task descriptions, scenarios, and state diagrams as a more complete representation of interface designs. Later, the maintenance process especially benefits from information on design decisions, often preventing a repetition of an unsuccessful design previously tried and rejected by designers. Implementers and evaluators also use discussion sheets to comment as early as possible on the design: implementers are in the best position to estimate the cost of implementing certain features; evaluators must document their reasons for suggested design changes.

IX. Experience with the UAN

We originally developed the UAN to communicate behavioral descriptions of our UIMS interface designs to implementers for construction and to evaluators for a pre-prototype view of the design, and we found it useful in this capacity. We used the UAN to conduct walk-throughs of our UIMS interface design and to check the implementation against the design. We found that we started using UAN symbology instead of prose while describing our thoughts during the walk-throughs. We also found design problems such as feedback occurring on the wrong user action.

We found that structured checkout (i.e., the process of verifying that an interface is implemented as specified) became quite easy because of the UAN. Our interface evaluator used the UAN task descriptions as a checklist. For each task in the list, the evaluator performed the indicated user actions and checked that the corresponding feedback and state changes occurred as written in the UAN. We estimated that approximately 80% of the design was implemented exactly as specified. Of the 20% that did not conform to design, approximately 10% was due to misinterpretation of the UAN by the implementers, and 10%

was due to their simply not wanting to implement as represented.

In order to determine more about the usefulness of the UAN, we are promoting its use in commercial, government, and academic development environments. In particular, the UAN is being used experimentally in the Human Interface Lab at Texas Instruments in Dallas, Texas, for design of a telephone interface. The Bureau of Land Management in Denver, Colorado, is procuring the development of a Geographical Information System for which the UAN was used to represent some prototype designs. An interface designer at the Naval Surface Warfare Center in Dahlgren, Virginia, struggling through a several-inch-thick stack of human-computer interface guidelines for the Navy, is using the UAN to document these guidelines precisely and to prevent repeated rereading of many lines of prose. The UAN is being used to represent several multimedia interfaces involving full-motion video and audio for a DVI (digital video interactive) application being developed for NCR Corporation. Interface designs for a UIMS and some applications systems in Project DRUID at the University of Glasgow (Scotland) have been represented with the UAN. A DEC U.K. interface designer used it to describe precisely what happens during a complex scrolling-in-a-window task for a new design. In the U. S., designers at DEC are using the UAN for the interface of a graphical editor. A data flow configuration system has been designed with the UAN at the Jet Propulsion Laboratory. This diversity of uses of the UAN indicates the broad range of interface styles it can represent.

In general, users of the UAN report that it is easy to learn to read and to write. They find its symbols and idioms to be mnemonic and intuitive. Perhaps more importantly, they like the thoroughness of the descriptions, and feel it facilitates communication between interface designer and implementer. They find it to be precise, concise, and easily extensible as needed for their particular environment. Negative comments are that UAN descriptions may be too detailed for use early in the design process, when too much specificity about the interface may limit the designer's creativity. One or two developers have commented that the symbols should be more expressive (e.g., they wanted to change the ~ to move_to), or that the symbols or columns did not allow them to represent their design fully.

We encourage extension of UAN symbols, columns, and any other feature by UAN users, so that the UAN approach will more completely support interface representation. For example, Sharratt (Sharratt, 1989a; Sharratt, 1989b) has introduced what could be called *cognitive data flow analysis* to the UAN. Two columns for GOMS-like operators are added to the UAN: user memory and cognitive operations. Examples of each are, respectively, RecallLongTermMemory(items), and LookAt(location) for(item). An interface analyst studies the user actions involved in a task and determines the memory and cognitive operations required to carry out those actions: "These cognitive actions can be viewed as the instructions given to the user carrying out the task before they perform the physical actions... ." (Sharratt, 1989b). These operations are listed in the appropriate columns. Sharratt has found that this tabular listing enables analysts to see the effects of memory loading and cognitive actions on task performance.

X. Software Tools

Work reported in this chapter is intended to support the interface development process through software tools and the evaluation of designs through analytical processing. We are presently exploring these uses of the UAN, particularly its support by software tools.

The primary UAN support tool, which we are currently developing, is a UAN editor that developers can use to design the interface of an interactive system. The tool supports textual entry of UAN task descriptions. Task description *by demonstration* (Myers, 1987) is being considered as well.

The tool also supports additional columns. For example, there are system events that occur asynchronously with respect to user actions (e.g., a clock updating itself) that cannot be described in terms of user actions. Other uses for extra columns include

- memory actions, memory loading, closure (Sharratt, 1989a; Sharratt, 1989b)
- cognitive and perceptual actions—seeing feedback and acting on it in a closed feedback loop mode, decision making (Sharratt, 1989a; Draper, 1989)
- semantic connections (to invoke computational functions, for semantic feedback, especially for interreferential I/O)
- user goals and intentions (i.e., Norman's theory of action (Norman, 1986))
- task numbering for cross-referencing of task invocations in large interface design structures

The UAN editor tool will also eventually be used to support other development activities such as implementation and interface evaluation. Other tools we are researching include tools for analytic evaluation of interface usability, rapid prototyping, code generation and translation, and generation of end-user documentation.

A. Analytic Evaluation

Analytic evaluation is an interface development activity that is applied to interface designs to predict and assess usability before even a prototype is built and tested. The model on which each analytic evaluation technique is based must be validated against user testing to determine its ability to accurately predict usability. Some types of analytic evaluation use direct user performance prediction metrics that predict elapsed times to perform user actions such as mouse movement (e.g., Fitts Law (Fitts, 1954)) and keystrokes (e.g., keystroke model (Card & Moran, 1980)). Cognitive, perceptual, and memory actions can also have associated performance times. Other types of analytic evaluation predict user performance indirectly by identifying inconsistencies and ambiguities in an interface, determining equivalency of tasks, and analyzing information flow among tasks (Reisner, 1981). We plan to apply analytic evaluation to UAN interface descriptions. A prerequisite is the inclusion of columns in UAN task descriptions for cognitive, memory, perceptual, and decision-making user actions, in addition to physical actions. Also, because this kind of analysis requires machine processing of task descriptions, descriptions must be even more formal, precise, and complete than those currently produced. Because UAN expressions will be parsed, the UAN must itself have a more rigorous grammatical definition (e.g., BNF-style production rules).

B. Rapid Prototyping

A rapid prototype is an early version of an interactive system with which users can interact in order to evaluate the system design. Constructional representation techniques are well suited for prototyping; their view of the interface design is the system's view. Constructional representation techniques allow direct execution, often by interpretation, of interface design representations or specifications. The system's part is played by the prototype as it is executing, allowing evaluation of the user's part as played by a human user. However, a behavioral representation of a design is the user's part. Running a behavioral description directly on the system would make the system appear to behave as a user. (There is some interest in doing just this, if the object is to study complexity of user behavior (Kieras & Polson, 1985), but this is not the goal in prototyping.) In other words, the representational domain an interface developer chooses determines which roles play opposites in the game of prototyping. Thus, behavioral representations must be translated to a constructional equivalent either before or during the prototyping process.

C. Code Generation and Translation to Constructional Domain

Both prototyping and generating executable code from UAN task descriptions require translation of design representations from the behavioral domain to the constructional. This kind of translation is not trivial, because it is more than a line-by-line translation between languages. It is translation from one context to another, requiring transformations in structure that can reach deeply into a design. Solutions to the translation problem will require formal understanding of structural, semantic, and syntactic connections between the two domains. The object-oriented paradigm seems to be the most suitable constructional model; user actions in the behavioral domain have, as their counterparts, events in the constructional domain. The translation process will involve identification of objects, classes, and methods from the UAN descriptions. For example, if a task description has the user action ~[file_icon-!], this implies an object that can be pointed to, and that must have at least two states of appearance, one of which is considered a highlighted state. Such an object must have methods that are appropriate for visual objects (e.g., show at a location, hide, highlight, de-highlight). Currently this translation is done manually by the interface implementer, and is easier to perform if the target language is an object-oriented language.

D. End-User Documentation Generator

Because the UAN describes how a user performs each task, the basic ingredients for user documentation are present. We are investigating how to automatically derive a minimal user's manual from UAN descriptions. In addition, maintaining integrity between the user manual and the implemented system is a common problem. A UAN tool to maintain the system definition, and other tools to translate these definitions into code and user manuals, can assure a match between manuals and system.

XI. Developmental Context of the UAN

Interface design occurs within the context of an overall system development effort, though in this chapter we focused only on the interface portion. In order to use the UAN effectively, interface developers must understand where in the development process it is best suited. We shall consider the star life cycle of Hartson and Hix (Hartson & Hix, 1989) and the six foci for interface design decisions of Casaday (see his chapter in this book) to help interface developers place the UAN in context. The life cycle shows in which interface development phases the UAN can be used, whereas the six foci show in what interface design decisions the UAN can be used.

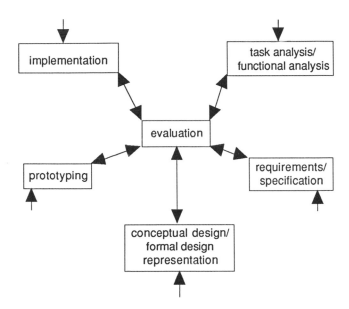

Figure 23. Star lifecycle for HCI design, reproduced from (Hartson & Hix, 1989) with permission from Academic Press

A. The Star Life Cycle

Hartson and Hix proposed an evaluation-centered life cycle characterized by iterative development of the interface, rather than the linear flow of the traditional waterfall model. They cited similar views by other researchers (Swartout & Balzer, 1982; Ramamoorthy, Prakish, Tsai, & Usuda, 1984), and their observations of how designers actually work, as motivation for their proposal. Figure 23 shows their star life cycle.

Within this star life cycle, we have found the UAN to be primarily useful in the conceptual design/formal design representation stage. In the conceptualization of an interface, an interface developer makes sketches of how the interface is to appear and behave. The UAN can be used to make quick notes that capture the desired interface behavior. The UAN provides a structured means of recording and studying the design as it evolves. The link between the interface design phase and the evaluation phase is readily supported by the UAN, since the degree of precision afforded by the notation allows a careful review of the design during design or cognitive walk-throughs (Polson & Lewis, 1990).

Since the UAN produces a behavioral design, translation to a constructional design must be made before the implementation phase can start. The UAN can, however, be used in the link from the implementation to the evaluation phase by using the structured checkout technique described earlier. Similar uses of the UAN are appropriate for the prototyping phase.

It is also possible to use the UAN in the task analysis/functional analysis phase. The UAN serves as a single representation both for the quasi-hierarchical task structure produced during task analysis and the specific action sequences produced during low-level design. The main difference between the two is the level of abstraction—UAN task descriptions at the high level are defined by temporal sequences of UAN task descriptions at the low levels.

In the requirements/specification phase, the UAN may be used as a short-hand for describing user actions, but we have not found it particularly useful otherwise during this phase.

B. Foci for Design Decisions

The chapter by Casaday presented six foci for design decisions made during interface development:

- system context
- user mental activities
- user physical activities
- functional interface design
- physical interface design
- implementation policies

Design decisions made at each of these foci must be captured both as a means for understanding why a design is a particular way and as a contract, or set of design guidelines, among designers who may be producing different parts of the interface. The latter is an important factor in the resulting consistency of the interface.

System context is the work the system does, irrespective of how a user might do that work. In behavioral terms, it is the task the system is being built to support. Decisions at this focus are independent of the specific system and of the user's private thoughts. This focus is not addressed by the UAN. Rather, it is typically embodied in a requirements document.

User mental activities refer to how the user thinks about the work to be done by the system—that is, what the user must know and think about in order to use the system. Decisions at this focus must account for the user's view of the tasks and for what the system does and how it does it. This focus is handled by task analysis. The UAN can be used as a means of representing the task structure at a high level. At lower levels, the UAN cognitive data flow analysis (Sharratt, 1989a; Sharratt, 1989b) can be used.

User physical activities refer to actions the user has to take to interact with the system, particularly through the hardware. This focus involves decisions such as when mouse clicks can occur. This focus is clearly supported by the UAN though its user actions column.

Functional interface design refers to the interface objects and operations that can be performed on those objects. Decisions at this focus are high level, device-independent, and semantic. The UAN addresses this focus in behavioral terms, that is, the actions a user performs to accomplish a task and the feedback and state changes caused by those actions. Complete support for this focus requires translation from the behavioral UAN representation to a constructional representation of the interface.

Physical interface design refers to detailed representation of the interface *look and feel*. This focus involves lower level syntactic decisions that result in specific interface objects, as well as their appearances, behaviors, and screen positions. This is supported by the UAN feedback column together with scenarios that illustrate screens, windows, and various other interface objects.

Implementation policies are design constraints such as standards, platforms, available resources, and ship dates. Decisions at this focus cover a broad range of issues that may be neither hardware nor software dependent. The UAN does not explicitly support this focus, for which decisions should be explicitly stated in a requirements document. Since these policies affect design decisions, their effects should be captured in the notes and discussion sheets of each task description.

XII. Summary

The UAN should be used through each development iteration as a means of representing the detailed design of direct manipulation interfaces, supporting design and cognitive walk-throughs, capturing design decisions, and conducting structured checkouts of implementation. Although the UAN is easy to learn to read, as with any language it takes time to write well. Based on our experience, we suggest that skilled designers, implementers, and evaluators be the primary users of the UAN.

User-centered interface design occurs in the *behavioral domain*. It requires that a designer maintain the viewpoint of the *user* performing tasks to interact with the computer. Thus, a tool-supported behavioral technique for representing the human-computer interface is needed to complement the constructional techniques needed for implementation. The User Action Notation (UAN) is a behavioral representation because it describes the actions a user performs to accomplish tasks, rather than the events that a computer interprets.

The UAN provides an articulation point between task analysis in the behavioral domain and design and implementation in the constructional domain;

with the UAN an interface is specified as a set of quasi-hierarchical tasks, with lower level tasks comprising user actions. Precision and clarity are obtained through associated feedback and system changes written in separate columns and in line-wise correspondence to actions. Because the UAN is a text-based representation, analytic evaluation of interfaces is possible.

Real world users of the UAN report it to be highly readable and writable with little training, because of its simplicity and natural mnemonicity. Use within numerous interface design and implementation projects has shown the UAN to be thorough, concise, and precise in conveying large complex user interface designs from designers to implementers and evaluators.

Acknowledgments

The Dialogue Management Project has received funding from the Office of Naval Research, the National Science Foundation, the Virginia Center for Innovative Technology, IBM Corporation, the Software Productivity Consortium, and Contel Technology Center. We also thank the UAN users who have given us valuable feedback on their experiences with its use, and the reviewers of this chapter for their thoughtful and helpful comments.

Sections and some figures of this chapter have been reproduced and/or adapted from a paper by Hartson, Siochi, and Hix which appeared in the July 1990 issue of ACM Transactions on Information Systems. (Copyright 1991, Association for Computing Machinery, Inc., reprinted by permission.)

References

Buxton, W. (1986). There's More to Interaction than Meets the Eye: Some Issues in Manual Input. In D. A. Norman, & S. W. Draper (Ed.), User Centered System Design (pp. 319-337). New Jersey: Lawrence Erlbaum Associates.

Card, S. K., & Moran, T. P. (1980). The Keystroke-Level Model for User Performance Time with Interactive Systems. Communications of the ACM, 23, 396-410.

Card, S. K., Moran, T. P., & Newell, A. (1983). The Psychology of Human-Computer Interaction. Hillsdale, New Jersey: Lawrence Erlbaum Associates.

Cardelli, L., & Pike, R. (1985). Squeak: a Language for Communicating with Mice. Computer Graphics, 19(3), 199-204.

Draper, S. (1989). Personal communication

Fitts, P. M. (1954). The Information Capacity of the Human Motor System in Controlling the Amplitude of Movement. Journal of Experimental Psychology, 47, 381-391.

Flecchia, M., & Bergeron, R. D. (1987). Specifying Complex Dialogs in ALGAE. In Proceedings of CHI+GI 1987 Conference on Human Factors in Computing Systems (pp. 229-234). New York: ACM.

Foley, J., Gibbs, C., Kim, W., & Kovacevic, S. (1988). A Knowledge-Based User Interface Management System. In Proceedings of CHI 1988 Conference on Human Factors in

Computing Systems (pp. 67-72). New York: ACM.

Gould, J. D., & Lewis, C. (1985). Designing for Usability: Key Principles and What Designers Think. Communications of the ACM, 28(3), 300-311.

Green, M. (1985). The University of Alberta User Interface Management System. Computer Graphics, 19(3), 205-213.

Green, M. (1986). A Survey of Three Dialog Models. ACM Transactions on Graphics, 5(3), 244-275.

Hartson, H. R., & Gray, P. (1990). Temporal Aspects of Tasks in the User Action Notation. Manuscript submitted for publication.

Hartson, H. R., & Hix, D. (1989). Toward Empirically Derived Methodologies and Tools for Human-Computer Interface Development. International Journal of Man-Machine Studies, 31, 477-494.

Hill, R. (1987). Event-Response Systems — A Technique for Specifying Multi-Threaded Dialogues. In Proceedings of CHI+GI 1987 Conference on Human Factors in Computing Systems (pp. 241-248). New York: ACM.

Hutchins, E. L., Hollan, J. D., & Norman, D. A. (1986). Direct Manipulation Interfaces. In D. A. Norman, & S. W. Draper (Ed.), User Centered System Design Hillsdale, NJ: Lawrence Erlbaum Associates.

Jacob, R. J. K. (1985). An Executable Specification Technique for Describing Human-Computer Interaction. In H. R. Hartson (Ed.), Advances in Human-Computer Interaction (pp. 211-242). New Jersey: Ablex.

Jacob, R. J. K. (1986). A Specification Language for Direct Manipulation User Interfaces. ACM Transactions on Graphics, 5(4), 283-317.

Kieras, D., & Polson, P. G. (1985). An Approach to the Formal Analysis of User Complexity. International Journal of Man-Machine Studies, 22, 365-394.

Moran, T. P. (1981). The Command Language Grammar: A Representation for the User Interface of Interactive Computer Systems. International Journal of Man-Machine Studies, 15, 3-51.

Myers, B. (1987). Creating Dynamic Interaction Techniques by Demonstration. In Proceedings of CHI+GI 1987 Conference on Human Factors in Computing Systems (pp. 271-278). New York: ACM.

Norman, D. A. (1986). Cognitive Engineering. In D. A. Norman, & S. W. Draper (Ed.), User Centered System Design (pp. 31-61). Hillsdale, NJ: Lawrence Erlbaum Associates.

Norman, D. A., & Draper, S. W. (1986). User Centered System Design. Hillsdale, NJ: Lawrence Erlbaum Associates,

Olsen, D. R. (1986). MIKE: The Menu Interaction Kontrol Environment. ACM Transactions on Graphics, 5(4), 318-344.

Olsen, D. R. J., & Dempsey, E. P. (1983). SYNGRAPH: A Graphical User Interface Generator. Computer Graphics, 17(3), 43-50.

Payne, S. J., & Green, T. R. G. (1986). Task-Action Grammars: A Model of the Mental Representation of Task Languages. Human-Computer Interaction (pp. 93-133). Hillsdale, NJ: Lawrence Erlbaum Associates, Inc.

Polson, P., & Lewis, C. (1990). Cognitive Walkthroughs: A Method for Theory-Based Design of User Interfaces. Paper presented at the CHI'90 Workshop: Taking Design Seriously: Exploring Techniques Useful in HCI Design, Seattle, WA.

Ramamoorthy, C. V., Prakish, A., Tsai, W. T., & Usuda, Y. (1984). Software Engineering: Problems and Perspectives. IEEE Computer, 17(10), 191-209.

Reisner, P. (1981). Formal Grammar and Human Factors Design of an Interactive Graphics System. IEEE Transactions on Software Engineering, SE-7, 229-240.

Richards, J. T., Boies, S. J., & Gould, J. D. (1986). Rapid Prototyping and System Development: Examination of an Interface Toolkit for Voice and Telephony Applications. In Proceedings of ACM SIGCHI Conference on Human Factors in Computing Systems (pp.

216-220). New York: ACM.

Sharratt, B. (1989a). MCA - an Approach to Task Descriptions and Usability Metrics Based on the User's Memory, Cognitive Operations, and Physical Actions. Unpublished manuscript, Scottish HCI Centre Working Paper, University of Glasgow, Scotland.

Sharratt, B. (1989b). Personal communication

Shneiderman, B. (1982). Multi-Party Grammars and Related Features for Designing Interactive Systems. IEEE Transactions on Systems Man and Cybernetics, 12(2), 148-154.

Siochi, A. C., & Hartson, H. R. (1989). Task-oriented Representation of Asynchronous User Interfaces. In Proceedings of CHI'89 Conference on Human Factors in Computing Systems (pp. 183-188). New York: ACM.

Swartout, W., & Balzer, R. (1982). On the Inevitable Intertwining of Specification and Implementation. Communications of the ACM, 25(7), 438-445.

Wasserman, A. I., & Shewmake, D. T. (1985). The Role of Prototypes in the User Software Engineering Methodology. In H. R. Hartson (Ed.), Advances in Human-Computer Interaction (pp. 191-210). Norwood, New Jersey: Ablex.

Yunten, T., & Hartson, H. R. (1985). A SUPERvisory Methodology And Notation (SUPERMAN) for Human-Computer System Development. In H. R. Hartson (Ed.), Advances in Human-Computer Interaction (pp. 243-281). New Jersey: Ablex.

10 Conceptual Modelling: A Look at System-Level User Interface Issues

ROBERT E. BRAUDES

TASC
Rosslyn, Virginia

I. Introduction

   User-computer interaction theory states that the design of a user interface should begin with an evaluation of the end users' view or *conceptual model* of the system being developed (Shneiderman 1987, Smith *et al.* 1982, Foley *et al.* 1990 and 1988, Rubinstein and Hersh 1984, Norman 1984, Norman and Draper 1986). However, in practice this is rarely found, and in fact very little research has been directed at the generation and analysis of these models.

   Two immediate questions are what are conceptual models, and why are they important? Briefly, conceptual models represent a user's view of an information system. They document entire *systems*, rather than *applications*. This means that the models describe objects and processes outside of the computer, for example, people, data sources, internal thought processes, etc. With this information, potential boundaries between the user and the computer can be evaluated to determine the most appropriate location for the user interface. Once this is known, the information that crosses the interface can be examined, with interaction tasks and techniques defined and prototyped.

   Another use of conceptual models is as an aid in selecting an appropriate metaphor for an application. Given a set of potential metaphors along with a model of a new system, a matching algorithm could be used to select applicable metaphors, which could then be tested with members of the user community.

   Conceptual models can also play two additional major roles in the development and construction of a complete application: a communications tool and an early sketch on which consistency and completeness verification can be performed. The development of conceptual models should occur during the requirements analysis phase of software development, when the task analysis of the system is performed. During this time, there should be a significant amount of interaction between the designers and representatives of the user community, in order to begin determining the requirements of the application. The completion of an initial conceptual model marks an important point in the development cycle when the system designer has an opportunity to discuss his or her view of the entire system with the end users in more than an informal way. This is because the designer has (or at least should have) taken a structured look at the system and has produced a *preliminary* definition of the entities, attributes, relationships, and actions that compose the system. The word preliminary is used because the initial view of the system will change as the application is built; this is discussed in other chapters of this book. Such an approach gives the designer and the users the ability to compare their views of the system for any areas of disagreement. These can then be resolved to ensure that the parties share an initial conception of the system. Again, it is to be stressed that this conception will evolve through prototyping sessions.

The structure imposed on the conceptual model also allows some verification of the model by bringing out omissions or inconsistencies. Software engineering principles state that the earlier in the life cycle such problems are noted, the better, and this philosophy of system development supports early problem identification.

Once a verified, agreed-upon model is available, it may be used as the blueprint for rapid prototyping. Ideally, the prototype will be automatically generated from the conceptual model, but this is beyond the scope of our effort. A prototype will most likely lead to identification of additional omissions, disagreements, extraneous sections, or other difficulties. These may be used to modify the model, with the model generation/modification and prototyping cycle continuing until the user and designer converge. The final model is a start for the subsequent system development effort.

II. ConMod: A Conceptual Modelling Research Tool

We have developed the *ConMod* (for CONceptual MODelling) System (Braudes 1990) for investigating these issues. ConMod is an extensible research tool, which allows us to investigate both the composition and analysis of these models. The tool has been developed in Smalltalk (Goldberg and Robson 1983), and makes use of the HUMBLE knowledge base shell (Piersol 1987).

The purpose of this chapter is to discuss generic conceptual modelling, rather than the specific ConMod system, and in particular the application of automated completeness and consistency verification to these models. This will be augmented with experience gained from using the tool. An example system, the Automated Bank Teller (ABT) discussed by Rubinstein and Hersh (Rubinstein and Hersh 1984), will be used to demonstrate the applicability to a "real" system.

While the ABT is a simple system, it is sufficient to show some of the advantages of developing and evaluating conceptual models.

III. Completeness and Consistency

Completeness and consistency represent two different concepts that are equally important when analyzing conceptual models. Completeness means that all items defined in a model are fully defined, or at least that the modeler is aware of any incompleteness. This is because some of the apparent inconsistencies in a model are actually due to holes whose filling removes the inconsistency. For example, assume that the role for an entity is left unspecified. Obviously this will cause great difficulties when evaluating role consistency (discussed later), and in fact the current ConMod knowledge base makes the assumption that all aspects of role consistency are inconsistent for entities to whom no role has been assigned. This will result in low confidence for the consistency of the model, when the problem is actually incompleteness. To help avoid these misleading situations, ConMod allows the modeler to evaluate completeness independent of consistency, and when both are evaluated, completeness verification is done first.

Consistency looks at different issues from completeness and has received more attention from the user interface community. One of the tenets of user interface software design is that user interfaces be consistent. A logical question is why is this so? As Baecker and Buxton stated (Baecker and Buxton 1987) one goal of user interface design is to "accelerate the process whereby novices begin to perform like experts." They asserted that giving the user a consistent interface style is a means to this goal. The first of Shneiderman's (Shneiderman 1987) eight "golden rules" for designing user-computer dialogues is to "strive for consistency," for reasons similar to those given by Baecker and Buxton. Consistency was also a major design goal in the development of the famous Xerox Star computer, with an explanation of possible "consistent inconsistency" presented in (Smith *et al.* 1982).

Given that consistency is important, why need it exist at a conceptual level? This was one of the major issues discussed at the ACM SIGGRAPH Workshop on Software Tools for User Interface Management (Olsen *et al.* 1987), especially in the groups discussing Goals and Objectives for User Interface Software (Betts *et al.* 1987) and Tools and Methodology for User Interface Development (Rhyne *et al.* 1987). Betts *et al.* (1987) stated that tools are needed to support the development of the conceptual model for a given application, with one of the functions of this tool set being to "evaluate the consistency and completeness of the definition" (p. 76). Rhyne *et al.* (1987) contained similar recommendations for tools to support the requirements and design phases of user interface design, and they argue that the early analysis of the design can substantially increase user acceptance of a system. They list five types of consistency that are important at this point in the development cycle: role, categorical, presentational, interaction, and metaphorical. Finally, additional support for the notion of conceptual consistency is found in (Rubinstein and Hersh 1984), (Norman 1984), and (Norman and Draper 1986).

The five types of consistency from (Rhyne *et al.* 1987) may be logically divided into three classes: abstract (metaphorical), conceptual (role and categorical), and stylistic (presentational and interaction). These classes provide a good start for developing a definition of conceptual consistency, but all five do not relate to the conceptual level, and not all aspects can be easily generalized across different domains and interfaces. We will discuss them to evaluate the appropriateness of inclusion in a generic definition.

Perhaps the highest level of consistency among the five is metaphorical consistency. The purpose of a metaphor is to allow the users of a system to transfer skills from a real-world situation, in which they have extensive experience, to the new system. One of the most common metaphors is the desktop metaphor first popularized in the Xerox Star (Smith *et al.* 1982), (Johnson *et al.* 1989). In the desktop metaphor, the computer's user interface is built to resemble a physical desktop, with manipulations in the interface mapped to interactions in the physical world. While the problem of appropriate metaphor selection is not directly addressed by the work described in this chapter, a potential linkage between conceptual modelling and metaphor evaluation is discussed.

The two stylistic aspects of consistency are not conceptual. Presentational consistency exists when the same object does "not appear in several representations which are visually unrelated." This aspect is concerned with the lexical level of the interface rather than the conceptual level and so is not appropriate for inclusion in determining consistency at the conceptual level. A similar argument holds for interaction consistency, which is concerned with ensuring that interaction tasks are implemented by means of the same interaction techniques. This is also at the lower level of the interface and so is omitted from the definition of conceptual consistency.

The remaining two dimensions, role and categorical consistency, are applicable at the conceptual level. But Rhyne *et al.*'s definitions are insufficient, so we have augmented them: Role consistency is concerned with having the user transfer across the structure of the roles in a system. This entails assigning roles to the various entities and ensuring similarity between the structures of objects with the same role. In order to determine whether two entities have the same role, we developed a list of seven types of role: agent, client, controller, data, data store, processor, and server. Use of the ConMod system made clear that an additional role exists in many systems, that of a *manipulated object*. These objects have some similarity to data, in that they are manipulated by the user, but actually have a more important role in a system than *data* implies. For example, a graphics primitive in MacDraw may be manipulated by the user in order to change its appearance. It is important that the modelling tool know that these objects have a special role in a system, and therefore a role type of *manipulated object* was added to the list. This list is extensible through the user-defined typing mechanism, which we will discuss, to add new role types that were not anticipated during the ConMod development.

A larger research issue is how to determine if two or more entities have *similar structures*. There are two parts to this problem. First, entities with the same role should have the same types of relationships and be related to similar objects. However, this may not be enough to allow the user to realize that the entities have the same structure. To reinforce the structural similarity, all entities associated with a given role should also have similar properties and characteristics, where *similar* means that all entities with the same role have properties and characteristics of corresponding types.

There is another type of role consistency that can be applied to conceptual models. In these models, there are actions that are requested by one or more entities. Entities that request the same actions probably have the same role in the system.

Categorical consistency is also concerned with the connections between entities and actions but associates the entities by types rather than by roles. This facet of consistency asserts that the user should be able to perform similar actions on entities of the same type and can be extended to verify that entities of the same type request actions of similar types.

Another form of categorical consistency may be called *stereotype* consistency. Here, one can develop a framework that contains the types of attributes, relationships, and actions normally associated with an entity of a given type. For example, assume that an entity of type *event* (the colloquial, not computer, sense) exists in a conceptual model. The framework could state that the entity should have an attribute containing the *date* or *time* of the event's occurrence. Similarly, the event should probably be affected by an action that processes it, which would have a type such as *query, respond, read,* or *consume*. Entities can also be checked to make sure that they are not contained in unexpected links. Continuing with the event example, events are usually not associated with *constraint, joins,* or *opposite* relationships.

A final type of categorical consistency is verifying that objects in the model with identical links should indeed be separate objects. For example, assume that there are multiple entities in a model that have the same set of relationship and requested action instances. There may be no discernable distinction between these entities. A potential solution is to merge the entities into a single entity, with the attributes and affecting actions combined as necessary. This merging of objects basically performs a *generalization* function on a model. This aspect of categorical consistency, *similarity* consistency, may also be used to identify cases in which several related objects should be *aggregated* into a higher level set. This aggregation serves to reinforce the similarity of the objects, without removing the individual object characteristics.

Besides being aggregated by roles and types, entities may be grouped by hierarchical relationships, such as "is a," "part of," "collected in," or "contained in." These relationships may be divided into two groups, one group (e.g., part of and is a) implies inheritance-type behavior, and the other group (e.g., collected in and contained in) does not. Conceptual consistency analysis must follow all appropriate inheritance paths (including multiple inheritance) during model evaluation.

IV.   The Structure of Conceptual Models

Now that a definition of conceptual consistency is available, the next issue is how to specify a conceptual model in a format whose adherence to the definition can be verified. Perhaps the easiest way is to look into the structure of the definition itself. The essence of the definition is the various objects and the links among them. This lends itself to an object-oriented paradigm, as discussed in (Myers 1989) and which has been used successfully in related systems, such as GWUIMS (Sibert *et al.* 1986), UIDE (Foley *et al.* 1989), and CREASE (Hurley

1989).

An object-oriented system necessitates enumeration of classes of objects. These classes should be selected to simplify the verification process and so should naturally match the different areas of the consistency definition. There are two major components of the definition: *role* and *categorical* consistencies, *categorical* consistency having the subcomponents of *stereotype* and *similarity* (discussed earlier). *Role* consistency requires various entities and their roles, so two natural classes would be *entity* and *role*. These entities are linked by various *relationships*, which form a third class of objects. The properties and characteristics employed to help determine similarity are an *attribute* class. Finally, the *actions* that are requested by and affect the entities in the model define a fifth class. The use of entity and action classes is also supported by the *categorical* consistency segment of the definition, while *stereotype* and *similarity* aspects of categorical consistency each support the use of the entity, relationship, attribute, and action classes. It is important to note that the entire consistency definition also calls for the use of some sort of typing mechanism within the class structure. Types are applicable to all classes but with a different set of types for each class. The initial types available to the user in ConMod are shown in Figure 1. It is clear that the initial set is not sufficient to address all possible application domains. This leads to the inclusion of user-defined types (which have the same status as the system-defined types).

V. The Automated Bank Teller

The ABT model represents a (intentionally incomplete) description of the automated teller machines used to deposit or withdraw money from a bank account. Access to the teller is controlled by an access card and an associated personal identification number (PIN). Figure 2 depicts the ABT model used in this example. In this figure, boxes are used to represent entities, lines to the side of the box are used to list attributes, and arrows are used to show (directional) relationships. The entity's name is listed inside each box, along with the type in parentheses and the role in brackets. Examples of two actions, *Make Deposit* are *Make Payment*, and shown in Figure 3.

Looking at the ABT model, several inconsistencies are apparent. From the view of role consistency, both the *Bank* and *Automated Teller* entities have the role *Perform Money Transactions*. However, the *Automated Teller* is associated with the attribute *Address* (of type *Location*), while the *Bank* is not associated with any location attributes. Similarly, the *Automated Teller* is associated with the relationship *Allows Access To* (of type *Control*), while the *Bank* is associated with the relationship *Holds* (of type *Maintain*). These differences will make it difficult for the user to generalize knowledge about objects that have the role *Perform Money Transactions*.

The ABT model as specified also has several categorical inconsistencies. For example, the actions *Make Deposit* and *Make Payment* have a similarity inconsistency. While both are requested by the *Customer*, *Make Deposit* affects the entities *Checking* and *Savings*, while *Make Payment* affects the entity *Line of Credit*. This inconsistency can have important implications on both hardware and

Entities	Attributes	Relationships	Actions	Roles
Container	Amount	Above/Below	Action	Agent
Data	Attribute	Before/After	Add	Client
Entity	Color	Collection	Begin	Controller
Event	Count	Component Of	Close	Data
Group	Date	Comprised Of	Communicate	Data Store
Language	Distance	Constraint	Consume	Manipulated
Number	Duration	Control	Create	Object
Organization	Frequency	Has	Cut	Processor
Person	Height	Inherits From	Destroy	Role
Place	Identifier	Joins	Duplicate	Server
	Location	Lead	Enter	
	Position	Located In	Erase	
	Size	Maintains	Enumerate	
	Shape	Opposite	Help	
	Speed	Owns	Interpret	
	State	Part	Join	
	Status	Portion Of	Leave	
	Time	Relationship	Measure	
	True/False	Same	Modify	
	Volume	Step In Process	Move	
	Weight	Subclass Of	Open	
	Width	Uses	Query	
			Read	
			Replace	
			Respond	
			See	
			Separate	
			Subtract	
			Talk	
			Teach	
			Terminate	
			View	
			Write	

Figure 1. Initial ConMod Object Types

software aspects of the user interface. Another categorical inconsistency is evident between the *Account* and *Checking* entities, assuming that inheritance is not included in the model. Both objects are defined to be of type *Container*, but the action *Make Deposit* does not affect the *Account*. While the ABT model and these inconsistencies are rather simple, they demonstrate the types of problems that can be hidden within conceptual models.

VI. Discussion

Analyzing models for conceptual consistency is an attempt to address user interface issues in the earliest stages of software development. The goal is to

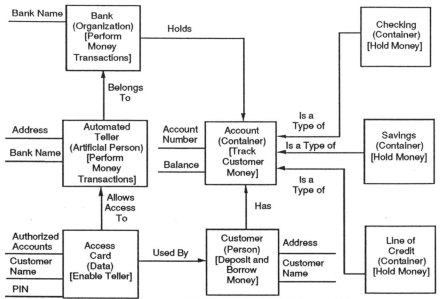

Figure 2. Automated Bank Teller (ABT) Block Diagram

derive an initial specification that is consistent, as inconsistencies at the conceptual level *cannot* be masked by a consistent syntactic design. For example, a graphics editor that has a conceptual model where polygons can be deleted but circles cannot will not be helped by a large *delete* button.

We understand that conceptual consistency contains both a domain-independent portion and a domain-dependent portion. However, it is impractical to develop a tool and a knowledge base that contain all potential domain-dependent information. The alternative is to build a knowledge base that is rich in domain-independent information and to provide hooks for domain experts to integrate domain-dependent knowledge. This is the approach we adopted for ConMod, with two modes of domain-dependent information entry provided: the addition of user-defined types into the system-supplied type structures and the facility to specify user-defined rules, which are integrated into the initial knowledge base.

The list of types contained in Figure 1 is not meant to be all-inclusive; it is meant to be broad enough to cover the requirements of most conceptual models. However, there are several cases where additional types are required, especially when trying to specify a model in the terminology of the user. To overcome this obstacle, ConMod allows the domain expert, and in some cases the conceptual modeler, to add domain-specific types to the model. The ConMod knowledge base, which codifies the completeness and consistency definitions, is intended to be useful across a wide variety of problem domains, so it contains domain-independent rules. However, a sizeable number of applications require conceptual consistency to also contain domain-dependent knowledge. There are other cases for which the built-in domain-independent knowledge is either inappropriate or at

Name: Make Deposit
Type: Add
Preconditions:
      Entity   State
        Automated Teller   Transactions Authorized
Postconditions:
      Entity   State
        Checking   Balance Needs Update
        Savings   Balance Needs Update
Affects Entities:
      Checking
      Savings
Requested By Entities:
      Customer
Relationships:
      None

Name: Make Payment
Type: Add
Preconditions:
      Entity   State
        Automated Teller   Transactions Authorized
Postconditions:
      Entity   State
        Line Of Credit   Balance Needs Update
Affects Entities:
      Line Of Credit
Requested By Entities:
      Customer
Relationships:
      None

Figure 3. Specifications for the *Make Deposit* and *Make Payment* Action
          Objects

the wrong level of granularity. The solution is to allow the ConMod user to write domain-specific rules and add them to the knowledge base.

Several conceptual models have been constructed using ConMod, to evaluate the feasibility of verifying their consistency. The first of these models is the automated bank teller (ABT), already introduced. The next two models, the Textra word processor and the MacDraw graphics paint system, are examples familiar to a wide audience. The specifications for these models were developed using IDL specifications (Gibbs *et al.* 1986) as templates. The initial ConMod models were then evaluated for completeness and consistency. The models were revised based on the ConMod reports and the updated models evaluated. This allowed comparison of the initial models with the updated models, to determine whether the suggested changes were appropriate.

The next model developed as part of the ConMod analysis process was a complete description of a hospital radiology department (Braudes *et al.* 1989). The radiology model, containing over 100 objects, was created to test the ability to process a large model. A unique feature of the radiology model is that it is not a traditional user interface and so demonstrates the ability of ConMod to handle different domains.

There are several features of the test models that are noteworthy. First, the models described entire systems, including the user, as opposed to solely modelling the portion of the system that was to be built into an automated application. This forms a more complete specification in that the interfaces between the system and the outside world are included. It also gives the system designers more flexibility in determining the appropriate system boundary during system implementation by showing them the effects of changing the boundary.

Whether to model within the boundary or across it determines when a model can be created. In the former case, the assumption is that preliminary design decisions have already been made, that the boundary has been decided. However, this is often not the case during the initial stages of system requirements definition. Usually, the entire system is analyzed to determine where the boundary should be.

There are some features of the conceptual consistency definition that should be addressed. For example, a potential conflict between the categorical and role consistency definitions became evident when building the test models. In the MacDraw model, we assigned the same role and type to all of the graphics primitives, which made one of the two classifications redundant. In fact, in many of the models the tendency to associate each entity type with a single role was enhanced by the consistency processing.

One of the main outcomes of the radiology model is that it demonstrates some of the shortcomings of categorical consistency. Five entities of type *Person* are contained in the model: the radiologist, the referring physician, the patient, the file room clerk, and the technologist. While these objects are all of the same type, they play substantially different roles in the model. Therefore, when categorical consistency verification tests were executed on the model, a large number of potential inconsistencies were reported. This represents a situation where role consistency should be given precedence over categorical consistency, as most of the "problems" were justified by the roles of the objects. This contrasts with the MacDraw model, where the role-related differences between a primitive object being text or being graphic should have significantly less impact on the affecting actions than the similarities from both being primitive object types in the system.

One of the major questions surrounding categorical consistency is whether it is too stringent for general applicability. This question actually has two parts: first, whether all entities of a given type should be involved in conceptual links of the same type, and second, whether stereotype entities can be developed for each type contained in the entity type structure. These issues are interrelated, because if the stereotype is appropriate, it can be used as the categorical consistency template.

In each of the models created to test the ConMod knowledge base, categorical inconsistencies of both kinds were found. In some cases, such as the person type from the radiology model, the links contained in the model were appropriate, and so the messages were not helpful. In many cases, the messages were generated by assigning an inappropriate type to an entity. Finally, there were several occasions where the model was in fact inconsistent.

One potential solution is to rely more on user-defined types and add user-defined rules to implement the stereotyping approach of categorical consistency to define both expected and unexpected links for the type. These stereotypes can be used to guide the development of the model, with verification logs reviewed and modifications made to the model as needed. This review process should be greatly assisted by the messages generated through the comparison of the structures of all entities having a given type.

One feature of the consistency definition that was more useful than anticipated was the analysis of objects that could be merged into a single object. The initial thoughts behind adding this to the knowledge base were that by allowing a model to be developed in any order, an object may accidentally be given two names when a single object was desired, or that two or more objects were included where only a single object was required. However, in several cases of test model evaluation, a series of objects was required, but those objects could be aggregated into a set with a single parent in order to more clearly show their similarity. For example, in the Textra model there is a set of delete actions, including *Delete Block*, *Delete Line*, *Delete Character*, and *Delete Word*. Similarly, the MacDraw model includes a series of create actions, one for each of the primitive objects. In both cases, the post-condition states for the action sets were identical, only affecting different entities in the respective models. This is compounded in the MacDraw model by having a multilevel entity hierarchy already defined. By specifying higher level delete and create actions (in the case of MacDraw, there were actually several levels of create actions defined), the entire set of entity-action links was simplified and more explicitly showed the relationships in the models.

VII. Future Work

The foundation has now been laid for continuing the conceptual consistency research in several areas. There will always be room for refinement of the conceptual consistency definition; the three areas of role, categorical, and similarity consistency are neither exhaustive nor complete, and so new facets should be identified and developed and the current definitions refined.

An additional research issue is extending the ConMod system both backward, to the evaluation of different metaphors for a system, and forward, towards the generation of prototypes based on the conceptual specification. The creation of a library of existing models or model components may be useful for metaphor determination, and systems such as UIDE and other UIMSs can be used to provide insight into the requirements for producing a prototype from the specification.

A final area of future work is a verification of the usability of the ConMod tool. NASA has plans to utilize the tool over the next few years, and a Canadian communications research organization is currently evaluating it. While the current research has demonstrated the feasibility of developing a conceptual modelling tool, the results of these efforts will demonstrate the general utility of the system.

VIII. Acknowledgments

I would like to acknowledge the workshop participants for their views and comments, and in particular those who reviewed this chapter. I would also like to thank the members of the George Washington University Graphics and User Interface Research Group for providing a stimulating environment for conducting this research. Finally, I thank Dr. John Sibert for his guidance and understanding.

Bibliography

Baecker, R.M. and W.A.S. Buxton, "Readings in Human-Computer Interaction: A Multidisciplinary Approach," Morgan Kaufmann, Los Altos, CA, 1987, 738 pages.

Betts, B., D. Burlingame, G. Fischer, J. Foley, M. Green, D. Kasik, S. Kerr, D. Olsen, and J. Thomas, "Goals and Objectives for User Interface Software," Computer Graphics, Volume 21, Number 2, April 1987, pp. 73-78.

Braudes, Robert E., "A Framework for Conceptual Consistency Verification," Doctoral dissertation submitted to George Washington University, 1990, 438 pages.

Braudes, Robert E., Seong K. Mun, John Sibert, John Schnizlein, and Steve Horii, "Workstation Modelling and Development: Clinical Definition of a Picture Archiving and Communications System User Interface," Medical Imaging III, in Proceedings of the SPIE, Volume 1093, 1989, pp. 376-386.

Foley, James, Won Chul Kim, Srdjan Kovacevic, and Kevin Murray, "Defining Interfaces at a High Level of Abstraction," IEEE Software, January 1989, pp. 25-32.

Foley, J., W.C. Kim, S. Kovacevic, and K. Murray, "UIDE-The User Interface Design Environment," Draft Report, Dept. of EE&CS, George Washington University, Washington, DC, 1988, 27 pages.

Foley, James, Andries van Dam, Steven Feiner, and John Hughes, "Computer Graphics: Theory and Practice," Addison-Wesley, Reading, Massachusetts, 1990.

Gibbs, Christina, Won Chul Kim, and James Foley, "Case Studies in the Use of IDL: Interface Definition Language," Report GWU-IIST-86-30, Department of EE&CS, George Washington University, Washington, DC, 1986, 32 pages.

Goldberg, A. and D. Robson, "Smalltalk-80: The Language and Its Implementation," Addison-Wesley, Reading, MA, 1983, 714 pages.

Hurley, William D., "A Generative Taxonomy of Application Domains Based On Interaction Semantics," Doctoral dissertation submitted to George Washington University, 1989, 316 pages.

Johnson, Jeff, Teresa L Roberts, William Verplank, David C. Smith, Charles Irby, Marian Beard, and Kevin Mackey, "The Xerox Star: A Retrospective," Computer, Volume 22, Number 9, September 1989, pp. 11-29.

Myers, Brad A., "User Interface Tools: Introduction and Survey," IEEE Software, January 1989, pp. 15-23.

Norman, Donald A., "Stages and Levels in Human-Machine Interaction," International Journal of Man-Machine Studies, Volume 21, 1984, pp. 365-375.

Norman, Donald A. and Stephen W. Draper, Editors, "User Centered System Design: New Perspectives on Human-Computer Interaction," Lawrence Erlbaum Associates, Hillsdale, New Jersey, 1986, 526 pages.

Olsen, D.R. Jr., D. Kasik, J. Rhyne, and J. Thomas, "ACM SIGGRAPH Workshop on Software Tools for User Interface Management," Computer Graphics, Volume 21, Number 2, April 1987, pp. 71-72.

Piersol, K., "HUMBLE V2.0 Reference Manual," Xerox Special Information Systems, Pasadena,

CA, 1987, 121 pages.

Rhyne, J., R. Ehrich, J. Bennett, T. Hewett, J. Sibert, and T. Bleser, "Tools and Methodology for User Interface Development," Computer Graphics, Volume 21, Number 2, April 1987, pp. 78-87.

Rubinstein, Richard and Harry Hersh, "The Human Factor: Designing Computer Systems for People," Digital Press, Bedford, Massachusetts, 1984, 249 pages.

Shneiderman, B. "Designing the User Interface: Strategies for Effective Human-Computer Interaction," Addison-Wesley, Reading, MA, 1987, 448 pages.

Sibert, J.L., W.D. Hurley, and T.W. Bleser, "An Object-Oriented User Interface Management System," Proceedings SIGGRAPH '86, published as Computer Graphics, Volume 20, Number 4, August 1986, pp. 259-268.

Smith, D.C., C. Irby, R. Kimball, B. Verplank, and E. Harslem, "Designing the Star User Interface," Byte Volume 7, Number 4, McGraw-Hill, Peterborough, NH, 1982, pp. 242-282.

11 Combining Task Analysis with Software Engineering in a Methodology for Designing Interactive Systems

JAMES A. CARTER JR.

University of Saskatchewan
Saskatoon, Saskatchewan, CANADA

Abstract

The Multi-Oriented Structured Task analysis (MOST) methodology balances the needs for consistency and completeness of structured specifications with the needs of both systems designers and systems users for flexibility and adaptability.

While providing considerable benefits to system designers, software engineering methodologies are generally lacking in their treatment of human-computer interaction design. Likewise, while providing considerable assistance to interaction designers, task analyses seldom are fully integrated within the software engineering of systems. The MOST methodology structures a task analysis and integrates it with more formal software engineering specifications and methods.

A hypertext based computer assisted software engineering tool, MOST-CASE, can be used to design interactive and even adaptive systems. MOST-CASE assists the designer with the acquisition of application knowledge, the analysis of acquired application knowledge (for consistency and completeness), the restructuring of application knowledge into a design, and the mapping designs onto reusable components (such as found in a UIMS).

I. Background

The importance of user interface design as a major component of systems design (and not just an afterthought or a peripheral event) is becoming widely recognized. Unfortunately, the method for accomplishing this is not as uniformly agreed upon. Proposed methods include two separate parallel activities, having interface design subsumed as an activity within system design, having system design subsumed as an activity within interface design, or integrating the two activities into a single design process. While the first three of these methods extend familiar methodologies, they all assume a clean partitioning of both design activities and their resulting system components. Moran (1981) stated that while people may distinguish the aspects of the system that the user interacts from their implementation, systems are almost never able to be partitioned this cleanly. Neither can the design of user interfaces be totally separated from the design of the functional system.

A new, more integrated method of design is needed to help the designer both to partition and to integrate the various interface and systems design activities. Such a method needs to be fully developed into an analysis and design methodology to be of practical use to actual designers. Wasserman (1985) described a methodology as a collection of development support tools and development management procedures unified in order to improve the various aspects of the software development process both in terms of quality and efficiency.

The central feature of any methodology is its model of the system to be developed. This model must meet a variety of needs. Both application and interface designers need it to assist in the design process. The end users need it to assure the system developed is suitable. The application needs it to be able to include all relevant components and features. This can best be accomplished by a methodology that has a sound basis and the ability to adapt to unforeseen or unusual circumstances.

The Multi-Oriented Structured Task Analysis (MOST) Methodology (Carter, 1990b; Carter & Hancock, 1991) includes the good features and overcomes the failings of existing human computer interaction and software engineering methodologies by combining the components of their models and allowing their alternative methods of use.

MOST supports all four design methods (while encouraging the interactive design of both the interface and the system components). It also allows designers to adapt the methodology to meet their needs and those of the system they are designing (rather than forcing them to pretend that they have conformed to irrelevant or inappropriate methodological requirements).

MOST promotes consistency in and between analyses and designs (rather than just demanding consistency to itself) and allows the modeling of alternate designs to meet the needs of different users or of users changing their needs over time.

This chapter describes the rationale for MOST and provides a high level discussion of its main components, methods, and uses. The details of the various components, methods, and uses are discussed elsewhere (Carter, 1990b), as are the various detailed task analysis questions proposed by MOST (Carter & Hancock, 1991).

II. Current Analysis and Design Methodologies

The main sources of software analysis and design methodologies are the fields of human-computer interaction and software engineering. Human-computer interaction methodologies generally focus on the user's viewpoint of the software system, while software engineering methodologies focus on the designer's view of the software system. While the overall system (of user + computer) includes both views, typical methodologies take only one view to the exclusion of others. Both approaches focus on modeling the application. The user is often modeled as a given "subsystem" that performs part(s) of the application. The designer is almost never considered in the modeling. A more wholistic view of the overall system is required to ensure the success of the overall design.

The current methodologies often have been developed from limited viewpoints (either software engineering or human factors) for use by experts, familiar with those viewpoints, to accomplish certain tasks in certain manners. This forces or reinforces the segregation of software engineers from user interface designers in development projects, which, in turn, often leads to inconsistencies and/or incompatibilities in the resulting system.

Software engineering approaches primarily decompose systems hierarchically in terms of functions and data. Structured systems analyses (Gane & Sarson, 1979) define processes as high level transformations of data structures to be followed by structured design (Yourdon & Constantine, 1979) identifying program modules, which act as detailed instantiations of the high level processes. Object-oriented analyses change their focus on these same components. They use data objects (rather than data flows) as their organizing principle and place a lesser emphasis on the functions that can be performed on/by the data (Coad & Yourdon, 1990). Wasserman's USE model (1985) includes the consideration of user transactions as well as tasks; however, it does not fully support user interface design or the analysis and design of tasks at the user's conceptual level.

Despite the variety of software engineering approaches (Olle *et al.*, 1982, 1983; Pressman, 1987), none explicitly model the user.

Human-computer interaction approaches deal with the connection between the highest level user task (referred to as the conceptual level by Foley & Van Dam, 1982; the task level by Moran, 1981; applications by Green, 1984; and abstractions by Coutaz, 1987) and the lowest level user interface components used to implement these user tasks (referred to as the lexical level by Foley & Van Dam, 1982; the interaction level by Moran, 1981; and presentation by Green, 1984 and Coutaz, 1987). These connections may be purely due to hierarchical decomposition or may involve control (as proposed by Green, 1984 and Coutaz, 1987). Moran (1983) and Foley *et al.*, (1987) addressed the typical weakness of high level conceptual modeling. These human-computer interaction approaches neither model users (or groups of users) nor data structures explicitly.

Design methodologies may violate the requirement of completeness in a number of ways. Mathematical (and some other formal notation) methods limit what information they specify to those concepts they can readily represent. They then guarantee the "completeness" of their specifications by accepting overall incompleteness of these limits in order to provide a provably complete subset. Proving completeness often is limited to checking for unmatched references (linkages) and incomplete specification of components and can seldom deal with whole components of a system that are missed entirely. Furthermore, the formalisms of methodologies tend to support the assertion that the methodologies are themselves complete and thus will produce complete designs. These two assertions are both unprovable and unconnected.

The majority of methodologies claim to classify all the important components of a system and all the relevant linkages between these components. Few methodologies go further than this. Roman (1985) suggested that consistency requires more than specifications being connected to each other. Consistency, also, requires that specifications don't contradict each other. The connection between design components and specifications with the real system is a further logical connection, which is needed but is often taken for granted.

Both software engineering and human-computer interaction methodologies also are notable in their omission of any explicit modeling of the user or users who will be coming in contact with the system. Such an explicit modeling of the user is an essential component in the design of an overall system model, which is, in turn, essential for the design of adaptive systems and which should be a part of the design of all systems (Carter, 1990a). The overall system model should go beyond assisting "the designer to create a conceptual model of the system for the user to assimilate" (Moran, 1981). It should assist the designer in creating a system that meets the expectations of the user, both conceptually and otherwise, without requiring the user unnecessarily "to assimilate" to user interfaces that are less than optimal. The needs of such explicit user models were discussed by Schweighardt (1990).

The recognition of different needs and characteristics between users (and even for a given user at different times) appears to challenge the attainment of designing a system that is both consistent internally and consistent with these various users at various times. However, upon further consideration, adaptivity can be allowed (and should be encouraged since it increases the external consistency of the system with the needs of the user at a given time) so long as the adaptation, itself, is done in a consistent manner.

Recently, Computer Assisted Software Engineering (CASE) tools have been developed to assist the software engineer in analyzing and designing systems. However, the current generation of CASE software only computerizes the textual and graphical editing and representation of data bases of traditional software engineering specifications. It neither significantly expands the coverage of these specifications (to include other relevant knowledge about the desired system and its users) nor makes use of the semantics of the knowledge related to the existing specifications.

III. The Usability of a Methodology

Designers will be most likely to use a methodology completely, correctly, and consistently if the methodology helps them in its use and in achieving the design of a complete, correct, consistent, usable system. Despite the availability of a variety of formal system development methodologies, designers seldom use any formal methodology completely, totally correctly, or fully consistently (Rosson *et al.*, 1988). Unfortunately, the benefits of the methodologies are often tied to their complete, correct and consistent use. Where designers are not forced to use methodologies, they often estimate the costs of utilizing a methodology to outweigh the benefits, and they therefore decide against fully using the formalized methodology. This is not to say that designers ignore or fail to utilize those techniques (from methodologies) that are beneficial (without necessarily associating them with a formal methodology).

In an attempt to provide apparent robustness, various methodologies have become "too prescriptive and difficult to use for real design tasks" while others focus on a particular design aspect (Preece *et al.*, 1987). The complexity of some methodologies may make designs susceptible to consistency errors, which will require additional complexity to identify and remove (Sharratt, 1987). Some methodologies resort to the use of "artificial concepts" (such as mathematical representations of systems) where consistency is handled easier than with "natural concepts", which may include contradictions that exist in the real world (Borigida *et al.*, 1985). The lack of global consistency in the design is often compensated by the demand for a high level of consistency in the design process. However, requiring designers to use design tools in a particular manner and sequence may limit both the productivity and the creativity of the designers.

Both software engineering and human-computer interaction methodologies generally impose strict top-down sequencing in an effort to control both completeness and consistency. When hierarchical methodologies delay making design decisions until the lowest possible levels, only the nodes directly below a node and designed after it will inherit these design decisions. Separate similar design decisions, in different parts of the hierarchical decomposition, may lead to similar and potentially equivalent but nonidentical resulting designs. In the absence of a bottom-up regrouping (as suggested by Moran (1983) or Foley *et al.*, (1987)) the consistency of design is localized within a number of different subsets of the overall design.

Although most methodologies expect a task analysis of the existing system as the basis for design, few actually provide a sufficient bridge between current user practices and those expected with the new system. Structured Analysis and Design methodologies generally are very explicit in their stripping of all physical information from the existing system model prior to the start of design (in the name of not being hindered by historical hang-ups). Rubenstein and Hersh (1984) advocated developing the new system model (use model) from the original task analysis but gave no developed methodology for either activity. Moran (1983) proposed an External Task - Internal Task mapping to overcome the conceptual mismatch between the way the user thinks and the way the system was designed.

To manage the growing complexity and size of analysis and design specifications, the majority of methodologies quickly reduce the set of potential instances of a system specification to a single instance of a system. However, the explicit modeling of all permitted instances of the system can provide a linked framework for both consistency and adaptivity. CASE tools can help manage the complexity of such specifications (e.g. by organizing them into useable subsets) and thus reduce the need to limit the amount of information retained throughout the analysis and design process.

IV. The Origin of the Multi-Oriented Structured Task Analysis Methodology

The MOST methodology grew from the elaboration of the ten task analysis questions of Rubenstein and Hersh (1984) to identify specific information required to answer each question. An informal normalization of the specific categories of information yielded four major interlinked foci of specification information (users, tasks, data, and tools) and an optional additional foci (constraints) that can be linked to any of the major foci.

Record formats for each of these foci were developed and further analyzed to find a number of common sets of information potentially shared between tasks and tools. These common sets of information were removed from task and tool records and developed into secondary records, which can be used with either or both tasks and tools. The five major interconnected foci of information are intended to encompass all of the information utilized in the various software engineering and human-computer interaction methodologies plus explicit user models.

A methodology for using the set of records was developed that utilizes a variety of knowledge engineering techniques to help attain consistency and completeness in analysis and design while facilitating flexibility and adaptability both in the development process and in the resulting product. The methodology explicitly recognizes that record layouts must be flexible enough to incorporate further information that may be found useful in the future. Thus, the detail information questions and the formal specification methods used in a particular record type can be modified as needed. It also recognizes that various designers and projects may favor either a phased (waterfall) or an iterative (prototyping) or a hybrid style of system development life cycle.

V. The Design Process and Environment of MOST

MOST recognizes that all design methodologies can be simplified to a cycle of two main processes: gathering information on what needs to be done and using the information to specify how this is to be accomplished. It accommodates both the classical phased model, which typically has one gathering (analysis) phase and one use (set of design, implementation, and testing) phase, and a prototyping model, which iterates through a number of gathering and using phases. It also allows the designer to proceed in a top-down, a bottom-up, or a combination manner, as required by circumstances and preferences. This view of the design process is supported by the findings of Rosson, Maass, and Kellogg (1988) that designers introspectively described their process of idea generation as composed of information gathering, information processing, and trying things out, given the close coupling of the latter two activities.

Human Factors Society's Human Computer Interactions Standards Group (HFSHCISG, 1989a) adopted several features features of MOST, with some slight modifications, to form the basis for their draft document on Design Processes for Human Computer Interactions (HFSHCISG, 1989b).

Design takes place in a nested environment consisting of the users' environment being analyzed and tools for it being designed within the designer's environment. The designer, in turn, is a user of analysis and design tools.

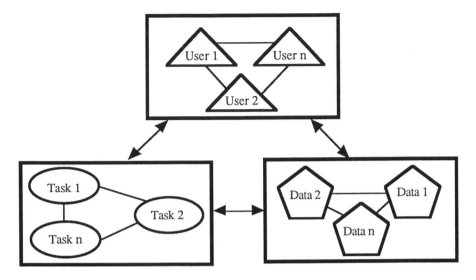

Figure 1. The User Environment

The users' environment is composed of sets of users interacting with sets of tasks and sets of data which also interact with each other (Figure 1). A key concept is the recognition that different users or groups of users interact with different tasks or groups of tasks to process different data or groups of data. Thus, systems grouping all user needs into a single statement will generally fail to meet the human-computer interaction needs of at least some of the users at least some of the time.

The designer's environment is composed of the user environment plus design tools and constraints (Figure 2). The distinction between tasks and tools is based on the separation of the functionality of the system from the implementation of this functionality (Jacob, 1983). Constraints add external requirements and standards that must be observed in the system development process. They are outside the set of tasks the system is to perform but constrain how the system is to perform those tasks.

The purposes of tools are to help people to accomplish tasks. Most system developments produce (or select) a tool or set of tools to help end users in their various tasks. Tools can and should help the designer to develop (or select) these user tools. In some cases a tool such as a word processor may be used both by the developer and the end user. By using tools to develop other tools, the designer is in a recursive relationship. This relationship caries over to end users, who use tools such as spreadsheets in their own development efforts.

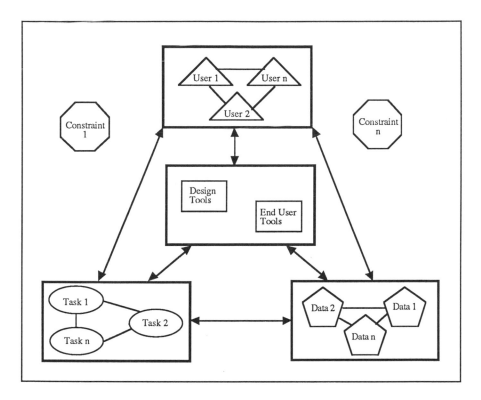

Figure 2. The Designer's Environment

While all types of user tools can be the desired outcome of the design process, the focus of this discussion is those tools that help in the design process. Tools help the designer to gather information on the user environment and to use this information to design a system. Specific tools may be used for either or both of these purposes. Tools can be developed to assist in either or both human factors engineering and/or software engineering. Methodologies and CASE tools for implementing methodologies both fall within the category of tools, as do programming languages and systems used by the designer. The MOST methodology takes the concept of tools one step further, by also considering the resulting software systems to be tools (even though these are tools for the user rather than tools for the designer). This is readily apparent when the resulting system is designed by the selection from a group of predesigned components. It is equally true where design involves the selection, modification, and arrangement of predesigned components where these components just happen to be programming language instructions.

VI. Record Types in MOST

All MOST records share a common structure. Each record format includes five major sections: Identification, Linkage, Details, Formal Specifications, and Usage , as illustrated in figure 3. The main distinction among different MOST record types are the categories of information found in the Details and Formal Specifications sections and thus the Usage of these records. This open structure provides MOST with considerable flexibility and extensibility.

```
Record Type:

Identification: Name of Particular Record

Linkage:
   - to records of the same type
   - to records of other types

Details:
   - a variety of prespecified detail types
   - provision to add other types of details

Formal Specifications:
   - for use by other CASE systems
   - for input to application generators

Usage:
   - how many records to use when and where
   - design guidelines for details
```

Figure 3. Sample MOST Record Layout

The first two sections of a MOST record are used to identify and organize the records. The Identification section requires a unique name for each record. The Linkage section identifies major relationships between a record and other records both of the same kind and of different kinds.

The answers to various task/systems analysis questions are stored in the Detail information section. MOST includes a comprehensive set of task/systems analysis questions (Carter & Hancock, 1991). These questions provide guidance to the designer and can be expanded, revised, or ignored as the situation requires. The detail information section also records how this information is or is not inherited from higher level records. Answers are recorded in the task analysis as they become known and are used and potentially modified in the design that follows. This detail information can include both functional and nonfunctional information as advocated by Roman (1985). The format of these answers is flexible so that the designer can determine how best to use them in a given design.

Details can be formalized by specifying them in the Formal Specifications section of a record. The formal specification section has no prescribed format. It is intended to take the format of any formal specification method (including any programming environment) that the designer wishes to use. The formal specifications can then be linked with one or more formal specification analyzers and/or application/program generators, depending upon the availability and desirability of such.

The Usage section information initially tells the user how to utilize the record based on its record type. In the future this section of the record may include detailed design rules or standards that correspond to various potential answers to questions in the details section.

VII. The Foci in MOST

The five major interconnected foci of information (users, tasks, data, tools, and constraints) are intended to encompass all of the information utilized in the various software engineering and human-computer interaction methodologies plus explicit user models such as those discussed by Schweighardt (1990). They also fully define the designer's environment. Each foci is composed of a directed acyclic network of records of a single focal type and allows both top-down and bottom-up development. Records in different foci are linked together, where appropriate, similar to the linkage between processes, data, and entities proposed by Shemer (1987). This linkage is described further in Carter (1990b) and can be illustrated as a knowledge space as in Figure 4.

The five foci of MOST gather and use the various types of information necessary for a complete representation of the designer's environment:

The user focus is used to structure information about groups of users, subgroups, and individuals. An acyclic network structure allows users and subgroups to be members of multiple higher level subgroups and groups while protecting the designer from having a subgroup as an ancestor of itself. The number of levels of records in a user focus depends upon the particular set of users and roles of these users that the system is being designed to accommodate. The detail of information in individual records within the user focus depends upon the structuring of the focus, level of the record within the focus, and the amount of information that applies equally to all records below that record in the focus. Thus, information is most general for the set of all users, less general for the main user groups, moderate for intermediate user groups, specific for user subgroups, and very specific for individuals. The most specific information recorded would be about individuals performing a particular role of theirs.

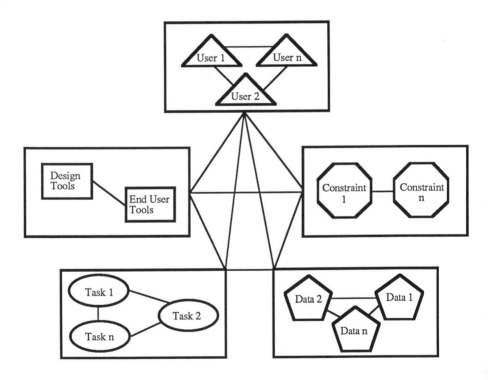

Figure 4. The Foci and Linkages Between Foci in MOST

The designer may specify and arrange multiple groupings and subgroupings to gain a better understanding of the different types of users, their characteristics and their needs. Users may be grouped by application(s) used, by type of use (end user vs. developer), or by level of experience (student vs. professional vs. instructor), or by any other grouping that helps in the analysis and design process. The designer should initially determine that each grouping is distinctive and thus adds to the understanding of the different users. An analysis of the knowledge contained in the resulting MOST records can later be done to improve the grouping structure.

Figure 5 illustrates how user information might be organized in some of these groupings for an analysis of various HyperCard users. In this illustration only identification and linkage information is shown. The records in this illustration all differ in terms of their linkages. Since a grouping of all experience levels would have the same linkages as that of all users and would provide no additional useful information, it is not included. Multiple groups could, however, have the same linkages and differ only in their detailed information. Where any differences (in linkages or in details) are significant, the designer should consider two or more records in the user focus to record these differences.

User focus information aids the suitable design of systems in general and user interfaces in particular for both nonadaptive and adaptive systems. Without this information, systems and interfaces tend to be designed for a mythical "average" user who is actually often based either on the "lowest common denominator" of capabilities or on the assumption of "expert use."

The information in the user focus assists in the design of nonadaptive systems by identifying the characteristics both of particular users and of reasonable subsets of users. Recognizing subsets of users can lead to the design of usable subsets of the system and the interface, as well as the design of a consistent overall system and interface. Characteristics of both individual users and subsets of users also can provide a basis for the design of user selectable or customizable options within the system and especially within the interface.

User focus information can also assist in the design of adaptive systems by recognizing the dynamic stages of user development - from that of a novice requiring considerable assistance through becoming an expert interacting with parts of or the whole system with a minimum of assistance. These varying stages of user developments generally involve a variety of "best" or "preferable" user interfacing techniques which may apply simultaneously to differing parts of the system, based on the user's experience with them. Information in the user focus can both facilitate the desired adaptation and be used to help control the consistency of the adapting interface throughout the user's involvement with it.

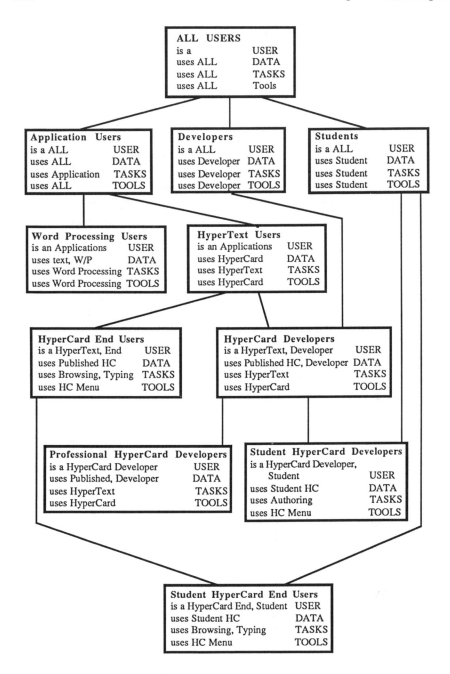

Figure 5. Identification and Linkage Information for a Sample User Focus

The task focus corresponds to nonprocedural user tasks that define the purposes of the users' interactions with the system. The task focus combines: the processes of structured analysis; the conceptual and semantic levels of Foley and Van Dam (1982), the task and semantic levels of Moran (1981), and the applications of Green (1984) and abstractions of Coutaz (1987). The combination of the conceptual/task and semantic levels of some of these models recognizes the multiple potential levels of decomposition between each of the applications, tasks (or user goals), subtasks (or user objectives), functions, and even variations of functions and further recognizes the need to accommodate the various models for decomposing them. The acyclic network structure (as opposed to the usual strict hierarchical structure of most methodologies) recognizes that some semantic functions are often utilized in a variety of high level tasks and further recognizes that applications can be accomplished by various groupings of semantic functions within various groupings of tasks. This structure is especially useful in investigating alternate conceptual designs.

As with the user focus, the designer may specify and arrange multiple groupings and subgroupings of tasks to gain a better understanding of the set of task requirements. Tasks may be grouped by the traditional organization of a task's procedures, by classes of functions, by classes of objects, or by any other grouping that helps in the analysis and design process. These various groupings provide the analysis knowledge that will help the designer in selecting, modifying, or developing a suitable grouping for the new system's design. The knowledge contained in the resulting MOST records can be analyzed, as with the user focus, to help the designer improve the grouping structure.

Where the semantics of the system to be developed are limited (either by the software being used for development, by a need for compatibility with some other existing system, or by some other valid reason) the set of allowable or existing semantic functions can be loaded into the task focus prior to commencing the task analysis. The structural decomposition of tasks can then be checked for consistency to evaluate how low level nodes correspond to the predefined semantic functions. While they should not contradict the predefined functions, in some circumstances they may elaborate them or define functions not currently included in them.

The semantics of the system may also be limited by identifying a potential error or slip as a task that "is-not-a(n)" instance of or part of some valid task. Knowledge of these invalid tasks can be used both to design interfaces which avoid them and to design user assistance to help avoid or to recover from them.

Entries in the task focus map directly to the set of tasks presented to users in a non-adaptive system and the set of possible tasks that a user might use in an adaptive system. In the latter case, a user might be currently using only a subset of these tasks (which therefore involves a second mapping).

The tools focus's primary purpose is to specify the resulting design of the desired system including implementations of tasks and interfaces to them. The tools focus combines the program modules of structured design, the syntactic and lexical levels of Foley and Van Dam (1982), the syntactic and interaction levels of Moran (1981), and presentations of Green (1984) and Coutaz (1987). Records in the task focus correspond to the procedural implementations that perform parts of one or more tasks in a particular physical manner.

The tool records can specify presentation (interface) tools, processing (function) tools, other types of procedural entities/tools, and even external noncomputerized tools, in addition to the dialogue tools that are specified by most of these models. Each distinctive type of tool can be arranged within its own hierarchy or acyclic network. Tool records can be arranged both in an acyclic network corresponding to the design of an implementation that meets the needs of the task focus and also in networks linked to the various appropriate types of tools to which they belong.

The multiple linkages of tool records recognizes that all systems are tools (to their user) and that systems are likewise built from other, more basic, tools. It allows, as in the case of predefined functions, the preloading of the tool focus with definitions of preexisting tools that will be used to create the desired system. Thus, the tools focus can be loaded with information about interface tools (such as a user interface management system (UIMS) and its components), programming tools (such as programming environments or fourth generation languages and their components), and manual tools.

Figure 6 illustrates how the tool focus can be used to design a specific tool. It includes some preloaded information on the components of a UIMS that will be used to implement the interface. Processing tools are being designed to meet the task requirements. The highest level processing task is to select a part of the application for the user to interact with. In this design, two UIMS tools are selected that each can be used to implement this task. This results in the design of a main menu and a set of quick keys.

The preloading of the tools focus can help the design process to evaluate the potential for selection and reuse of existing tools prior to the creation of new tools. This is especially important where this creation might create inconsistencies for the user. As new tools (including new systems) are created they can be added to the preloaded set of tools for use in future designs.

In addition to accelerating user interface development and making it more modular, Rosson, Maass, and Kellogg (1988) found that a UIMS can provide design assistance "through the automation of interface design recommendations or principles" (so that designers need not know all the relevant research literature), "and through an increase in consistency" (by including reusable modules of interface code). Preloading records describing a UIMS (to be used in the system's development) into the TOOLS focus allows MOST to integrate these forms of design assistance within the overall system development process.

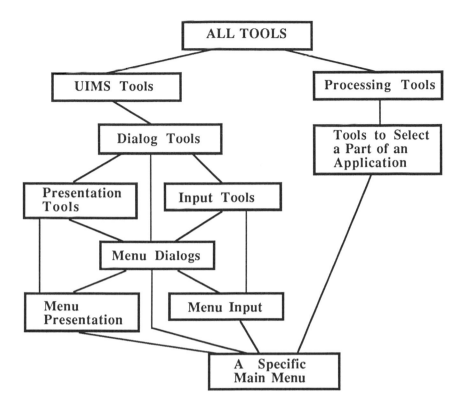

Figure 6. Using the Tool Focus to Design Multiple Interfaces for a Processing Function

Rosson, Maass, and Kellogg (1988) found actual designers to be split between their separating or not separating the design of the user interface from that of the rest of the system. Their choice was found to be related to characteristics of the projects, the tools, and the designers preference. MOST's approach (allowing preloading both human-computer interaction and software engineering tools within a single interlinked tools focus) assists designers in developing consistent interfaces that meet the needs of both the users and the system regardless of their approach to separation of the user interface.

Information on human-computer interaction tools and software engineering tools may also be preloaded into the tools focus to assist the system developer in gathering and using information (rather than to be used as potential components of new systems. In some circumstances this preloaded information might be used for both purposes.

Analyses can be performed on the tools focus to ensure the global as well as localized consistency of designs contained therein. Alternative designs can be developed and evaluated in parallel (by experienced designers). The organization of the tools focus can also suggest how users, in either a nonadaptive or an adaptive system can be given their choice of equivalent tools to perform various tasks.

The data focus organizes all information about the user's application data whether external, internal or both external and internal to the system. The data focus can be used for either or both data flow oriented (as in structured analysis and design) or object oriented data analysis. When used with data flow analysis, the data focus includes the concepts of data flows, data stores, data structures, and data elements. Typically users, tasks, and tools are linked to data flows, which are linked in the data focus below data structures. Data stores and data elements are also linked below corresponding data structures. The acyclic network structure is necessary to allow data elements to be linked to a variety of data structures.

When used with object oriented analysis, the data focus includes the concepts of classes, subclasses and instances of (data) objects. Typically users, tasks, and tools are linked to instances, which are linked in the data focus below classes and subclasses. The acyclic network structure allows instances to inherit the properties and attributes of multiple classes and subclasses.

By allowing both forms of data analysis, MOST is uniquely able to assist designers wishing to convert from more traditionally (data flow) designed systems to object oriented systems.

Entries in the data focus map directly to the set of available data presented to users in a nonadaptive system and the set of possible data that a user might use in an adaptive system. In the latter case, a user might be currently using only a subset of the data (which therefore involves a second mapping).

The constraints focus organizes standards externally imposed upon a system by the organization(s) it will be used for, by legislation, or by a standards setting body. Some example organizational standards can include goals, objectives, policies, finances, and development standards and procedures. Constraints can control design factors, including usability, customization, adaptability, and some aspects of consistency.

It is important to distinguish between external constraints and internal constraints. The latter are part of the user, task, tool, or data records to which they apply. Only external constraints are dealt with in the constraints foci, in order that it supplement rather than duplicate the other information. Thus, a task that constrains the user is treated as a task, while a law that constrains what the user can legally do (regardless of the circumstances) is treated as a constraint.

Whereas the other four foci are required components of all systems development, constraints may or may not exist. Likewise, different groups of constraints may apply to each systems development project. Because of this and the external nature of constraints, their organization is both less likely to be structured and less crucial in the success of the development. The important organizational principle for the constraints foci, is that constraints be readily identifiable to the designer so that they can be linked to the appropriate records in the other foci.

VIII. Analysis and Design Using MOST

The methodology for using the records and their linkages within MOST is designed to cooperate with the designer rather than to force the user to serve the methodology. Rosson, Maass, and Kellogg (1988) found actual designers are almost evenly split between using a phased development approach and an incremental development approach. They also found that the choice of design approach was related to several project characteristics, as well as to designer preference. MOST can be used in either a phased (waterfall) or an incremental (prototyping) manner (generally composed of an sequence of waterfalls incrementally performing analysis, design, and development).

To gather information a MOST task analysis is documented by filling out the various types of MOST records (as required and as suggested by the usage information). The details section of the records assists the designer in identifying important information, without restricting the designer to limited types of codable information (as formal specification languages generally do). These records are structured according to the appropriate linkage information both within and between foci. This structuring can be greatly facilitated by using a hypertext system as a documentation tool (as described by Conklin, 1987).

A completed MOST analysis will include an analysis of the various types of users and the structure of their relations to each other; the existing tasks and their structure (and tasks not currently done that should be part of the application); the logical contents and structure of the data; the existing tools and structured groups of tools (both those being used currently for the application and those available for future use (or reuse) by the application); and any constraints upon the design of a new system.

A typical method of analysis consists of identifying information provided to the analyst/designer; determining an appropriate initial location for this information within the MOST structure; adding, changing, and/or deleting information in MOST records, and changing links between MOST records; and analyzing the resulting documented information to determine further areas of information to investigate and identify. MOST is compatible with a variety of knowledge acquisition techniques (including those suggested by Munsen *et al.*, 1986; Jacobson and Freiling, 1987; and Kitto, 1988) which can be readily implemented within a computerized (CASE) tool to support MOST.

To utilize information, a MOST design utilizes the linked sets of records to get a consistent description of what is to be designed. The designer selects or adds tool descriptions to meet the design needs and links these tool records appropriately to produce a use model of the new design. Both the task analysis and the design can be done in any order (top-down, bottom-up, or random) and either as separate phases or together to meet the needs of the situation and of the designer. The linkages in MOST provide a flexible structuring and restructuring of records as they are added or re-added.

A completed MOST design will have transformed the MOST task analysis by adding new tasks and potentially restructuring the set of tasks; adding physical structure to the data; and designing the tools and their structure that will specify the new system (and its interfaces) that will meet the user's needs. The majority of secondary records linked to tasks should now be linked also to the tools that will be used to implement those tasks. If desired or required, the informal information contained in the details section of the MOST records can be transformed into formal information in the formal specifications section.

These transformations can be assisted and/or evaluated with a number of tools and techniques. A unique feature of MOST is how its linkages support the analysis of informal information. Factoring, as discussed by Foley *et al.* (1987), uses the bottom-up grouping of parameters to make them global (or at least modal) parameters to provide consistency to design. Factoring of the use model involves developing tool classes that govern the consistency of individual tools via the property of inheritance. Tsai and Ridge (1988) identified four software engineering techniques (coupling, fan-in, span of control, and cohesion) that can be used in "expert transformations" of MOST specifications from requirements specifications (application knowledge acquisition) to design specifications (using knowledge). Formal specifications can be transferred to existing formal specification analyzers.

The MOST methodology assists the designer in the production of consistent designs. External consistency is possible due to the inclusion of explicit models of users, tasks and the linkages between them and internal components (tools and data). MOST's structuring promotes internal consistency. The MOST methodology can act like a metasystem (by being able to include other formal specification systems within it) and can add its consistency controls to those of other methodologies. This flexibility allows the MOST methodology to be consistent with the designer's needs, as well as the needs of the system being designed.

The adaptive components of an adaptive system can be incorporated within a MOST analysis and design by creating a special adaptive TASK under which all other tasks and tools operate. This allows the existence of alternate versions of tasks linked to various users, tools, and data. The MOST user focus provides the explicit user model required to control the adaptivity. State variables to keep track of adaptation can be designed in the data focus similarly to other internal system variables. Adaptive tools can be defined to implement the adaptive tasks. The linkages in the MOST analysis and design include the paths by which consistent adaptation can take place. The heuristics of adaptivity can be distributed throughout the various MOST records, as required, both as informal detail information and/or as formal specifications. The flexibility of the MOST record structures and methodology can be used to accommodate future design requirements as the levels of adaptive computer systems advance.

IX. Developing a CASE Tool to Support MOST

The MOST methodology has been used successfully for the analysis and design of a variety of systems. MOST has been used manually for a project scheduling and management system, a resource scheduling and management system, and an accounting system. It has been used with a dBASE III data base of MOST specification records for an information archiving and retrieval system.

In each of these developments, a set of MOST records provided the main analysis and design documentation, replacing both a task analysis and traditional software engineering specifications. While these projects demonstrated the feasibility of MOST, the volume of records and linkages in each system limited the designers ability to make use of the knowledge contained in the MOST specifications of the systems. It was generally agreed by the designers involved in these projects that MOST is both well suited to and in need of the benefits of automation. The positive results of these projects have provided the basis for the development of an automated CASE tool to support MOST.

A prototype computer assisted software engineering tool to support MOST was recently developed in the Knowledge Engineering Project at the University of Calgary. In that project, MOST was used as the methodology to analyze and design a CASE tool MOST-CASE to support the MOST methodology. The tool was developed in HyperCard (c).

The use of a rapid prototyping approach supported by the latest prototype of MOST-CASE resulted in a number of useful findings. The most general of these findings was that MOST was fully capable of and very helpful in analyzing and designing a tool to support itself. We believe this to be a more rigorous test of the capabilities of a methodology than has been reported for other methodologies. At the same time, it should be expected as a partial proof of the consistency and completeness of any methodology. Various particular findings from our prototyping were analyzed using the MOST methodology and led to a number of major improvements in the usability of MOST-CASE. Some of these cases are discussed in the following examples.

The overall prototyping process has been driven by the philosophy of "using the tool to investigate the requirements and design of the tool." The initial windowing design specified the support of 1 window, 2 or 3 (horizontally split) windows, 4 windows (split in quadrants), or 5 windows (composed of four quadrants with a thin horizontal window across the bottom). This design came from the requirement to simultaneously show one record for each of up to the five main foci to give a comprehensive view of the environment of a tool being designed. No more than five record windows would be supported due to both physical screen limitations and because only one record per focal type was expected to be used at once. When secondary records were to be used, it was expected that they would replace the tool or task record they elaborated in its window. Prototyping with MOST uncovered the additional need for multiple windows to have different records from the same focus, to support analysis rather than just design, by allowing the analyst to distinguish between the record currently being documented and its parent and sibling records.

The prototyping approach discovered that some methods used in MOST could be used more universally than first envisaged. Inheritance, initially adopted for simplifying and then analyzing informal detail information, was also found necessary and useful in simplifying uses linkages. Likewise, flexibility of quantity and content of detail questions was achieved by having the detail headings be entered (or pre-entered) as the details of the top level node of every focus (and of each set of secondary records).

MOST's knowledge structure continues to meet the needs or to be able to meet the needs of other methodologies. The IBIS model (as discussed in Conklin &Begeman, 1989) which documents issues, positions, and arguments, and the ISAAC model (Conklin, 1989) which documents issues, alternatives, analysis, and comments, can both be incorporated into a MOST knowledge base as attributes of MOST linkages. These and other ideas are being developed for incorporation (as an option) into both MOST and MOST-CASE.

MOST-CASE currently supports the entry and browsing of knowledge bases MOST records. A sample MOST-CASE screen layout, illustrated in Figure 7, includes up to five windows for combinations of user, task, data, tool and constraint records (or browsers for these or secondary task/tool records).

The designer can select a record in one focus (e.g., a user) to start with and then select a uses linkage in that record to a record in another focus (e.g., a task). The combined uses linkage information in both of these records can suggest a third (e.g., a data) record, which can be combined to suggest further records (e.g., a tool record). Where no records in a focus are suggested to be linked to the other records currently selected, a browser for that focus can be used to examine whether or not there are any records that should be, but are not currently, linked. The designer can also use browsers in the various foci to browse up or down any "is-a" linkages from existing selected records to investigate the potential for generalization, specialization, or substitution of the various records. The designer then can add, change, or delete linkages or records to produce the desired design and to resolve inconsistencies.

The hypertext implementation of MOST provides a visual representation extending software engineering's domain. It facilitates the translation of externally domain structured knowledge (MOST's informal specifications) into an internal form suitable for manipulation by a software engineering expert system to be developed. Use of hypertext browsers with MOST assist the software engineer in visualizing the relationships between particular records and the rest of the knowledge base. By facilitating the simultaneous viewing of multiple (potentially interlinked) records, a hypertext interface to MOST provides a synergistic view of the currently acquired knowledge that can guide the software engineer in both the gathering of further knowledge and the use of existing knowledge.

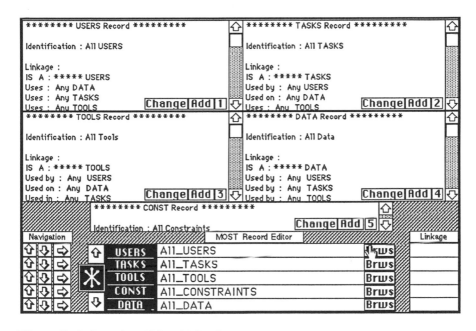

Figure 7. A Sample MOST-CASE Screen

A variety of software engineering techniques can be integrated within MOST so that they are invoked only when requested or when absolutely necessary so as to avoid disturbing the software engineer's trend of thought. When invoked, they provide "a basis for effective integration between expert and expert system, with the human expert continuing to have the role of managing the inductive process" as suggested by Gaines (1988).

Work is currently under way to expand the editing capabilities in MOST-CASE prior to its release to support the MOST methodology. In the next generation of the MOST project, we will develop knowledge analysis routines to provide expert software engineering and human factors engineering advice to the analyst/designer using MOST-CASE. We will start with the inheritance of informal specifications and move to transforming informal to formal specifications.

References

Borigida, A., Greenspan, S., and Mylopoulos, J., 1985. Knowledge Representation as the Basis for Requirements Specification, *Computer,* April, pp. 82-90.

Carter, J., 1990a. The Dimensions and Degrees of Adaptation: A Synergistic Analysis, *Proceedings of the 34th Annual Meeting of the Human Factors Society,* October, pp. 336-340.

Carter, J., 1990b. Juggling Concern for Completeness and Consistency With Concerns for Flexibility and Adaptability Using MOST, Proceedings of the 34th Annual Meeting of the Human Factors Society, October, pp. 341-345.

Carter, J.A. and Hancock, J.P., 1991. A Context for Designing Adaptations: The Multi-Oriented Structured Task Analysis (MOST) Methodology, to appear in *SIGCHI Bulletin.*

Coad, P. and Yourdon, E., 1990. *Object-Oriented Analysis,* Yourdon Press, Englewood Cliffs, NJ.

Conklin, J., 1987. Hypertext: An Introduction and Survey, *Computer,* September, pp. 17-41.

Conklin, J., 1989, Design Rationale and Maintainability. *Proceedings of the 22nd HICCS.*

Conklin, J. and Begeman, M.L., 1989, gIBIS: A Tool for All Reasons. *Journal of the American Society for Information Science.*

Coutaz, J., 1987. PAC, An Object Oriented Model for Dialog Design, *Human-Computer Interaction: Interact'87,* North-Holland, pp. 431-436.

Foley, J.D. and Van Dam, A., 1982. Fundamentals of Interactive Computer Graphics, Addison-Wesley Publishing Company, Reading, MA.

Foley, J.D., Kim, W.C., and Gibbs, C.A., 1987. Algorithms to Transform the Formal Specifications of a User-Computer Interface, *Human- Computer Interaction: Interact'87,* North-Holland, pp. 1001-1006.

Gane, C. and Sarson, T., 1979. Structured Systems Analysis, Prentice-Hall, Englewood Cliffs.

Gaines, B.R., 1988. Knowledge Acquisition and Technology. Boose, J.H. and Gaines, B.R. (Eds) *Proceedings of the Third AAAI Knowledge Acquisiton for Knowledge Based Systems Workshop.* pp. 8-1 - 8-20, Banff.

Green, M., 1984. Report on Dialogue Specification Tools. Pfaff, G.E. (Ed) User Interface Management Systems, Springer-Verlag, Berlin, pp. 9-20.

HFSHCISG, 1989a, Human Factors Society Human Computer Interactions Standards Group meeting held at Santa Clara, CA, January 11-13.

HFSHCISG, 1989b, Human Factors Society Human Computer Interactions Standards Group Draft Document on the Design Process.

Jacob, R.L.K., 1983. Using Formal Specifications in the Design of a Human-Computer Interface, *Communications of the ACM*, April, Vol. 26, No. 4, pp. 259-264.

Jacobson, C. and Freiling, M.J., 1987, ASTEK: A Multi-Paradigm Knowledge Acquisition Tool for Complex Structured Knowledge. Boose, J.H. and Gaines, B.R. (Eds) *Proc. 2nd AAAI Knowledge Acquisition for Knowledge Based Systems Workshop.* pp. 11-0 - 11-19, Banff.

Kitto, C.M., 1988, Progress in Automated Knowledge Acquisition Tools: How Close Are We to Replacing the Knowledge Engineer? Boose, J.H. and Gaines, B.R. (Eds) *Proc. 3rd AAAI Knowledge Acquisition for Knowledge Based Systems Workshop.* pp. 14-1 - 14-13, Banff.

Moran, T.P., 1981. The Command Language Grammar: a Representation for the User Interface of Interactive Computer Systems, International Journal of Man-Machine Studies, 15:3-50.

Moran, T. P., 1983. Getting Into a System: External-Internal Task Mapping Analysis, *CHI'83 Proceedings,* pp. 45-49.

Munsen, M.A., Fagan, D.M., Combs, D.M., Shortliffe, E.H., 1986, Using a Domain Model to Drive an Interactive Knowledge Editing Tool. Boose, J.H. and Gaines, B.R. (Eds) *Proc. AAAI Knowledge Acquisition for Knowledge Based Systems Workshop.* pp. 33-0 - 33-11, Banff.

Olle, T.W., Sol, H.G., and Verrijn-Stuart, A.A. (eds), 1982. Information System Design Methodologies: A Comparative Review, North-Holland, Amsterdam.

Olle, T.W., Sol, H.G., and Tully, C.J. (eds), 1983. Information System Design Methodologies: A Feature Analysis, North-Holland, Amsterdam.

Preece, J., Woodman, M., Ince, D.C., Griffiths, R., and Davies, G., 1987. Towards a Structured Approach to Specifying User Interface Design, *Human-Computer Interaction: Interact'87,* North-Holland, pp. 415-421.

Pressman, R.S., 1987, *Software Engineering,* McGraw-Hill, New York, NY.

Roman, G.-C., 1985. A Taxonomy of Current Issues In Requirements Engineering, *Computer*, April, pp. 14-22.

Rosson, M.B., Maass, S., and Kellogg, W.A., 1988. The Designer as User: Building Requirements for Design Tools from Design Practice, *Communications of the ACM*, November, Vol. 31, No. 11, pp. 1288-1298.

Rubenstein, R. and Hersh, H., 1984. *The Human Factor: Designing Computer Systems for People,* Digital Press, Maynard, MA.

Schweighardt, M.F., 1990. Facilitating Adaptation While Controlling its Consistency With a Context Management System, *Proceedings of the 34th Annual Meeting of the Human Factors Society,* October, pp. 346-350.

Sharratt, B.D., 1987. Top-Down Interactive Systems Design: Some Lessons Learnt From Using Command Language Grammar, *Human- Computer Interaction: Interact'87,* North-Holland, pp. 395-399.

Shemer, I., 1987. Systems Analysis: A Systemic Analysis of a Conceptual Model, *Communications of the ACM,* June, Vol. 30 No. 6, pp. 506-512.

Tsai, J.J-P. and Ridge, J.C., 1988. Intelligent Support for Specification Transformation, *IEEE Software*, November, pp. 28-35.

Wasserman, A.I., 1985. Developing Interactive Information Systems With the User Software Engineering Methodology, Human-Computer Interaction: Interact'84, North-Holland, pp. 611-617.

Yourdon, E. and Constantine, L.L., 1979. Structured Design, Prentice-Hall, Englewood Cliffs.

12 PRODUSER: PROcess for Developing USER Interfaces

M. GREGORY JAMES

University of California
Irvine, CA

I. Motivation

Although tremendous advances have been made in the study of human computer interaction in areas such as user modelling, graphical interaction, and user interface management systems, there is still no clear prescription for actually designing a user interface. Several high-level models have been proposed that address the important cognitive relationships between users and computers (Card, Moran, & Newell, 1983; Norman, 1984; Shneiderman, 1980) and that identify critical issues on which developers should focus when creating user interfaces (Foley, & Van Dam, 1982; Shneiderman, 1987). However, there has been less work on refining and elaborating these models into specific sequences of development steps. This leaves the novice or intermediate user interface developer with little guidance on *how* to develop user interfaces.

Taking Software
Design Seriously

235

Research in software engineering has focused a great deal of effort on understanding how to develop software. There are numerous examples of process models that have been created and used in the construction of various systems (Balzer, Cheatham, & Green, 1983; Benington, 1987; Bischofberger, & Keller, 1989; McCracken, & Jackson, 1982; Royce, 1987). Each of these models addresses various aspects of software development with different degrees of effectiveness. Unfortunately, all of these models are lacking in their ability to help user interface developers construct better user interfaces.

The solution to both problems may be found in a marriage of software engineering process modelling with the user-centered advances in human computer interaction research: Process models can provide the rigor and structure for integrating the human-computer interaction advances. Together, these two disciplines can guide developers in the design and construction of the user interface aspects of a software system.

PRODUSER (PROcess for Developing USER-interfaces) is such a marriage. PRODUSER defines a framework for integrating, coordinating, and focusing existing and future human-computer interaction research. The sections below are a discussion of PRODUSER and its development. PRODUSER is intended to serve as a demonstration that by applying software modelling to user interface development, an explicit, understandable, generally applicable, and evaluatable process for developing user interfaces can be created, which, when supported by a development environment, is easy and powerful to use and which yields a high quality user interface for a given software system.

II. Overview

PRODUSER consists of a process for developing a broad range of user interfaces and an environment for supporting the execution of the process. It is particularly appropriate for medium and large scale software systems because of the significant time and effort involved in executing the process. While other processes may be equally valid, PRODUSER provides a means for representation and a level of detail that have not been previously presented for user interface development. Hopefully many other development processes will also be elaborated and made explicit so that they can all be evaluated for appropriateness and effectiveness. The environment part of PRODUSER is called the *PRODUSER Environment* and together with the process program (the representation for the process) they are referred to as the *PRODUSER System*.

Before describing PRODUSER in detail, some software engineering background must be provided. PRODUSER employs the *spiral model* process model for software development. Section III A. describes the spiral model and why it is a powerful choice for user interface design. Section III B. explains *process programming*, a means for expressing processes, which is used to represent the PRODUSER process.

Section IV describes PRODUSER. Topics include the requirements and design for the PRODUSER process program (after all, a process program is still a program, and therefore it should be developed like one), how the spiral model was adapted to the task of user interface design, a discussion of key implementation issues, a description of the PRODUSER Environment, and a discussion of applying PRODUSER to a medium-sized software system. Finally, section V presents conclusions and outlines work planned for the future.

III. Software Engineering Background

A. *The Spiral Model of Software Development*

The spiral model is a risk-based model of software development that "can accommodate most previous models as special cases and further provide guidance as to which combination of previous models best fits a given software situation" (Boehm, 1988, pp. 64–65). There are several aspects of the spiral model that will benefit user interface development. These will be discussed after a brief overview of the spiral model.

1. Overview

Barry Boehm stated that the "primary functions of a software process model are to determine the *order of the stages* involved in software development and evolution and to establish the *transition criteria* for progressing from one stage to the next" (Boehm, 1988, p. 61). Several process models exist and have been used explicitly or implicitly on many software projects. Probably the best known is the waterfall model (Royce, 1987). Others include the code-and-fix model, the evolutionary development model, the transform model, a prototyping enhancement to life cycle models, and the star model which focuses on user interface development (Balzer, Cheatham, & Green, 1983; Benington, 1987; Bischofberger, & Keller, 1989; Hartson, & Hix, 1989; McCracken, & Jackson, 1982). Phase-based models (such as the waterfall) are more appropriate for developing systems with well-understood capabilities where the challenges are in identifying and specifying the components and interactions (examples include payroll and accounting systems). Evolutionary models (such as prototyping) are best used on systems involving complex interactions (particularly human interaction) where trying the system may be the only way to be sure that it meets the needs of its users (examples include word processing or graphical editor programs). The spiral model is an effort to take advantage of the strengths of existing models and to provide additional support by focusing attention in high risk aspects of development for a given system.

The spiral model can be graphically represented as a spiral starting in the center of the intersection of horizontal and vertical axes and moving clockwise and outward. The horizontal axis represents progress made through each of the steps and the vertical axis represents the cumulative cost of applying the model. A *cycle* is one rotation around the spiral and most of *phases* of development are one cycle long. Figure 1 (in section IV) is a visual representation of the spiral model adapted to user interface development; how it was adapted is discussed in section IV.

One key aspect of the spiral model is the "underlying concept that each cycle involves a progression that addresses the same sequence of steps, for each portion of the product and for each of its levels of elaboration" (Boehm, 1988, p. 65). In other words, regardless of whether one is engaged in a requirements analysis cycle or a coding cycle, one engages in the same sequence of steps. There are four quadrants in the model, as shown in Figure 1. The first is to determine the objectives, alternatives, and constraints for the cycle. Secondly, the alternatives are evaluated in terms of identifying and resolving the risks. Next, the product for the cycle is developed and verified. Finally, the next cycle is planned and must be committed to by those controlling the project before it is initiated.

There are four phases in the standard spiral model: (1) the initial project concepts and purpose, (2) the software requirements, (3) the software product design, and (4) the detailed design, coding, and testing leading to the implementation. Since this is a fairly standard set of steps in a software process model, no further detail will be provided here.

Boehm explains how "the spiral model can accommodate most previous models as special cases" (Boehm, 1988, p. 64) of the spiral model by adjusting the use of the model to meet the needs of a particular project. If a project has many high-risk issues, then an evolutionary approach to development using a series of prototypes may be useful. The emphasis would be on developing prototypes of increased reliability and utility, and there would be less effort spent on developing complete specifications of each aspect of the project. In a less risky project, a more traditional waterfall model can be the most beneficial in that it requires the emphasis on specifying the interfaces and design for the software. In this case, there would be little effort spent on evaluating the risk items and much on the product development phases of each cycle. For more information on the spiral model, see Boehm's original article (Boehm, 1988); (Boehm, & Belz, 1988) identifies some enhancements to the model. Boehm's tutorial on risk management (Boehm, 1989) provides a comprehensive examination of that topic.

2. Advantages for User Interface Design

Boehm described several advantages to the spiral model (Boehm, 1988). These same advantages make a case for why the spiral model is the most appropriate model to apply to user interface development. Note that in its original form, as was stated previously, it does not sufficiently address the topic of user interface development; however, it can be adapted to focus on this topic in a significantly beneficial manner. The first advantage is that the spiral model can behave like other process models, if warranted. For example, in low risk situations with a well understood set of capabilities, applying the spiral model is much like applying a traditional waterfall model. In situations of higher risk, the model acts like an evolutionary model. It does not have the evaluation-centered structure of the star model; however, there is an emphasis on assessing risk, evaluating alternatives, and regular evaluation. In addition, the spiral model provides more guidance as to the relationships among the phases and mechanisms of development more effectively than the star model, particularly for larger projects. Moreover, the spiral model can employ various development techniques such as automated software generation or formal product development directly. Of course, usually there will be a combination of these abilities and needs, which the spiral model can also handle. This flexibility is as important when developing user interfaces as it is when developing software products, and therefore the spiral model is an excellent choice for user interface development.

A second major contribution of the spiral model is the emphasis on *software risk management*. Software risk management allocates the most resources to the development decisions that it identifies as having the highest a priori probability of being wrong, or having the highest cost if made incorrectly, or the lowest expected utility. For example, a standard problem in user interface design is making certain that a particular presentation of capabilities is appropriate for those who will be using the system. Prototyping is a common method for modifying the presentation in response to users' evaluations before the designers commit many resources to any particular presentation. User interface development is especially vulnerable to high risk so incorporating risk management directly in the process model is especially appropriate. Prototyping is just one of many techniques available for reducing risk; for a complete tutorial, see (Boehm, 1989).

Other advantages of the spiral model include an early focus on reuse when identifying alternative choices for a particular decision, an integrated mechanism for evaluating both hardware and software alternatives during the same process, allowance for expected changes during the life of the product by identifying this as an objective early in the process, and efficient resource allocation. Each of these advantages is important to user interface development.

B. Process Programming

Osterweil observed that software developers "develop and evolve so large, complex, and intangible an object as a large software system without the aid of suitably visible, detailed and formal descriptions of how to proceed" (Osterweil, 1987, p. 6). Process programming is one technique for addressing this problem. The first subsection below contains a definition and description of process programming, and the following subsection identifies the advantages of process programming for user interface design.

1. Overview

To begin with, one must assume that one employs processes in order to accomplish various tasks. A process can be defined as a complete specification of all of the activities necessary to perform a certain task. This includes the decisions to be made, the sequencing among the decisions, the relationships among the decisions, the objects or products used in or produced by the process, and the relationships among the objects or products. Processes may be private, particular to a small group, or public and broadly defined, but usually they are not explicitly represented. Instead, they are either in a person's mind, part of the local folklore, or written in a procedural manual, which may not be accessible, legible, or comprehensible. This can be a problem if one wants to analyze a process for quality, convey a process to another person, or simply modify a process to accommodate new parameters.

Process programming is one answer to this set of problems. Process programming is "the activity of expressing software process descriptions with the aid of programming techniques" (Osterweil, 1987, p. 4). There are several gains from applying programming (in the traditional computer programming sense) to the problems of process description. First, the description is formal and, therefore, analyzable. Second, the important objects that must be created are identified and defined explicitly. Third, accounting for future changes and enhancements is a natural capability, because modifiability is at the foundation of programming. Fourth, reusing various aspects of a process is possible because of the formality of the representation. Fifth, there is a possibility that various parts of the process can be automated, in the sense of being directly compilable and executable on a computer. Finally, the simple fact that the process is explicitly represented allows for enhanced communication about the process among various people.

One of the elements distinguishing process programming and traditional programming is the ability of the former to invoke human beings as processors. This allows the process phases that are difficult to express to a computer to be left to humans. This is a powerful capability, but it can be abused. For example, there are many aspects of a set of requirements for a software system that cannot be programmed in a general way to handle all specific cases. Therefore, there must be many places in a process program for doing requirements that would require a human decision. Since the process for building requirements is so human intensive, there is a temptation to collect all the requirements generation into a single, simple, function call on a human. While this may be convenient for the process programmer, it does not help the human processor define the requirements. A more useful process would include guidance as to what decisions need to be made about requirements and what the relationships among those decisions should be. Then, with this structure in place, the human processor can be polled for a decision.

A key research task is identification of the characteristics of a language that would be useful for process programming. One theory is that there must be several domain-specific languages. Another is that one language should be developed that has all the capabilities that will ever be needed to handle multiple domains. In the interim, process programmers can either define their own domain-specific languages by defining the constructs necessary to meet their needs, or they can use an existing process programming language, such as APPL/A (Sutton, 1989; Sutton, Heimbigner, & Osterweil, 1988), to help evaluate whether this process programming language can be used in the developer's particular domain.

2. Advantages for User Interface Design

Most of the advantages of process programming for user interface development are the same as the advantages for software engineering. Developing a user interface for a medium to large scale system is a challenging and complex activity. Those engaging in this activity can employ many different processes and different kinds of processes in order to accomplish this task. Although there have been some examples of successful user interfaces and, therefore, successful processes, none of these processes has been recorded in detail. Therefore, these processes are difficult to repeat, evaluate and improve, communicate to others, and directly support with tools or automation. Process programming provides a mechanism for recording processes in detail so that these difficulties can be addressed. In addition, processes or parts of processes can be reused.

Two things are *not* true about process programming. First, it does not suggest that there will be only one correct process for any given activity. On the contrary, it provides a means for identifying several processes for any given activity and then evaluating the processes to understand the best uses and circumstances for choosing one over another or how to modify existing processes and create new ones for evolving needs. Second, process programming does not limit the scope or content of any particular process program or set of process programs. For example, it does not suggest that user interfaces processes must be representable in a Pascal-like language and performed in a sequential and procedural fashion. The claim of process programming is that by explicitly representing processes, the processes can be improved. Therefore, whether the representation mechanism is Pascal-like, Prolog-like, or somewhere in between, the benefits can still be realized.

IV. The PRODUSER System

PRODUSER is a process for the development of user interfaces based on the spiral model of software development and represented as a process program. Issues of coordinating with a software project, modelling the users of the system, evaluating and incorporating the most current technology, and choosing abstract and eventually concrete representations of a system's capabilities are all addressed in the process program. Even if PRODUSER's process is not the one and only process for user interface development, it is a detailed and concrete representation of *a* process, which can then be analyzed, debated, modified, and enhanced.

A. *Requirements*

The concept of requirements for PRODUSER is a combination of what Richard Fairley calls *system definition* and *software requirements definition* (Fairley, 1985). The system definition is produced during the planning phase of a project and addresses such issues as defining the problem to be solved, determining goals of the project, and noting constraints on the system. "The goal of software requirements definition is to completely and consistently specify the technical requirements for the software product in a concise and unambiguous manner, using formal notations as appropriate." (Fairley, 1985, p. 88) All of these activities are referred to as *requirements* for PRODUSER.

In order to define the requirements, one must consider what capabilities the system should provide and why (not how they will be provided) and what contributions the system should make besides the set of capabilities identified (studying new research issues, solving a problem in a new way, providing a better and faster solution to previous approaches, etc.). The following subsections contain the requirements for PRODUSER.

1. Define a Process Model for Developing User Interfaces

A process model identifies the phases of development for a process, the basic sequencing within and among the phases, and the products produced in each phase. Such models provide guidance and a framework for developing software systems and are dramatically lacking in the field of user interface development. A user interface development process model could help organize and focus the field of human-computer interaction research and, if it is used as the basis for PRODUSER's process, it would increase the general applicability of the process. Since PRODUSER is an effort to provide a framework for HCI research, developing an explicit process model is a logical requirement.

Many kinds of process models exist, each with various strengths and weaknesses. In the design section, one particular model will be selected and justified. Of course, it may be that using process models, or one process model in particular, is not as useful as one might expect, but even that information would be useful to know. By choosing one approach and elaborating it to the point of being able to apply it to the development of specific user interfaces, it can be determined which aspects of the model are useful and which are not. Then the model can be modified, or new models can be evaluated, and a better, more appropriate model can be developed.

2. Incorporate Risk Management in the Model

One of the biggest problems facing user interface development is the question of how useful and well-received a new interface will be. Often, a great deal of time and resource are invested in developing a well thought out and powerful interface, only to find out that the users of the system had something completely different in mind. At that point it is very difficult and expensive to change the interface, and the project may have to be abandoned.

A well-known means of minimizing this problem is to prototype a system before all of the time and energy have been invested in developing a complete product. While this is useful and a good idea, there are other ways of reducing the risk in developing a bad user interface. Other examples of risk reduction techniques include staffing, team building, cost and schedule estimation, and incremental development, among many others. *Risk management* provides a framework for locating and controlling or reducing risks. It is only recently being studied for software engineering and appears not yet to have been applied to user interface development. This is unfortunate since user interface development is especially vulnerable to bad decisions. Therefore, a fundamental requirement of PRODUSER is to incorporate risk management into its process in order to improve the quality of user interfaces.

3. Develop and Explicitly Record a Process from the Process Model

Subsection IV A 1. defines the term *process model*. While a process model and a process appear to have a great deal in common, a process will be defined for PRODUSER as a complete specification of all of the activities necessary to perform a certain task. This includes the decisions to be made, the sequencing among the decisions, the relationships among the decisions, the object classes that must be defined, and the relationships among the classes. Classes can be either those that record decisions or those that are the end product of engaging in the process: the specification of the user interface.

The task for PRODUSER's process is that of developing user interfaces. Since the process model that will satisfy the requirement specified in section IV A 1. will define the phases and products for each phase for user interface development, then it should serve as the structure for the PRODUSER process. While this may sound like a design decision (how should the process be structured), it is actually a requirement for

PRODUSER: the process must be derived from the model. The reason this is important is so that both the model and the process can be evaluated for correctness and utility. If the two were inconsistent with each other, then it would not be possible to make a case that both were correct.

An additional requirement of the process is that it be recorded in a concrete manner. Without concreteness, it would be difficult to assess its quality, communicate it, or modify it. Since the process is a fundamental component of PRODUSER, it is important that it be explicit, understandable, and evaluatable.

4. Allow the Process to Apply to Small and Large Scale Projects

One of the challenges is to create a process that is easy to use and cheap enough for small projects and powerful enough for large ones. This is not a new problem, nor has it been solved very often. PRODUSER's primary focus is the larger projects — systems requiring significant, creative, and intensive human-computer interaction. However, perhaps with a strong support environment that is helpful, logical, flexible, and powerful PRODUSER may be applicable to smaller projects as well.

5. Incremental Gain for Incremental Investment

Using the complete PRODUSER process program requires a great many resources, including people to perform many tasks, time to research, explore, and resolve the high-risk issues, and computer support both to record the information collected and to support prototyping and simulations. However, this research effort is based on the contention that this investment will result in an effective, powerful user interface that is well-received by users. Moreover, if the investment is made in the early stages of the project, rather than throughout its life, as has been done traditionally, the investment will be much more cost effective with PRODUSER than without.

There may be situations where a user interface developer has a fairly good idea of what he or she wants in an interface but would just like some help in making sure that no major issues have been left out. For example, he or she may not be concerned with all of the risk management that PRODUSER encourages or may not want to do complete evaluations of the various user interface products. As long as he or she realizes that PRODUSER may not produce the same degree of success if shortcuts are taken, it would be desirable for PRODUSER to offer some shortcuts. In other words, PRODUSER should be flexible enough to help even those users who do not wish to use the full set of capabilities. Without this flexibility, users may be afraid to use PRODUSER because of the investment of time and energy. Clearly it is a goal for PRODUSER to be used, and therefore every effort ought to be made to provide capabilities that will increase PRODUSER's user population.

6. Focus on Early Phases of User Interface Development

PRODUSER is based on the contention that developing the user interface for a software system is a subtask of developing the entire system. However, it is an important subset that is not well understood, will dramatically affect a software system (especially if done improperly), and has its own set of challenges that are not faced in any other subsets. Therefore, this subset is worthy of special attention, which is one reason PRODUSER is important.

A related assumption is that the unique challenges of user interface development are primarily those found in considering the requirements and specification (or design) of the user interface. The actual implementation of a user interface involves the same tasks and skills necessary as implementing the rest of a software system. PRODUSER will focus on the requirements and specification of the user interface, because that is where the largest benefit will be realized. Although it is certainly true that the implementation can affect the specification (for which PRODUSER must allow), the problems of implementation are not as specific to user interface development.

B. Design, Implementation, and Use

While a significant amount of progress has been made on the design and implementation of the PRODUSER system, it is still a work in progress. As such, some of the design and much of the implementation has not yet been completely fleshed out. In spite of this, PRODUSER has been used on one example. This section will present the current state of the design, the implementation strategy, and a description of applying PRODUSER to a software system.

PRODUSER is composed of two major parts: (1) a process that is represented as a process program and derived from PRODUSER's process model, and (2) the PRODUSER Environment that will consist of several support tools for developing user interfaces. The structure of PRODUSER's process is taken directly from an adaptation of the spiral model to user interface development that serves as PRODUSER's process model; this adaptation is discussed in section IV B 1. Section IV B 2. discusses the PRODUSER Environment and the four tools currently planned. Most of the implementation is not yet available; however section IV B 3. describes the plan for PRODUSER's implementation. Section IV B 4. is a discussion of applying PRODUSER to a medium-sized software system under development, namely PRODUSER.

1. PRODUSER's Process

Section III A 2. presents a discussion as to why the spiral model is an excellent choice to serve as a basis for developing a process model for developing user interfaces. Figure 1 is a visual representation of such a process model hereafter referred to as PRODUSER's process model. There were two major influences on the selection or identification of the phases for PRODUSER's process model. First was the original spiral model's phases, which correspond to the traditional software engineering development phases. Second, Foley and Van Dam's language model (Foley, & Van Dam, 1982) and, in as much as it is similar, Shneiderman's syntactic/semantic model (Shneiderman, 1980; Shneiderman, 1987) were strong influences. The nature of these influences will be described after the phases are identified.

There are three phases in PRODUSER's process model. First is the *Requirements*. This phase is for identifying the general input and output capabilities for the user interface, developing a model of the expected users of the system, and identifying technical constraints that will impact decisions about the user interface. The second phase is the *Abstract Specification* phase. Activities during this phase include organizing the input and output capabilities into an appropriate structure for the user interface and identifying the parameters for each, selecting and defining the interaction mechanisms that will be employed, and determining the appropriate style or styles of interaction. The third and final phase is the *Concrete Specification*. This phase provides a complete specification of the user interface by attaching the user interface capabilities to instances of the abstract interaction mechanisms in a manner governed by the styles of interaction. After the Concrete Specification is complete, the user interface is completely defined.

In order to see the first influence on the model, one can think of the three phases of PRODUSER's model as being analogous to the requirements, preliminary design, and detailed design that are part of most traditional software development life-cycle models. As in the case of software models, once the detailed design (or Concrete Specifications) are complete, then the next phase is implementation. Foley and Van Dam's language model suggest that users interact with user interfaces at several different levels, all of which need to be addressed in the design. The levels they discuss are conceptual, semantic, syntactic, and lexical. If the last two were to be combined, then these three phases would directly correlate to PRODUSER's three phases. It is interesting to note that although these influences appear to be derived from quite different domains, they turn out to be quite similar to each other. In any case, both appear to be relatively well accepted within their domains, and, therefore, the three phases of PRODUSER's model appear to be derived from solid foundations.

Because PRODUSER's process model is based on the spiral model with the intent of benefiting from the advantages of that model, it seems only logical to use the same steps in PRODUSER's model as were used on the original software model. Therefore, the identities and sequences of steps in PRODUSER's process model are plan, determine the objectives, alternatives, and constraints, assess and then control the risk, develop the

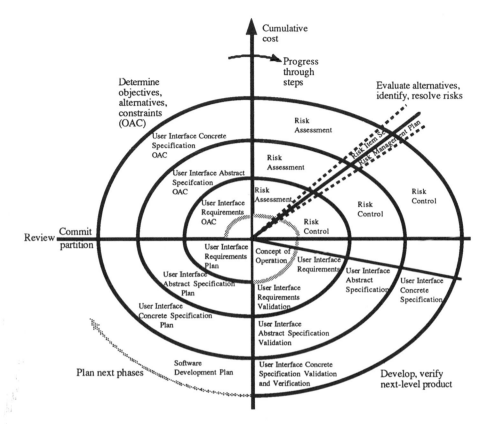

Figure 1. Adaptation of the spiral model to user interface development.

product, and then validate the product for each of the three phases. The general activity in most of these steps is fairly clear from the name.

The planning step produces a plan for development for each phase. Determining the objectives, alternatives, and constraints step will yield a prioritized list of each of these. Assessing the risk will result in a risk item set, while controlling the risk will begin by producing a risk management plan and will end by recording the results of the risk reduction techniques employed and how they will affect the development of the user interface. All of the products described so far use the same structure for each phase of development.

Producing the phase's product results in the phase's product being defined. Not surprisingly, each phase will produce a different kind of product, that will each be referred to by the same name as the phase during which it was developed. The evaluation phase produces a version of the phase's product that has been modified according to the results of the evaluation.

Since PRODUSER's process is represented as a process program, then for all intents and purposes the process program is PRODUSER's process. The major components and object classes are derived directly from PRODUSER's process model. The process program incorporates concurrency, structured revisiting of previous activities as necessary for redesign, and consists of a hierarchy of objects for storing the specification of the user interface. Further discussion would require examining the detailed design and the actual code of the process program.

2. PRODUSER Environment

PRODUSER's process provides user interface developers with the definition of how to proceed through the activity of developing a user interface. What is not addressed in the process itself is how to handle the myriad of administrative details nor what assistance and support capabilities are available to the developer. The PRODUSER Environment addresses these needs. In this subsection, all of the capabilities envisioned for the environment will be described, including some of which will be developed for the first version and others that require further research before they can be realized.

Plans for version 1.0 include a structured data object editor, a graphical object editor, and a set of feedback mechanisms that provide visual and textual feedback about the state of PRODUSER and the currently executing process. Later versions are expected to have a comprehensive help and tutorial subsystem, a risk management support environment, the data collection and evaluation system that is part of Arcadia (called Amadeus), and a user interface evaluation system that will provide static and dynamic evaluation of a current user interface as far as it is defined.

PRODUSER guides user interface developers in the activity of specifying a user interface, which is recorded in the PRODUSER objects. The *Structured Data Object Director* assists in the task of recording values in the objects. It allows developers to move through the objects they want to define, to input and manipulate values using a keyboard, mouse, and function keys, and to validate values based on the data type of the field in which they appear.

The *Graphical Object Director* allows users to conveniently and efficiently create and manipulate the graphical aspects of a user interface. While not all interfaces include graphics, the trend today is toward a dominance of graphical user interfaces. It is expected that the Graphical Object Director will be used both to define abstract interaction mechanisms as well as component collections (screen shots). The Graphical Object Editor provides developers with predefined user interface components to which they can attach behaviors. (Behaviors will be programmed in the first version; in later versions there may be more sophisticated means of defining behaviors.) They can also use more generic, predefined objects or plain bit manipulation in order to define graphics to which they can attach behavior. Because there are behaviors involved, developers are likely to want to test their creations, and so they can request that an object or set of objects be prototyped, which will execute the behavior dynamically. Finally, rather than starting from scratch, there may be previous graphical objects that a developer or his or her colleagues have created. This object library can be browsed and objects copied from it in order to prevent having to start from scratch.

There are four feedback mechanisms that are planned for the PRODUSER Environment. While each is rather simple, and the user can choose to have them displayed or hidden, they can provide useful information about the state of the system. The first, called *Executive PRODUSER – State of the Model*, is a visual representation of PRODUSER's process model, which is highlighted to indicate how far a developer has proceeded through the model at the current moment. The second, called *Executive PRODUSER – State of the Process*, is an expanded visual representation of the flow of control of the process program. This representation indicates which processes are currently active, which ones have been visited already and are dormant, which ones have not yet been visited at all, and how many times each of the paths have been travelled, which serves as a history of what and how much revisiting has been done. The third feedback mechanism is a simple representation of the physical function keys that indicates what functions or capabilities are attached to each (since developers will be able to attach whatever capability they want to whatever function key they want, this representation needs to be dynamic rather than static). Finally, there is a message window that displays the current messages for all of the active tools in one location. While each tool has its own, attached message area, this central location allows for all messages to be displayed even if all of the tools are not.

The other four subsystems for the PRODUSER Environment are not as well defined as these. In fact, some of them are not even well enough understood in the research community to know how such systems should even work. However, with each of these systems in place, PRODUSER would include an environment unparalleled in capability for user interface development. Therefore, these systems are part of PRODUSER's future, but the details of their capabilities are rather sparse at this time.

Assistant PRODUSER is the equivalent to a help system. However, besides providing context specific help about how to work with a particular tool or what type of information is required in a given field of an object, it also will provide tutorial assistance on how to develop user interfaces. When a developer is not sure what options are available to them or what the strengths and weaknesses of the options are for a particular section of PRODUSER's object hierarchy, the tutorial can provide them with the current research on this area. It will not so much tell them what to do as give them the alternatives and let them decide which is best for their needs.

The *Safety Inspector* is an environment for performing risk management. It provides help on selecting risk reduction options, assists in the setting up of those risk management techniques that require computer assistance, and helps record the results of risk reduction activities.

Accountant is the data collection and evaluation capability. In fact, the Accountant that will be used first is named Amadeus and is part of the Arcadia system. It provides for automatic data collection during the execution of a process or tool, as specified by the Amadeus users. This data can then be evaluated in various ways to improve the functioning of the process or tool. For PRODUSER, it would be especially desirable if this could not only be used for evaluating PRODUSER and the PRODUSER Environment, but also for the user interfaces created by PRODUSER.

Critic is a user interface evaluation system. It will take as input the user interface specification in its current state and evaluate it in terms of consistency, completeness, and correctness, according to the Requirements part of the specification. In addition, it is a goal for Critic to be able to evaluate the user interface in terms of current research trends and a qualitative assessment of the interface.

3. PRODUSER's Implementation

PRODUSER is implemented as a process program not a traditional program. Therefore, it is reasonable to expect that PRODUSER's process program must be executed in an environment that supports process execution. Arcadia (Taylor et al., 1988) is an example of a process-based environment that supports many software development activities. It will serve as the platform upon which PRODUSER will run.

Arcadia is focusing on the components and interfaces that are necessary in order to support software development. Some of the fundamental components include an object manager, a user interface manager, a process interpreter, and a data collection and evaluation manager. Domain-specific systems or applications can be constructed on top of these components to support all facets of software development. PRODUSER is one of these systems. PRODUSER's process program can be interpreted by the interpreter, its objects are managed by the object manger, human-computer interaction is done through the UIMS, and data can be collected for evaluation through the data collection and evaluation manager. PRODUSER's Environment is a suite of tools that will be managed by Arcadia to be used as the process program is executing. This is the basic implementation plan for the PRODUSER system (Figure 2).

4. Applying PRODUSER to PRODUSER

Although the entire PRODUSER system is not yet up and running (see section IV C.), it is still important to try to obtain an early evaluation of the usefulness of the fundamental ideas proposed in PRODUSER. A preliminary version of the PRODUSER

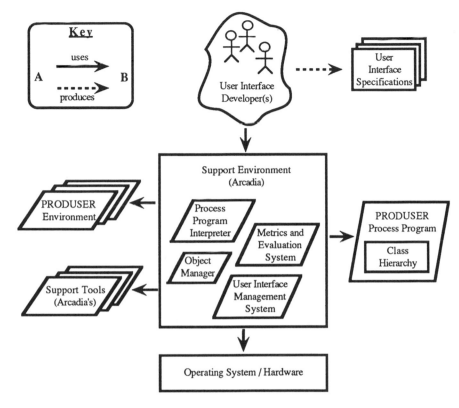

Figure 2. Overview of the major components of the PRODUSER system.

process program has been completed. This process program was hand executed on the PRODUSER system itself. The primary purpose of this activity was to determine what it is like to use PRODUSER. It will be important in the near future to evaluate the benefits of PRODUSER, as opposed to alternative user interface development processes and support environments (see section V), but that will not be the topic in this section.

Using PRODUSER to develop a user interface is analogous to using a travel agent to plan a driving vacation. The agent can provide maps indicating how to get from one place to another, lists of hotels, restaurants, and places to visit along the way, but it is up to the traveler to decide what route to take, where to stay, what to eat, and what to do. It is the collection of the traveler's decisions that determine the characteristics and contents of the vacation. PRODUSER provides user interface developers with direction and a framework of decisions, but it is still up to the developer to actually make the decisions that lead to the construction of the user interface.

Applying PRODUSER to PRODUSER meant starting at the beginning of the process program and moving through the various phases of development. Nearly 100 pages of specification were generated during this activity. This section will identify some of the issues that are addressed during the process and some examples of the decisions that were made.

The first phase was to identify the requirements for the system. This means identifying all of the input and output capabilities for the software system, identifying the characteristics or a model of the expected users of the system, and recording any constraints that will be imposed on the user interface. For this application, the capabilities are those previously identified as version 1.0 of PRODUSER, namely the structured data editor, the graphical editor, and the feedback of the current state information. Users were identified as being heavy users of the system for concentrated periods of time, not necessarily people with extensive software development expertise but usually with some expertise about the system for which the user interface was being developed. One example of a constraint is that Arcadia is planning to adopt the OPEN LOOK user interface. Since PRODUSER will execute within Arcadia, in order to be consistent, it should also conform to the OPEN LOOK standards.

Phase two of the PRODUSER process required detailed specifications of the input and output capabilities, identification of general styles of interaction, and selection of hardware and software components to be used for the concrete specification. PRODUSER reminded the developer that the second and third of these is constrained by OPEN LOOK. In particular, OPEN LOOK uses a direct manipulation, graphically based interface, and it defines a number of generic interaction components. These were directly included as part of the abstract specification.

The detailed specifications required making precise decisions about the capabilities of the software system. For example, when manipulating a line of text in the structured editor, will there be separate commands for move, copy, and delete? Or only a copy command with an option to delete or keep the source? And when recalling the line of text, should there be both insert and overlay commands? Or one place text command with a preset option of inserting or deleting? Note that all of these capabilities are provided by the software system; the issue is how to provide users with access to them. The choices are made based on the needs of the user as determined in the requirements phase. In these examples, performance is expected to be a more important criteria than learnability. In addition, it was decided in the requirements that users are likely to get used to working with one style or another (such as insert or overlay). Therefore, the number of commands was kept streamlined: there is a copy command with a delete option and a place text command.

Although the abstract specification phase of PRODUSER precisely defined the capabilities and general interaction components of the system, the two are not connected until the concrete specification phase. It is during this phase that commands are placed on software and hardware buttons, groups of commands are organized into windows or subwindows, and the high level organization of the user interface is put into place. These decisions are influenced by the constraints identified in the requirements and the organization of capabilities and style of interactions identified in the abstract specification. This is also the phase that will require extensive risk management, particularly prototyping, to assist in the verification of the decisions.

C. Current Status

Version 1.0 of PRODUSER consists of a process program that is written in an Ada-based language. The primary purpose for this version was to create the first process program in a free-form language that could accommodate any needs that might arise. However, there is no compiler or interpreter for this language, so the version 1.0 process program cannot be executed. Version 2.0 will be written in APPL/A (Sutton, 1989; Sutton, Heimbigner, & Osterweil, 1988). APPL/A (A Process Programming Language based on Ada) is formally defined and an APPL/A to Ada translator, called APT, is working and available to PRODUSER. In order to manage the more sophisticated relation capabilities defined in APPL/A, an object manager must be employed. Triton is an object manager that can support APPL/A. A working version of Triton exists and is available to PRODUSER. APPL/A, APT, and Triton are all part of the Arcadia environment.

At this time, there is no PRODUSER Environment. As was discussed previously, the environment can be divided into a version 1.0 or *minimal* environment and a *complete* environment. The minimal environment would only include the structured data editor and the graphical editor, along with some degree of graphical state feedback. The complete environment would be the minimal environment plus everything else defined in section IV B 2. above. For the short term, only the implementation of the minimal environment is being considered. In particular, two implementation options have been identified. First, the tools in the environment could be built from scratch in order to maximize interoperability and the exact set of available capabilities. Second, existing tools could be tied together, since there are many existing tools that serve nearly identical functions.

V. Conclusions and Future Work

PRODUSER addresses a problem that is in desperate need of a solution: the need for a framework to incorporate the significant advances in human-computer interaction research. While HCI research has yielded many powerful results, most of the focus has been on small, isolated aspects of the problem. PRODUSER focuses on the large problem of user interface development. It does not attempt to define a new, definitive, unique process. Instead, it suggests a process, based on existing work, that can serve as a framework to integrate the representations, the design techniques, and the assessment methods that have been proposed. Another contribution of PRODUSER is to apply software engineering process modelling to this goal of defining a general process. PRODUSER is based on the assumption that there is a benefit to attaching structure and organization to this complex and diverse activity. Certainly not all aspects will benefit, but PRODUSER also attempts to maintain a flexibility to allow for those unstructured activities that must remain as such.

Many of the claims PRODUSER makes are still hypotheses. Although it has been applied to one system, without actually executing the process program and allowing several people to use PRODUSER, it is difficult to determine the correctness and utility of the process and certainly the PRODUSER Environment. As was discussed in section IV C. the near term goal is to provide a working version of the PRODUSER system so that it can be better assessed. In any case, there are still benefits realized by the very activity of addressing the problem, such as better understanding of the problem and its complexities. PRODUSER is based on sound software engineering methodologies that should prove beneficial to the task of creating high quality user interfaces.

Acknowledgements

This work was supported in part by the National Science Foundation under grant CCR – 8704311 with cooperation from the Defense Advanced Research Projects Agency under Arpa order 6108, program code 7T10; and National Science Foundation under grant DCR – 8521398.

The author gratefully acknowledges the feedback and insights from fellow contributors Tom Dayton, Bob Braudes, Deborah Hix, and particularly to editor John Karat for including me within this distinguished group addressing this important topic. In addition, I am grateful for the continuing support from the Arcadia consortium. I would especially like to thank Richard Taylor and Richard Selby for their guidance and patience throughout the development of this research.

References

Balzer, R., Cheatham, T. E., & Green, C. (1983). "Software Technology in the 1990s: Using a New Paradigm," *IEEE Computer*, 39–45.

Benington, H. D. (1987). "Production of Large Computer Programs," Reprinted in *Proceedings of the Ninth International Conference on Software Engineering*, Monterey, CA, 299–310.

Bischofberger, W., & Keller, R. (1989). "Enhancing the Software Life Cycle by Prototyping". *Structured Programming* (pp. 51–63). New York, NY: Springer-Verlag.

Boehm, B. W. (1988). "The Spiral Model of Software Development and Enhancement," *IEEE Computer*, 21(5), 61–72.

Boehm, B. W. (1989). *Tutorial: Software Risk Management*. Washington, DC: IEEE Computer Society Press.

Boehm, B. W., & Belz, F. C. (1988). "Applying Process Programming to the Spiral Model," In *Proceedings of the 4th International Software Process Workshop*, May, Association for Computing Machinery.

Card, S. K., Moran, T. P., & Newell, A. (1983). *The Psychology of Human-Computer Interfaces*. Hillsdale, NJ: Lawerence Erlbaum Associates.

Fairley, R. E. (1985). *Software Engineering Concepts*. New York, NY: McGraw-Hill.

Foley, J. D., & Van Dam, A. (1982). *Fundamentals of Interactive Computer Graphics*. Reading, MA: Addison-Wesley.

Hartson, H. R., & Hix, D. (1989). "Toward Empirically Derived Methodologies and Tools for Human-Computer Interface Development," *International Journal for Man-Machine Studies*, 31, 477–494.

McCracken, D. D., & Jackson, M. A. (1982). "Life-Cycle Concept Considered Harmful," *Software Engineering Notes*, 7(2), 29–32.

Norman, D. A. (1984). "Stages and Levels in Human-Machine Interfaces," *International Journal of Man-Machine Studies*, 21, 265–375.

Osterweil, L. (1987). "Software Processes are Software Too," In *Proceedings of the Ninth International Conference on Software Engineering*, Monterey, CA, 2–13.

Royce, W. W. (1987). "Managing the Development of Large Software Systems: Concepts and Techniques," Reprinted in *Proceedings of the Ninth International Conference on Software Engineering*, Monterey, CA, 328-338.

Shneiderman, B. (1980). *Software Psychology: Human Factors in Computer and Information Systems*. Boston, MA: Little, Brown, and Co.

Shneiderman, B. (1987). *Designing the User Interface: Strategies for Effective Human-Computer Interfaces*. Reading, MA: Addison-Wesley.

Sutton, S. M., Jr. (1989). *Working Report on the Revised Definition for the APPL/A Programming Language* (CU-89-05). Department of Computer Science, University of Colorado.

Sutton, S. M., Jr., Heimbigner, D., & Osterweil, L. J. (1988). *Programmable Relations for Managing Change During Software Development* (CU-CS-418-88). University of Colorado, Boulder, CO.

Taylor, R. N., Belz, F. C., Clarke, L. A., Osterweil, L. J., Selby, R. W., Wileden, J. C., Wolf, A. L., & Young, M. (1988). "Foundations for the Arcadia Environment Architecture," In *Proceedings of ACM SIGSOFT '88: Third Symposium on Software Development Environments*, Boston, MA, 1–13.

13 A System for Specifying and Rapidly Prototyping User Interfaces

CHRIS ROUFF

TRW
Systems Engineering & Development Division
Carson, California

ELLIS HOROWITZ

Computer Science Department
University of Southern California
Los Angeles, California

I. Introduction

Rapid prototyping of user interfaces allows a designer to produce a proposed interface in a short time, to easily experiment with different approaches to the interface, and to allow end users to try it early in design, when it is most cost effective to make changes. The primary hinderance of producing a prototype is the amount of code needing to be handwritten. Reducing the programming reduces the designer's reliance on a programmer, decreases development time, and leaves the interface more modifiable (which supports iterative design).

Taking Software
Design Seriously

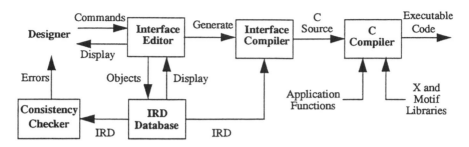

Figure 1. Components of RPP.

We are currently developing a methodology and system for prototyping user interfaces, called RPP (Reduced Programming Prototyper). This system and methodology allow a designer to

- interactively lay out the graphical components of the interface,
- combine components into hierarchical groups,
- specify the control flow between interface components and groups,
- define constraints between interface components, and
- define semantic feedback between the interface and the underlying application,

without writing any code. As the interface is being constructed, its components, flow of control, constraints, and semantic feedback are represented by a formal model, which can be used as the interface specification. This specification can be compiled into C code with calls to the OSF/Motif X window toolkit [10].

Figure 1 shows the structure and components of RPP. An interface designer interacts with RPP through an interface editor. As the designer draws the components and defines relationships between them, the definition of the interface is saved onto a formal structure, called an IRD, which can be checked for inconsistencies and incompleteness. The designer produces an executable version of the interface code by issuing the generate command, which causes the interface compiler to read in the interface representation and compile it into C code with calls to the Motif toolkit and X library. At this point the source code is compiled and linked with any user written functions, which then can be executed by the designer.

In the remainder of this paper we discuss related work, discuss the components of an interface, describe the methodology a designer follows to specify the interface, and define the formal representation of the interface components and their interaction.

II. Related Work in Prototyping Tools

There are three basic types of prototyping [17]: storyboard or slide shows, Wizard of Oz simulation, and testable simulations. The storyboard or slide show is a predefined set of screens displayed in a predetermined order, the Wizard of Oz type of prototype uses a person behind the scenes to drive the interface, and the testable simulation is a fully functional user interface that can be tested by the end user. RPP addresses the testable simulation type of prototyping. Production of this kind of prototype requires the largest investment in time and money so it is often integrated into the final product [2]. Current tools for producing testable simulation prototypes can be divided into three groups: UIMSs (User Interface Management Systems), IDTs (Interactive Design Tools), and high-level language based systems.

A UIMS's primary goal is to separate the user interface from the application. It can be defined as a system that provides a component for the presentation of the visual part of the interface, a component for the definition of the dialogue between the user and application, and a component for defining the interface between the UIMS and the application program [5]. The separation of the interface from the application allows different interfaces to be tried without modifying the application. Two current UIMSs are Serpent [1] and TeleUse by TeleSoft. Serpent and TeleUse both provide an interactive design tool for defining the layout of an interface, a dialogue language (Slang in Serpent and D in TeleUse) for describing the flow of control of the interface, and a specification language for defining the interface between the UIMS and application. Both systems use X windows [15] for presenting the visual component.

IDTs are similar to interactive graphics editors but allow users to place interface objects such as buttons, lists, menus, and icons, instead of graphics objects such as circles and lines. Many IDTs also allow the designer to specify application functions to be executed when a particular input occurs (e.g., a button press). Most systems produce source code definitions in a programming language or layout description language that represents the screen layout. The dialogue portion of the interface is then written in a programming language, or if part of a UIMS, in a dialogue language that uses the earlier generated definitions. A large number of IDTs have been written, often as part of UIMSs or other development systems. Some of these systems are Dialog Editor by Cardelli [3], Interface Builder by Next [7], Prototyper by SmethersBarnes [14], XBuild by Nixdorf Computers[18], and Dev Guide by Sun Microsystems. HyperCard [4] and OSU [8] also allow interface objects to be interactively laid out on the screen but differ from the other systems in that a limited amount of sequencing can be specified. In HyperCard the designer defines a series of cards with common backgrounds and differing foregrounds and links them together through button presses and other interactions. In this way, simple flow of control between cards can be defined without the need for any programming, though the Hypertalk scripting language can be used for more advanced schemes. OSU allows sequences of Macintosh interface objects to be specified based on user inputs. Peridot [12] is another system that lets a designer interactively lay out and construct interface objects by demonstration.

The third type of prototyping systems are based on high level programming languages that have specific constructs for displaying and manipulating user interface objects and usually have capabilities to call functions written in a conventional programming language. Examples of these types of systems are Winterp [9], Garnet [13], and Tooltool [11]. Winterp is based on XLISP and the Motif widget set. It allows easy definition of widgets in X windows and has the power of programming in LISP. Like Winterp, Garnet is Lisp based and provides a high level interface to X windows. Garnet also provides mechanisms for defining constraints between objects as well object manipulation. Tooltool is based on SunView and acts as a mediator between the windowing system and an application. The designer defines what interface objects will be used and maps inputs to these objects into inputs for the application and maps outputs from the application onto the user interface.

RPP differs from these systems in that it allows the definition of complex sequencing of the dialogue, constraints, and semantic feedback, interactively without using a dialogue programming language. The application still needs to be programmed, but for prototyping purposes a mock up facility is supported that simulates the call and return of application functions allowing the application routines to be simulated. Previous prototyping systems have relied heavily on programmers to code any complex sequencing of the interface and in many cases to also define the layout of objects. With the exception of Peridot and Garnet, none of the systems allow the designer to define constraints between objects of the interface. None of the systems allow hierarchy of frames of the interface to be grouped together to reflect visual and flow-of-control similarities.

III. Components and Interaction of an Interface

To produce a prototype with a minimal amount of programming, an overall structure that describes the components and their interrelations needs to be defined. The building of this structure is then reflected in the methodology that a designer follows to produce an interface. We define a user interface to consist of

- graphical objects,
- flow of control,
- semantic actions, and
- constraints.

The graphical objects are made up of the graphical images that are visible to the user, the control portion defines an ordering on the appearance of the objects, the semantic actions define how the interface interacts with the application, and the constraints define interrelations between the objects. The following sections discuss each of these parts.

A. Graphical Objects

The graphical objects consist of the buttons, menus, dialog boxes, text, and other items that are directly visible to the user. These objects can be divided into two groups: those that contain other objects and those that are atomic. The container objects are called windows and the others graphics. Graphics that appear at the same time inside a window are grouped together into frames. When control is transferred from one frame to another, the content of the window is cleared and a completely new set of graphics is drawn. An example of a series of frames is a transaction based system, such as a database browser, in which query fields are filled, and query results are displayed by erasing the contents of the window and displaying a list. Since modifications to a frame sometimes need to be made without erasing the entire frame, a second type of frame is defined, called a subframe. Modifications can consist of (but are not limited to) display of dialog boxes, addition of menus, lists, error messages, or help.

Some user interfaces are a series of frames, others are a single frame with subframes that continually modify the original frame, and others are a mix of these. An example of a frame oriented user interface is a transaction based system where data in fields of a form are filled, with new frames and fields appearing depending on the items selected or the values entered. An example of a single-frame oriented interface is a graphics editor, in which a single frame is displayed and changes are continually made to it. Most systems contain both types of frames. There may be several frames that make up the interface but are modified with dialog boxes and error and help messages that continually update or modify the original frame.

B. Flow of Control

Flow of control defines how the interface will change on inputs from the user or values returned by the application and represents an ordering on the interface objects over time. There is also an implicit flow of control defined by the windowing system (in this case X) that allows the input focus to be changed from window to window and graphic to graphic. This usually takes the form of moving the cursor from one window or graphic to another with the window or graphic that the cursor is over being the object that receives input. Control among frames and subframes is explicitly defined since it requires the interface to be modified.

C. Semantic Actions

Semantic actions are the operations that drive the application. These actions are tied to the events that are associated with the flow of control. When an event occurs, a semantic action can be performed. These actions can take the form of calls to user written functions, programs, or file input/output. These actions can also reference or set variables that represent attributes of graphics being displayed. This allows the user to pass data to the application and allows the results of calculations in the application to be printed or change the display.

D. Constraints

Constraints occur when an attribute of an interface object becomes dependent on a value computed in the application or the attribute of another object. Constraints are one way that an application displays its output. Examples of attributes that an application might set are the label, position, size, or color. These attributes can reflect values computed by the application. The second type of constraint occurs when an attribute of one object is dependent on the attribute of another. Examples are an object's position depending on another (e.g., when one object moves the other follows), and objects sharing a color.

IV. Prototyping an Interface

To prototype a user interface a designer follows these steps:

1. The windows that are to appear in the interface are drawn.
2. Frames that are to appear in each of the windows are drawn.
3. The sequence in which the frames are to appear are defined.
4. Events are specified that determine when a sequence is to be taken.
5. Constraints between the components are defined.
6. Semantic feedback among the interface, the application, and the constraints are defined.
7. The specification is converted to C and X Windows code.

All interface objects are drawn in an interactive editor that allows the designer to place objects on the screen exactly how they will be seen at execution time. At any point in these steps the designer can repeat or reduce previous steps. This allows mistakes to be corrected, enhancements to be made, or different techniques

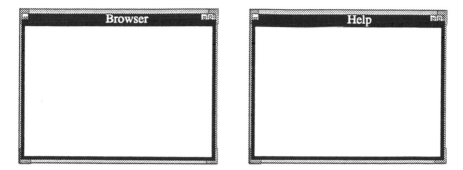

Figure 2. Two top level windows.

to be tried, thus supporting iterative design. The following sections describe each of these steps in more detail.

A. Defining Windows

A designer begins a prototype by defining the windows in which the interface is to appear. A window can be defined as either a top level window or a subwindow. Multiple top level windows can exist and each window can have multiple subwindows. Appearance times for windows can also be specified, which defines when the window will be displayed. The appearance time can be the same as the parent's or when control is transferred to the object. If it is the same as the parent's, then whenever the parent appears, the object also appears. If the window is a top level window and does not have a parent, then it appears at the start of the application. Appearance when control is transferred to an object is how pop up windows, dialogs, and other transitory windows are defined.

When specifying a window, its initial position and size are given by the designer. If it is a subwindow, its parent window is selected from the already defined windows. Next defined are the attributes of the window, such as the width of its border, its dimensions, and its appearance time. Figure 2 shows two windows after specification. They are both top level windows, the left window (*Browser*) being the main window and the right window displaying help information.

B. Defining Frames and Subframes

After a window is defined, a series of frames is drawn to represent the appearance of the interface at a different points in time. Frames can be defined in one of three ways: by the designer explicitly defining the graphics that make up the frame, by the designer defining a frame to be a modification of a previously de-

Figure 3. Three frames of the bookstore query system.

fined frame (subframe), through semantic feedback from the application, or by a dependency on another graphic.

Hierarchies of windows, frames, or graphical objects can be defined by grouping together those sharing common attributes such as graphical objects, flow of control, or attributes (e.g., color). Groupings allow common attributes to be defined once for the entire group instead of individually for each item. A group of objects can be used like any other object: they can be listed as the source or destination of a sequence, graphics or attributes can be assigned to them (which are persistent across all frames and windows in that group), semantic feedback can be associated with them, and they can belong to other groups. Grouping similar objects together produces a consistent user interface by providing these benefits:

- Persistent objects only need to be defined once.
- Persistent objects appear in the same place and look the same over the frames in which they appear.
- Identical flow of control properties need be defined only once.
- Objects with the same flow of control operate similarly.
- Modification of a shared object or sequence only has to be done once.

Figure 3 shows examples of frames that could be defined in the two windows shown in Figure 2. Two frames are shown in the *Browser* window and one frame in the *Help* window. The frame on the left in the *Browser* window is the initial frame listing a choice of queries that can be made. The center frame is the frame displayed if the first query is taken. The third frame (rightmost) is the first frame of the *Help* window that is displayed whenever a help button is pressed. All the frames of the *Browser* window could be grouped together so the help button would only have to be defined once and will appear in each frame of the *Browser* window in the same place and operating in the same manner, thus ensuring consistency in the look and operation of the button in all the frames of the browser.

C. Defining Flow of Control between Components

Once the windows, frames, and subframes are specified, the flow of control of the interface is defined by ordering the frames. The ordering consists of a set of sequences, each having a source and destination object. The source object can be a graphic, frame, subframe, window, or group. The destination of the sequence can be a frame, subframe, group, or window. Each sequence is assigned a value indicating what input initiates it. Input can be in the form of keystrokes, mouse button clicks, mouse movements, a value read from a file, or a value returned from a user written function. Allowing inputs from the user or outputs from a program to initiate flow of control allows the interface to be either user driven, application driven, or a combination of both. Actions – graphical operations, user written routines to be executed, values read or written to files – also can be assigned to sequences, which are executed when the sequence is taken.

D. Defining Constraints on Objects

Constraints can be defined on objects or flow of control of the interface. Constraints among objects (either windows or graphics) can be defined by declaring that a value of an attribute of one object is dependent on an attribute of another object. This is useful for defining such things as shadows, groups of objects whose positions are defined relative to one another, and objects with equivalent attributes such as the same foreground color. When defining an attribute of an object to be defined relative to an attribute of another object, a simple formula can be applied to the original attribute to transform it to a value for the new object. This transformation can be done by selecting the appropriate attributes of each object whose relationships are to be maintained or by explicitly naming the attributes involved and the transformation to be applied to those attributes.

Constraints on the flow of control is where multiple events in multiple objects must take place before a sequence can be taken. An example is when a user has to select an item from multiple menus before the next frame is displayed or a value must be entered into a text field and a button pressed before execution can continue. Constrained and unconstrained flow of control can occur in the same frame, thus allowing the user to get help, quit, or skip the frame.

E. Defining Feedback to Objects

Input may be passed from the interface to the application, and the results returned to the interface for display or for modification of the interface appearance. Passing values between different parts of the interface allows a value input to one graphic to affect a second graphic without going through the application. A simple transformation formula can also be applied to these values to account for off-sets. Values can be read from files as well as passed from the application. This allows quick mock-ups of the interface before the application is written, and re-moves the need for a programmer from the early stages of the interface design. Values can also be saved to files. The values passed to the application are not re-stricted to input but can be attributes of a widget, such as position or dimension.

F. Generating the Interface

The interface specification can be converted to UIL (User Interface Language) [10] and C code with calls to Motif and X window routines, compiled, and then linked with user written functions. The UIL defines the initial appearance of the interface objects, the C code implements the flow of control of the interface, and modifications are performed through calls to Motif and X toolkit routines. Values defined as semantic feedback are stored in shared data structures, which can be read and written to by application functions. When the shared data values are changed, the corresponding attribute of an object is updated.

V. Interface and Interaction Representation

As an interface is specified, it is mapped onto an interface representation dia-gram (IRD), which represents its structure, flow of control, interrelationships, and semantic feedback. This diagram models the structure and interaction between the graphics and application. The interface objects themselves are not addressed, because it is assumed that the interface designer was given a predefined set of ob-jects (such as the Motif widget set) and has no control over their functionality, only in how they are used. Such low level actions as highlighting menu items are defined by the object and are not addressed in this model. The IRDs are not seen by the designer but are what drives the prototyping process. The designer only sees the actual interface objects in the editor. The following sections describe IRDs and how interface specifications are mapped onto them.

A. Representing Components of the Interface

IRDs, which are based on statecharts [6] [16], can be defined as hierarchical transition diagrams in which nodes either stand for themselves or contain subdi-agrams. It is this hierarchy of nodes that is used to represent the levels of win-dows, frames, and graphical objects of an interface. An interface is mapped onto the node structure by first representing the entire interface as a root node of an IRD, the top level windows as children of the root node, subwindows as child nodes of the window's parent, frames as children of window nodes, and graphics as children of frame nodes. If a window contains subwindows, then the window has two types of children: frames and a subwindow. Grouping of nodes (such as frames or graphics) are represented by enclosing them in superstates with the group possibly spanning across windows, frames or other groups. Groups are treated like any other node. They can have transitions, semantic feedback, constraints, or other attributes that apply to all the nodes inside the group.

There are other types of nodes. Default nodes are starting subnodes in a window or group. A history node remembers the last subnode executed that can be used after control is temporarily interrupted. A diversion is a group of nodes that are executed as an aside to the current flow of execution, and a termination node stops execution of the application.

B. Representing Sequencing between Components

The sequences in an interface are represented by transitions that connect nodes of the IRD. Transitions are defined as tuples containing a source and a destination node, a value indicating when the transition can be taken, and actions to be executed. The circumstance for a transition to be taken, the semantics associated with a transfer of control, and the actions executed when the destination is reached, all depend on the types of nodes involved. If a window is the source of a transition, then whenever control is in the window and the value listed on its transition occurs, then the transition is taken and control given to the destination node. If a frame is the source of a transition, the transition is taken whenever the listed input occurs among the frame's graphics. If a graphic is the source of a transition, then whenever the listed input occurs inside, the graphic control is transferred.

The type of a destination node determines the result of the transition. If the destination is a window node, then until control leaves the window all inputs are applied to the nodes in that window. The window must then transfer control to its start state: a group, frame or graphic. If the destination is a group then, like a window, its start state is given control. If the destination is a new frame then the graphics in that frame are displayed in the window; if it is a modified frame, the graphics are modified. Finally, if the destination is a graphic, such as a dialog box, then only that graphic can receive input; this forces the user to acknowledge a message or input a value before continuing with any other part of the interface.

Unlike transition diagrams and state charts, IRDs do not require nodes to have transitions entering and leaving them. This is due to the fact that not all objects change the state of the interface and not all receive input. An example of the former is radio buttons, which simply set a variable, and an example of the latter is a label.

An example of transitions between different interface components is shown in Figure 4. In this example there are two windows. **Window 1** has two frames and

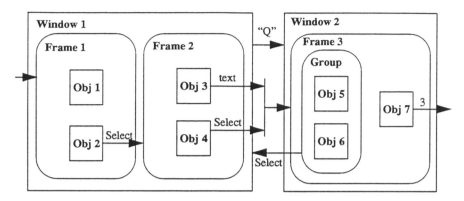

Figure 4. Transitions between different components of an interface.

Window 2 has one frame. The default start node for **Window 1** is **Frame 1**. This is where execution begins when control is given to **Window 1**. When **Frame 1** receives control through the transition, it will display objects **Obj 1** and **Obj 2**. **Obj 1** does not have any transitions entering or leaving it. It could be a radio button, a text widget, or an object whose sensitivity has been turned off, like an invalid menu item. **Obj 2** has a transition leaving it with a destination of **Frame 2**. This means that whenever the event "select" occurs in **Obj 2**, then **Frame 2** is drawn. **Frame 2** has an example of constrained flow of control. Control can only be transferred from **Frame 2** to **Window 2** when text has been entered into **Obj 3** *and* **Obj 4** has been selected. **Window 2** has an example of a group of objects (**Obj 5** and **Obj 6**) that might share some attribute or common flow of control.

C. Representing Semantic Feedback

Semantic feedback between the interface and application is represented through data feedback transitions (DFT) and application feedback transitions (AFT). These transitions show flow of data instead of flow of control. A DFT transfers data from the user interface's object supplying the value, to a parallelogram representing a variable containing a data value shared between the interface and the application. An AFT has as its source a shared data value and as its destination a node representing the widget that is to be affected by the data. The values that flow between the interface and the application can be attached to any attribute of a widget, such as its position, size, label, or ability to accept user input.

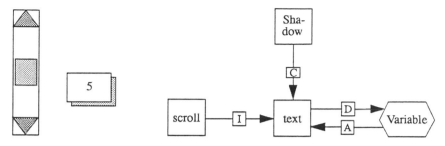

Figure 5. Scrollbar, text widget, and corresponding IRD.

D. Representing Constraints on Components

Constraints between widgets are represented similarly to the above semantic feedbacks. An interface constraint transition (ICT) has as a source the node representing the widget that is to be constrained, and as a destination the node representing the object that the source is being constrained to. An equation is associated with the transition that represents the transformation of the source widget's value to the destinations widget's value. Constraints can be used on widgets to force them to maintain positions relative to each other or for one widget to display an attribute of another.

An example of semantic feedback and constraint between widgets, with the resulting IRDs, is shown in Figure 5. On the left side of Figure 5, a scrollbar and a text widget with shadow are shown. The text widget displays a value relative to the location of the slider in the scrollbar. The right side of Figure 5 is the IRD representing the widgets. The square labeled "variable" represents a value shared between the interface and the application. The transitions from the scroll node and shadow node to the text node represent constraints. The transition between the text node and the variable node represents the data feedback, and the transition from the variable to the text node represents application feedback. Additional constraints between the scrollbar and the text widget could be defined to keep the widgets a fixed distance from each other. In such a situation, one widget's position would be constrained by the other via an offset added to the original value.

E. Example of a Representation

Figure 6 is the complete IRD of the Browser interface described in the second section. The interface being specified is for a system that allows patrons of a bookstore to query the availability of books. At any time the user can move from the Browser window to the Help window, page through the Help window, and return to the Browser. Subsequent movement to the Help window resumes execu-

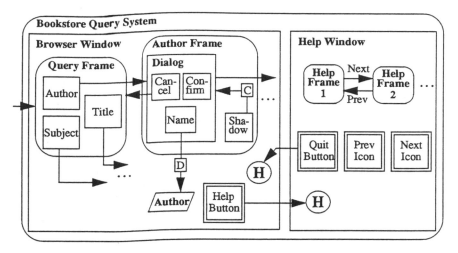

Figure 6. IRD representation of interface in Figure 2.

tion where it left off.

The outer node (Bookstore Query System) contains the entire interface description. The two states (Query and Help) in the root state represent the two windows
of the interface. The nodes in the Query node represent the frames that appear in
that window and correspond to the first two frames in Figure 3. The four nodes in
the Book node and the three nodes in the Author node represent the widgets in
each of the frames that receive input. The Name node in the Author node does not
have a transition leaving it because input to that widget does not cause any changes in the interface. The circles with the H in the middle are history states that return control to the last executed node; if no node has been executed, the default
node is used. The transition from the Query node to the history node represents
an input that can be executed anytime to take the user into the Help window.

VI. Conclusion

The system described here allows a wide range of user interfaces to be easily
and quickly prototyped by an interface designer with little and in some cases no
assistance from an applications programer. It allows the interface components,
their relationships, flow of control, constraints, and semantic feedback to be interactively laid out directly on the screen. The designer specifies the interface by defining windows, frames, subframes, and the graphics within them. The frames and
graphics can then be grouped together for easy specification of persistent objects
and identical flow of control. The grouping supports consistency of the objects'

appearance and operation across the interface and reduces the time to modify persistent objects.

The IRDs are capable of representing the structure, flow of control, constraints, and semantic feedback of the interface. The hierarchical structure of the IRDs allows them to represent the nested components of the interface and the grouping of the objects and their flow of control. It also has constructs for representing the execution of semantic actions of the application, feedback from the application, and constraints between graphics and the interface.

References

1. Bass, L., Hardy, E.J, Hoyt, K., Little, R., and Seacord, R. C. (1988). *Introduction to the Serpent User Interface Management System.* Technical Report CMU/SEI-88-TR-5, ADA200085, Carnegie Mellon University, Software Engineering Institute, March.
2. Boehm, B. (1984). "Prototyping Versus Specifying: A Multiproject Experiment," *IEEE Transactions on Software Engineering*, SE-10 (3), May, 290-302.
3. Cardelli, L. (1988). "Building User Interfaces by Direct Manipulation," *Proceedings of the ACM SIGGRAPH Symposium on User Interface Software,* Banff, Alberta, Canada, October, 152-166.
4. Goodman, D. (1987). *The Complete Hypercard Handbook*, Bantam Books, New York.
5. Green, M. (1985). "Report on Dialogue Specification Tools," in *User Interface Management Systems*, edited by Gunther E. Pfaff, Springer-Verlag, 9-20.
6. Harel, D. (1989). "On Visual Formalisms," *Communications of the ACM*, May, 514-528.
7. Interface Builder (1989), *NeXT Systems Reference Manual*, Chapter 8, NeXT Inc.
8. Lewis, T., Handlooser III, F., Bose, S., and Yang, S. (1989). "Prototypes from Standard User Interface Management Systems," *IEEE Computer*, 51-60.
9. Mayer, N., Shepherd A., and Kuchinsky,A. (1990). "Winterp: An Object-oriented, Rapid Prototyping, Development Environment for Building Extensible Applications with the OSF/Motif UI Toolkit", *Xhibition '90 Conference Proceedings*, San Jose, May, 49-64.
10. *Motif Programer's Guide, Open Software Foundation* (1989), Open Systems Foundation, Cambridge, MA.
11. Musciano, C. (1988). *Tooltool Reference Manual.*
12. Myers, B. (1988). *Creating User Interfaces by Demonstration*, Academic Press, Boston.
13. Myers, B., Giuse, D., Dannenberg, R., Vander Zanden, B., Kosbiew, D., Marchal, P., Pervin, E., and Kolojejchick, J. (1989). *The Garnet Toolkit Reverence Manuals: Support for Highly-Interactive, Graphical User Interfaces in Lisp*, Tech. Report CMU-CS-89-196, Carnegie Mellon University, Computer Science Department, November.
14. *Prototyper Reference Manual* (1987), SmethersBarnes.
15. Scheifler, R. and Gettys, J. (1986), "The X Window System," *ACM Transactions on Graphics*, April, 79-109.
16. Wellner, P. (1989). "Statemaster: A UIMS Based on Statecharts for Prototyping and Target Implementation," *Proceedings of the ACM SIGCHI '89*, April, 177-182.
17. Wilson, J. and Rosenberg, D. (1988). "Rapid Prototyping for User Interface Design," in *Handbook of Human-Computer Interaction*, edited by Martin Helander, North-Holland.
18. *XBuild User's Guide* (1990), Nixdorf Corp, Cambridge, MA.

14   Rapid Prototyping: An Effective Technique for System Development

HAROLD H. MILLER-JACOBS
TASC
Reading, Massachusetts

Introduction

Software development for computer systems is a constantly evolving process—new techniques emerge that facilitate the development process. In the last few years one of the most powerful techniques to emerge is rapid prototyping of the user interface. Rapid prototyping, in this context, refers to the quick representation of what a user would actually see on the display when sitting down to operate the system. It not only presents a visualization of what the operator has to work with, but in so doing it also defines the basic functions that the system will perform. This perspective and its associated clarity facilitates the software development process.

Rapid prototyping has emerged for two primary reasons: shortcomings of the traditional development process, and the availability of software tools that facilitate the rapid prototyping process. The chapter begins with a description of the traditional development process and its problems. The techniques of rapid prototyping and how it is used in the systems development process come next, followed by an example and definition of the rapid prototyping process come next. The

Taking Software
Design Seriously

benefits of rapid prototyping and the tools that facilitate its application are then described. Finally addressed are some concerns about the rapid prototyping process and its future.

The Traditional Systems Development Process

Systems development for at least the last twenty years may be described broadly as a multistep process. The first step is the generation of detailed specifications of what the system should do, as well as its operational characteristics. Specifications for most systems acquired by the U.S. government have been multivolume tomes that describe in excruciating detail the system's characteristics down to such details as the response times to operator queries. Several large organizations have specification generating systems that automatically turn out these multivolume documents often referred to as "boiler plate" material. These documents, while tailored to the specific system being addressed, contain much of the same standard material that is usually desired by the procuring agency.

The second step is building the system based on the specifications. Readers of these specifications examine the document trying to separate the important information from the boiler plate. Their task is to extract the essence and recreate what the writers of the specifications had in mind. The process of conveying information from the writer of the specification to the reader is at best a difficult one, confounded by all the extraneous material. The system is then built to conform to the reader's interpretation of the specification. It is no wonder that the system envisioned by the writer may not match the system reconstructed by the reader of the specification!

The third step is testing and evaluating the system that was built to the original specification. In too many cases, the tests reveal that the system does not comply with the requirements envisioned by the specification architects. Something usually gets lost in the translation between specification and product, and invariably the requirements have changed. This results in costly modifications and schedule delays.

Finally the system is delivered to the users. In many cases delivery may be characterized as throwing the system over the wall to unsuspecting users (see Figure 1). The users have had little previous insight into the features of the system — what it will do and how it will operate. They might have attended various design review meetings and even participated in several technical interchange meetings with the developers. Yet upon delivery there is often disappointment and sometimes disaster.

Why the Process Doesn't Work

The process does not work because it is based on the misconception that a system can be specified a priori and then built to those specifications. It is assumed that writers of specifications know and understand all of the details of the system

TRADITIONAL APPROACH TO
SYSTEMS DEVELOPMENT

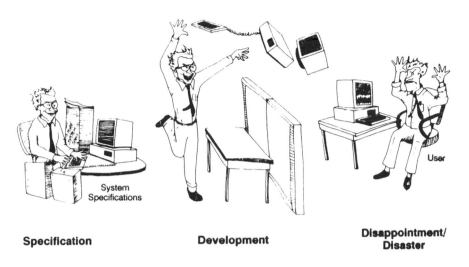

Specification **Development** **Disappointment/ Disaster**

RAPID PROTOTYPING APPROACH
TO SYSTEMS DEVELOPMENT

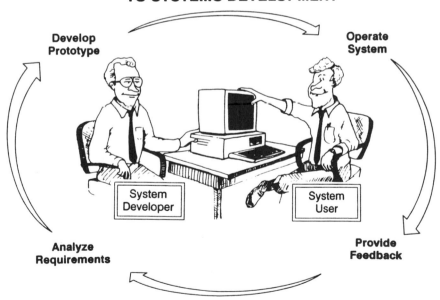

Figure 1 Traditional and Rapid Prototyping Approach to Systems Design/Development

under development. It is also assumed that once stated, the requirements are fixed; experience has shown that specifications evolve as the system develops. For example, as a particular function of the system is examined in detail it often leads to subfunctions or other functions that could not have been foreseen. Specifications are dynamic documents that are not easily dealt with by the traditional development process.

Even if the requirements were fixed, the assumption is that the writer can accurately articulate all of the relevant information to a reader in a specification. Assuming the document were carefully written, read, and analyzed, the probability of having the information accurately conveyed is low. Written specifications containing voluminous amounts of boiler plate that must be sifted for the relevant information probably impede rather than enhance communication.

Another reason for failure is that the actual operators are usually left out of the development process with no opportunity for providing feedback. Even when users are involved, they only examine a high stack of design documents that rarely convey the important aspects of a system. These documents usually describe system details and do not provide the necessary overview. Even design reviews can get bogged down in trivial issues and not convey the important information that the users need to provide meaningful feedback.

What Can Be Done?

Recognizing that there is a need for some sort of system specification and given the aforementioned limitations, what can be done? The proposal here is to use the rapid prototyping approach as a dynamic specification. This means that the system specification should be primarily a graphic representation of what the user interface would look like. The graphics should not be a design of the interface but rather a representation of the primary functions that the system should perform. It also should not be a final version until well into the developmental process. This allows for orderly modifications as the specifications evolve.

Rapid Prototyping: Definition

Rapid prototyping is the construction, early in the system development cycle, of an initial visualization of the operator interface. It is usually done with little or no computer coding, after a quick analysis of the system. In many cases the initial prototype can be generated in several days. The aim is to develop the user interface to resemble the actual operational system.

In general, the rapid prototyping approach works as follows (Figure 1): The developer quickly analyzes the requirements of the system and ascertains the functions that are needed by the user. A computer platform and tool are selected, and an initial prototype is then developed that incorporates a small subset of the functionality. The selection of the platform and tool is relatively straightforward; the selection of the functions is more difficult, requiring expertise in user interface design.

The prototype is then shown to the user who provides feedback to the developer. Often this is the first time the user confronts the issues of how the system will actually work. Invariably, this feedback modifies the original requirements, and these modifications are incorporated in the prototype. The process of reviewing and updating the prototype may continue for several iterations. The term rapid prototyping has been used in the literature to refer to processes that speed up the systems development process. Connell and Shafer (1989, p. 23) define evolutionary rapid prototyping as an "easily built, readily modifiable, ultimately extensible, partially specified, working model of the primary aspects of a proposed system." Tanik and Yeh (1989, p. 9) refer to prototyping as the "process of developing a scaled-down version of a system to use in building a full-scale system."

While these approaches to rapid prototyping convey the essence of speeding up the system development process, they basically prescribe a relatively faster method of developing code to implement a portion of system functionality. The definition advocated in this chapter is that the important element is the visual representation of the system, that is, the user interface of the system. By actually seeing the user interface, the functionality of the system becomes much clearer.

A key part of the definition is "rapid." Advocates of rapid prototyping specify various fourth generation languages (4GL) as needed to expeditiously generate the prototype. Using a 4GL may no longer be considered rapid, since far quicker prototypes can be generated using tools specifically designed or adapted for the purpose.

The term prototyping is also often used in the context of event simulation. While this is a related use of the term, traditional event simulation is a complex and long term process. While the payoff may be great, it lacks the speed of development and feedback that is the hallmark of rapid prototyping.

An Example of a Rapid Prototype for Defining Requirements

While rapid prototyping can be used throughout the development process, the most effective use is at the early stages, when requirements are being defined. Figure 2 illustrates an application developed with rapid prototyping as part of the requirements definition process. This implementation is a concept for a weather workstation to be used by meteorologists in developing forecasts for dissemination to the public. The purpose of the prototype was to identify the various functions that a meteorologist might use in generating a forecast; it was not the final user interface for the system. It was developed on a Sun workstation using the DataViews Graphics Software package from V.I. Corp.

The major portion of the screen is devoted to a graphics map, depicting the area of interest. Across the top, in the rectangular boxes, is a row of major functions that a meteorologist may use in generating the forecast. These include all the steps from the Monitoring of Status to the Distribution and Dissemination of the forecast products, in this case the entire U.S. These are actually menu buttons that have

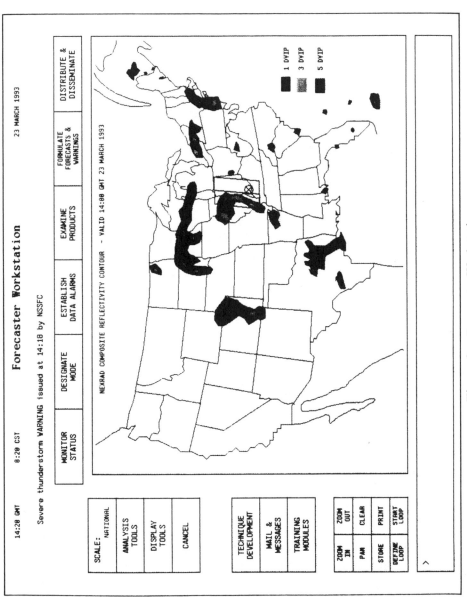

Figure 2 Forecaster Workstation

associated submenus when activated. In the prototype, clicking on one of these buttons opens up its associated submenu.

Down the left side of the screen are also menu buttons for tools that an operator may use in performing the various forecasting functions. In addition there are tools for manipulating the image, such as Zoom, Pan and Store. In the prototype some of these buttons were functioning.

To verify that the listed functions were the primary ones needed by a meteorologist, a scenario was developed that started with a thunderstorm warning. A message containing the general WARNING, which was issued by the National Severe Storms Center, is listed near the top of the screen. The prototype was designed to enable the meteorologist to perform all the steps needed to verify the extent of the thunderstorm and to issue a local warning. Approximately a dozen subsequent screens were developed that tracked the various functions used and enabled a simulated operation of the system. These were then shown to meteorologists, and their comments were incorporated into the prototype. When working interactively with the prototype it appeared as if it was an actual system with limited functionality. This realism facilitated informative feedback and was an essential part of clarifying the requirements.

The major benefits of this approach were that it incorporated in several screens a representation of what was thought to be the primary functions needed by a meteorologist to perform the required tasks. There were definitely errors and omissions, which were easily corrected. The major benefit, however, was the time saved by using this approach. After a quick analysis was performed to understand the basic functionality, the actual initial implementation of the prototype took less than a week!

Benefits of Rapid Prototyping

Rapid prototyping facilitates the development process by providing an early view of the operator interface and, by extension, the entire functionality of a system. In particular, it clarifies requirements and helps ensure that designers are tracking the users' goals. Rapid prototyping is becoming one of the most effective and efficient tools in developing sophisticated workstations that incorporate graphics and text.

Specifically, rapid prototyping serves these purposes:

- **It enables the visualization of the system requirements**. Requirements may not be fully known, and even if known they are difficult to specify. While a limited number of written requirements and specifications are needed, visualized requirements in a graphic format convey far more information to the system developer. Rapid prototyping makes it possible to actually look at the requirements rather than extract them from a collection of words.

- **It provides a common frame of reference for developers and users**. One of the most difficult parts of any development program is to ensure that accurate information is conveyed between the system specifiers and the developers. Even among the developers there may be misunderstandings, as each has a different discipline and frame of reference. Written requirements are subject to interpretation; visualized requirements eliminate potential uncertainty and misunderstanding. There is rarely a question of *what* was meant by that?

- **It enables inputs from users early in the development process.** In the traditional development cycle, users may get a glimpse of what the developers have in mind at formal reviews, such as at the Critical Design Review. The actual interface is viewed after the initial design is completed. Through rapid prototyping, users get to examine the interface before the initial design is completed. They can then provide feedback in a timely manner and have their ideas reflected in the evolving design.

- **It enables an iterative development cycle.** It is difficult (if not impossible) to specify all requirements of a system beforehand. In any system, changes to requirements always surface once the project has gotten underway. New functions are needed that could not have been foreseen. Rapid prototyping enables these emerging requirements to be incorporated in the system design without major effects on cost and schedule.

- **It facilitates the early testing.** In the conventional development approach, test and evaluation takes place after the system is built. Changes are then difficult and expensive to incorporate. With rapid prototyping, testing can be done before any code is written! Operators can exercise parts of the system and evaluate their usability. Difficulties can be analyzed and the changes reflected in the design. As development progresses, the prototype can be updated accordingly, with testing continuing throughout the development process.

Rapid Prototyping Tools

Various software packages have been used for rapid prototyping, from simple drawing packages such as Macdraw to sophisticated graphics packages such as DataViews. At the Association for Computing Machinery's conference on Computer-Human Interaction (CHI '90), participants in a Special Interest Group on rapid prototyping tools reported over forty software packages being used for rapid prototyping. Most of the reported tools were not designed specifically for rapid prototyping purposes; rather they were adapted from a variety of software applications, as they possess characteristics that enable rapid prototyping to varying degrees of usefulness.

Tool Characteristics

Tools differ along several dimensions; many provide for interactive capability, and some can evolve to become the actual user interface. Some are coding facilitators that enable the generation of essentially higher order code, whereas some enable the direct and graphic representation of the user interface. Tools should be selected to incorporate the characteristics most appropriate for the applications. These characteristics include the following:

- **Graphical Construction of the Interface** — The tools that are easiest to use enable the development of the interface by positioning graphical objects directly on the screen. For example, a button can be selected from a menu, placed anywhere on the display, labelled, and linked to a subsequent action, such as a subsequent screen. Tools that permit this type of interface building, rather than writing code, are the ones that are truly rapid.

- **Static or Dynamic Representation** — Many of the tools can generate dynamic screens where it is possible to see data changing in response to some function, such as an ongoing chemical process. Other tools, such as MacPaint, are restricted to simply paint static screens that cannot represent changes in the underlying data. Dynamic representation is usually required for interfaces that represent an ongoing process or that require animation. For applications involving only the entering and viewing of data, as for example an insurance data base, the dynamic feature may be of limited value.

- **Interactive Capability** — Most tools provide for the ability to interact with the screen; that is, the user can provide an input that can cause another screen or some action to occur. This is a critical feature for most applications, as it best represents a real system by providing feedback to operator actions. There is a wide variety of interactive capabilities. Many tools can respond to a user input and display a subsequent screen, and others can actually accept inputs in the form of text or data and respond accordingly.

- **Discard or Evolve** — The tools may be divided into two groups. One group contains tools that generate prototypes, with the prototypes being discarded once the actual program is written. They serve their purpose during the critical requirements phase. The other group contains tools that generate prototypes, which can evolve to become the user interface of the actual application. When the prototype evolves to the actual application, it will usually fall into the class of software tools referred to as a User Interface Management System (UIMS). A characteristic of a UIMS is that it is a separate module in the software set apart from the other application code. The advantage to this approach is that either the user interface or the applications code can be modified without affecting the other.

Tools at the higher end of the cost spectrum are usually the ones that can evolve to become UIMSs. The ability to evolve is a positive feature, but it may not always be the best approach. Tools in this category require more memory and may be more time consuming, thereby compromising some of the speed of rapid prototyping. Even when using a tool that can evolve to become the front end of the application, it is important to trade off the costs and benefits to determine which is the best approach. For interfaces that are relatively simple with few functions and screens, there may be insufficient reason for having the prototype evolve to become the actual interface. When the tool manufacturer requires a license for each host computer, it may not be cost effective to maintain the rapid prototyping tool on the target system.

- **Code Generation** — Many of the software tools used for rapid prototyping can generate a programming language code for use in an application. The ability to generate code is usually considered a positive feature, but as in the discard or evolve feature, it may not be necessary or desirable. For tools that evolve to become the user interface, code generation may not be relevant, as the prototype itself is the interface. For others, the code generation capability is valuable in expediting system development.

- **Portability** — Tools can be designed for use on a single platform, such as Prototyper on the Mac or Dan Bricklin for DOS machines. Some tools provide the capability of developing a prototype on one platform and running it on another; prototypes can be developed on a Sun, for example, and run on a Silicon Graphics machine. Some tools are even designed to be used with different operating systems. DataViews and SL-GMS, for example, have versions that can be used in Unix and VMS environments. Tool developers recognize the advantages of portability and newer packages are heading in this direction.

Tool Listing

As the value of rapid prototyping becomes evident, more tools that facilitate the process are being developed. Table 1 lists some of the more popular tools that are in use in the PC, Mac, and graphics workstation platforms as of this writing. These are only representative of the types of tools that are available.

Table 1 Some Representative Tools for Rapid Prototyping

PLATFORM	TOOL	COMPANY
PC	Choreographer Demo II (Dan Bricklin) Easel Protoscreens	Guidance Technology, Pittsburgh, PA Sage Software, Beaverton, OR Easel Corp., Woburn, MA Bailey & Bailey, Ogden, UT
Macintosh	HyperCard SuperCard Plus Prototyper	Apple Computer, Cupertino, CA Silicon Beach Software, San Diego, CA Spinnaker Software, Cambridge, MA SmethersBarnes, Portland, OR
Graphics Workstation (e.g., Sun, Silicon Graphics, DEC)	DataViews LUIS SL-GMS TAE Plus VAPS	V.I. Corp, Northampton, MA Lockheed, Austin Div., Austin, TX SL Corp., Corte Madera, CA COSMIC, University of Georgia, Athens, GA Virtual Prototypes, Inc., Montreal, Canada

Rapid Prototyping as Part of the System Development Process

Among the primary benefits of rapid prototyping is the speed with which initial prototypes can be developed. In relatively short order a system interface can be constructed that can assist in zeroing in on the essential requirements. It is, however, important to note that other elements in the software development cycle must be present so that rapid prototyping is meaningful. Rapid prototyping by itself is very seductive, but other essential elements of the software development process must be present for the prototype to be of any value.

In particular, the most important element that must accompany rapid prototyping is system analysis. In this context, system analysis refers to the process of examining and understanding who will use the system and what they want to do with it. Note that there are two elements of the analysis process. The first is an understanding of the characteristics of the user. Often this is considered trivial and unimportant and is, therefore, neglected. In reality, unless the system is designed for the intended user, much documentation, training, and costly change will be required before the system can be effectively used.

The experience, educational level, capabilities, and mission of the intended users must be understood, as well as the environment within which the system will be employed. Will there be different types of users that the system must accommodate, such as infrequent as well as expert users? Are the users high school graduates or skilled professionals? Do they have any computer background? Will the system be used in an office environment or a high stress field situation? Are responses required immediately; are critical operations involved such as in a power plant? These questions must be addressed as part of the analysis process.

The other key part of the analysis is an examination of the functions that are to be performed by the system. Various types of analysis can be used in conjunction with rapid prototyping to understand and capture the functionality of the system. Some of the common types of analyses include the following:

• **Functional Analysis** — An identification of the functions that the system is to perform. A common technique is to examine the primary functions and then subdivide each of these into components. The process continues for several levels of detail until all the functionality is identified. Each of the identified functions is then analyzed to determine the the hardware, software and operator interactions required. Rapid prototyping can be used to simulate the major functions.

• **Operational Sequence Analysis** — An examination of the operations that a user would perform when operating the system. The operations are identified sequentially as if they were being performed. This is particularly effective for systems that follow a standard order for use. When using interactive rapid prototyping it is relatively easy to capture a sequence of operations.

• **Critical Operations Analysis** — If a system encompasses certain critical operations, such as controlling a manufacturing process, the analysis should focus on these critical operations for the rapid prototyping phase. Other operations can be examined after an initial version of the rapid prototype is constructed.

- **Scenario Building** — A technique wherein a particular user and a particular scenario of operation are postulated as a starting point for identifying all the elements of system. This technique is particularly effective with rapid prototyping, as it is quick and initially only covers a subset of the system functionality.

It is important to emphasize that the rapid prototyping approach does not replace the analysis process; rather it can accelerate and facilitate it. The analysis need not be complete before the rapid prototyping starts. Some analysis, however, is required for the prototype to have a purpose. One can argue that in the past an inordinate amount of time was spent on the analysis process with little to show for it but a stack of documents that were only marginally related to developing the system. The rapid prototyping approach enables the analysis process to have a usable output.

Another step in the development process that is important to use with rapid prototyping is usability testing. Usability testing verifies the operability of the system with actual users. Traditionally this type of testing occurs at the completion of the design phase of development. Unfortunately at this point in the development cycle it is costly and time consuming to make changes to the system. As mentioned previously in the listing of benefits, rapid prototyping permits and even encourages testing prior to the design phase. During this predesign phase it is relatively easy to incorporate changes. Finally, after the design is completed, usability testing should again occur to verify system operability.

Concerns When Using Rapid Prototyping

Like every innovative development, rapid prototyping has its limitations and drawbacks. While these must be addressed, they do not negate the benefits. The most common pitfall is inadequate analysis. The importance of the analysis phase has been discussed in the previous section. Alavi (1984) reported that the prototyping process was difficult to manage and control, but these shortcomings did not outweigh the potential benefits. Several other difficulties and pitfalls that have been identified when using the rapid prototyping approach:

- **"Wow, It's Almost Done"** — Because the prototype looks so much like a completed system, customers get the mistaken idea that the system is almost finished — even when told very clearly that it is only a prototype! It must be emphasized to customers that what they are viewing is only a simulation and not the actual system.
- **Unattainable Expectations** — Because of the ease and speed with which prototypes can be constructed, it is easy for the system developer to prototype something that cannot be delivered within the allocated time and budget. It is important to ensure that the prototype is realistic and falls within the plan of what can be accomplished.

- **Contractual Documents** — The current format of contracts, especially the established acquisition specifications of governmental procuring agencies, cannot accommodate rapid prototyping. Their specifications require certain Data Item Deliverable documents that can detract from the benefits of rapid prototyping by focusing on paperwork rather than engineering! Contractual vehicles are needed that will permit the rapid prototyping approach to replace some of the paperwork in the procurement process.

- **Infringement On the Design Process** — When rapid prototypes are used as a visual specification, they can be viewed as infringing on the design process, which is supposed to follow the specification phase. By having a representation of the user interface, the charge can be made that the interface is already designed! This can be a serious drawback to developing fresh ideas during the design phase. When a rapid prototype is used as the specification, it must be clearly stated that it is not to be misconstrued as the design. Design is still needed to address system integration and performance issues such as response time, error handling, and help functions.

- **Users That Are Never Satisfied** — The iterative approach of rapid prototyping has its down side. Users can become greedy and ask for items or functions that are beyond the scope of the project. "It was so easy for you to to give me X, why can't you give me Z?" Experience using rapid prototyping has shown that this is not a major problem, but the potential for abuse does exist. In these situations it is important to clearly define the scope of the project and to set limitations on the process.

The Future for Rapid Prototyping

Rapid prototyping can be viewed as one of a series of emerging techniques that will streamline the entire system development process. Other such developments include the use of off-the-shelf hardware and software and the use of computer aided software engineering (CASE) tools. Some even consider rapid prototyping tools to be a subset of CASE tools. One thing is certain, the traditional development model (sometimes referred to as the waterfall model) is fading.

In addition to the efficiency of system development using rapid prototyping, another key factor favoring this approach is the increasing emphasis on the importance of the system user. Years ago, systems were driven by the demands of hardware limitations. The important criteria in system development were elegance and compactness of the code, so as not to waste precious memory. We are technologically past that now and can focus on the more important elements of the system, namely the user.

Initiatives such as Total Quality Management or Quality Function Deployment focus on the needs of the user or customer (King, 1989). The rapid prototyping approach advocated here is founded on the user interface as the driving force in system design. As these initiatives become more prevalent in U.S. industry, so will approaches that emphasize the user.

References

1. Alavi, Maryam, "An Assessment of the Protoyping Approach to Information Systems Development," *Communications of the ACM*, Vol 27, No. 6, June 1984.
2. Boar, Bernard H., *Application Prototyping: A Requirements Definition Strategy For the 80s*, John Wiley & Sons, New York, NY,1984.
3. Connell, J.L. & Shafer, L.B., *Structured Rapid Prototyping: An Evolutionary Approach to Software Development*, Yourdon Press/ Prentice Hall, Englewood Cliffs, N.J., 1989.
4. King, Bob, *Better Designs in Half the Time: Implementing Quality Function Deployment in America*, Goal/QPC, Methuen MA, 1989.
5. Tanik, M.M. & Yeh, R.T. Rapid Prototyping in Software Development. In Rapid Prototyping: Developing Systems for the Future. Computer, Vol 22, No. 5 IEEE Computer Society, May 1989.

15   Tools for Task Analysis: Graphs and Matrices

JOHN F. McGREW

Pacific Bell

San Ramon, California

I. Introduction

The purpose of task analysis is to transfer knowledge from one group of people to another for system development. Task analysis is the description and analysis of the content, structure, and relationships of the job related task performed by a person. The task knowledge is usually gathered by a human factors specialist and then analyzed and structured to meet the needs of the recipients. The recipients are the system development teams for functional analysis, task allocation, requirements, design, implementation, and testing.

The transfer is most effective when the method for describing the knowledge about tasks is common to both groups. Unfortunately most professions have different ways of describing their content. This difference is particularly large between computer system developers and their clients. The clients usually described their tasks by documents or text, while system developers describe computer systems by requirements, schematics, programming languages, algorithms, and structures such as trees. Even within the systems development community there are different methods for describing task knowledge. For instance, the format and structure used by the requirements team is different from that used by the design team.

There are many techniques for doing a task analysis; some are esoteric and used only by an individual, some are used by a small group, and some are mandated by organizations. The output of almost all of these methods is difficult to use for the different people or processes in the systems life cycle.

Experience with several system development projects has shown that in practice knowledge transfer is incomplete, or not done at all. Usually the only people who understand the user's tasks are the ones who created the task analysis. It is not uncommon for a detailed task analysis to be done and then left on the shelf. The knowledge contained in the task analysis is never effectively transferred to the other groups involved in a system's development. The reason for this is a lack of methods and tools for the transfer of the knowledge in the task analysis to the other concerned groups in the development process.

The tools and method described here enable a task analysis to be done so that the knowledge about the tasks is analyzed and then transformed into the different formats needed by the different groups involved with a system's design. Several things must be done for a successful task analysis:

- construct a map of the task domain,
- analyze the map's contents,
- determine who will receive the analysis, and
- transform the task mapping into a format that the target audience can use.

The mapping of the task domain has two characteristics: it is user centered and it is a cognitive mapping. The focus of the task analysis is the user's interaction with the task, not the system being developed. Converting the contents of the task analysis into system concepts comes later. If the focus is on the system being developed, the users will be forced to conform to the system rather than the system being designed for the user. If the task analysis contains future system architecture terms, schematics, and concepts, then it is not user centered.

In keeping with being user centered, the task analysis is a description of how the users think about and interact with their tasks. It is a cognitive mapping. Just a listing and description of the task elements does not constitute a task analysis. The task analysis must include how the user organizes, sequences, and interacts with the tasks. After it is understood how the tasks are structured and performed, they can be allocated in the system to either the machine or the user. The determination is based on a match between the the task characteristics and the machine or the user's abilities.

Once the task information has been mapped and analyzed, the contents are transformed into the formats and structures used at the different stages of system development. Several of the major uses and formats of the task analysis used are

- functional analysis (functional flows and task functional descriptions);
- requirements (task descriptions and relationships);
- task allocation (task description, type, and relationships);
- design (task relationships, structure, and content);
- implementation (task structure and content); and
- testing (task test criterion).

One of the bottlenecks in system development has been finding a representation common to these different formats and a method for converting from one format to another. This chapter describes a system for doing a task analysis, analyzing it, and converting it to the different formats required.

Basic to this system is the ability to represent the same information in different ways. It is well known that a change in representation can facilitate problem solving. The problems in the transfer of information encountered during the task analysis, requirements specification, and design phases of software development can be resolved by taking advantage of two additional methods of representation in addition to the traditional text description and outline. These methods of representing information are graphs and matrices. These methods have been used to generate and verify task descriptions, analyze and simplify the relationships among tasks, generate data structures such as networks and trees, and derive content for menus and screens.

In the sections that follow, the four purposes of this system will be described. The first section will describe how graph methods can be used to facilitate the gathering of information from users or experts and to increase the validity and consistency of such information. The second section will discuss the use of a matrix for the analysis of the relationships among tasks elements. It will point out redundancies and suggest complexity reducing reorganizations. The third section will illustrate the use of a matrix for design by using the concept of the clique and cut points to suggest a better organization of the information. Finally the fourth section will show the conversion of the information into menus.

II. The Use of Graphs for Task Description and Verification

This description and discussion of graphs is not intended to be precise or detailed but to demonstrate in a general way their uses and benefits for task analysis. A graph is a collection of points connected by lines. The points are called nodes, and the lines are called edges, arcs, or links. The nodes can be used to represent events, objects, or processes. The links represent relationships between the nodes. This relationship can be unidirectional between two nodes (a one way link from node A to node B) or it can be bidirectional between two nodes (a two way link between nodes A and B). A graph in which the links have a value or are labeled is called a network.   For an introduction to graphs and their use, see Busacker and Saaty, 1965, Deo, 1974, Harary, 1969, and Temperley, 1981.

There are many examples of graphs in uses. Hardware wiring diagrams, software architecture schematics, functional analysis bubble charts, and many other applications are all types of graphs. In fact the tree used extensively by software engineering is a type of graph (an acyclic digraph).

A graph commonly used to describe ideas is a semantic net (Quillian, 1967). A semantic net is used to describe the relationship among concepts, such as family relationships. The people are represented as nodes and the links are labeled with the different relationships (sibling of, child of).

The type of graph used in this analysis is one in which only the nodes are labeled and the links or edges are not labeled.   There is assumed to be a consistent relationship among all of the nodes; in fact, part of the method is to find such a consistent relationship. The relationship used in the example below is "needs access to or is connected to." Since a node can represent anything, different types of relationships themselves, such as sibling of or child of, can be placed on nodes. This eliminates the need to label the links.

The advantage of this type of graph is that it can be converted to an adjacency matrix for analysis. If the links have different values as in a semantic net, then it is not possible to convert the network to an adjacency matrix. In fact a difficulty with semantic nets is that they were large, complex, and hard to understand. Furthermore, until recently not much analysis has been done with them.

There are several reasons for using a graph to represent a task analysis. First, a graph provides a good representation for the relationship among the task elements. The usual method for describing the task in a task analysis is a text description. This textual description often is in outline format. This style of presentation implies that the structure of the task is the list structure of the outline even if this is not the intent. The real structure, if collected at all, is buried in the textual description. While designers agree that the list is usually not a good representation for task relationships, it is the one that is immediately available, and therefore it is often the one used.

A graph provides a map of the user's task by representing the tasks as nodes and the interrelationships as links. The graph provides a method for visualizing the interrelationships and complexities of the task. The graph avoids implying a structure for the task that is an artifact of the method of presentation. By using a graph, the designer can immediately grasp the complexity of the relationships among the tasks.

Another benefit of using graphs is that the visual representation provides feedback during the acquisition of the information. Experience has shown that the users seldom realize the full implications of their statements about a task. The immediate visual feedback to the user provides the implications of what has been said about a task.

For this reason it is often useful to sketch a graph of what a user is saying about a task as information about the tasks is being gathered. The sketch provides immediate feedback and helps clarify the task description. In fact it often forces the user to think about the task from perspectives that he or she has not considered before. In several instances, relationships that the user was not aware of have been discovered, and in one instant, a missing piece of information about the task was identified. The result is a confirmation of the validity of a design early in the design process.

The use of graphs enables validity and reliability checks during the development of the task analysis Reliability refers to how consistent the data are; if you did the task analysis at a different time would you get the same results? Validity refers to how accurate the task analysis is. The validity of a set of data is limited by its reliability. The task analysis can be no more accurate (valid) than that core of tasks that remain consistent with each iteration.

A further aid in establishing the reliability and validity is the checking of the symmetry of the relationships among the tasks. The relationship among the tasks is checked from each direction. For instances, if you have four tasks A,B,C, and D, you first ask about the relationship of A to B, C, and D. Then when you are doing B, you ask about the relationship of B to A, C, and D, etc. In essence each link is checked from multiple directions.

Because it is easy to visualize and grasp the relationships among tasks in a graph, previous work can be quickly reviewed and changes quickly made. By reviewing the previous work as new work is done, the graphs stabilize over the course of the task analysis. By the time the task analysis is finished, it is highly reliable.

Graph theory has a well developed mathematical basis. There are many theorems, algorithms, and techniques that can be use for the analysis of a task analysis's content. Concepts like connected components, cut points, and shortest paths are useful for understanding the task and designing interfaces (Even, 1979, Gibbons, 1985, Golumbic, 1980, and Tarjan, 1983). In the example to follow, the concepts of a connected component and a cut point will be used to analyze and simplify the structure of a task analysis.

Finally, graphs can be transformed into the format needed by the people who use the information. The trees, data flow diagrams, state transition diagrams, and network schematics used in software development are all types of graphs. The graph used to represent the task analysis is a form basic to those already being used by design engineers.

The methods described in this chapter have been used on several projects at two institutions. The projects have included large ongoing system designs, a proof-of-concept prototype for an expert system, and redesign and update of an existing systems. The size of the task analysis has ranged from about 50 to over 300 task elements.

The example presented here succinctly demonstrates the principles. This example is used to show how the technique works rather than as an example of a complete task analysis. The example uses only the top level of an analysis that was eight levels deep.

This is a description of the top level activities of the meteorologist in the centers that control air traffic between airports (McGrew, 1987, McGrew, 1990). The descriptions of the tasks given here are brief and capture only the essence of the task;

the actual task descriptions are more detailed.   The twelve top level tasks are as follows:

1. Start. Start the shift or shift relief.
2. Assess Short Term Weather. Analyze the weather for the next two hours.
3. Construct & Disseminate CWA. Generate the Central Weather Advisory.
4. Assess Long Term Weather. Analyze the weather for the next 12 hours.
5. Construct & Disseminate MIS. Generate the Meteorological Impact Statement.
6. Construct Shift Briefing. Generate the weather briefing for the air traffic controllers.
7. Brief Weather Coordinator. Brief the weather coordinator for the air traffic controllers.
8. Monitor Weather. Keep track of the weather as it develops and changes.
9. Low Priority Tasks. Training, reports, administrative duties.
10. Brief Incoming Meteorologist. Brief the incoming meteorologist for the next shift.
11. High Priority Tasks. Weather analysis for aircraft in trouble or severe   weather developments.
12. End. End of shift.

During the task analysis, the graph for each task is constructed, used for feedback, and verified with the task expert. These initial graphs are usually sketches done by hand and used to guide the discussions about the tasks and their structure. When the sketches stabilize they are drawn as a final graph.

Figures 1 through 12 show the connectivity for each of the tasks. Each task is represented by a node (small circle) in the graph. Tasks (nodes) that are related are connected by a line (edge). The line is solid with no arrowheads for bidirectional connections and dashed with an arrowhead for unidirectional connections.

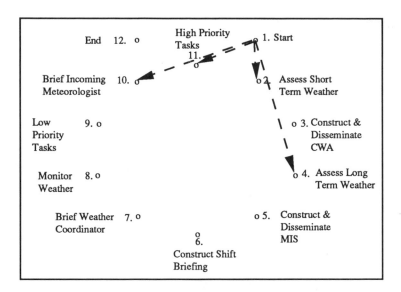

Figure 1. Graph for Start of Shift. The dashed lines indicate a one way connection in the direction of the arrowhead. Figure adapted with permission from the author, *McGrew, John F.*, Operations Engineering Resource Center Report, 1987.

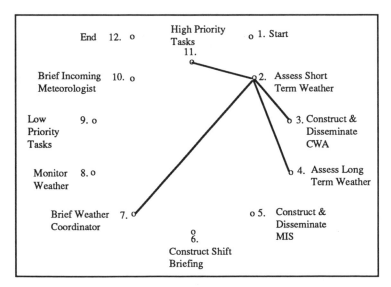

Figure 2. Graph for Assess Short Term Weather. The solid lines indicate a two way connection between nodes. Figure adapted with permission from the author, *McGrew, John F.*, Operations Engineering Resource Center Report, 1987.

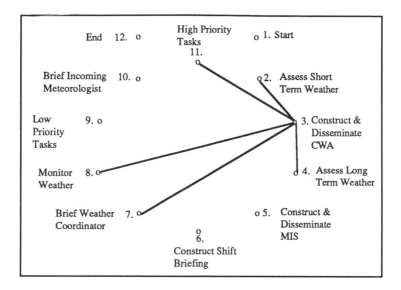

Figure 3. Graph for Construct and Disseminate CWA. The solid lines indicate a two way connection between nodes. Figure adapted with permission from the author, *McGrew, John F.*, Operations Engineering Resource Center Report, 1987.

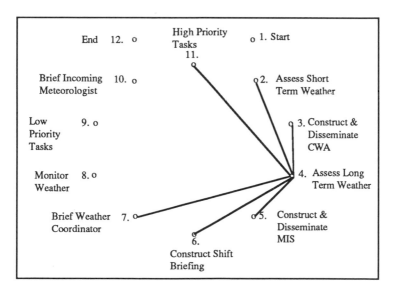

Figure 4. Graph for Assess Long Term Weather. The solid lines indicate a two way connection between nodes. Figure adapted with permission from the author, *McGrew, John F.*, Operations Engineering Resource Center Report, 1987.

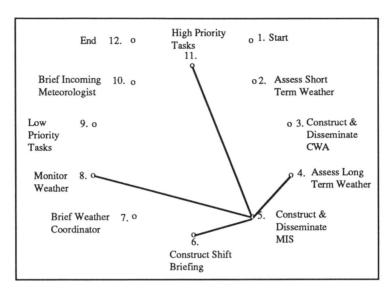

Figure 5. Graph for Construct and Disseminate MIS. The solid lines indicate a two way connection between nodes. Figure adapted with permission from the author, *McGrew, John F.*, Operations Engineering Resource Center Report, 1987.

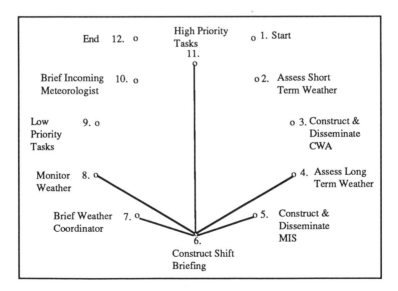

Figure 6. Graph for Construct Shift Briefing. The solid lines indicate a two way connection between nodes. Figure adapted with permission from the author, *McGrew, John F.*, Operations Engineering Resource Center Report, 1987.

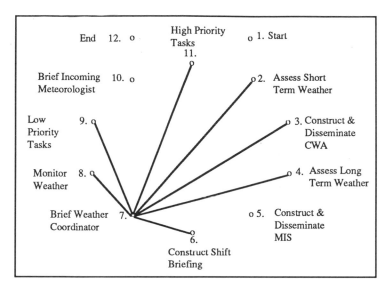

Figure 7. Graph for Brief Weather Coordinator. The solid lines indicate a two way connection between nodes. Figure adapted with permission from the author, *McGrew, John F.*, Operations Engineering Resource Center Report, 1987.

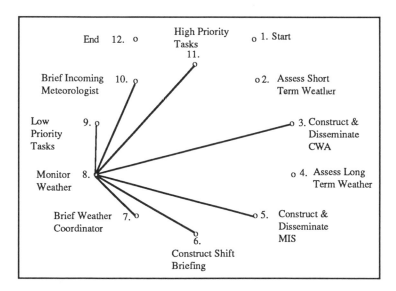

Figure 8. Graph for Monitor Weather. The solid lines indicate a two way connection between nodes. Figure adapted with permission from the author, *McGrew, John F.*, Operations Engineering Resource Center Report, 1987.

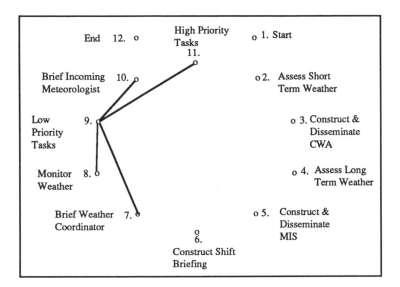

Figure 9. Graph for Low Priority Tasks. The solid lines indicate a two way connection between nodes. Figure adapted with permission from the author, *McGrew, John F.*, Operations Engineering Resource Center Report, 1987.

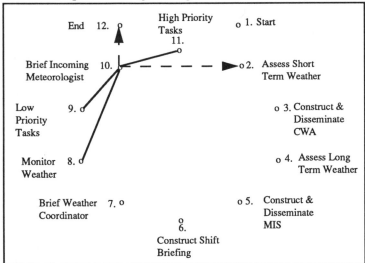

Figure 10. Graph for Brief Incoming Meteorologist. The dashed lines indicate a one way connection in the direction of the arrowhead. The solid lines indicate a two way connection between nodes. Figure adapted with permission from the author, *McGrew, John F.*, Operations Engineering Resource Center Report, 1987.

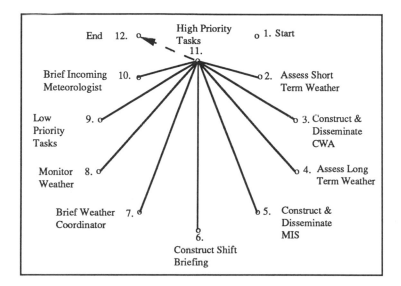

Figure 11. Graph for High Priority Tasks. The dashed lines indicate a one way connection in the direction of the arrowhead. The solid lines indicate a two way connection between nodes. Figure adapted with permission from the author, *McGrew, John F.*, Operations Engineering Resource Center Report, 1987.

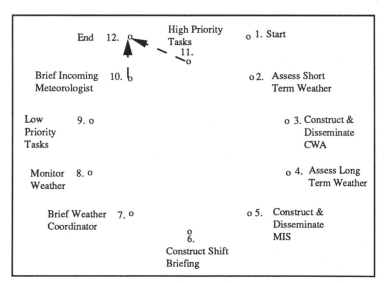

Figure 12. Graph for End of Shift. The solid lines indicate a two way connection between nodes. Figure adapted with permission from the author, *McGrew, John F.*, Operations Engineering Resource Center Report, 1987.

The basis for a connection is the need by the meteorologist to have access to the other tasks when processing information about the weather. For example, Figure 1 and 10. It also shows that he will not need access to the tasks not connected by a line.

It is also easy to see that some tasks have more connections than others. Tasks 4, 7, 8, and 11 have many connections. Eleven is actually connected to all the others except for 1 (start). Task 11 is a high priority task; these are the actions taken when there is need for immediate weather information for an aircraft in an emergency situation. This is also a low frequency task, so in the final design there needs to be a consideration of the trade-off between high priority and low frequency.

Figure 13 is the composite of all of the individual graphs. It shows the overall connectivity and complexity for the twelve top level tasks. From the graph, one gets an overall appreciation for the complexity of the task. There are multiple paths that can be taken to and from the other task. This reflects the way that the meteorologist performed the weather analysis. The user interface design must allow for this complexity.

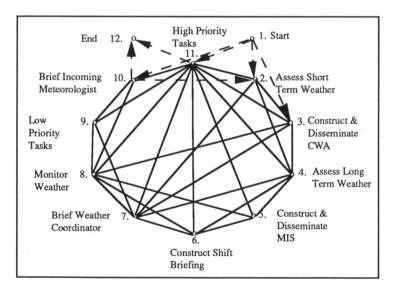

Figure 13. Combined Graph of the Twelve Tasks. The dashed lines indicate a one way connection in the direction of the arrowhead. The solid lines indicate a two way connection between nodes. Figure adapted with permission from the author, *McGrew, John F.*, Operations Engineering Resource Center Report, 1987.

There are various shapes that can be used for the graph. Experience with different ways of presenting graphs has shown that the simplest way to arrange the nodes is on the circumference of a circle. If there are a lot of nodes, it is possible to use concentric circles to arrange the nodes.

No single representation can show everything. While the graph is a good mechanism for facilitating the gathering of information about tasks and showing the relationships, overall structure, and complexity among the tasks, it is difficult to use in analysis.

As there is much gained in the shift from text to graph, there is much to be gained in the shift from the graph to an adjacency matrix. An adjacency matrix shows which nodes are connected by an edge (i.e., are adjacent) in a graph.

III. Analysis of the Task Interrelationships

The conversion of a graph to an adjacency matrix provides further details about the task analysis and makes it easier to apply analysis techniques. Figure 14 shows the the conversion of the graph in Figure 13 to an adjacency matrix. Each task element becomes a row and a column in the matrix. The tasks numbers that are listed along the sides and top of the matrix are the same as in the task outline and graph. If the task elements are connected with a line in the graph, a 1 is placed in the cell at the intersection of the row and column representing the tasks. If the tasks are not connected the cell is left blank. If each task is considered connected to itself, there is a 1 in the intersection of the row and column cell for a task. If there are no connections between the task elements, the cell is left blank. Figure 15 shows the resulting matrix.

The matrix will be symmetrical if all of the connections are bidirectional. If there are unidirectional connections in the graph, then the matrix will be asymmetrical. If the matrix is symmetrical, then the information in it can be represented by just the upper triangular or lower triangular matrix. In practice, the matrices of task analysis are seldom symmetrical.

The sums for each row and column provide data about each task element. The row sums indicate the number of elements to which the row heading is connected. This

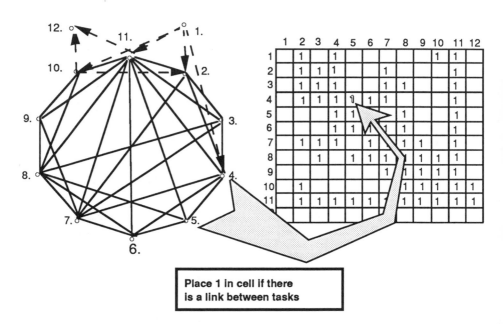

Figure 14. Converting a Graph to an Adjacency Matrix. Figure adapted with permission from the author, *McGrew, John F.*, 1990.

gives a number for the spread of effect of the task. It also indicates the number of potential paths that can be taken from that task to other tasks. This number is called the out degree of a node in graph parlance.

The column sums at the bottom of the matrix indicate the number of elements that have access to a task. This number can give an indication of the potential frequency with which this task will be needed by the others. This number is called the in degree of a node.

From this information, prioritization based on a task's effect can be made. If necessary, it is also possible to gather information about the frequency of use of a tasks or its importance. This information can be represented in additional matrices. In this example this information was not systematically collected.

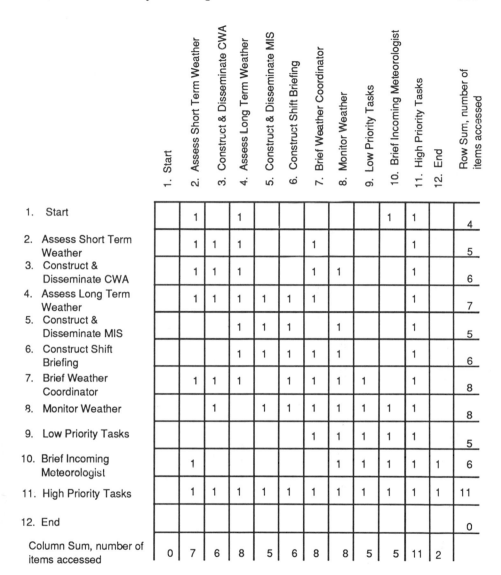

	1. Start	2. Assess Short Term Weather	3. Construct & Disseminate CWA	4. Assess Long Term Weather	5. Construct & Disseminate MIS	6. Construct Shift Briefing	7. Brief Weather Coordinator	8. Monitor Weather	9. Low Priority Tasks	10. Brief Incoming Meteorologist	11. High Priority Tasks	12. End	Row Sum, number of items accessed
1. Start		1		1						1	1		4
2. Assess Short Term Weather		1	1	1			1				1		5
3. Construct & Disseminate CWA		1	1	1			1	1			1		6
4. Assess Long Term Weather		1	1	1	1	1	1				1		7
5. Construct & Disseminate MIS			1	1	1		1				1		5
6. Construct Shift Briefing			1	1	1	1	1				1		6
7. Brief Weather Coordinator		1	1	1		1	1	1	1		1		8
8. Monitor Weather			1		1	1	1	1	1	1	1		8
9. Low Priority Tasks							1	1	1	1	1		5
10. Brief Incoming Meteorologist		1						1	1	1	1	1	6
11. High Priority Tasks		1	1	1	1	1	1	1	1	1	1	1	11
12. End													0
Column Sum, number of items accessed	0	7	6	8	5	6	8	8	5	5	11	2	

Figure 15. The Adjacency Matrix for the Twelve High Level Meteorologists Tasks. Figure reproduced with permission from the author, *McGrew, John F.,* 1990.

The matrix can also show patterns of connections that are difficult to determine from a graph. Along the diagonal from the upper left to the lower right of the matrix there are clusters of ones representing related tasks. These are tasks that are often done together or right after each other. Therefore, it is important to keep these clusters together in the design process. These clusters along with some basic concepts from graph theory can be used for design purposes.

In order to get the clusters of 1's diagonally, in a matrix one interchanges the rows and columns. Each time that a row (or column) is moved, the corresponding column (or row) must also be moved to the same relative position in the matrix. For instance, if row five is moved to the second row in the matrix, then column five must be move to the second column in the matrix. In order for the permuted matrix to be isomorphic (of the same structure) to the original matrix, it is necessary to keep the rows and columns corresponding to each other in the same relative position.

Getting a 1 in each cell of the main diagonal of the matrix, and if possible the diagonals immediately above and below it, will show a complete path through the tasks. The path presented by the diagonals in Figure 14 corresponds to the path along tasks (1, 2, 3, 4, 5, 6, 7, 8, 9, 10, 11) in the overall graph (Figure 13). This is the sequence of events after permutation of the rows and columns. It also corresponds to the sequence of events frequently followed by the meteorologist.

As a further illustration of analysis, two concepts from graph theory can be identified in the matrix representation of the task analysis. The concepts are those of a clique or (connected components) and cut points. A clique is a part of the graph (subgraph) whose nodes are connected with each other. If the clique has three nodes, its graph will look like a triangle; if it has four nodes, then it will look like a rectangle with its diagonals connected, and so forth.

Figure 14 has at least four possible cliques. They are along the diagonal, and some of them are shown by a square outline in Figure 16. The grouping in the middle does not have all of its cells filled and therefore is not a clique. It actually contains two cliques of three tasks, one in the upper left and one in the lower right.

A goal of the design process is to keep as many tasks together as possible. This cuts down on the number of menus, commands, or machine state traversals that must be made by the user. In this case the large middle square is highly connected, only four of its 25, (25 = 5 x 5), possible cells are not filled. The degree of connectedness can be set by the designer; it is a matter of design trade offs rather than a rigidly set principle. If there are readily available cliques in the matrix, it makes the design process easier. However if a few cells are not filled in a potential cliques, the

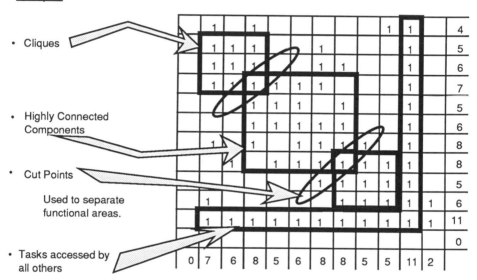

Figure 16. Some Graph Structures as Represented in an Adjacency Matrix. Figure adapted with permission from the author, *McGrew, John F.*, 1990.

constellation of tasks can nevertheless be considered as a connected unit. Since most of the cells are filled in this middle grouping, it makes sense to consider them as a whole

Cut points are nodes (it may be one node) in a subgraph that, when removed, will disconnect the graph into two or more separate graphs. In Figure 16, the cut points are indicated by an ellipse between the outlined cliques. It should be obvious that one would want to keep the cliques together and partition at the cut points if the design calls for dividing up the task elements into logical or functional areas.

IV. Applications of the Analytical Results to Design

An example of how to use the information obtained by the analyses of the task elements follows from the identification of the cliques and the cut points as illustrated in section II.

We have seen the overall relationships among the task elements in the graph (Figure 13). The analysis of the matrix of the graph suggests that there is a simpler, more compact, easier to understand graph of the high level tasks.

The cliques identified in Figure 15 can be considered functional areas because they are closely related. When users are working with one of these items, they are likely to want access to the other items in the cliques. These items should be kept together during analysis and design.

One of these functional areas is concerned with the assessment of the weather. This includes tasks 2, 3, and 4. These tasks assess the short term and long term weather. Another functional area is concerned with briefings. This includes 4, 5, 6, 7, and 8. These tasks construct and disseminate the briefings about the weather, along with the continual monitoring of the weather.

Task 4 is in both of these groupings. Since task 4 is interconnected with both groupings, it can be included in both groups. Redundancy is useful in user interface design. Providing information in more than one place saves the user from having to search for it in the middle of problem solving or task execution. Although the elimination of redundancy is a good principle in software and hardware engineering, it is not necessarily a good principle in user interface design. Removing redundancy from the user interface can increase the workload for the users by making them search in different places for items.

The third functional area is monitoring the weather and other duties. Tasks 8, 9, and 10 monitor the weather during the day, along with the execution of administrative, training, and other low priority tasks. Again there is redundancy in this grouping; task 8 is in this and the previous grouping.

The fourth functional area is high priority tasks. This is task 11, which includes the actions taken to determine the weather conditions that might affect an aircraft during an emergency situation. Because of its importance and the fact that it is connected to all other tasks, it is considered as a group by itself.

These four groupings allow a simpler representation for the top level tasks. Each area is condensed into a node. The nodes are then graphed with the relationship that connected the original groups. The redesign of the task structure is given in Figure 17.

The simplified structure is a strongly connected graph of the four elements, Assess Weather, Briefing, Monitor Weather, and High Priority Tasks. The connections from Assess Weather to Briefing to Monitor Weather to Assess Weather are all one way links. These one way connections are shown as a counterclockwise flow in

Condense, Simplify, and Regraph

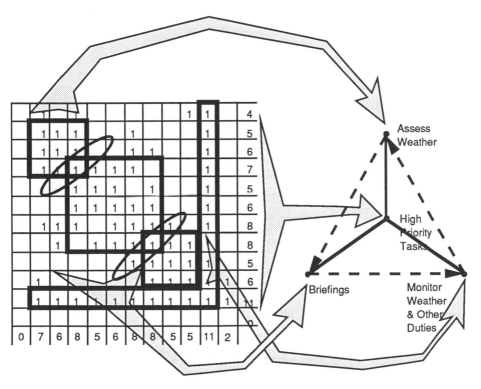

Figure 17. Transformation of Structures Identified in an Adjacency Matrix into a Graph. This simplified graph represents the underlying structure of the twelve tasks. Figure adapted with permission from the author, *McGrew, John F.*, 1990.

Figure 17. This flow is indicated in the matrix by the sequence of the cliques along the matrix diagonal. The fourth element, High Priority Tasks has two way connections to each of the other three elements. This is because it is necessary to reach this element from any of the others and then to return.

A comparison of the two graphs, the original graph and the graph after the analysis and simplifications, can be seen in Figure 18. The process of analysis using the matrix has shown an underlying simpler structure for the tasks done by the meteorologist. This simpler structure provides the basis for the transfer of information to the other members of the design team. This simpler graph can be transformed into other formats that meet the needs of the design process. One such transformation will be demonstrated.

The transformation will be into interface widgets. This is an example of the transformation of the task analysis information into high level interface design structures. A widget is a user interface device for interaction with the computer

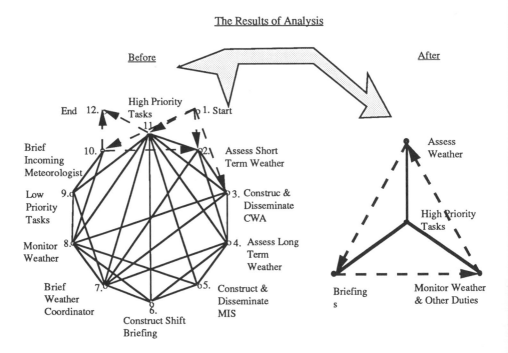

Figure 18. Comparison of the Graphs for the Tasks before and after Analysis with an Adjacency Matrix. Figure adapted with permission from the author, *McGrew, John F.*, 1990.

system. Examples are the various icons used in graphic interfaces, windows, radio buttons, scrolling arrow and boxes, and the different types of pull down or pop up menus. The widget in this example will be menus.

The transformation of the graph structure into widgets is done by means of spanning trees. A spanning tree is a tree that includes each node of a graph but not necessarily all of its links. There is a type of spanning tree called a minimal spanning tree, which is the smallest tree that spans a graph. It is smallest in the sense that it has the fewest number of links. For each graph there is a set of minimal spanning trees. For example, a completely connected graph has four nodes, A, B, C, and D (it would look like a rectangle with both of its diagonals connected) will have several different possible minimal spanning trees. One possible minimal spanning tree would be A connected directly to each of the other nodes B, C, and D. Another possibility would be A connected to B, which is connected to C, which is connected to D. The first tree is one level deep (one step from A to B, C, or D) while the other is four levels deep (A to B to C to D). Which spanning tree selected depends on the design situation: a highly structured linear process with sequential access to the menus, or a more flexible structure requiring more expertise to use.

Generating the spanning tree organizes the cyclic task interactions into a hierarchical structure. The use of a minimal spanning tree to start the process ensures that this is done in the best possible manner. The final result will not necessarily be a minimal spanning tree because of the addition of branches and nodes to accommodate cycles in the graph. This hierarchical structure is a representation that is commonly used in software design and engineering.

V. Generating Menus

Menus are generated from the simplified graph by converting the graph to a spanning tree, expanding that tree to include all of the original tasks, and generating the menus from the expanded tree. Figure 19 shows the result of generating a spanning tree from the simplified graph. The one way connections in the graph from A to B to C are converted to a tree with A at the top (root) going to B, which in turn goes to C, which in turn returns to A. The two way connections of each of the nodes to D is represented in the tree by connecting D to each of A, B, and C. This tree captures the essence of the task as described in the simplified graph. The user goes

Generate a Spanning Tree

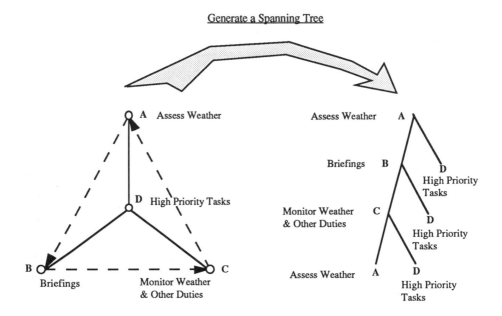

Figure 19. The Generation of a Spanning Tree for the Simplified Graph. Additional branches and leaves have been added to the tree for the cycles in the graph. Figure adapted with permission from the author, *McGrew, John F.*, 1990.

from task A, Assess Weather, to B, Briefing, to C, Monitor Weather & Other Duties, and back to task A as required. At the same time, no matter which task the user is involved in he or she can go immediately to task D, High Priority Tasks. Although the minimal spanning tree is the starting point, the spanning tree that is generated may not be minimal. It may be necessary to add branches to the tree for the cycles in the graph. This was done for the branches to the High Priority Tasks at nodes B and C and for Assess Weather at node C.

While this tree captures the essentials of the tasks, it lacks the details necessary to generate the menus for the user interface. To get the details it will be necessary to expand the tree to include the contents of the original graph.

The tree to include is expanded by adding back the tasks that were condensed to make the simple graph's nodes. The best source for this information is the adjacency matrix. By going back to the groups outlined in the matrix (Figure 15) it is possible to expand the tree at each level. Figure 20 shows the result of this expansion. In addition the tasks needed at the start of the day or shift are added to the expanded tree.

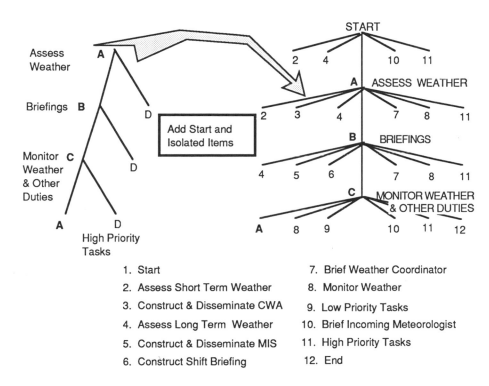

Figure 20. Expanding the tree of the Simplified Graph to Include the Details Contained in the Original Graph. Figure reproduced with permission from the author, *McGrew, John F.*, 1990.

There is considerable redundancy in the expanded tree. For example, task 4, Assess Long Term Weather, is included at the tree levels for Start, Assess Weather, and Briefings. The principle is to keep together tasks that are logically connected even if that means considerable redundancy in the user interface structure. This reduces the cognitive and work load on the user by placing it on the machine. We are designing the interface to fit the user's needs, not retraining the user to conform to the machine.

Again, there are design trade-offs in the placing of tasks in the expanded tree structure. Level B, Briefings, in the expanded tree could contain eight items but it only contains six. The other two items, task 2 and 3, would come from the connections to task 7, Brief Weather Coordinator (see Figure 15). In this case, tasks

2 and 3 have been left off because of their tighter coupling with level A, Assess Weather. Since the mapping of the task domain is complete, explicit, and easy to grasp in the graphs and matrix, it is possible to see the consequence of making design trade-offs. Here the consequence is minimal.

The final step is to convert the expanded graph into the appropriate widgets, in this case, menus. This is done by going across the expanded tree at a given level and constructing a menu, as in Figure 21. Each menu has access to the relevant tasks and

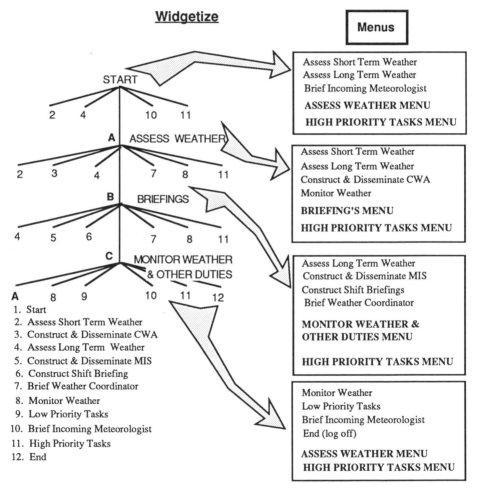

Figure 21. Converting the Expanded Tree into the Appropriate Widgets for the User Interface Design. Menus are used here for illustration only. Figure reproduced with permission from the author, *McGrew, John F.*, 1990.

to the other needed menus. The menu construction is such that at any given place in the menu structure all of the necessary task elements are present but none of the unnecessary ones. We can make this claim with confidence because we have a mapping of the task domain and can clearly identify what is needed when.

Figure 21 shows menus that could be constructed from the tree. Again there have been some choices made on what to include on a given menu, particularly if a task can be included on most of the menus.

VI. Conclusions

This chapter was an overview of a method based on graph theory and matrix algebra, for transfering the information in a task analysis to the system development team. This was done by identifying concepts in graph and matrix theory that relate to design problems that have surfaced in my experience. The relevant graph and matrix concepts were identified without specifying the details or the algorithms. The specific content and details are available in the cited references. Schanevelt, 1990, McDonald & Schaneveldt, 1988, and Hartson 1990, are some additional sources for converting networks to menus. An excellent source for investigating graph theory with a computer is Skiena, 1990.

References

1.   Busacker, Robert G. and Saaty, Thomas L. *Finite Graphs and Networks: An Introduction with Applications.* McGraw-Hill, New York, 1965.

2.   Deo, Narsingh. *Graph Theory With Applications to Engineering and Computer Science.* Prentice-Hall, Inc., Englewood Cliffs, NJ, 1974.

3.   Even, Shimon. *Graph Algorithms.* Computer Science Press, Inc., Rockville, MD, 1979.

4.   Gibbons, Alan. *Algorithmic Graph Theory.* Cambridge University Press, New York, NY, 1985.

5.   Golumbic, Martin Charles. *Algorithmic Graph Theory and Perfect Graphs.* Academic Press, New York, NY, 1980.

6.   Harary, F. *Graph Theory.* Addsion-Wesley, Reading, MA, 1969.

7.   Hartson (Ed.). *Advances in Human-Computer Interaction, Volume 1.* Ablex Press, Norwood, NJ, 1990.

8. McDonald and Schvaneveldt. "The Application of User Knowledge to Interface Design." In R. Guindon (Ed.), *Cognitive Science and its Application for Human Computer Interaction.* Ablex Press, Hillsdale, NJ, 1988.

9. McGrew, John F. "Graph Methods For Task Analysis." Operations Engineering Resource Center Report. Jet Propulsion Laboratory, 1987.

10. McGrew, John F. "The Use of Graphs and Matrices in Task Analysis." Poster Session at BellCore Symposium on User Center-Design. Somerset, NJ, May 7-9, 1990.

11. Quillian, M.R. "Word Concepts: A Theory and Simulation for Basic Semitic Capabilities." *Behavioral Science* 12.5 (1967), 410-430.

12. Schvaneveldt (Ed.). *Pathfinder Associative Networks: Studies in Knowledge Organization..* Ablex Press, Norwood, NJ, 1990.

13. Skiena, Stenven. *Implementing Discrete Mathematics: Combinatorics and Graph Theory with Mathematica.* Addison-Wesley, Redwood City, CA, 1990.

14. Tarjan, Robert Endre. *Data Structures and Network Algorithms.* Society for Industrial and Applied Mathematics, Philadelphia, PA, 1983.

15. Temperley, H.N.V. *Graph Theory and Applications.* Halsted Press, New York, NY, 1981.

16

The HUFIT Planning, Analysis and Specification Toolset: Human Factors as a Normal Part of the I.T. Product Design Process

BERNARD J. CATTERALL,
BRONWEN C. TAYLOR and
MARGARET D. GALER

The HUSAT Research Institute
Loughborough
Leicestershire
United Kingdom

I. Introduction

A recent international conference on the theme of marketing ergonomics (Noordvijk, Netherlands, June 1988) achieved its impetus in response to a telling comment by Gallaway (1985). In calling for more practical and usable tools and techniques from the ergonomics/human factors community he stated that "...doing fantastic technical work is of little benefit to anyone if others don't have a need for, know about and use the information developed."

The work of the HUSAT Research Institute (Human Sciences and Advanced Technology) in the ESPRIT (European Strategic Programme for Research and Development in Information Technology) HUFIT Project — Human Factors in Information Technology — has reaffirmed that in order to be influential in a hard-edged business environment, ergonomics/human factors must be both demonstrably cost-effective and provided in a form which allows its knowledge base and expertise to be implemented appropriately. As users and applications differ, so the human factors tools and techniques required successfully to address the detailed problems that arise must themselves differ.

Additionally, tools and techniques must be developed which are sufficiently generic to be effective and usable in a range of design processes. Using this approach, the ergonomics/human factors practitioner is not directly involved in the final delivery of ergonomics expertise. Rather, he or she facilitates that delivery by providing suitable tools, techniques and methodologies, and through training.

The HUFIT Planning, Analysis, and Specification (PAS) Toolset described here arose as one of the many outputs of the large-scale HUFIT research and development project, which demonstrated a need to develop high-level, easy to use tools for the designers of generic products in information technology supplier companies. A further requirement, arising from the relative dearth of human factors practitioners in IT supplier companies, was that the tools should be usable without any support from human factors practitioners.

The Toolset, therefore, was designed to be easy to use by design teams with little or no previous human factors expertise, within the constraints of the product life cycle, and was intended to yield relevant, usable and timely information. Most importantly, the tools were designed to be both design-methodology and design-system independent. In essence, the aim was to enable designers themselves to take a user-centred design approach as a normal part of the product design process (Galer 1989; Taylor & Bonner 1989; Catterall, Allison & Maguire 1989).

To that extent, the tools developed are procedural, tailorable and therefore context-specific, being operable at levels suitable to the time allocation and personnel involvement appropriate to a given design window. The individual items of the Toolset are intended for use by personnel in marketing, product planning, design and development, testing, quality assurance, documentation and so on. The tools address user and task issues at the crucial early planning phases of the product development cycle. They are delivered to designers via training seminars.

II. The Research Background

The HUFIT Project represented the HUSAT Research Institute's first step into large-scale collaborative projects funded by the Commission of the European Community (CEC). Begun in December, 1984, after exploratory studies as early as 1983, the project was the flagship for human factors in the Office Systems division of the ESPRIT programme.

Its two main areas were research on Advanced Integrated Interfaces led by the project prime-contractor, the Fraunhofer Institute (Fhg-IAO) from Stuttgart, and secondly, research into human factors requirements for the information technology product design process led by HUSAT. A third set of activities recognised the need for an information dissemination role to ensure that project outcomes were made widely available to the European information technology community. HUSAT's HUFIT Planning, Analysis and Specification Toolset, therefore, represents only one of many outcomes of the HUFIT project as a whole. It developed in direct response to the results of the research phase of the project, which identified the needs of information technology product designers for human factors. It is interesting to note that the Toolset was not initially a planned outcome of the project at all — rather, as requirements became apparent, so the tools were iteratively developed in response, becoming a coherent set only after much work on their integration.

Early research (conducted mainly with designers in the HUFIT project industrial partner companies - ICL, Philips, Siemens, Bull and Olivetti) demonstrated the wide variability in design approaches of information technology supplier companies. Equally important was that there were also wide variations in the ways individual design teams within a company chose to or were able to implement a given design process. Information flows were often inadequate, and existing human factors tools and techniques were thought to be either largely inappropriate, usually having been developed with a specific, and often inappropriate, design methodology in mind, or requiring skilled human factors support at all times. Access to that kind of skilled human factors support was not widely available. There were not enough trained human factors specialists to go around and where they did exist, their inputs were often restricted to a given limited window in the design process, such as offering ergonomics design guideline advice or conducting usability evaluations for interface design. Moreover, many companies had no clear business case for including human factors.

HUSAT's view of the required scope of human factors tools in IT product design is based on socio-technical system theory and the principles of user centred design. These lead to the premise that human factors must be considered at all stages in the product life cycle — during requirements capture, specification, design, evaluation and implementation.

II.1. Socio-Technical Theory

Socio-technical theory, based on early studies in the coal-mining industry (Trist & Bamforth 1951), established that human and organisational issues cannot be considered in isolation from the technology, and as such the interdependences between the social and technical systems are fundamental to the effectiveness of any work organisation. Fragmented, piecemeal human factors projects concerned solely with any given design problem *in isolation* have, in general, failed to deliver effective solutions from either the viewpoint of the design organisation or of the user organisation (Eason 1989).

In the context of socio-technical system theory it is understood that only a more holistic approach to the development and exploitation of information technology systems and products will produce real and lasting benefits for their users. Similarly, the theory largely discredits the view of human factors as an optional contributor playing a largely negative role where, for instance, it exists only for end-process usability evaluations. Human factors issues, properly incorporated into the wider socio-technical strategy of the organisation, become an integral part of an effective business solution to information technology systems design. The cost-effectiveness of a given human factors approach can then be judged according to the same criteria as the other business factors affecting product or systems development — where positive effects may be demonstrable in widely separate sections of the total socio-technical system. The need, therefore, is for an holistic view of human factors input rooted within the social and technical constraints of the client organisation and within the business constraints of the design process itself.

II.2. User-Centred Design

The basis of HUSAT's work is that design which fails adequately to account for human factors will restrict the effective use of any information technology development. The HUFIT approach, therefore, advocates a user-centred design strategy where designers, planners, managers and marketeers, in fact all people involved in the design process are required to take explicit account of the requirements of users, their tasks (in the way that they actually perform them rather than in the way that they are intended to perform them) and the social and technical environments in which they interact. Any approach which seeks to limit consideration of user and task issues to the design stage is severely flawed. Equally, those which restrict human factors inputs to one point in the technical design, and which fail to involve user and task inputs at the earliest possible stages in the product or systems design life cycle will fail to deliver the benefits that are available from a more comprehensive approach.

User-centred design implies the active participation of users in the design process. This participation should be comprehensive and not simply part of an end-process evaluation procedure which seeks to identify design faults (usually too late for effective rectification). It should be part of an evolving and iterative design process. Users may, for instance, be actively involved in the specification procedure, in rapid-prototyping trials, throughout the quality assurance process and in the development of system implementation strategies, with a view to managing the process of organisational change.

II.3. The Human Factors in System Design Project

A source of invaluable information for the development of the HUFIT PAS Toolset was the outcome of another of HUSAT's research projects. The UK Alvey programme's "Human Factors in Systems Design" project (Eason & Harker 1989) proposed a number of implications for a successful human factors input to the systems design process. These focus on the need for a wide range of methods tailored, or tailorable, to the specific requirements of the different design contexts. No single approach, they argued, could possibly hope to address the widely varying contexts in which real design occurs. The major contextual forces revealed in the project survey were

- Generic versus bespoke (or tailor made) developments — each with different levels of user identification and/or participation
- Supplier versus user developments — exploring the nature of the customer/contractor relationship
- The size of the design project — as a determinant of the need for formality or flexibility in the human factors input and whether human factors experts or the designers themselves make the input
- Constraints — the need for an human factors input to function within the normal financial and technical constraints of the design process

Any successful human factors approach to systems design should be able to define the boundaries of its intended use in these terms. Perhaps the most important criterion for a successful human factors input is that of financial viability. For user issues to be explicitly considered as a normal part of the design process, their value must be obvious to those making financial decisions.

III. The HUFIT Planning, Analysis and Specification (PAS) Toolset

The PAS Toolset developed by the HUFIT project team at HUSAT addresses high-level human factors issues during the conception and planning phases of the product life cycle. Other HUFIT products address different stages in design. The PAS Tools also link to another tool on user-computer interface design. Together, they comprise an easily usable and effective human factors methodology for design teams with little or no human factors experience and with little access to specialist human factors support. Where such expertise exists, the individual tools may be used in a modular fashion or can be tailored to fit existing company methods. The Toolset as a whole has been found useful as a framework onto which more detailed techniques can be added.

The tools were developed iteratively in a series of workshops with designers in information technology supplier companies, and with human factors practitioners, during continuous assessment and evaluation. As a result the tools became simpler, rather than more complex, and more structured. Demonstrations of the tools on-line were developed to show how the tools could be implemented. However, as the mechanisms for using the tools are in multidisciplinary workshops, the paper versions of the tools are easier to use. The on-line version can be used for data recording and to carry forward the data from one tool to the next. The exception to this is the functionality matrix that utilises the advantages of spreadsheets in completing the matrix. The main delivery mechanism for the tools is by training seminars in which the participants receive the tools and are shown how to use them.

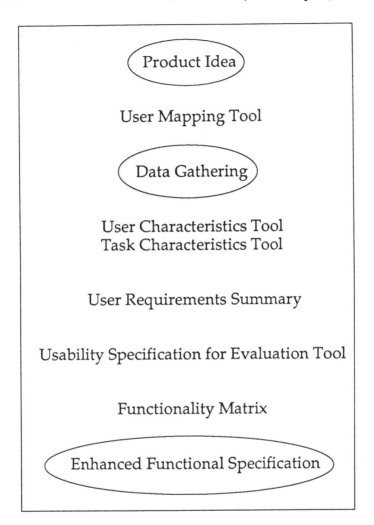

Figure 1. The PAS Toolset

Considering user and task requirements throughout the design process in an integrated fashion is crucial to the development of successful information technology products. Figure 1 shows how the six tools in the PAS Toolset fit together. They are integrated in that each one draws information from the previous tools and develops the information further. Each one also produces outputs which are of use to various participants in the development stages of the product life cycle. The tools are described next.

III.1. *User Mapping Tool*

This tool is intended for use very early in the product life cycle, when a product idea is being considered. The tool is used in four steps. The first is to identify users and stakeholders, i.e. all those who will use the product or who have a stake in it. The job goals for these groups are identified in step 2 to examine the benefits (step 3) and costs (step 4) of using the proposed product.

The information gathered in the User Mapping Tool is important for the later planning activities, since it identifies the users whose tasks will have to be supported by the product and who, therefore, form the basis of further data gathering and analysis. In drafting the PAS tools, we recognised that during the manufacture of generic office products it is not always possible or necessary to mount a full scale study of users in the field. There may be data already available in the company from previous studies, or information may be obtained from training, sales and maintenance personnel about the use of existing similar products. The information gathered by the User Mapping Tool is used in the subsequent tools to generate product requirements.

Product ....   User Mapping : Groups : Cost Benefits

Column 1: Identify User Groups and Stakeholders for this product	Column 2: Decide on the task goals for the user groups	Column 3: Potential benefits to each group from this product	Column 4: Costs to each group of using or choosing this product.
End Users Direct Users			
Indirect Users			
Remote Users			
Other Stakeholders Purchasers			
System staff: Customer dp staff Support System Maintenance			

Figure 2. Layout of the User Mapping Tool

III.2. An Extract from an Example of the User Mapping Tool in Use

The product example is a public access point to a training courses database (Training Access Point - TAP).

Column 1: Identify user groups and stakeholders for this product

End Users
Direct Users

- *Any member of public over 16 years, may be unemployed or employed*

- *Careers advisers for public*

- *TAP agents*

- *Personnel officer, etc. in small businesses*

etc.

Column 2: Decide on the task goals for the user groups

End Users
Direct Users

- *Unemployed — to find work therefore to increase employable skills. Employed — to use leisure time or improve skills for present or future job*

- *Help clients find suitable jobs or training for job*

- *Provide information service on training*

- *Improve skills of workforce*

etc.

Column 3: Potential benefits to each group from this product

End Users
Direct Users

- *Easier access to wide range of information. May be more comfortable making repeat enquiries from machine than from careers officer, etc.*

- *Quick access to wide range of information .*

- *Better service to public if terminals widely available*

- *Better information for staff, skills increase*

etc.

Column 4:   Costs to each group of using or choosing this product

End Users   • *Time to learn system.*
Direct Users   *Fear of using VDU?*

                     • *Time to learn system*

                     • *Time to learn system, more complex tasks.*
                       Extra tasks of inputting data, user support, etc.

                     • *Time to learn system, staff time to use it*
etc.

These columns would be presented in the layout shown in Figure 2 and hence will read across the table. The comments in columns 2, 3 and 4 refer to the users specified in column 1.

III.3. User Characteristics and Task Characteristics Tools

Experience in bespoke product design has shown that various attributes of the users, their tasks and their context are important for the design of successful information technology products. Traditional systems analysis methods do not usually consider these attributes. The User and Task Characteristics tools provide structured methods by which planners and developers can include these issues in product plans. These tools complement analysis of task content using any of the charting techniques available.

The tools elicit a general description of the direct user groups and their task environment and conditions. This highlights unusual or important factors that will affect the use of the product. They then concentrate on the user and task characteristics known to be important in the design of office technology. At each step, product requirements are derived to meet the user and tasks characteristics.

The information generated by these tools is useful in many stages of the design process. The product requirements feed into the product specification. The descriptions of the user groups and their task conditions are used in testing for developing appropriate user tests. The information is also useful to all groups in product development, including documentation and training developers, by focussing their activities on the correct users and tasks.

User Characteristics

In the table below write the user characteristics for this product under the headings given. You may think of other characteristics for your product. The accompanying notes explain the headings and give examples of product requirements which match the user characteristics.

User group	User Characteristics	Product requirements
Frequency of Use	How often will the user use this product?	
Public	Mostly first time users or very infrequent. May return to system after months or year	Need very supportive dialogues easy to learn to use and to remember
Careers advisers	May be frequent users	Need short cuts, maybe special search facilities
TAP agents	Frequent users	Need good input dialogues, etc.
Discretion to use	Can the different users decide whether or not to use the product?	
Public	Very high level of discretion, can ignore system or abandon search for any reason	Needs to be attractive and easy to use and give results quickly
Careers advisers	High discretion, can use other information sources	Needs to meet their needs and be quicker to use than other sources
TAP agents	Not discretionary user	Can train in complex tasks
etc.		

Figure 3. An Extract from an Example of the User Characteristics Tool in Use - TAP Example

III.4. The User Requirements Summary

The product requirements generated in the User and Task Characteristics Tools are collated into a summary which may be inserted into the product functional specification. The process highlights conflicts arising from the requirements of different user groups or different characteristics. These conflicts may be resolved now or flagged for special attention during development and testing. The requirements are also redistributed in this tool to suit the structure of the development process; for example, information for training and documentation personnel are separated out for use by their development groups.

III.5. The Usability Specification for Evaluation Tool (USE)

The research carried out in the company design teams showed that designers often encounter problems because of lack of clarity in the product specification. A formal specification might not be written before development begins, or the specification might be unclear. Decisions taken to meet problems encountered during design also change the specification but this is not always recorded. If the product is then evaluated according to an out-of-date or incomplete specification, it is difficult to reach any satisfactory conclusions about the quality of the product or the steps needed to improve it. For these reasons, a method that clarifies product goals in the planning stages is useful to both designers and evaluators. This led to the development of the USE — Usability Specification for Evaluation — tool. This tool is linked to the other Planning, Analysis and Specification tools drawing particularly on the information developed in the User and Task Characteristic Tools.

The USE tool comprises tables which provide a structure to lead the planner, designer and evaluator through a series of steps until the specification of product goals and criteria is complete. The steps are supported by suggestions for the sort of goals which may be set and examples of the tests and measures.

The tool includes a set of preparatory tables that gather the necessary data about the users and their tasks and their work environment. The core of the tool is the Usability Specification for Evaluation table, which helps identify the separate elements of usability for testing. The table leads the designer through four steps:

1. Defining usability goals for the product. The designer is encouraged to set high level human factors goals that are specific to the product and measurable.
2. Setting tests to find out if the goal is met. Keeping the test specification closely linked with the goals ensures that realistic goals are set.
3. Identifying measures to use in the test. With the help of examples and notes it is possible for designers to find tests and measures, including subjective assessment as well as the more frequently discussed metrics involving timings and error rates.
4. Setting criteria for judging success or failure. Two levels of criteria are set, a desired and a minimum level.

When completed, this table provides a high level plan for all user evaluations of the product. The goals and tests are product specific and practical. Goals specified here may indicate issues for performance and technical testing. Indeed, the same format could be used to specify technical and business goals for product evaluations.

A further table shows how this information is expanded to form a test plan. It divides the test procedures into the different kinds of testing to be carried out, such as performance tests, user trials in the laboratory and field testing. At this stage it is necessary to specify which user groups will be required, the kinds of tasks to be carried out and so on. In this way a high level test plan is developed.

III.6. An Extract from an Example of the Usability Specification for Evaluation Tool in Use

Column 1: Define Product Usability

List the usability goals which the product must meet in order of priority.

1. Users must be able to learn to use the terminal and get a result within a few minutes.

2. The public interface must be usable by the majority of the public, including groups with low education levels or slight physical handicaps.

Column 2: Test Specification

Choose one or more test procedures. Decide who will do what and how.

1.   Use a wide range of users in lab tests, working through a set of standard tasks.

2.   Use a wide range of users for user testing in lab and field trials.

Column 3: Measures

List the measure(s) appropriate for the tests chosen.

1.   Time to get information on set tasks from first contact.

2.   % of users able to get going and complete their enquiry.
User comments.

Column 4: Criteria

Decide on the desired and minimum levels.

Desired Level

1.   95% to success in 5 minutes.

2.   90% able to complete enquiry.
90% satisfied.

Minimum Level

1.   80% in 5 minutes.
Rest within 10 minutes.

2.   75%
75%

These columns would be presented in a four column layout and hence will read across the table.

III.7. The Functionality Matrix

Having completed the user requirements specification phase, the design team must then amalgamate these requirements with the proposed technical specification in order to begin the process of functional decomposition — iteratively describing functional requirements to the level of detail required for coding.

The Functionality Matrix contributes to this process by cross-referencing user and task requirements with the initial functional specification in a first-pass assessment procedure. Designers, prior to system building or prototyping, are able to assess the degree to which the proposed functionality specification is likely to meet the requirements of the users and tasks.

In business terms, the Matrix provides an explicit mechanism for assessing user and task issues in the context of the other business trade-offs of product development. The Matrix also acts as an aid to efficient project management by providing a permanent record of these trade-offs. Human factors information becomes an integral part of the design process which seeks to arrive at a value-added and enhanced functional specification.

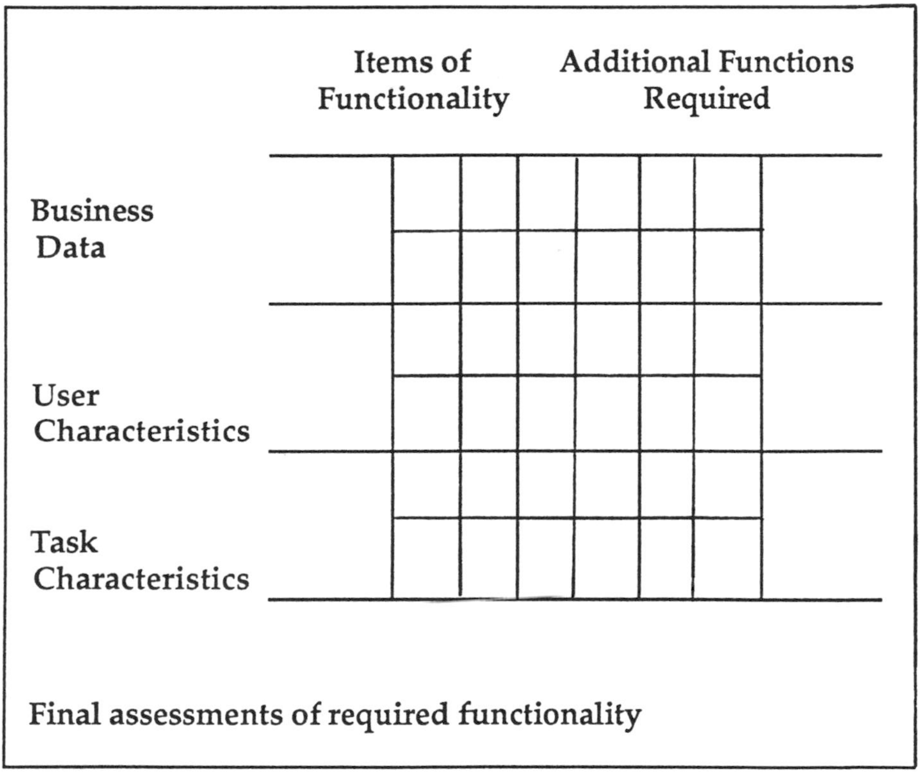

Figure 4. A Schematic Representation of the Functionality Matrix

An important feature of the Toolset as a whole, and of the Functionality Matrix in particular, is that it places human factors considerations in the context of the other business constraints. The trade-off procedures which operate are recognised and recorded explicitly. The tools establish data recording mechanisms to capture the information for use by all parties in the design process. The data will also be of considerable benefit to later redesigns or new developments.

III.8. The Current Status of the Toolset

The Planning, Analysis and Specification Toolset was developed with designers over a period of three years from 1986 to 1989. The Toolset is delivered to designers and more recently to human factors practitioners by training seminars. The seminars have been run by HUSAT since 1988 and continue in a variety of forms to the present time. The designers and human factors practitioners who attend the seminars receive the paper versions of the tools with which they have been working and are able to take them back for use within their own companies. HUSAT has also developed an on-line demonstration of the tools. This demonstration shows how the tools could be implemented within an on-line environment in a company. It is not intended as a stand alone package. The tools are designed for use in workshops, and as such the paper versions of the tools are easier to work with in this forum. The on-line version does not facilitate group discussion as access to the screen and keyboard is limited. However, the on-line version is useful for recording the outcomes of the discussions and in carrying forward the decisions into the next tool.

III.9. Examples of the Tools in Use

The tools were developed in an iterative fashion with designers in IT companies, and evaluation was an integral part of this iterative design process. Hence, the tools changed and developed in response to the comments from users.

  The tools are presented in the form of training seminars to a wide variety of potential users. A review of what the participants planned to do with the tools after attending the seminars has shown that a number of people involved in teaching computer scientists, systems engineers and other types of engineers, information technology students, as well as ergonomists, intended to incorporate the HUFIT Toolset in their courses.

  Other people, who were for example, working in companies developing consumer and information technology products, intended to take the HUFIT Toolset concept and build it into the procedures already in operation in their company. The Toolset was designed to be modular to facilitate this approach, and it is clear from feedback from course participants that this has been appreciated. For example, a number of companies have implemented the Functionality Matrix during the design of their products or systems, where the company already had methods for producing user and task information. A major British defence system manufacturer has used the Functionality Matrix in developing a space station, another defence system manufacturer has used the Functionality Matrix for the development of components. The company reported that it was very useful and they would continue to use and develop it. In this instance the completed Functionality Matrix covered three walls of their office! A company concerned with building nuclear power stations in the UK has used the

Functionality Matrix as an evaluation tool to assess the implications of the system specification for the workers in the power station, and they will also use it for assessing prototypes of components.

Feedback from the human factors practitioners who have used the Toolset indicates clearly that they can see its applicability beyond the information technology, office systems area and have used it in different applications. This is because the Toolset is a process, a way of making people address user and task issues in a structured fashion. Examples of the various applications include the specification of office furniture, the design and evaluation of a washing machine, the evaluation of a retractable dog lead, as well as the defence system applications already mentioned.

A company specialising in the design of system and product documentation reported that the principal advantage of the Toolset was that it encouraged the inclusion of people from documentation and training departments in the early stages of design and provided information to these departments.

A company who develop AI products assessed the usefulness of the Toolset for their product development process by reviewing the output from a completed set of forms. They had not been trained in the use of the Toolset. Their comments included:

"The User Mapping workshop is on the whole a very useful section. This sort of precis now comprises part of the ***, ***, and *** documents It is, however, useful to have this sort of structure to outline the market niche, and highlight the user domains into which the system will fit."

"The User Mapping table again is an excellent way of structuring user requirements and, unlike SSADM techniques, forces the analyst to pay more attention to user groups."

"The User Characteristics section again seems well structured. I found the Task Knowledge section to be not as detailed as I would have liked on the product requirements section. I feel the product requirements could be expanded and more detail given. I accept that these are covered in more detail in the Task Characteristics section."

"The Task Environment and Conditions section is useful."

"The Task Characteristics section is useful."

"The Functionality Matrix I found very difficult to understand. This may be due to my inexperience in interpreting these matrices. It may also be due to the huge amount of information being expressed in a single document."

"The Usability Specification for Evaluation is possibly the singularly most important output from the entire analysis in development terms. Here for the first time we have a description of the users' (human factor) requirements. It is exceptionally useful to have this sort of information available in a tabular format, as it allows the development department to test against it. This is exactly what one of the functions of our 'Client Support' testing step is about. We are now able to test the developed system against a known (and agreed) set of objectives. If there is one justification for HUFIT, this must be it."

This assessment also raises another and significant point with regard to evaluation of the Toolset, namely commercial confidentiality. Very few companies are prepared to be mentioned by name or even have details of their products or design processes quoted.

The HUFIT Toolset is also being used and developed in a number of European research and development projects in the ESPRIT and RACE programmes.

IV. The Case for Using the PAS Tools

In this practitioner-as-enabler approach to the provision of human factors expertise, the initial thrust of the tools must be their promotion of a positive and immediate sense of achievement in their users. The aim is to demystify human factors concepts without trivialising them and providing confidence to the user by indicating that a more detailed level of analysis and support lies behind their use.

During the development of the Toolset we became acutely conscious of the need to present human factors issues as *a normal and achievable part of the product design process* rather than as a set of complicated, optional procedures for already hard-pressed design teams. There is undoubtedly a conflict in adopting complex, leading-edge methodologies emanating from academic or even industrial research bodies and the day-to-day needs of designers to solve immediate and short term difficulties within an achievable timeframe. How often, for instance, are designers heard to say of human factors papers or presentations, "Very interesting, but too specific/complex/costly/lengthy for me or my company. Give me something I can use!" It is this concern in relation to product specification that the HUFIT Toolset addresses.

To be really effective in a commercial environment, it is essential to be able to cost and plan the uptake of human factors tools. Information technology businesses do not have the time or resources to speculate on the uptake of tools and techniques that carry too high an investment or training overhead. They must be convinced that there is a quantifiable and acceptable risk involved in any speculative uptake.

Much effort was expended in the HUFIT project in putting together an effective business case for human factors to accompany training in the use of the tools themselves. In common with a number of other authors in this area, we were not entirely satisfied with our efforts and so chose to attack the problem from another viewpoint.

IV.1. The Value Added Benefits Method

After many discussions with business managers in the information technology field we made contact with the Institute of Management Accountants in London who recommended the cost-benefit analysis approach adopted by Meyer and Boone (1987) in their book *The Information Edge.* Although the book was written to assist managers in user organisations in assessing the benefits or otherwise of information technology implementations, the principles translated well to assessing the effectiveness of human factors tools, techniques and methodologies in corporate product development.

To implement any new tools and techniques widely in an organisation, the management must be actively involved from the outset. In the case of the HUSAT work within HUFIT, this was achieved by the provision of outline adoption strategies for the PAS Toolset and its component parts. This allowed the formulation of a first-phase cost/benefit analysis. This is based on the need for quantifying value-added benefits — that is to say, those benefits which may be accounted for in terms of organisational and product effectiveness. Justification and measurement of these value-added benefits is part of a continuum — from an outline of the specific application of the tools through their impacts and perceived benefits to an evaluation of these benefits.

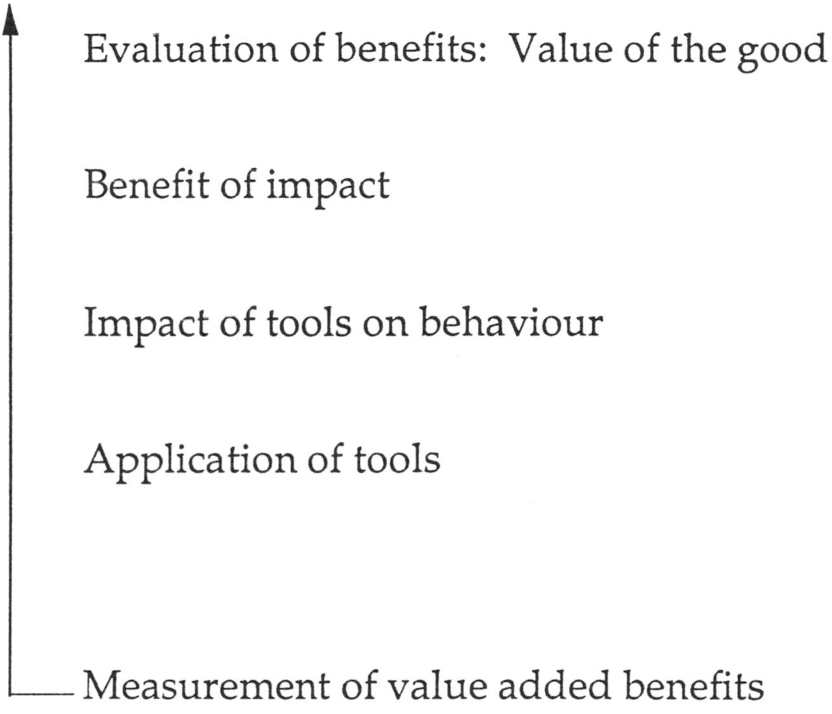

Evaluation of benefits: Value of the good

Benefit of impact

Impact of tools on behaviour

Application of tools

Measurement of value added benefits

Figure 5. The Measurement of Value-Added Benefits (After Meyer & Boone, 1987)

As can be seen from the diagram, four steps to measurement are proposed:

Application:	What tools are used for what and by whom?
Impact:	How do the tools change behaviour?
Benefit: organisation?	Why is the change in behaviour good for the
Evaluation:	What is the value of the good?

IV.2. Benefit Assessment for the PAS Tools

As an example, the following is a top-level description of these steps in relation to the HUFIT Toolset as a whole, which can then be further quantified and detailed in relation to the individual tools themselves:

Application	• Product planners • Designers at all stages of the product life cycle • Marketeers • Technical authors • Quality assurance staff • Human factors staff • Management
Impact	• Defects in product plans and prototypes are corrected upstream • Planners collect and use relevant data in product specification • Produces a better technical specification • Establishes a recording procedure for change control mechanisms • Evaluates products against relevant user goals • Targets marketing activities more accurately • Separates responsibilities more clearly
Benefits	• Reduced costs of correcting defects downstream • Improved matches of products to users and tasks • Improved quality of first designs • Improved communication and trade-off decision making • Improved usability of released products • Increased competitiveness • Improved coordination for product management
Evaluation	• Comprehensive human factors input across the product life cycle • Parallel strategies for managers and designers • Suitable levels of analysis and advice for different needs • Core tools usable with little or no HF background • Tailorable to corporate strategy • Short training times • Full expert back-up • Demonstrably cost-effective

The technique offers a systematic, positive view of any given example. It can be further developed to the level of a fully costed implementation plan, by estimating values for each identified benefit. These savings can be set against training costs. Having involved managerial, marketing, financial, and technical decision makers in the design process itself, it becomes much easier to identify quantifiable gains in cost categories of the kind suggested. Bids for adoption are thus couched in terms that will carry greater weight with managers allocating budgets.

Increased revenues	- Identifiable incremental scales - New business activity - Increased odds of closing
Accelerated revenues	
Reduced costs	- Operating costs - Production costs
Increased odds of a quantifiable gain	
Reduced risk of a quantifiable loss	

Figure 6. Quantifying Value-Added Benefits (Meyer and Boone, 1987)

V. The Need for Coordinated Marketing and Training

V.1. Marketing Requirements

For tools like these to be fully effective, they must be marketed and supported. Marketing and training material must meet the different requirements of managers and of designers. This two-level simultaneous approach facilitates a more efficient implementation of human factors in information technology product design. Managers need to know not only the benefits for their product opportunities but also the role they must play in implementation and facilitation of the use of the human factors tools. Personnel involved directly in the design of IT products must understand how to put human factors into practice in the context of their own work. For managers, the emphasis is on human factors *opportunity* whereas for designers it is on *context-specific application*. Adoption may then be initiated either top-down, across a department or company, or bottom-up by committed individuals. It is essential to ensure that appropriate marketing material is available for whichever adoption strategy is implemented.

V.2 . Training through Seminars

The main delivery mechanism for the HUFIT PAS Toolset is a seminar training programme on the concepts of user-centred design and on the techniques required for adoption and tailoring of the tools. This training seminar shows product designers how to use the tools and introduces human factors concepts in the context of commercial product design. Most importantly, it concentrates on showing how the procedures contribute cumulatively, and positively, to the design process itself.

Lectures	Practical Exercises
	User Mapping Tool
Data Gathering	
	User Characteristics Tool
	Task Characteristics Tool
	User Requirements Summary
	Usability Specification for Evaluation Tool
Principles of Interface Design	
	Functionality Matrix
	User-Computer Interface Design Tool
Discussions of design plans and demonstration of prototypes	
Implementation strategies	

Figure 7. An Outline of the Seminar Structure for Designers

The seminar is practical, based on a series of exercises that allow designers to use the tools with data from an interface design exercise from HUSAT's recent consultancy experience. The seminar was developed for designers who do not have human factors expertise and indicates what the designers can expect to be able to do for themselves and where human factors expertise is essential.

Typically about 15 people take part in the seminars at each time. This number enables group activities to be undertaken with ease. Participants include software engineers, systems, analysts, programmers, technical researchers and industrial designers from a wide range of companies in the UK, Scandinavia and continental Europe. Although the Toolset was originally designed for office systems applications, as a result of its position in the Office Systems division of ESPRIT, participants from other market sectors including railway signalling, video recorders, telecommunications and defence systems have also found the seminar useful. The seminars are evaluated, and the following are comments from participants:

"I learned some useful techniques which this company can use."
"The Functionality Matrix is a neat idea!"
"I would have found the user checklists more useful if they were structured to fit in with a structured method."
"Content good, sound and extremely pragmatic."
"I expect all the information will be useful, especially the Functionality Matrix, which will be very helpful."

A seminar for human factors practitioners has also been developed to meet frequent requests from practitioners who want to use the tools themselves or who want to be able to train the designers in their own companies. The practitioners have an interest in employing the tools as a structured framework within which to perform their own analysis and specification work. They also use the tools as a framework for interaction with designers. In this way designers and human factors practitioners can work together within a common framework. In the practitioners seminar the exercises have been shortened and sessions have been added. These added sessions are an outline of the training strategy recommended for the introduction of the tools, a discussion of the possible implementation and tailoring strategies and costing implications. The human factors practitioners specialising in consumer product design and evaluation are using the HUFIT Toolset successfully in a number of non-IT product developments. The consultants specialising in IT are using the Toolset as part of their service repertoire.

The seminars have been running successfully since 1988 and will continue beyond the end of the HUFIT project into the early 1990s. In the future it is more likely that HUSAT will offer the seminars for designers or practitioners as in-house tailored seminars. This is as a result of comments received that individual designers would have preferred that their colleagues also knew about the tools. They could then return to a more supportive environment for using the tools in their own companies. Another observation was that because the participants came from a variety of application areas, their interests in the Tools were often not the same. This made group working slightly more difficult.

V.3. *Training through Distance Learning*

Another delivery mechanism for the HUFIT Toolset is currently under development as a series of distance learning packages. The HUFIT package will cover not only the PAS Toolset but also a wealth of related information in the form of a primer for planners, designers and evaluators detailing the tools and techniques required to initiate user-centred design throughout the product life cycle. It will be extended to include elements of interface design, product testing, and usability evaluation.

The series will comprise

i)   A management overview

- Selling the concept of user centred design
- Outlining the human factors tools and techniques in the series
- Outlining the implications for management of adopting the tools
- Implementing the PAS Toolset
- Placing the tools in the context of the business requirements of commercial product development

ii)   A set of four binders for planners, designers and testers of IT products

- Planning and analysis techniques
        Data gathering, data representation, deriving user
        requirements, organisational implications, job design criteria
- The PAS Toolset
- Interface design
        Five stage proactive guidance using structured checklists
- Evaluation
        Usability specification, planning, laboratory and field testing,
        human factors in quality assurance.

iii)   A tutors and trainers pack

- To enable company trainers to run their own courses in the PAS Tools and to assist university and other technical lecturers to incorporate the techniques in appropriate teaching modules.

The distance learning series is expected to be generally available in both Europe and the USA during 1991.

VI. Summary

The aim of the HUSAT component of the HUFIT project has been to develop tools and methods which enable the wide variety of people who design generic IT products to themselves take account of human factors as a normal part of their role within the design process they are currently operating and in a cost-effective way. To accommodate the constraints in which these people operate, the tools are high-level and structured, procedural and tailorable, enabling product designers, planners and marketeers to adopt a user-centred design approach from the earliest stages of the design process.

The PAS Toolset was developed iteratively in workshops with designers in information technology supplier companies and with human factors experts during continuous in-house assessment and evaluation. By late 1988 a seminar programme for designers to support the delivery of the tools had been launched. This ran throughout 1989 and has continued beyond the end of the HUFIT project (Nov 1989) into the 90s. The tools were redrafted in mid-1989, and software demonstrators have been developed.

The HUFIT Toolset aims to present human factors issues as a normal and achievable part of the product design process. It takes a practitioner-as-enabler approach and promotes a positive and immediate sense of achievement in its users. To be really effective in a commercial environment it is essential to be able to cost and to plan the adoption of human factors tools. Companies must be convinced that there is an acceptable level of risk and that this can be quantified. HUSAT adapted the Value Added Benefits method to assess the effectiveness of human factors tools in corporate product development.

It is important to note that the HUFIT Toolset is currently delivered mainly by a practical training seminar that also covers a variety of additional concerns, such as data gathering techniques and management support strategies by lectures or supporting materials. The tools are available through attendance at one of the public seminars or by presentation to individual clients in-house. Publication in the form of a series of distance learning manuals is currently in progress.

The HUFIT Toolset provides product design teams in IT supplier companies, who have little or no expertise in human factors, with a set of high-level tools for the effective input of user and task information into the planning, analysis and specification phases of the IT product life cycle. The HUFIT Toolset was designed to meet the requirements of generic IT office systems product design because the contract was part of the Office Systems division of ESPRIT. However, as a result of reports on its use in other applications we believe that the Toolset does have wider applications. Its use is seen as a first but vital step in adopting a more comprehensive user-centred design approach. It has been found to be particularly useful where there is either resistance or logistical limitations to the adoption of a value-added human factors input as an equal component with all the other value-added business factors involved in information technology product development.

References

Catterall, B.J. (1990). "The HUFIT Functionality Matrix," *Human Computer Interaction, INTERACT '90, Proceedings of the IFIP TC 13 Third International Conference on Human Computer Interaction, (377-381),* (D. Diaper, D. Gilmore, G. Cockton and B. Shackel, eds). North Holland, 1990.

Catterall, B. J. and Galer, M.D. (1989). "Marketing Ergonomics — What Are We Selling and To Whom?", *Proceedings of the International Marketing Ergonomics Conference 1989,* International Ergonomics Assoc., Noordvijk, Holland, June, 1989.

Catterall, B. J., Allison, G. and Maguire, M. (1989). "HUFIT: Specification and Design Tools", *Proceedings of the Ergonomics Society Annual Conf., Contemporary Ergonomics 1989 (97-*102), (E. D. Megaw, ed). Taylor and Francis, London.

Eason, K.D. (1989). "Designing Systems to Match Organisational Reality." In *People and Computers V (57-69),* (A. Sutcliffe and L. Macaulay, eds), Cambridge University Press, Cambridge.

Eason, K.D. and Harker, S.D.P. (1989). "Human Factors in Systems Design," ALVEY/SERC Project MMI080, HUSAT Memo No 461, February, 1989.

Galer, M.D. (1989). "From Conception to Use — Human Factors in the Product Design Process," ESPRIT PROJECT 385 — HUFIT Final Report, December, 1989.

Galer, M.D. and Taylor, B. C. (1989). "Human Factors in Information Technology — ESPRIT Project 385," *Proceedings of the Ergonomics Society Annual Conf., Contemporary Ergonomics 1989,* (82-86), (E. D Megaw, ed), Taylor and Francis, London.

Galer, M.D., Taylor, B.C., Dowd, M., Catterall, B.C., Allison, G. and Maguire, M. (1990) "An Integrated Human Factors Input to Human Factors in the Design of Information Technology Products." In *Computer Aided Ergonomics,* (526-544), (W. Karwowski, A. H. Genaidy and S. S. Asfour, eds), Taylor and Francis, London.

Gallaway, G.R. (1985). "Marketing Ergonomics: Influencing Developers, Managers and Customers," *Proceedings of IXth Congress of the International Ergonomics Assoc.,* Taylor and Francis, London.

Hannigan, S.and Herring, V. (1987). "Human Factors in Office Product Design — European Practice." In *Cognitive Engineering in the Design of Human-Computer Interaction and Expert Systems,* Vol. 2, (225-232), Proceedings of 2nd Int. Conf. on Human-Computer Interaction,Hawaii, Aug. 1987, (G. Salvendy, ed), Elsevier, North Holland.

Meyer, D.N. and Boone, M.E. (1987). *The Information Edge,* McGraw-Hill, New York.

Taylor, B. C. (1989). "HUFIT: User Requirements Toolset," *Proceedings of the Ergonomics Society Annual Conf., Contemporary Ergonomics 1989,* (87-91), (E. D. Megaw, ed), Taylor and Francis, London.

Taylor, B. C. (1990). "The HUFIT PAS Tools," *Human Computer Interaction, INTERACT '90, Proceedings of the IFIP TC 13 Third International Conference on Human Computer Interaction, (371-376),* (D . Diaper, D. Gilmore, G.Cockton and B.Shackel, eds). North Holland.

Taylor, B. C. and Bonner, J. (1989). "HUFIT: Usability Specification for Evaluation," *Proceedings of the Ergonomics Society 1989 Annual Conf., Contemporary Ergonomics 1989* (92-96), (E. D. Megaw, ed), Taylor and Francis, London.

Trist, E.L. and Bamforth, K. (1951). "Some Social and Psychological Consequences of the Long-Wall Method of Coal-Getting." In *Human Relations,* Vol. 1, 3-38.

17 Requirements Specification and the Role of Prototyping in Current Practice

SUSAN HARKER

*Department of Human Sciences/HUSAT Research
Institute
Loughborough University of Technology
Loughborough
Leicestershire
United Kingdom*

I. Introduction

The HUSAT Research Institute is committed to the exploration of ways of improving the effectiveness and usability of human factors inputs to design processes. This commitment is based on a user and task centred approach, where the needs of designers and the nature of design processes provide the starting point for identifying the requirements placed on the form and content of human factors inputs to the design of computer systems. The process of design which is of interest includes all stages of development, from initial conception and feasibility studies through to the introduction of the computer system into the end user environment.

A number of projects, carried out as part of research and development programmes sponsored by national bodies and the European Community, have contributed to the development of our understanding of these design processes and the designers involved in them. The projects have offered the opportunity to explore the provision of human factors inputs to the design of computer systems. The main basis for the findings reported in this chapter was a project concerned with Human Factors in the Design of Information Technology Systems (Harker et al,1990), sponsored by the UK Alvey programme. This provided the opportunity to study and analyse the design process in some detail. The approach adopted sought to cover the range of design activities representative of the UK environment. The overall purpose of the investigation was to develop an understanding of current and future design practice and to establish criteria for the form and content of human factors inputs to the design process.

II. Studying the Design Process

The methods used to study design processes were based upon longitudinal studies of ongoing design activities in a range of supplier companies and user organisations. Ten cases were studied in this way and form the backbone of the study. Interviews were conducted at regular intervals with participants in the design activity and, where possible, the research worker would attend group meetings and discussions. Relevant documents were read when available. A further twenty cases were surveyed retrospectively and in less detail but with the purpose of reviewing the generality of the conclusions over a wider range of design environments. In these cases a smaller number of the participants in the design process were interviewed and some documentation was reviewed.

In constructing the sample, the aim was to cover a diversity of design contexts based upon the design of applications for use in commercial and industrial environments. None of the cases studied involved the development of military systems. The main dimension used was concerned with the design of generic or off-the-shelf products, and bespoke design in which products or systems were commissioned and developed for specific task applications for specific user groups within an organisation. In bespoke developments a distinction was made between design undertaken on a contractual basis by a supplier company for a client and design undertaken within the user organisation for its own users on an in-house basis. When generic products are introduced into an organisation there are a number of design decisions and adaptations which form part of the design process within the organisation. This created a further category with cases involving the in-house use of generic products. The number of cases in each category in the sample is shown in Figure 1. In practice the boundaries between the categories was much less clear-cut than this, and there were continued on both dimensions. For example, a number of the generic products actually had their origins in in-house bespoke developments, either for the supplier company itself or for another organisation from whom it had been purchased. In another case the development of a bespoke system by a supplier was taken back under the control of the user organisation when the development ran into difficulties. Thus the genesis of individual applications was quite complex.

	In-house	Supplier
Bespoke	Organisations developing tailor-made systems for their own use.	Software suppliers developing applications for specific clients.
	N = 7	N = 9
Generic	Organisations purchasing products and adapting them for their particular needs.	Software suppliers developing applications for general client needs. Domain specific but not client specific.
	N = 3	N = 11

Figure 1. The Sample — Classification of the 30 Cases

Another dimension which was relevant to sampling concerned the scale of the design activity being undertaken, which had two separate components, one concerning the absolute size of the system being developed and the other concerning the size of the design team involved in development. Generally speaking, cases classified as small, occupied less than 24 man months of effort per year. However, these small cases tended to increase in overall size as development proceeded and could often be classified as substantial development activities by the time they were complete.

III. Overview of the Design Process

Individual cases were written up and used to produce a framework for the activities taking place within the design process. It is clear that there is a considerable diversity in the activities which took place within the design processes studied, and they certainly cannot be described by one invariant linear sequence. Nevertheless, there are a number of activities which figure as significant elements in the overall process of design as we have defined it. Five of these activities were selected for detailed examination in view of their importance with respect to human factors issues. These are

- Requirements capture and specification
- Prototyping
- Design and build
- Evaluation
- Implementation and support in user organisation

All these topics are interrelated, and it is not possible to discuss the role of user-centred design in relation to any one topic isolated from the others. However, one of the most obvious outcomes of the research was the finding that the processes of requirements capture and specification were regarded by design teams as the most problematic elements in the design process. The main factors underlying this were concerned with the technical aspects of requirements capture and specification. However, it was apparent that these processes also involved user issues, and observation of the difficulties encountered showed that many of the problems were concerned with identifying user and task needs. This observation is consistent with the findings of an Esprit Workshop on Requirements Capture (1988).

The use of prototyping as a way of establishing a design which would meet users' needs provided a topic which was of particular interest in relation to the provision of human factors inputs to a more user centred design process. The benefits of prototyping are widely accepted as desirable by the human factors community, and it is therefore of interest to review its role in current design practice. The effects of different design contexts on the processes of requirements capture and specification are discussed, and then the role of prototyping is examined in greater detail.

IV. Requirements Capture and Specification

There were distinct differences in the ways in which requirements capture and specification took place, depending upon whether the design was for a generic product or for a bespoke product. These have particular significance for the utilisation of a user centred approach to the determination of user requirements.

Generic Products

Perhaps the most significant factor relating to human factors inputs in the design of generic products was the extent of the constraints operating on specifications. Thus, while the thrust of much HCI work is to identify radical solutions to user problems, the practical situation was that many of the interface decisions were preempted by long-standing structural considerations such as the existing installed base and the need for consistency with what had gone before, as well as with de facto standards and house styles.

Another finding was that there was clear evidence that user requirements tended to be heavily influenced by a marketing view of purchasers as users rather than operators as users. Purchasers were regarded as checking off features in competing products, whether their end users actually required these features or not. This frequently resulted in the over-specification of functionality and created demands for development work, which reduced the opportunities for spending time on more focussed areas of end user need.

Where opportunities to influence the nature of the system and the user interface did exist for generic products, it could be seen that difficulties arose for a number of reasons. It was not simply a question of commitment to a user centred approach, nor indeed the availability of the resources. Design teams lacked the means to engage with user needs and found it difficult to identify and specify end user requirements. They had relatively little knowledge about user characteristics and tended to use stereotyped views of the user-task demands. This is probably not surprising, given the tradition of developing technology driven products which characterised the suppliers in the sample. These suppliers did regard this tradition as inadequate and were seeking ways to understand their users and their tasks better. They were keen to obtain methods that would help with this process, provided this help could be made available in a timely and usable way. In the context of the time scales of design cycles typical in these samples, where an iteration for enhancement might be from 6-12 months, extended studies of use would be precluded. Human factors inputs must be based on the creation of knowledge bases to which designers can be given access together with the introduction of systematic techniques for exploring the issues which arise in relation to specific products. Examples of suggested ways of achieving such economies are discussed by Galer et al. (1990) and Nielsen (1990).

When requirements had been established early in the planning stages, another problem arose, which has been labelled "design drift." This might occur when a series of enhancements were spread over a long period of time or when a large number of designers were involved. The nature of, and reasons for, a particular form of specification might get lost as design proceeded and new designers became involved, with the result that they could introduce a new set of assumptions unrelated to earlier stages. Thus, the communication of user requirements and the rationale underlying them was another important area for a potential contribution to improving interface quality.

Ways of formally communicating the basis of the specification of user and task requirements can be linked to the systematisation of the processes for exploring such issues in the planning stages. By creating records of the decisions made, it is possible to diffuse this information both across the expanding design team and along the design process, as it moves into other areas of technical development. This is not to suggest that such decisions are immutable nor that they are not open to elaboration as design progresses through iterative stages. By ensuring that there is clear evidence of the reasoning that is current, it is possible to assess the impact of proposed changes and developments and to rework the specifications accordingly. One way of addressing these issues is provided by the modular tool set developed within the Esprit HUFIT project (Catterall et al., 1991).

User organisations identifying their requirements for generic products also showed evidence of difficulties with the systematic specification of user requirements. There was little evidence of formalised techniques being used and a common experience was the development of an array of software applications which provided little basis for consistency or integration. In one of the cases where a systematic procurement policy had been pursued, the task of determining what applications were likely to be most useful was left to those individuals who were motivated to take a lead, and the systems fell into disuse when these local experts were no longer available. In smaller organisations the choice of an application or product was often made on arbitrary criteria relating to price or an individual's experience. The identification of requirements would then emerge from operational experience of use (or disuse) of the product. This can be related to the dissatisfaction expressed by small and medium sized enterprises in relation to their experience of computer products (Wroe, 1986).

Bespoke Products

At the opposite end of the continuum from the design of generic products lies the design of products tailored for a specific user or organisation. In these cases there is a much clearer commitment to the identification of user and task requirements, and there are a range of structured design methods which explicitly recognise the need to create user specifications which have to be negotiated and agreed with user representatives. Unfortunately, the evidence from our investigations suggests that the scope of the user requirements considered is often limited to the logical data processing elements. There is little support for the identification of organisational and psychological factors, which should structure the nature of the system being delivered. It is also evident that while there is formal recognition of user involvement, there is no support to the users to provide feedback in an informed way. They may receive a specification presented in an entirely technical form and/or be given a very short time to digest and agree with its contents. Prototypes could be seen to exercise a powerful effect in providing users with a specification which they found meaningful.

The philosophy underlying the most widely adopted methods for large scale bespoke developments in the UK is based on a "waterfall" model with reliance being placed on the adequacy of early stages of analysis as the basis for elaboration later. The expectation is that the use of a systematic analytical framework will give rise to a "right first time" solution. As the project moves from feasibility and initiation stages into detailed specification, it is common for responsibility for design to be divided between different teams. The responsibility for coordinating the various parts then requires a substantial project management effort, which can inhibit innovative technical and user centred solutions. It was apparent, in cases where structured methods were used, that when developers discovered some deficiency in the specification which they wished to rectify, it proved hard to mobilise the iteration of all the earlier stages and to deal with the impact on current parallel activities. The problem was perceived in terms both of the resources already invested and the management overhead required to change things. This difficulty is probably endemic to most large scale developments involving functional devolution of responsibility.

This increasing rigidity also caused considerable frustration to users if they became aware of things they wanted to change. They would often find that their requests were rejected or they were assured that some change already in hand elsewhere would alleviate the problem that concerned them. Particular difficulties were experienced in projects where operational policy was changing while the system was being developed. This meant that many of the requirements had actually changed by the time the initial specification was complete. There seemed to be a need for some way of formally identifying potential areas of uncertainty so that design could proceed on the basis of offering sufficient flexibility to accommodate the variance which might arise.

There were some differences between suppliers developing bespoke systems for other organisations and organisations developing systems for their own use.

While it is, in principle, easier for the developer of any bespoke system to gain access to the information underlying user, task and organisational requirements, the preparation of a specification for a customer can run into a variety of problems. Potential customers were reluctant to spend a lot of time working through requirements with a number of different suppliers, and therefore access to information might be limited. Some suppliers, particularly small ones, found it difficult to recoup the cost of a specification exercise, if it was done thoroughly, in advance of the submission of a tender. Clearly there was some pressure to adapt the specification in order to maximise the chances of acceptance as part of a competitive tender. Finally, it has to be said that the tendency to underestimate the demands on development effort required for a particular system seems to be endemic to all software development processes!

The Effect of Size

The major advantage experienced by small development teams was the ease of communication which they could enjoy. Thus, the danger of ambiguity and misunderstanding in relation to the production of the specification was reduced. They also tended to respond with greater flexibility to feedback about the design as it progressed. The scope for iteration of the specification and a more evolutionary approach to development was clearly greater in small development teams. Large developments with a complex array of users not only created problems for coordination within the design team but also posed problems for the integration of the different, and potentially conflicting, user requirements.

V. Prototyping

The purpose of this section is to examine the contribution of prototyping to the design processes which were studied and to examine the relationship between developments in the technical capacity to prototype information technology systems, trends in design practice, and the potential impact of these on the future of user centred design. In this context, prototyping was taken to be the process of producing versions of the system to be used as the basis for consideration of their implications for the user, as opposed to the prototyping of the intrinsic technical viability of a solution. Even when this restriction was applied, there was still a great diversity in what forms user oriented prototyping might take within design processes. In fact it is possible to prototype almost any aspect of the user-system interface including hardware and organisational issues, and there were examples, within the sample, of both these types of activity, as well as prototyping of software issues. This diversity was reflected in the wide range of views and opinions expressed by the interviewees as to what constituted prototyping.

The technology is offering an ever increasing range of possibilities for prototyping, which are eagerly adopted by research staff in both academic and commercial environments. However, it is less apparent that the techniques which are now available are being taken up for main-line development activities. It is instructive to examine the reasons for this and to consider what needs to be done to realise the potential benefits of prototyping for the creation of human-computer interfaces which satisfy their users' requirements.

The Use of Prototyping

In reviewing the activities which actually occurred in relation to the prototyping of software aspects of development, it was found that nineteen out of the thirty cases in the sample did engage in some form of user oriented prototyping, as defined above. The extent to which prototyping was used by each of the categories is illustrated in Figure 2.

Bespoke: In-house   Bespoke: Supplier

    100%   56%

Generic: In-house   Generic: Supplier

    0%   63%

Figure 2. Percentage of Sample Engaging in Prototyping

All the in-house cases producing bespoke applications did some prototyping. These developers had the advantage of greater opportunities to present prototypes to users within their own organisations. There were a number of components involved in the increased ease of access to users. One simple advantage is that there was a greater probability that development was taking place quite close to some potential users. It was also easier to arrange contact within a single organisation. External suppliers were likely to be less readily received by user groups. For example, in one case it was not possible for the external suppliers to communicate directly with end users because of problems with industrial relations.

In contrast, the in-house group using generic products contained no case in which prototyping was used. This is despite the fact that all the products required some configuration and could be adapted to specific organisational requirements, albeit within fairly narrow limits. This raises interesting questions for adaptive products, which are seen as an important future scenario for matching specific user needs. Users are not equipped, in the current situation, to take advantage of adaptability by exploring the options available. They are far more likely to fix on a single solution and implement it without any testing. This is entirely consistent with the data emerging from earlier work on the use of adjustable hardware. It is evident that it will be necessary to install an infrastructure to educate users and provide on-going support if they are to take advantage of adaptability and prototyping power built into software.

Suppliers are more variable in their use of prototyping, but over half the cases in both the bespoke and generic groups did engage in some form of prototyping. One might have expected that there would be more evidence of prototyping activities in the bespoke category, but the restricted use of prototyping may be attributed to the kinds of barriers created by the need to gain access from one organisation to another. When suppliers did prototype bespoke developments they would usually have gained similar rights of access to those enjoyed by an in-house developer and would have access to relevant users within the client organisation. Suppliers developing generic products were equally likely to be using some form of prototyping The effects of the absence of direct end users and tasks has implications for the ease with which users can be involved in the prototype evaluation. Suppliers of generic products found it more difficult to evaluate prototypes with typical users, particularly when the products were for rather specialised markets and their prototyping activities were more restricted in scale.

VI. "Static" versus "Dynamic" Prototyping

An examination of the activities that actually took place in relation to the prototyping of software aspects of development, identifies two main approaches, which have been labelled "static" prototyping and "dynamic" prototyping. The former was characterised by the creation of prototype interfaces and dialogue components that could be demonstrated but that could not be used directly. Dynamic prototyping was the creation of some form of prototype which could be tried out with "hands-on" use. If the sample is broken down on the basis of the distinction between these two, the picture in Figure 3 emerges.

In-house Bespoke		Supplier Bespoke	
Static	Dynamic	Static	Dynamic
7	4	3	4
100%	57%	33%	44%

In-house Generic		Supplier Generic	
Static	Dynamic	Static	Dynamic
0	0	4	5
		36%	45%

Figure 3. Static v. Dynamic Prototyping

While all the in-house developers of bespoke applications did some static prototyping, only four of them did any dynamic prototyping. Dynamic prototyping would tend to involve more resources for both development and evaluation. This concern for a more economical approach explains why some of the in-house bespoke developments restricted themselves to static prototyping. The picture in the supplier groups is different. While some suppliers only do static prototyping some of the suppliers only do dynamic prototyping. It should also be noted that there is more dynamic than static prototyping in both the bespoke and the generic groups. There is no obvious explanation for these differences on the basis of the attitudes to resources, the size of the developments or the extent of user involvement.

When suppliers did prototype bespoke developments they would usually have gained similar rights of access to those enjoyed by an in-house developer and would have access to relevant users within the company.

VII. Design Context

The nature of the design process does appear to distinguish between the different ways of using prototyping, as shown in Figure 4.

In-house Bespoke   Supplier Bespoke

Structured design methods (3)   Structured design methods (2)
Exemplars (2)*   Process (3)*
Demo (1)*
Process (1)*

                                                                Supplier Generic

                                                    Ad hoc checking of parts (7)**

*   Part of requirements capture and specification.
**   Quality assurance.

Figure 4. Design Contexts for the Use of Prototyping

Structured Design Methods

Prototyping took place where structured design methods were used for bespoke developments, either in-house or by suppliers. In these cases an important role for the prototyping activities appeared to involve reassuring users that progress was being made. This could lead to a conflict of interest between those developers who wished to get feedback on the currently proposed solution and those who wished to represent the development in the most favourable way.

Prototyping for Specification

Bespoke developments which did not involve structured design methods gave rise to a number of examples where prototyping formed the basis of the design process. In particular it was used by suppliers for requirements capture and specification. These organisations tended to be smaller companies working on relatively small scale developments with a limited amount of manpower. They used fourth generation languages as the basis for formulating a possible solution to the user requirements. In some cases the prototype might form the starting point for the ultimate technical solution or it might be thrown away and implemented in a different technical form. The successful use of a prototype in this context, as a way of negotiating a specification with a client, could also be a source of problems. In at least one of the cases, a small supplier organisation had difficulty trying to recover the value of the initial work it had carried out. This company relied on its ability to produce specifications which met the client's needs, but it might not succeed in capturing the subsequent development work.

Organisational Impact

In-house development of bespoke applications included some cases where the use of prototyping was the basis for exploring issues relating to longer term use within the organisation. Some of the prototypes were used as exemplars, where they also played a part in contributing to the specification of both the technical and organisational changes to be introduced.

Quality Assurance for Generic Products

The striking characteristic of the use of prototyping for generic products was that the developers in these cases used prototyping to examine specific issues which were thought to be potentially problematic. It was likely that only a limited subset of the design would be prototyped, and this was usually done to check for anticipated problems. The main role of prototyping appeared to be a form of quality assurance. Prototyping did not involve comparison of alternatives and there was little evidence that it formed part of an iterative or evolutionary approach to design. One factor which should be born in mind is that most of the examples in this category involved enhancement rather than new products, so that the outcome of any prototyping was reviewed against previous versions of the product.

The sample contained few cases involving innovation in generic products. The one case of an innovative product which was studied longitudinally had plans to prototype but had not yet reached the stage at which this was due to take place, when the study concluded. The team involved had no intention of using it as the primary basis for developing the application. This contrasts with a commitment to prototyping as a stimulus to innovation and evolution, such as that described by Tang (1991). This approach appears to be characteristic of research and development environments supported by large supplier companies. In this study the sample was intentionally directed at developments which had been selected for commercial exploitation. Work being carried out entirely in research and development laboratories was therefore excluded. However, there was no evidence that any of the cases studied had their origins in this kind of environment.

VIII. Actors

Prototyping activities were generally conducted by systems analysts and development staff, although, in some of the bespoke cases, these roles might be filled by users, who had been seconded to the development team to represent user interests. In no case was any of the work done by an interface designer with a specialist role. In some cases human factors specialists were involved, but these people were usually involved in the conduct of prototyping trials and, in one case, used a prototyping tool to build a replica of the proposed design.

The most surprising omissions from the prototyping activity, given that the prototyping being studied was aimed at the evaluation of the implications for users, were potential users. Only half the sample of bespoke cases actually used the prototype with representatives of end users. In some cases the development staff built both static and dynamic prototypes and then made their own judgements about their impact on users. In other cases the prototypes might be used with user management or a steering committee, but end users would have no experience of them at all. The problem of recruiting representative users for the testing of prototypes of generic products has been discussed elsewhere (Harker 1987). While it is relatively straightforward to find representatives of office and administrative users within a supplier organisation, it can be extremely difficult to find more specialised groups of users, for example, personnel managers in small to medium sized companies.

It would seem that if the view that prototyping of user interfaces is now an "almost universally accepted principle" (Baecker and Buxton, 1987), is to come to fruition in commercial settings, it will be necessary to convince developers that the opportunities provided by the new development environments must be coupled with a serious commitment to involving users in development and the creation of the means to involve them. While it was evident that members of the design teams were aware of these issues, they felt that they could not be dealt with before a range of other more structural problems had been addressed.

IX. Barriers to Successful Prototyping

The most commonly cited difficulties with respect to the use of of prototyping as a way of promoting user centred design were resources, perceived value, fit with the design process and timing.

Resources

Except in the cases where the designers used the prototyping approach as the centre of their requirements capture and specification process, the most common difficulty cited concerned the resources required for prototyping. It was the most usual reason given for the absence of any prototyping activity, but even those people who did prototype said that resources were a great concern. Clearly the building of prototypes creates a demand for skilled personnel and may occupy development machines, thus competing with what has traditionally been regarded as the main part of the development process.

Perceived Value

The problem of using scarce resources was related to perceptions of the value of prototyping. Many of the people who were positive about the use of prototyping still said that they found it difficult to justify to management on the basis of the benefits that it conferred, since there appeared to be little concrete evidence which they could use to convince other people that investing the resources   in prototyping would yield benefits in terms of development quality and save overall design resources in the longer term.

Fit with the Design Process

In some cases, as has already been noted, the use of prototyping actually forms the basis of the design process. In other cases the use of prototyping, which carried with it the notion of iteration and change, was ill-matched with the design philosophy adopted. This was particularly noticeable in connection with structured design. In these circumstances it was not unusual to undertake some static prototyping of screen layouts for demonstration purposes, but the notion of building a dynamic prototype which might identify requirements for change provided a formidable and, in some cases, unacceptable challenge to the logical build-up of the design. Thus, there were examples in the survey where dynamic prototyping had been undertaken, but little attention was paid to the results because they appeared to demand too many radical changes to the substantial volume of design decisions which had already been undertaken. In some of these cases, which all arose in relation to bespoke developments, the onus for dealing with the need for change was passed on to the installation processes, where extra training or user support might be recommended.

In the generic product category the ad hoc nature of the prototyping created less problems because it was invoked on a "need" basis. However, it was apparent that the design processes typical of these environments would create considerable demands for changes, if prototyping was to be used in a more systematic and proactive way. The cases studied included designers who were keen to see Computer Aided Software Engineering (CASE) tools being used. Such tools should offer greater potential for early prototyping. However, it should be noted that despite the enthusiasm which was expressed, the suppliers of generic products in our sample were a long way away from achieving automated software tooling in their developments and thus lacked access to tools which might facilitate early explorations of potential solutions, prior to specification. It is still open to question whether this may reflect some of the difficulties which we experienced in building up our sample, since this finding appears to create most surprise among those engaged in education and research. Nevertheless, the promise of CASE tools does not appear to have been realised by any of the development processes which we studied. This is consistent with LeQuesne's (1988) work on the use of Integrated Project Support Environments, which shows that the introduction of tools to support teams of individuals working on large scale developments appears to place considerable administrative loads upon the design process, which are regarded as unacceptable by the individuals.

Timing

One particular problem associated with the fit between **prototyping** and of the design process concerns timing issues. As has already been indicated, there is great reluctance to change designs which are shown to be unsatisfactory, when prototype tests are run late in the day. The implication that design effort has been wasted creates a great deal of discomfort, and while users may feel more confident in asking for changes, it can create conflict within the development team. The people who were most satisfied with the results of prototyping were the people who used it as part of specification and requirements capture. They were concerned with bespoke developments and were the developers most likely to use some sort of automated tooling.

X.   The Benefits of Prototyping

This analysis raises a number of issues about the how prototyping should be used in the future. However, the first question which must be addressed, concerns the reality of the benefits of prototyping in creating more usable products. Direct evidence of the effects of prototyping would be hard to establish, and the assessment of its impact has to be inferred. The case studies do not yield consistent evidence that prototyping improved the quality of the designs which emerged. Both users and developers were very satisfied with its contribution to the specification of relatively small bespoke systems. In the large bespoke developments, there was evidence that users felt much better equipped to make meaningful judgements about proposed design solutions after they had seen and tried prototypes. The difficulty in these cases was that the prototyping appeared to take place too late and at a time when the developers were unwilling to act on the feedback they received. Suppliers of generic products were satisfied with their prototyping activities, and there was evidence that it was used to correct designs which offered a poor match with user and task needs. In one case, a product which had been under development for six months was cancelled when it was the subject of a very negative prototyping review.

   This picture suggests that prototyping can have positive effects but that the extent to which potential benefits are realised is heavily dependent upon the circumstances in which it is used. There is evidence to suggest that it can be used most effectively in the early stages of the development cycle and that it provides a valuable medium of communication between users and designers. It would therefore seem to have a role in requirements capture and specification, particularly in relation to the identification of user needs and the creation of feedback which can be directly related to the process of design.

XI. Implications for Prototyping as an Aid to Requirements Capture and Specification

Given the problems of integrating prototyping activities into design, these activities need to be focussed in a selected range of design contexts. The greatest potential lies in bespoke developments, where one is specifying for a known task and a user population which can be directly involved in the evaluation of prototypes. This can be achieved in both supplier and user led developments. Suppliers of generic products should be able to make use of prototyping as an aid to capturing user requirements in the conceptual stages of design, but they may find prototyping less practical for the specification of detailed user requirements, for which other forms of human factors input will be needed.

The introduction of generic products within user organisations raises interesting questions about prototyping. There was no evidence in this study to suggest that users were willing or able to use adaptive and configurable products as a means of testing alternatives provided as part of generic applications. However, there is a view of users as designers exploring and implementing options in generic products, which has been discussed by Nardi (1990). In principle users should be able to develop their generic products and implement them in response to emerging and evolving requirements. However, for this to be possible they will need support and training to go with the technology. Even the use of basic hardware adaptations has been shown to be very sensitive to previous user experience (Jorgensen and Sauer, 1990).

The design processes themselves must have certain characteristics if they are going to permit effective use of prototyping activities. The process must be explicitly iterative in character and allow for feedback and change, if prototyping is to influence the specification. In one of the cases, the role of an extensive prototyping exercise was undermined by the central design team refusing to reconsider their original specification, on the grounds that there was no time or resource allocated for this purpose in their project management plan. Prototyping is also likely to have more significant effects in a design environment where the iterative approach is based on the evolution of the development and uptake of applications, rather than an approach based on a single radical implementation strategy. This will allow prototyping and pilot studies to reflect the full range of user, task and organisational issues and to modify the design in the course of its development.

Given these circumstances it will still be necessary to develop strategies for the use of prototyping which are well matched to the particular circumstances of a given context of use.   Systematic evaluation procedures will need to be developed, and it will be necessary for developers to overcome the inherent difficulties associated with involving users in evaluation and to establish ways of doing this. It will also be necessary to pay more attention to the development of software support and simulation tools. While the power to prototype interactions has increased rapidly over the past five years, there are still inherent constraints which are imposed by the tools currently available and which demand that some choices are made before any prototypes can be tested.

Whatever the technical tasks, perhaps the most significant challenge will be the need to create the cost-benefit case to justify the use of prototyping. It is only when it can be institutionalised as a part of the design process and is accepted by all members of the development team, that prototyping will be able to yield the full potential for creating a much better match between users and their systems.

References

Baecker, R.M. and Buxton, W.A.S. (1987). "Readings in Human-Computer Interaction: A Multi-disciplinary Approach," Morgan Kaufman Publishers, Los Altos, California.

Catterall, B.J., Taylor, B.C. and Galer, M.D.(1991) "The HUFIT Planning, Analysis and Specification Toolset: Human Factors as a Normal Part of the I.T. Product Design Process." In *Taking Software Design Seriously*, Academic Press, Boston, 1991.

ESPRIT (1988). Report on Esprit Workshop on Systems Requirements Capture and Handling, Commission of the European Communities, Noordvijk, The Netherlands.

Galer, M.D. (1989). "From Conception to Use Human Factors in the Product Design Process," ESPRIT PROJECT 385 - HUFIT Final Report.

Galer, M.D., Taylor, B.C., Dowd, M., Catterall, B.C., Allison, G. and Maguire, M. (1990). "An Integrated Human Factors Input to Human Factors in the Design of Information Technology Products." In *Computer Aided Ergonomics,* (526-544), (W. Karwowski, A. H. Genaidy and S. S. Asfour, eds), Taylor and Francis, London.

Harker, S.D.P. (1987). "Rapid Prototyping as a Tool for a User Centred Design." In *Cognitive Engineering in the Design of Human-Computer Interaction and Expert Systems*, (G. Salvendy, ed), Elsevier, Amsterdam.

Harker, S.D.P. and Eason, K.D. (1990). "Human Factors in Systems Design: An Investigation of Human Factors Inputs to the Information Technology Design Process," Final Report on Alvey/SERC Project MMI 080, SERC Grant No. GR/D 29468.

Harker, S.D.P., Eason, K.D., Poulson, D.F. and Parkes, A. (1987). "Classifying the Target for Human Factors Output." *Proceedings of the Annual Alvey Conference*, UMIST, Manchester.

Jorgensen, A.H. and Sauer, A. (1990). "The Personal Touch: A Study of Users' Customization Practice," *Human Computer Interaction, INTERACT '90, Proceedings of the IFIP TC 13 Third International Conference on Human Computer Interaction,* (D. Diaper, D. Gilmore, G. Cockton and B. Shackel, eds). North Holland.

LeQuesne, P.N. (1988). "Individual and Organisational Factors and the Design of IPSEs." In *The Computer Journal, 31, 5.*

Nardi, B. (1990). "Participatory Design of Computer Systems." *Proceedings of CHI '90 - Empowering People*, (Chew, J.C. and Whiteside, J., eds), Seattle.

Nielsen, J. (1990). "Big Paybacks from 'Discount' Usability Engineering." In *IEEE Software, 7, 3.*

Tang, J. (1991) "Applying Video-Based Interaction Analysis Methods in the Design of New Technology." *Taking Software Design Seriously*, Academic Press, Boston 1991. In this book.

Wroe, B. (1986) "Contractors and Computers: Why Systems Succeed or Fail," Ph.D. Thesis, Loughborough University of Technology.

Index